LEGAL EDUCATION AT THE UNIVERSITY OF VIRGINIA

Legal Education at the University of Virginia

Tradition and Transformation

Edited by Meggan F. Cashwell,
Randall N. Flaherty, and Loren S. Moulds

UNIVERSITY OF VIRGINIA PRESS
Charlottesville and London

The University of Virginia Press is situated on the traditional lands of the Monacan Nation, and the Commonwealth of Virginia was and is home to many other Indigenous people. We pay our respect to all of them, past and present. We also honor the enslaved African and African American people who built the University of Virginia, and we recognize their descendants. We commit to fostering voices from these communities through our publications and to deepening our collective understanding of their histories and contributions.

University of Virginia Press

Printed in the United States of America on acid-free paper

First published 2025

1 3 5 7 9 8 6 4 2

ISBN 978-0-8139-5379-3 (hardback)
ISBN 978-0-8139-5380-9 (ebook)

Library of Congress Cataloging-in-Publication Data is available for this title.

Cover art: Law students in the classroom, c. 1971.
(Records of the *Virginia Law Weekly*)
Cover design: Will Brown

CONTENTS

FOREWORD

As a historian of legal education, I've long considered place essential to understanding law schools. But I never appreciated the importance of location to a law school more than I did in reading *Legal Education at the University of Virginia: Tradition and Transformation.* As the authors of this outstanding volume make clear, its presence in Mr. Jefferson's University has shaped UVA Law. The former president envisioned an "academical village" where, for much of the nineteenth century, professors, their wives, children, and enslaved servants lived and worked with law students. But as the essays also demonstrate, where Jefferson wanted the law school to serve the present, its past enslaved UVA Law for much of its history.

Its faculty and administrators proved crucial in creating a southern jurisprudence that rationalized and advanced the causes of slavery, secession, and segregation. They promoted a patriarchal conception of property rights that eradicated financial independence for all women, whether married or single, and reduced beloved law professor John B. Minor's widow and daughters to penury after his death, despite their decades of service to UVA Law. Faculty and administrators developed a curriculum that eschewed the case method of instruction that Harvard began popularizing in 1870 for lectures, textbooks, recitation, and memorization until the 1930s. Like other elite law schools (think Harvard), they perpetuated themselves by restricting hiring largely to their own graduates through the 1950s to preserve "the school's distinctively 'southern' and 'Virginian' atmosphere." They did not require an undergraduate degree for admission until 1961.

Like other leading law schools, theirs catered to white Protestant men. The first woman to receive her degree from UVA Law, Elizabeth N. Tompkins (Law 1923), was so miserable after a year among her male counterparts, who were "more repulsive than snakes" and who made up "this mob of crawling humanity [that] has destroyed any liking that I might have once had for men," that she wanted to drop out and complete her studies at "Richmond College night School of Law." When UVA Law finally admitted an African American man, Gregory H. Swanson, to its LLM program after he had successfully sued to win admission in 1950, it isolated him *and* spread the myth that he had dropped out before he met the residency requirements. When Elaine R. Jones (Law 1970), UVA Law's first Black alumna, applied to the school, she fully anticipated rejection, since Virginia had paid for her equally well-credentialed African American friend, Patricia A. King, to go to Harvard. As at other law schools, what diversification in student body and curricular modernization occurred came largely as a response to student demand from the 1960s through the 1980s. No clinical legal education program existed until 1976.

Real change required real money. In the 1990s, Dean Robert E. Scott ushered in a new era of financial self-sufficiency for UVA Law when he launched what became "the most successful capital campaign in the history of legal education" up to that point. It made possible new Law Grounds, a reduction in the student-faculty ratio, a more diverse student body, and better financial aid offers. Dean John Jeffries (Law 1973) won the financial independence for UVA that any flourishing law school needs, and his successors have continued to control the school's finances.

These developments enabled the Law School to rebrand itself. Like other national law schools, UVA had begun its dance with interdisciplinarity in the 1970s when a withering job market in the humanities and social sciences enticed interested individuals into attending law schools and teaching at them instead. To remain competitive, UVA Law now had to tighten its embrace of other disciplines and hire more faculty members with advanced degrees. To ensure that theoretical professors did not neglect students' need for practical training and hands-on experience, it had to increase its clinical and experiential offerings. And thankfully, given our benighted present, it strengthened its commitment to turning out graduates who see public service as essential to the practice of law.

Would Thomas Jefferson recognize the contemporary school? I like to think so. He might be surprised to see a woman at its helm and the rich ideological, geographic, racial, and sexual diversity of the student body, of course. But as Risa Goluboff, who served as dean of the Law School during the writing of this volume, indicates in her illuminating epilogue, UVA Law today is the culmination of Jefferson's initial view of a law school embedded in the larger intellectual currents of the university, assumed to the special training lawyers need to enter legal practice, and committed to the values of public service. The more things have changed, the more they have stayed the same.

This rich volume is even more remarkable because of its production under Law School auspices. As might be expected from "an art form by and large designed to separate alumni from their money," generally "the hero of the history of a law school turns out to be the institution itself."[1] But only the most mossbacked reactionary would celebrate the story of UVA Law during the nineteenth and early twentieth centuries presented here. The authors have focused attention on many persons UVA Law once marginalized, as well as its inconvenient past. They have produced a model history of a venerable institution. Bravo!

Laura Kalman

Note

1. Alfred S. Konefsky and John Henry Schlegel, "Mirror, Mirror on the Wall: Histories of American Law Schools," *Harvard Law Review* 95, no. 4 (February 1982): 833, 836, 835.

ACKNOWLEDGMENTS

This project has been a deeply collaborative one, involving not only the editors and contributors but also a wide network of colleagues, librarians, archivists, and researchers. In presenting this volume, we are acutely aware of the many contributions, both seen and unseen, that have made this work possible. We are fortunate to be surrounded by such a wonderful community of scholars and friends—we are deeply thankful for the support they have provided.

First, we wish to express our gratitude to J. Gordon Hylton (Law 1977), who played a foundational role in the conception of this curricular history project. Gordon was an esteemed friend, a wonderful colleague, a respected historian, as well as an alumnus of the Law School. He helped shape the genesis of this volume through insightful conversations about the history of legal education and by contributing his own scholarship early on. His legacy permeates this work, and we are honored to continue the project he so passionately believed in.

We are grateful to Risa Goluboff, who served as dean during the drafting of the first two books in this series of histories of the Law School. As a champion of the project, her unwavering support and intellectual leadership have proven instrumental to the series, not only through contributing chapters to this volume but also by playing a pivotal role in ensuring the success of both volumes.

This series has spanned the tenure of two library directors whose support has made it possible. Taylor Fitchett realized the possibilities of an expansive series of histories of the Law School about the people who worked, taught, and attended here. She believed that the project should originate within the library and its special collections—her leadership indelibly improved the building, interpretation, and promotion of its archival collections and interpretation of the Law School's history. The library's current director, Amy Wharton, continued this legacy and helped bring the project to fruition.

Cecilia Brown, the former Law School archivist, provided intellectual support and decades of deep institutional knowledge, and this book is a legacy to her collegiality and able stewardship of the Law School's archives. Daniel Cavanaugh capably took the reins as the new archivist following Cecilia's retirement and provided invaluable support to this project.

We cannot overstate how important Jane McBrian was to this project. She meticulously read drafts, fact-checked, formatted texts, and checked citations. Jane also tirelessly contributed to research, digitization, transcription, and project management. We owe her an enormous debt of gratitude.

Addison Patrick brought her special kind of magic to nearly every aspect of this project. In addition to coauthoring a chapter for this volume, Addison played a key role in research and ideation, helping shape the direction of the work from its earliest stages.

Philip Herrington created an enduring and elegant first volume on the Law School's architectural history, demonstrating the value and importance of undertaking institutional histories like this one.

As a research fellow, James Ambuske had his hands in many projects including the history of slavery at the University, expansion of our digital archives and methodologies, and scholarship on legal education in the early republic. Jim also provided essential advice as we started up our *Legal Knowledge* podcast.

Students and interns provided background research woven throughout this volume. We wish to acknowledge the following: John Modica provided groundbreaking research and histories of slavery at the University; Cannon Lane examined how the early library was used by students; Ana

Teresa Atiles, Courtney Davis, Margaret Doyle, Stefani Mitrovic, Cynthia Okoye, Lauren O'Neill, and Day Robins transcribed student notebooks; Mara Guyer provided research and transcription. Rebecca Barry coproduced the *Legal Knowledge* podcast, which shaped the direction of the project in numerous ways. Logan Heiman played a critical role in the development of our website on slavery and UVA Law. Additionally, numerous law students contributed as research assistants; they are thanked accordingly in individual chapters.

Colleagues at Main Grounds were helpful collaborators. Our team was a regular presence at the Albert and Shirley Small Special Collections Library, and the staff there deserve a big shout out for their assistance and knowledge. The materials housed there provide access to critical primary sources, while their expertise informed our research. Worthy Martin from the Institute for Advanced Technology in the Humanities (IATH) and Jefferson's University: Early Life Project (JUEL) has long been a valuable mentor. James Zehmer in the historic preservation department provided special access tours of the Academical Village along with research assistance. Holly Robertson was a regular source of inspiration and helped uncover remarkable materials that greatly enriched our research and helped shape the narrative of this project.

Our thanks go to the staff at UVA Press, especially Nadine Zimmerli, whose guidance and encouragement made the book immeasurably better.

And finally, we wish to express our deepest thanks to our families for their patience, love, and support throughout this long process. To Taylor Cashwell, David Flaherty, and Kelly Moulds, we are endlessly grateful.

NOTE ON STUDENT DESIGNATIONS

The first time a University of Virginia student is mentioned in a chapter, we follow their name with a school designation, such as Law to denote UVA Law School, and their final year of enrollment. The year notation, therefore, is not necessarily a date of graduation or evidence of graduation. Many law students in the nineteenth century did not earn a degree but nonetheless used their academic legal training to pass the bar or engage in other professional pursuits.

The following abbreviations are used in the designations:

Law	School of Law
GSAS	Graduate School of Arts and Sciences
College	College of Arts and Sciences

LEGAL EDUCATION AT THE UNIVERSITY OF VIRGINIA

Introduction

ELAINE R. JONES enrolled at the University of Virginia School of Law in 1967 because it was time to do something different. She had been an academic standout at Howard University as an undergraduate and was now in her second year in the Peace Corps in Turkey. When she decided to apply to UVA for law school, Jones knew she had the grades and should be admitted. But as a Black Virginian, she expected rejection. Jones was aware that Virginia had recently paid tuition assistance to her Norfolk, Virginia, friend and fellow academic star, Patricia A. King, to attend Harvard Law School rather than admit her to the UVA School of Law. Jones anticipated the same answer, and she was ready to be a test case. To Jones's surprise, UVA admitted her. She weighed her options. After deliberating, Jones rested on her certitude that there was a larger world out there than what she knew, and to function in it, she had to be exposed to it. She said yes to Virginia.

In 1970, Elaine Jones became the first Black woman to graduate from UVA Law School. She would go on to lead the NAACP's Legal Defense Fund and become a national leader in civil rights litigation. Her professional drive came from her Virginia childhood. In Norfolk, Jones grew up with segregated housing and segregated schools. As an elementary student, she decided to become a lawyer to do something about it. She had applied to UVA for law school because she was a Virginian, and UVA was her state school, but the world of UVA was foreign to Jones. Throughout the school's history, it had shaped its mission to nation and state around training white lawyers, and predominantly men, for positions of leadership. As a Black woman, Jones knew nothing about UVA, including its Law School, and she believed UVA knew nothing about her. But it was time for both to try something new.[1]

Central to the Law School's history has been the school's often fraught work to find guidance in its mission while navigating change. A pressing question underlies this work: What is the mission of a law school? Assessing mission has shaped the UVA Law School from its very start. Commitment to excellence in legal training has been a historical through line at UVA Law, but for whom? At UVA particularly, what is the responsibility of a prominent state law school to its state and nation? Those with the authority to answer these questions at the Law School held significant sway over who could enroll, what was taught, and who taught it. All of these decisions engendered debate, whether from inside UVA Law or from outside its Grounds, even from voices not invited as faculty or students. Despite the national cache that the Law School has always held due to its Jeffersonian founding, UVA Law's transition from being the preeminent southern law school to a leading national law school did not occur until the mid-twentieth century. This elicits important questions of how the Law School made this transition and why. Elaine Jones's story reveals that expanding the Law School's mission to bring students into new contact with the larger world has been a long and unsettled process. As the chapters in this volume illuminate, the addition of new voices to the Law School faculty and student body, particularly in the postwar era, was a driving force in pushing the school to national stature. *Legal Education at the University of Virginia: Tradition and Transformation* explores this question of mission over the Law School's two-hundred-year history.

UVA's position has given it a distinct vantage point to view foundational shifts in American legal history and legal education. As a state university, as a member of an elite cohort of national law schools, and as a devotee to training public servants in law, UVA Law has found itself distinctly positioned to feel the push and pull of these forces. For much of its history, UVA offered the preeminent southern alternative to the Harvard model of

American legal education. Created in the same historical moment in the first quarter of the nineteenth century, the UVA and Harvard law schools were shaped in their infancy by Thomas Jefferson and Joseph Story, two early national Republicans who nonetheless became foes over national policy. In that same philosophical split lay the divergence of UVA from its northern elite peers. As Daniel R. Coquillette and Bruce A. Kimball write, Harvard's competitive advantage in its early years was its national and cosmopolitan worldview.[2] Story's Harvard taught the legal architecture of a commercial society and built a consciousness of national law grounded on veiled sectional interests.[3] UVA began with a similar premise of infusing parochial legal education with a national, cosmopolitan framework: international and constitutional law were core parts of the mission of the Law School from the start. UVA espoused the cosmopolitan nature of its curriculum as critical for training statesmen leaders. But just as Harvard was grounded in New England, UVA's cosmopolitanism in its first century was grounded in the southern perspective.

For much of its history, UVA Law played a lead role in the construction of southern jurisprudence.[4] The Law School of the nineteenth century was deeply rooted in its southern location, with students and faculty coming predominantly from Virginia and from other southern states. Adding to this insularity, most of the school's faculty positions in its first hundred years were filled by Law School alums, including a number from the same Davis-Minor family. The nineteenth-century Law School was far more parochial than its current instance, but as such—indeed, because of its regional preeminence and the draw of the Minor name—the school still held undeniable repute among the national community of legal professionals, but especially within the American South. Throughout the 1800s, the focus of UVA Law remained on constitutional law and property, each reinforcing the lessons of the other around southern interests such as enslavement, states' rights, and segregation. A small, core group of courses, grounded in national and Virginia law, constituted the Law School curriculum under the direction of a teaching faculty that did not expand beyond two law professors until 1896. In contrast to its northern elite peers, the Law School in its first one hundred years maintained standard courses of study for all students and did not include specialized courses on federal or commercial law.[5] The entrenched Law School methods of this period through which the school had made its name—teaching legal principles from a lecture and textbook model, serving as an undergraduate professional school enmeshed within UVA's liberal arts environment, and educating only white men—slowed the Law School's willingness to change, even as legal education evolved nationally.

The chapters in this volume reveal the seismic shift that the Law School underwent in the mid-twentieth century as three core, interrelated dynamics came to bear on the teaching of law at UVA: the professionalization of legal education; changing student and faculty demographics; and new pressures to become a national law school. Competition from emerging southern law schools, most especially Duke and the University of North Carolina, pushed the Law School to bring its curriculum, teaching methods, and admission standards in line with new national, professional standards and to become an elite national law school, not simply a regional leader. By mid-century, World War II and its aftermath finally pushed Law School administration to incorporate specialized education on national and international legal topics, particularly on law and business, and to begin hiring new faculty of national repute to teach these topics. The changing environment for federal constitutional law in this time, particularly around education and civil rights, brought new questioning of the Law School's admissions policy and amplified calls for the Law School to reexamine who it served and who it should educate. Into this moment stepped Gregory H. Swanson, who sued for and won his right to enroll at the Law School as the University's first Black student in 1950. These expansions of curriculum, of national prominence, and of demographic diversity were monumental changes in their time, though the chapters in this volume show how much of the Law School's current institutional makeup is a product of the twenty-first century.

The major institutional changes that the Law School has undergone over the past two hundred years have transpired in dialogue with the Law School's history and mission. With every relocation to a new physical home at UVA, the Law School has sought to reconstruct the residential dynamic of Jefferson's Academical Village and continue the idea of a collegial community of lawyers that has always distinguished it among its peers. Historically, this created an inward-looking tradition with significant implications. The nineteenth-century law classroom and residential spaces became intellectual echo chambers, where white male students and faculty could see their success as birthright and support one another, undistracted and unchallenged, in becoming the statesmen they believed their society needed. For over a century, the Law School excluded women and people of color, while it taught the laws that denied them equal rights. UVA Law's move to Clark Hall and then to its current North Grounds location in 1974 has increased the independence of this professional school from UVA's Academical Village. The significant demographic diversification of the law student body in the past ten years means that the Law School is now building its collegial community of lawyers at North Grounds with an array of voices and perspectives that increasingly reflect the society around it. That these enrollment and curricular shifts were bolstered significantly in the 2000s by the Law School's new arrangement for financial self-sufficiency from Virginia state budgets offers another important dialectic with the Law School's history and founding mission. Gregory Swanson, Elaine Jones, the Virginia Law Women, the Gay and Lesbian Law Students Association (now Lambda), and the diversity of students who have passed through the Law School were essential in pushing these changes and in reshaping the worldview of the Law School to become wider, more professional, and more competitive on a national level.

Curriculum served as the initial lens through which this volume's contributors set out to study UVA Law's two-hundred-year history, but the varying interpretive lenses represented across the fourteen contributors allow for a more complex analysis of UVA Law and American legal education. Critically, this project reveals that legal education—the act of teaching the profession of law—comprises both classroom learning and the culture of a place, specifically the social preparations for being a lawyer. The scope of this book, therefore, extends outside formal instruction to encapsulate the wider forces that shaped the Law School and to center the perspectives of individuals and communities beyond the dean's office and faculty appointments.

Contributors represent a diversity of fields including legal, southern, cultural, and social history. Some contributors have spent their careers teaching at UVA Law and have a personal and professional familiarity with the institution; four graduated from the Law School. Several contributors bring expertise about the history of UVA, particularly the histories of slavery and emancipation, the Civil War, anti-Black racism, and student activism. Others have expertise in the history of the law and legal culture in the United States. This framework expands the definition of legal education. Ultimately, contributors tell an integrated story about the development of UVA Law as a southern institution, embedded both within local culture and national currents.

Central Themes

Jefferson looms large in the history of the UVA Law School. His founding influence imbued the school with the seeds of its ongoing debate over mission. As a former US president and revolutionary hero, Jefferson anointed UVA with concomitant state, regional, and national purpose, especially to rank with excellence as an academic law program on all three of those levels. He inaugurated a new university curricular model that placed philosophical inquiry on par with learning technical skills. Jefferson supported liberal education for "those persons, whom nature hath endowed with genius and virtue."[6] These contributions have helped make the Law School's history a protracted reaction to its founding.

The pedestal Jefferson inhabits as the Law School guidepost, however, is far too exclusive. A multitude of persons and perspectives have shaped this legal community. As David T. Konig observes in the inaugural chapter, Jefferson designed the University of Virginia to draw southern white men away from the monopolistic hold of northern universities. At UVA, his carefully selected faculty would train elite young men to be expert practitioners in their respective fields and, ideally, to be southern statesmen. And yet, as Konig shows, even as the first law professors invoked their own stewardship of Jefferson's legacy, they immediately adapted his distinct interdisciplinary vision toward new ways of thinking. John Tayloe Lomax, the first law professor, taught Sir William Blackstone before Sir Edward Coke, despite Jefferson's strong preference that Coke precede Blackstone. One of his successors, Henry St. George Tucker, taught southern states' rights theory with a new militaristic emphasis. As Randall N. Flaherty shows, John B. Minor aligned his law curriculum with scientific inquiry but grounded it on identifying legal truths, rather than Jefferson's emphasis on intellectual curiosity.

Critical for this volume is the observation that law teaching extended into UVA's distinct environment of the Academical Village. In a residential space for collegial study, a feature the Law School has always claimed as a core identity trait, the homogeneity of faculty and students takes on great pedagogical import. The nineteenth-century legal education with which students engaged at UVA was premised on gendered and racist notions of legal personhood and provided the justifications for slavery in the United States, as well as the subjugation of women and legal dependents. Justene Hill Edwards analyzes the law classroom as a site of proslavery rhetoric and ideology in the antebellum period. As enslavers themselves, UVA Law professors trained their students to use the law to preserve and perpetuate the institution of slavery. Faculty and students interacted daily (and sometimes violently) with enslaved persons whose coerced labor maintained the University's operations and supported the student experience. These chapters correspond with later essays to demonstrate the significant change that comes to a law school from expanding the diversity of voices who lead lectures and populate classes.

Women and African Americans were deeply implicated within the Law School's pedagogy from the outset as subjects through which white male students came to understand the law and the operations of broader society. In her chapter, Laura F. Edwards studies the wider domestic environment of UVA, where the wives and daughters of law professors informally trained law students in the art of propriety and decorum. These women, whose lives were deeply intertwined with campus life, tried to exercise their own legal agency and navigate increasingly restrictive coverture laws—which were supported and taught by UVA Law School professors. As Anne M. Coughlin explores in the subsequent chapter, during this same time women fought to be lawyers despite laws and ideologies prohibiting them access to the bar. A select few white women gained entry to the Law School as students in 1920, though women's admission remained nominal until after World War II.

Themes of race and gender are narrative threads that connect these chapters across time. Elizabeth R. Varon's examination of the Civil War and Reconstruction reveals that by the close of the nineteenth century, the Law School had set itself apart as an elite southern institution with national aspirations. Simultaneously, it had produced a generation of lawyers who went on to establish and uphold Jim Crow laws, including a state constitution that disenfranchised Black Virginians. A. E. Dick Howard and Catherine A. Ward's chapter continues those themes well into the twentieth century with their study of constitutional law. As they observe, and as Gregory Swanson's story illustrates, it took integration and a national civil rights movement before Law School faculty and students helped turn the tide in favor of democracy for all Virginians. Risa Goluboff, Randall Flaherty, and Biruktawit M. Assefa illuminate Swanson's successful but difficult work to desegregate the Law School in 1950. Despite Swanson's acceptance in the classroom, he was prohibited from participating in the full milieu of life and learning at UVA and in Charlottesville. His story reveals the importance of individual plaintiffs, students, and other changemakers to this institutional history.

Amid curricular and community change, tensions emerged at the Law School over its identity as a state school with regional recognition and national ambitions—another key thread of the book. Konig argues that Jefferson always intended for UVA and the Law School to have national prominence and to be a leader among top academic law programs such as that at Harvard. When John Minor took over the law professorship from 1845 to 1895, he continued to look to Harvard as his main competitive foil. And yet, as Flaherty demonstrates, the law school that emerged from Minor's tenure was one of regional and distinctly southern prestige. G. Edward White argues that it took several decades for the Law School to find a balance between its sometimes dueling state, regional, and national identities. Younger faculty largely drove this shift by bringing newer trends in legal education—namely the case method—to Virginia Law in the 1920s and 1930s. As UVA Law strove to keep pace with its peers through the twentieth century, Law School leaders insisted the institution maintain the qualities they believed made the school unique: the small section in the 1L year, the accessibility of faculty, and an amicable law school community.

Claudrena N. Harold challenges this notion of civility at UVA Law, highlighting a culture of activism among women and minority student groups in the 1970s and 1980s who felt the Law School was too homogeneous and too slow to enact meaningful change. The Black Law Students Association and Virginia Law Women pressed the administration to diversify the Law School's faculty, student body, and course offerings. Their demands also represented a push and pull between students and administrators over the lawyer's purpose and the need for legal education to evolve with the times.

Meggan F. Cashwell and Addison R. Patrick's chapter contends that in the 1980s and 1990s the Law School cautiously incorporated interdisciplinary and clinical training into its curriculum in line with national trends and intentionally kept at bay more progressive pedagogies such as critical legal studies. Meanwhile, Law School administrators and students continued to negotiate the meaning of the UVA Law community, one that by this time had physically relocated to a new and expanded law complex at the University. The notion of UVA Law as its own modern "Academical Village" permeated Law School conversations and framed the next era of UVA Law—one that brought financial independence, curricular innovation, and an increasingly diverse student body.

Risa Goluboff, the twelfth and first female dean of UVA Law, closes the book with her perspective on the Law School over the past two decades—an institution now boasting an international reputation and a school that achieved greater demographic and curricular diversity in 2024 than at any other moment in its history. With this recognition of UVA Law's progress comes an acknowledgment that the work is far from done. What is the mission of a law school today, and how will law curricula adapt to deep legal debates, both nationally and regionally, around issues of free speech, admissions in higher education, and human rights? The epilogue issues a charge for the Law School—that it continues to train capable lawyers and legal professionals by providing an educational experience fostering inclusion and excellence.

Methodology

The forum of the classroom for tracing changes in legal education is central to this volume. Universities, particularly UVA and those in the South, have received important scholarly attention as broad spaces for social and intellectual learning, particularly around issues of race.[7] Fixing a lens on the classroom is made difficult by the sources, which are typically handwritten student notebooks. Faculty publications, university catalogs, student magazines and journals, and decanal papers are more widely accessible, and more legible. Alongside those commonly used institutional records, student notebooks provide a roadmap of curricular change and insight into the ways the UVA Law School responded to broader social, cultural, and legal developments. As the recent project to digitize Litchfield Law School student notebooks reveals, student notes are remarkably illuminative, but they are hard to work with due to their sometimes perplexing internal organization, marginalia, and scribbles—the very humanness that makes them historically valuable. While they have been underutilized as a historical source, the essays that follow reveal them to be invaluable in chronicling the history of the curriculum and the Law School as a whole, especially in the nineteenth century when there were fewer institutional records and personal accounts. Contributors' varied uses and interpretations of these notebooks not only set this volume apart from others on US legal education but lay the groundwork for similar studies.[8]

Student notebooks have allowed contributors to investigate the order of the curriculum, the minutia of lectures, and the evolution of how professors interpreted key legal developments. They provide glimpses into how students absorbed and interpreted legal principles, often inflected by prevailing sociopolitical norms. Early notebooks showcase foundational legal theorists such as Coke and Blackstone and illuminate how the faculty grappled with their ideas. Student notebooks from the early twentieth century illustrate how UVA Law initially resisted the popular case method championed by Harvard in the 1870s and instead adhered to a more traditional textbook and lecture style of teaching. In the 1930s and beyond, student notebooks show that faculty adopted a hybrid approach between the two methods until the Law School eventually adopted the case method in full. As the Law School slowly diversified in the latter half of the twentieth century, so did law lectures and, in turn, student notes. More modern student notebooks indicate an interdisciplinary shift in the curriculum beginning in the 1970s as law students

A single page of notes created by law student Corwin Levi (Law 2005) for the course Employment Discrimination in 2003. (Arthur J. Morris Law Library Special Collections, University of Virginia)

began to study the impact of the law on broader society as well as the intersections of the law with adjacent fields. While the format of student notebooks and related materials has evolved and expanded—ranging from highlighted casebooks to crib sheets and test notes—their role in capturing the academic experience remains essential. These artifacts continue to provide a tangible connection to the classroom experience across generations.

To capture the environment for legal learning at UVA and the larger cultural collection of legal knowledge, this book draws on correspondence, recollections, and other firsthand accounts from individuals historically barred from formal legal education. The daughters of John Minor left behind a letter trail that documents daily life in a Law School faculty household and the long-term impact of coverture's restrictions in the South. The correspondence of Elizabeth N. Tompkins, the Law School's first woman graduate in 1923, indicates that while Tompkins succeeded academically inside the law classroom, she was largely excluded from the school's male-dominated culture. Gregory Swanson recalled similar experiences in which he felt prohibited from participating in the full range of opportunities afforded white students.

Just as the project brings together scholars across disciplines, the sources collected here capture legal education as the cumulative product of countless minds and lives. Collectively, the chapters illuminate how conceptions of law and pedagogy were shaped through complex interactions between administrators, professors, students, and the legal community. While the book focuses specifically on UVA Law, it sheds light on broader themes within the history of legal education, including its intersections with race, gender, and power. This diversity of evidence makes visible the many threads woven into the tapestry of UVA Law and its curriculum across two centuries.

Purpose

This volume is a part of a larger movement at UVA and UVA Law to understand its full history and legacy. As a part of this charge, in 2011 the Arthur J. Morris Law Library created a postdoctoral fellowship to support ongoing scholarship about the institution. The first major product of this effort was *The Law School at the University of Virginia: Architectural Expansion in the Realm of Thomas Jefferson* by Philip M. Herrington (GSAS 2006, 2012).[9] This volume is the second, with Meggan Cashwell spearheading the project during her time as fellow from 2019 to 2023. Since Herrington's publication in 2017, the Special Collections department at the Law Library—which shepherds the institution's archival collections—has produced numerous digital and physical exhibitions, a podcast, historical walking tours, and a reimagined oral history program, all in service of making the Law School's history accessible to a wider audience.[10] The materials and stories uncovered in these initiatives critically inform the work done in this volume on curricular change.

While there have been and continue to be many institutional histories on US universities, the history of American legal education is, in many respects, an emerging field.[11] Since Julius Goebel Jr.'s foundational 1955 study of Columbia Law School, which emphasized the work of deans in the development of academic legal education, critical studies of American law schools have taken a broader look at the people and the forces that have shaped the teaching of American law.[12] This volume, accordingly, places the UVA Law School within the broader national context of legal history and legal education, particularly US race and gender relations. The essays found here build on the work of Laura Kalman on Yale Law School as well as David Coquillette and Bruce Kimball's histories of Harvard Law School as models in our conceptualization of the volume. Kalman, Coquillette, and Kimball take an analytical and contextual approach—one that recognizes that many individuals shaped the development of these institutions over time.[13] In addition, several studies on UVA and UVA Law have helped lay the groundwork for our study.[14] John Ritchie (Law 1927), a former UVA Law faculty member, wrote a history of the first one hundred years of the Law School in 1978.[15] A few years later, W. Hamilton Bryson (Law 1968) published a volume of short biographies of legal educators in Virginia.[16] There is also ongoing scholarship that continues to explore legal education in the early republic, including Thomas Jefferson's intentions in establishing the University of Virginia. *The Founding of Thomas Jefferson's University,* edited by

John A. Ragosta, Peter S. Onuf, and Andrew J. O'Shaughnessy, brings to light the significance of UVA to the development of higher education in the nineteenth century.[17]

Legal Education at the University of Virginia expands on current scholarship that explores the intersections of slavery and higher education. Alfred L. Brophy's *University, Court, and Slave* studies the university's relationship to slavery in the United States. Brophy highlights faculty at UVA, including the Law School, who advanced a proslavery ideology during the antebellum period.[18] This volume builds in particular on Maurie D. McInnis and Louis P. Nelson's *Educated in Tyranny: Slavery at Thomas Jefferson's University* and Kirt von Daacke and Andrea Douglas's *After Emancipation: Racism and Resistance at the University of Virginia* in illuminating how UVA was, and still is, deeply connected to and embedded within its surrounds. *Educated in Tyranny* has helped shift the field toward understanding the teaching of slave mastery and white supremacy at southern colleges, namely UVA. *After Emancipation* incorporates an interactive format among academics, alumni, students, and community members to reveal how UVA and its surrounds have shaped each other, both through the University's perpetuation of legacies of slavery and through traditions of activism by Charlottesville's Black community.[19] Additionally, authors in *Charlottesville 2017: The Legacy of Race and Inequity* pick up on the lessons of the city's white supremacist march in August 2017 with essays that reveal anew how injustices and prejudices of the past, many that UVA and the Law School helped perpetuate, remain in the present, particularly in Charlottesville, calling out for redress.[20] Building on these works, this volume identifies the antebellum and postbellum law classrooms as sites deeply intertwined with their society.

Legal Education at the University of Virginia contributes to the Law School's ongoing efforts to grapple with its history and build a more just future by bringing forward the diversity of voices that have shaped the University of Virginia School of Law since its founding and continue to shape the school today. Our approach strives to be both honest and holistic. The history of UVA Law cannot be told, as these essays prove, without broadening the definition of changemakers within legal education. Combatting archival and historical silences requires the inclusion and contextualization of traditionally excluded persons such as women, people of color, LGBTQ+ individuals, and other marginalized communities. In elevating voices, sources, and stories that have been neglected, this volume aims to move closer to an authentic accounting of our shared history.

Notes

1. Elaine Jones, interview by Julian Bond, 1 November 2000, interview transcript, Explorations in Black Leadership, University of Virginia, https://blackleadership.virginia.edu/transcript/jones-elaine; Elaine Jones, interviewed by Julieanna L. Richardson, 6 March 2007, A2006.151, The HistoryMakers Digital Archive, https://www.thehistorymakers.org/biography/elaine-jones-41; UVA Law Elaine R. Jones Portrait Dedication Ceremony, 14 May 2022, transcript available: https://www.law.virginia.edu/news/videos-podcasts/dedication-portrait-elaine-r-jones-%E2%80%9970.
2. Daniel R. Coquillette and Bruce A. Kimball, *On the Battlefield of Merit: Harvard Law School, the First Century* (Cambridge, MA: Harvard University Press, 2015), 3, 38–39.
3. R. Kent Newmyer, "Harvard Law School, New England Legal Culture, and the Antebellum Origins of American Jurisprudence," *Journal of American History* 74, no. 3 (December 1987): 818.
4. For a discussion of southern jurisprudence around slavery and the legal academy's role in shaping it, including UVA faculty as authorities on proslavery thought, see Alfred L. Brophy, *University, Court, and Slave: Pro-Slavery Thought in Southern Colleges and Courts, and the Coming of Civil War* (New York: Oxford University Press, 2016).
5. Newmyer, "Harvard Law School," 820, 825; Coquillette and Kimball, *On the Battlefield of Merit,* 171.
6. "79. A Bill for the More General Diffusion of Knowledge," 18 June 1779, in James P. McClure and J. Jefferson Looney, eds., *The Papers of Thomas Jefferson, Digital Edition,* (Charlottesville: University of Virginia Press, Rotunda, 2008–2025), 2:527, https://rotunda-upress-virginia-edu/founders/TSJN-01-02-02-0132-0004-0079.
7. Maurie D. McInnis and Louis P. Nelson, eds., *Educated in Tyranny: Slavery at Thomas Jefferson's University* (Charlottesville: University of Virginia Press, 2019); Kirt von Daacke and Andrea Douglas, *After Emancipation: Racism and Resistance at the University of Virginia* (Charlottesville: University of Virginia Press, 2024); Craig Steven Wilder, *Ebony & Ivy: Race, Slavery, and the Troubled History of America's Universities* (New York: Bloomsbury Press, 2013); Brophy, *University, Court, and Slave.*
8. Jason Eiseman, Whitney Bagnall, Cate Kellett, and Caitlyn Lam, "Litchfield Unbound: Unlocking Legal History with Metadata, Digitization, and Digital Tools," *Law and History Review* 34, no. 4 (November 2016): 831–55; Coquillette and Kimball use student notebooks as one of their key sources in *On the Battlefield of Merit.*
9. Philip Mills Herrington, *The Law School at the University of Virginia: Architectural Expansion in the Realm of Thomas Jefferson* (Charlottesville: University of Virginia Press, 2017).
10. Related projects designed and curated by UVA Law Special Collections include The 1828 Catalogue Project: The First Law Library of the University of Virginia (digital repository); Slavery & The UVA School of Law: A History (digital repository and exhibition); A Virtual Walking Tour: The Historical Landscape of North Grounds; Virginia Law Women 50: A Collaborative Oral History Project; Marshaling May Days:

UVA Law and the 1970 Student Anti-War Movement; and 50 Years of the Black Law Students Association: Chronicling Five Decades of Black Student Activism, Service, and Community at the University of Virginia School of Law. In addition, the *Legal Knowledge* podcast is designed to be an extension of the volume. In the first season, coeditor and podcast host Meggan F. Cashwell interviews the first six authors. For more on UVA Law Special Collections and to access the above initiatives, visit https://archives.law.virginia.edu.

11. A few of note include Arthur E. Sutherland, *The Law at Harvard: A History of Ideas and Men, 1817–1967* (Cambridge, MA: Belknap Press, 1967); Robert Stevens, *Law School: Legal Education in America from the 1850s to the 1980s* (Chapel Hill: University of North Carolina Press, 1983); Marian C. McKenna, *Tapping Reeve and the Litchfield Law School* (Dobbs Ferry, NY: Oceana Publications, 1986); Steve Sheppard, ed., *The History of Legal Education in the United States: Commentaries and Primary Sources,* 2 vols. (Pasadena, CA: Salem Press, 1999); Anthony T. Kronman, ed., *History of the Yale Law School: The Tercentennial Lectures* (New Haven, CT: Yale University Press, 2004).
12. Julius Goebel Jr., *A History of the School of Law, Columbia University* (New York: Columbia University Press, 1955).
13. Laura Kalman, *Legal Realism at Yale, 1927–1960* (Chapel Hill: University of North Carolina Press, 1986); Laura Kalman, *Yale Law School and the Sixties: Revolt and Reverberations* (Chapel Hill: University of North Carolina Press, 2005); Coquillette and Kimball, *On the Battlefield of Merit;* Daniel R. Coquillette and Bruce A. Kimball, *The Intellectual Sword: Harvard Law School, the Second Century* (Cambridge, MA: Belknap Press, 2020).
14. Others include *A Sketch of the History of the University of Virginia Together with a Catalogue of Professors and Instructors, the Graduates in Law and Medicine, and the Masters and Bachelors of Arts since the Foundation of the University* (Washington, DC: Henry Polkinhorn, 1859); John A. Ragosta, Peter S. Onuf, and Andrew J. O'Shaughnessy, eds., *The Founding of Thomas Jefferson's University* (Charlottesville: University of Virginia Press, 2019).
15. John Ritchie, *First Hundred Years: A Short History of the School of Law of the University of Virginia for the Period 1826–1926* (Charlottesville: University Press of Virginia, 1978).
16. W. Hamilton Bryson, *Legal Education in Virginia, 1779–1979: A Biographical Approach* (Charlottesville: University Press of Virginia, 1982).
17. Ragosta, Onuf, and O'Shaughnessy, *Founding of Thomas Jefferson's University.* See also Steven J. Macias, *Legal Science in the Early Republic: The Origins of American Legal Thought and Education* (Lanham, MD: Lexington Books, 2016); McKenna, *Tapping Reeve and the Litchfield Law School.*
18. Brophy, *University, Court, and Slave.* See also Leslie M. Harris, James T. Campbell, and Alfred L. Brophy, eds., *Slavery and the University: Histories and Legacies* (Athens: University of Georgia Press, 2019).
19. McInnis and Nelson, *Educated in Tyranny;* von Daacke and Douglas, *After Emancipation.*
20. Louis P. Nelson and Claudrena N. Harold, eds., *Charlottesville 2017: The Legacy of Race and Inequity* (Charlottesville: University of Virginia Press, 2018). See especially Risa Goluboff's essay, "Where Do We Go from Here?"

Jeffersonian Foundations of Legal Education in Virginia, 1779–1845

David T. Konig

Dedicated to the late Professor Gordon Hylton, who passed away after beginning an essay for this volume on the founding of the University. A devoted teacher and selflessly generous friend, he deserves recognition for sharing his insights and encyclopedic knowledge of the Law School's history.

IN AUGUST 1818 Thomas Jefferson convened the "Commissioners of the University of Virginia" to meet, "as by law required at the tavern in Rockfish gap on the blue ridge," to draft a report as the basis for establishing "an university, to be called the 'University of Virginia.'"[1] Already aware of disagreement among those who would be attending, he had arranged with James Madison to "confer on our campaign" in advance of the meeting to support his plan for the University.[2] Such preparation—lawyerly in its meticulous concern for detail and scrupulous control of process—was typical of Jefferson, and it foreshadowed his close management of matters large and small for the Law School well before the University opened in 1825. During construction he earned a reputation for being "particular in the matter of books as in everything else" and, apocryphally, for "inspect[ing] every brick used in the University building."[3] Until his death he would bring to the pursuit of reforming legal education the same attention that characterized his preparation for court.

Jefferson's commitment to the success of the University became the consuming project of his last years, "the last of my mortal cares, and the last service I can render my country."[4] In 1845, more than a quarter century after ground was broken and four law professors later, the buildings he had designed stood completed as a monument to their founder, but his efforts had bequeathed a problematic legacy.

Student, Teacher, and Builder

The Rockfish Gap commissioners began by quickly settling the contentious matter of a location—ratifying Jefferson's choice of Charlottesville—and by affirming a general mission statement for the University that echoed similar calls across the nation to educate leaders for a republic: "training up able Counsellors to administer the affairs of our Country," and, through "education, advancing the prosperity, the power and the happiness of a nation."[5] The task, however, encountered challenges that tested his lawyerly skills and political dexterity. When the commissioners met to consider his agenda for a law school, Jefferson was prepared for "much difference of opinion" about its broadly conceived liberal arts curriculum. As he reported, "Some good men, and even of respectable information, consider the learned sciences as useless acquirements."[6] Because the report would have to seek funding by the legislature and private subscription, he had to use his lawyerly drafting skills to choose his words carefully and to sidestep contentious subjects. In the final report, therefore, he was intentionally vague about legal education, leaving enough of the curriculum unstated to provide wide discretion to the professor of law chosen by the University rector—who, it was no secret, would be Jefferson.

Jefferson's careful planning produced a report that embodied his long-standing vision of education on "a plan so broad & liberal & modern, as to be worth patronising with the public support, and be a temptation to the youth of other states to come, and drink of the cup of knolege & fraternize with us."[7] To make that vision a reality, the campus he designed would "consist of distinct houses or pavilions, arranged at proper distances on each side of a lawn . . . in each of which should be a lecturing room with from two to four apartments for the accommodation of a professor and his family."[8] Taking personal control of the project to ensure that the University would conform to his wishes, he defied the relentlessly encroaching aches and debility of old age to ride more than three miles over rugged terrain from Monticello to "go . . . to the College ground to see what is done & doing" at the site he had surveyed.[9] Construction required a large labor pool, and Jefferson's choice to assume supervision of construction brought him into close contact with the dozens of enslaved laborers among the workers and artisans who carried out this massive project. Those who built the first pavilions, and then served their occupants, were the vanguard of the hundreds of enslaved Virginians who worked at the University before Jefferson's death in 1826, and the hundreds more who toiled there until 1865. Leveling, clearing, and terracing the rough terrain that he had surveyed, they gave literal

1805 portrait of Thomas Jefferson by Rembrandt Peale. (New York Historical Society)

shape to the University he designed. Using the artisanal skills befitting his vision, many were entrusted to follow his exacting detail on the interior instructional spaces that constituted the built environment of the pavilions. Professors and their families resided in these pavilions, and when John Tayloe Lomax commenced lecturing as the University's first law professor, he and his family shared Pavilion III with the enslaved Black servants who lived in the Pavilion's dark and dank basement. Their largely domestic duties serving the free white labor force, whose monumental efforts remain visible today, were as unacknowledged as they were indispensable—a fact that Justene Hill Edwards and others in this volume seek to make clear.[10]

Jefferson's educational vision also reflected his experience as a student at the College of William & Mary. Jefferson and the other young men who entered the College of William & Mary in 1760, in Williamsburg, brought with them an unquestioned assumption that, as members of the landed elite, they could confidently expect to enjoy their status among a hierarchy of wealth and privilege. Before long, however, Jefferson came to disdain a society where "the man who powders most, parfumes most, embroiders most, and talks most nonsense, is most admired."[11] This coming of age coincided with his introduction to the "first views of the expansion of science & of the system of things in which we are placed," and as he wrote in his "Autobiography," it "probably fixed the destinies of my life."[12] His studies led him to question, and then to oppose, the hierarchies he had known since childhood and to commit himself to "forming a system by which every fibre would be eradicated of antient or future aristocracy; and a foundation laid for a government truly republican."[13] He came to appreciate the transformative power of education, and as he recollected to his grandson in 1808, he recalled asking himself, "Which of these kinds of reputation should I prefer? That of a horse jockey? A fox hunter? An Orator? Or the honest advocate of my country's rights?"[14] The choice was clear, and as a member of Virginia's revolutionary legislature revising Virginia's code of laws in 1779, he proposed "A Bill for the More General Diffusion of Knowledge" so that "those persons, whom nature hath endowed with genius and virtue, should be rendered by liberal education worthy to receive, and able to guard the sacred deposit of the rights and liberties of their fellow citizens." A "liberal education" in a republican state should be made available "at the common expence," he emphasized, lest "the happiness of all should be confided to the weak or wicked."[15]

By 1786 the bill had failed to advance to a final vote and was abandoned, representing a conspicuous defeat of what he regarded as "by far the most important bill in our whole code," falling victim to a legislature that refused to appropriate the necessary tax revenue to support liberal, republican education for qualified young men of any social rank. A disappointed Jefferson could only lament to George Wythe "that the tax which will be paid for this purpose is not more than the thousandth part of what will be paid to kings, priests and nobles who will rise up among us if we leave the people in ignorance."[16] The price of public ignorance, he would argue in support of public funding thirty years later, remained steep: "If a nation expects to be ignorant & free, in a state of civilisation, it expects what never was & never will be."[17]

Reading law in Williamsburg expanded his education, enabling him to observe the colony's high court, a busy hustings court, and a county court. Although his practice would involve few criminal cases, what Jefferson witnessed in the civil courts amply confirmed what "the higher branches" of science taught him about the human propensity for evil. Virginia courtrooms introduced him to the unseemly side of Virginia society, where law became an empirical matter as much as a philosophical study, and which led him to admit, "I was bred to the law; that gave me a view of the dark side of humanity."[18]

Remaking the Landscape of Legal Training

Jefferson's college years coincided with the intensifying imperial crisis, and colonial resistance to Parliament immersed him in England's historic Whig tradition, which taught that English liberties were never safe from despotism. Like nearly every law student of the day, his study of law began with Sir Edward Coke's gloss and translation of Sir Thomas Littleton's fifteenth-century text on *Tenures,* which appeared posthumously in 1628 as the first of his four-volume *Institutes of the Lawes of England.*[19] By the time Jefferson encountered *Coke on Littleton,* as its first volume was commonly known, it had assumed iconic status, remaining the basic introduction to the study of English law into the next century. Of Coke's legacy, Jefferson wrote to Madison in 1826, "a sounder whig never wrote, nor of profounder learning in the orthodox doctrines of the British constitution, or in what were called English liberties."[20] But Coke was also an accomplished conveyancer who extolled property rights and their protection under law. He praised "the rules of good pleading" as "the heart-string of the Common Law" and forensic skills as "necessarie to a compleat Lawyer."[21] Jefferson did not lose himself in the philosophical abstractions of the law, and he was neither the first nor the last to recognize and respond to a dilemma that others teaching law confronted then and now: how legal education must reconcile the teaching of law as an academic inquiry with the demands of instruction in its technical procedures.[22]

Wythe had directed Jefferson to attend the courts that met in Williamsburg and to learn by observing the colony's best pleaders. After Jefferson concluded his studies, Wythe added a moot court for his students and required that they participate in mock trials and model legislatures, habits that Jefferson also passed on to the many students who read law under his guidance, emphasizing them as "the only method by which a student can discover his own powers, and decide for himself his future enterprizes."[23] Jefferson was not the only practitioner who looked with disapproval at the ill-trained lawyers swarming over the legal landscape, and the changes wrought by independence only deepened his concern. Debt recovery, the instability of paper currency, and conflicting land claims pitted Virginians against one another, and the ideal of the lawyer shifted from public service toward private claims. The very meaning of legal practice and the education of lawyers shifted, too, as the increasingly attractive potential of a lucrative career swelled the ranks of ambitious young men taking advantage of Virginia's standards for admission to the bar, which were among the most lax in the nation.[24]

In his appellate practice, Jefferson had seen many cases appealed from county courts where poor lawyering skills had eroded clients' confidence in the legal system and its practitioners. As he prepared to leave the presidency in 1808, he had no desire to return to practice. "I know that no profession is open to stronger antipathies than that of the law," he observed in 1808 when a discouraged William Wirt, who would go on to become

Engraving of the Rotunda and Lawn, completed by B. Tanner and featured in Herman Boye's Map of Virginia, 1827. (Albert and Shirley Small Special Collections Library, University of Virginia)

one of the most skilled and eminent lawyers in Virginia, thought of giving up the law.[25] Restoring public confidence in the bar and the rule of law required better trained practitioners and more learned judges. The revolutionary impulse to democratize bench and bar in 1779 gave Jefferson pause when he considered the effect of opening appellate practice, which had been limited to an elite cadre of lawyers, to all practitioners. He reconsidered and abandoned the idea, explaining to Wythe the need to keep "the bar of the general court a proper and an excellent nursery for future judges," which would be possible only "if it be so regulated as that science may be encouraged and may live there." Without higher educational standards "this can never be if an inundation of insects is permitted to come from the county courts and consume the harvest."[26]

One remedy was to replace the system of office apprenticeship and to professionalize legal education. Little support existed for professionalization until independence created the conditions conducive to taking such a step. Since 1774 Tapping Reeve had been training apprentices—his first was Aaron Burr—in the parlor of his home in Litchfield, Connecticut, then a commercial, cultural, and legal center. But his reputation as an attorney, and the success of his former students, attracted a growing enrollment, which led him to begin lecturing to students in groups. In 1784 he had a small schoolhouse built to accommodate students who traveled to Connecticut, and in 1798 Reeve was joined by James Gould to share the teaching. Their curriculum was organized according to Blackstone, and its substance was national, not local, and private law, not criminal or constitutional.[27] Many young Virginians traveled north to Connecticut, as the proprietary model offered an attractive alternative to apprenticeship.

No rigid or uniform pedagogical model existed to be emulated—some proprietors of these private law schools lectured, while others did not—but the basic structure of reading law and preparing for practice pointed toward the future of legal education committed to satisfying the demand for better instruction in the practice of law, while also providing the imprimatur of professional rigor by teaching within a vaguely articulated academic system of "science." Of legal education at Litchfield, Timothy Dwight, president of Yale College, wrote contemporaneously, "Law here is taught as a science . . . as a regular well-compacted system," but what he meant by "science" took many forms, from the superficial application of scientific metaphor to adherence to scientific methods of inquiry. Nevertheless, Litchfield prioritized practical instruction, and Dwight noted that prospective students seeking a career in law would be "taught the practice of being actually employed in it."[28]

The rise of the proprietary law school pioneered by Reeve transformed the landscape of American legal education, a change made immensely easier by the publication of Sir William Blackstone's *Commentaries on the Laws of England* (1765–69), based on his Oxford lectures.[29] Ironically, Blackstone had not intended the work to be a primer for the thousands of American practitioners who came to regard it as indispensable. Rather, he designed it for "every gentleman and scholar: and an highly useful, I had almost said essential, part of liberal and polite education" for "gentlemen of independent estates and fortune." His *Commentaries,* therefore, would provide a "few leading principles," to "form some check and guard upon a gentleman's inferior agents, and preserve him at least from very gross and notorious imposition."[30]

The *Commentaries* quickly displaced *Coke on Littleton* as the required introduction to law for American students, a development that Jefferson later deplored, believing it to be dangerously "tory" and, moreover, a superficial shortcut for lawyers at the growing number of proprietary schools or those who read Blackstone on their own. As plans for the University proceeded in 1812, Jefferson revisited his opinion of the pedagogical suitability of the *Commentaries* and derisively remarked that "a student finds there a smattering of every thing, and his indolence easily persuades him that if he understands that book, he is master of the whole body of the law."[31] Yet that was precisely its greatest attraction, and the *Commentaries* sold a thousand copies in the colonies before its first American edition appeared early in the next decade. Not only did it supply faculty at American proprietary law schools with structure for teaching their courses and content for their lectures; it also provided students with a text that Jefferson admitted was "most lucid in arrangement," although only a "summary" that "lacked therefore the species of merit" of Coke and other great jurists.[32] Many aspiring law students read law with Jefferson in his retirement, and he grudgingly recommended Blackstone as "their last book, after an intermediate course of 2. or 3. years." The *Commentaries,* Jefferson remained convinced, "is nothing more than an elegant digest of what they will then have acquired from the real fountains of the law."[33]

Even so, students found much in what the better proprietary law schools provided that office mentors could not: better reference libraries, shared study with fellow students, connections for placement as practitioners in the offices of judges or eminent lawyers, a prestigious veneer of formal training in jurisprudence, and more attention from a professional faculty. Universities seeking to attract tuition-paying law students responded by providing lectures in law delivered by eminent legal scholars, but these courses taught law as jurisprudence or political science, and they ignored the technical training that students sought. Struggling to compete, universities hired eminent legal figures, but even the stature of a James Wilson at Pennsylvania or a James Kent at Columbia could not overcome student indifference to academic lectures, and universities soon abandoned their offerings in law.[34] The success of proprietary schools forced Jefferson to consider how to maintain legal education as an "excellent nursery for future judges" while also attracting tuition-paying students in a hurry to practice.[35]

In Virginia in 1825 Jefferson's University would have competition from William & Mary, but also from two successful proprietary law schools:

Creed Taylor's, formally organized in Needham in 1821 but begun in Richmond in 1810, and Henry St. George Tucker's newly opened school in Winchester in 1824.[36] Taylor explained the shape of legal education: "The *law-school* was established, not with a view to lectures by the patron, but for the purpose of aiding and assisting the student in the art and science of pleading: in other words, to instruct him how to conduct the business of a client." Taylor gave token acknowledgment to legal theory, but the basis of his course was contained in his *Journal of the Law-School,* a misnamed tome of legal forms, pleadings, statutes, and precedents. This would be the basis of a program centered on moot court exercises in which students argued simulated cases, first at a common law moot court and then in chancery, followed by appeal. Though his eighteen-month program of instruction was only an introduction to practice, it was adequate to launch a legal career or to supplement an ongoing practice, and it purported to elevate its material within a "scientific" framework.[37] Taylor had participated in the Rockfish Gap meeting in 1818, and he was the first signatory to its report.[38] His successful but long-forgotten law school represented the growth of the proprietary model of legal education that laid the basis for reform by preparing students for what to expect in the courtroom and, equally important, how to keep clients out of court by drafting documents that would not be challenged. Taylor's law school is significant for what it reveals as typical of its time, foreshadowing in its broad outline a curriculum sympathetic to Jefferson's wishes but more suited to accommodate the needs of prospective lawyers.

Jefferson's years of training law students who came to Charlottesville to read law under his direction had exposed him to another educational reality: the need to reach students of vastly different capacities. To accommodate the range of abilities they brought, he drew up and submitted a request that the library purchase books to provide for "the advocate a learned assistant" and for "the court an indisputable authority," as well as original sources for the scholar.[39] After history, its legal items comprised by far its largest category, an exhaustive compilation of more than three hundred fifty titles, equal to those for politics and religion combined. Its intended users would find not only treatises and reports but also practical manuals, abridgements, digests, and arguments of lawyers in major cases.[40] *Coke on Littleton* appeared on the list, but memories of his own days as a student had left Jefferson with reservations about its suitability to all students as an introduction to the common law. In 1814 he labeled it a "jumble" that "loses much of it's value by it's chaotic form," which he knew would be unwelcome to many would-be lawyers.[41] On first encountering Coke in 1762, even a student of Jefferson's ability had written in discouragement to his best friend, "I do wish the Devil had old Cooke, for I am sure I never was so tired of an old dull scoundrel in my life."[42]

By the time he concluded his reading law under Wythe's direction, however, he came to realize "that upon the whole the advice of these old fellows may be worth following."[43] He had discovered Coke's "artificial reason" of the law, the historically grounded jurisprudence that made the common law more accessible to a legal profession serving a republic of freeholders, and leading him finally to agree with "old Cooke" that this method would "open some windowes of the Law to let in more Light to the Student by diligent search to see the secrets of the Law."[44] Jefferson's much-quoted advice to a relative "disposed to the study of the law" in 1790—"All that is necessary for a student is access to a library, and directions in what order the books are to be read"—was thus not glib dismissal; rather, it offered advice on understanding what Coke meant when he wrote that "the common Law it selfe is nothing else but reason, which is to be understood of an artificial perfection of reason."[45] Properly understood, this "artificial perfection" was a process of *perfecting*—in its older sense of *to perfect* or improve, by which common law principles were historically derived, "gotten by long study, observation, and experience . . . because by many successions of ages it hath been fined and refined by an infinite number of grave and learned men."[46]

In expounding the common law as an intellectual skill, Coke and the common lawyers of his era began the long process of elevating the authority of judge-made precedent that emerged from the English experience—and, for Jefferson, with equal reason from Virginia's. Students in every department of the University would find in their library "not merely the best books in their respective branches of science . . . but such also as were deemed good in their day, and which consequently furnish a history of the advance of the science."[47] Virginia law students would thus learn American law as defined and validated by American

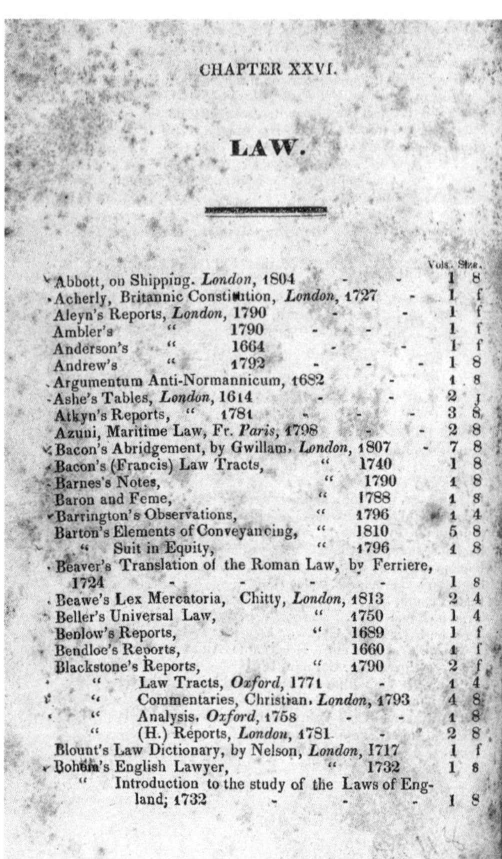

CHAPTER XXVI.

LAW.

	Vols.	Size.
Abbott, on Shipping. *London*, 1804 - -	1	8
Acherly, Britannic Constitution, *London*, 1727 -	1	f
Aleyn's Reports, *London*, 1790 - -	1	f
Ambler's " 1790 - -	1	f
Anderson's " 1664 - -	1	f
Andrew's " 1792 - - -	1	8
Argumentum Anti-Normannicum, 1682 -	1	8
Ashe's Tables, *London*, 1614 - -	2	j
Atkyn's Reports, " 1781 - - -	3	8
Azuni, Maritime Law, Fr. *Paris*, 1798 - -	2	8
Bacon's Abridgement, by Gwillam, *London*, 1807 -	7	8
Bacon's (Francis) Law Tracts, " 1740	1	8
Barnes's Notes, " 1790	1	8
Baron and Feme, " 1788	1	8
Barrington's Observations, " 1796	1	4
Barton's Elements of Conveyancing, " 1810	5	8
" Suit in Equity, " 1796	1	8
Beaver's Translation of the Roman Law, by Ferriere, 1724 - - - -	1	8
Beawe's Lex Mercatoria, Chitty, *London*, 1813	2	4
Beller's Universal Law, " 1750	1	4
Benlow's Reports, " 1689	1	f
Bendloe's Reports, 1660	1	f
Blackstone's Reports, " 1790	2	f
" Law Tracts, *Oxford*, 1771 -	1	4
" Commentaries, Christian, *London*, 1793	4	8
" Analysis, *Oxford*, 1758 - -	1	8
" (H.) Reports, *London*, 1781 -	2	8
Blount's Law Dictionary, by Nelson, *London*, 1717	1	f
Bohun's English Lawyer, " 1732	1	8
" Introduction to the study of the Laws of England; 1732 - - -	1	8

Law titles included in the 1828 Catalogue of the Library of the University of Virginia, copy owned by law professor John A. G. Davis. The catalogue lists the contents of the original UVA library selected by Thomas Jefferson. (Albert and Shirley Small Special Collections Library, University of Virginia)

experience that produced authoritative precedents. Jefferson took note of the power of precedent when practicing law in the 1760s, commonplacing a 1703 King's Bench opinion by Chief Justice John Holt, whom he called "the greatest lawyer England ever had, except Coke": "where is the same reason there is the same law; like reason doth make like law."[48]

It was not until 1822, when Jefferson discovered John H. Thomas's *Systematic Arrangement of Lord Coke's First Institute*, that he found an edition of *Coke on Littleton* that presented the artificial reason of the law in a manner that made it more accessible to those pursuing the status of a "reputable lawyer" without diminishing its value to the academically inclined student aspiring to be an "adept" scholar.[49] Thomas had reorganized the "jumble" of *Coke on Littleton* according to "the plan of Sir Matthew Hale's analysis," which demonstrated "that it is not impossible, by much Attention and Labour, to reduce the Laws of England at least unto a tolerable *Method* and *Distribution.*"[50] Hale's "method and distribution" was a taxonomy of law according to the historical purposes and needs of the English people and provided a method to classify and apply law to decide cases.[51] Hale had previously reorganized *Coke on Littleton,* helping make it more comprehensible, and Thomas's 1818 edition included "a new series of notes and references to the present time: including tables of parallel reference, analytical tables of contents, and a copious digested index." Jefferson included Hale's *Analysis* along with Thomas's *Systematic Arrangement* in his 1825 catalogue, calling the latter "the most essential & immediately necessary" text for the new law curriculum. Although no professor of law had yet been appointed, and despite the widespread preference for Blackstone, Jefferson remained insistent that *Coke on Littleton* would be "the first book which will be put into the hands of our law Students, and will in fact be the elementary book of the school." With classes about to begin, he had been unable to find any copies in the United States, and he wrote to his booksellers in Boston that they must import Thomas's expensive London edition. "I think it advisable," he wrote, "to lose no time in giving you notice of it."[52]

Jefferson devoted countless hours between 1814 and 1826 to tinkering with a curriculum that would be a model of legal education for a republic consistent with nature's order, not church dogma, and in Thomas's *Coke on Littleton,* he believed that he had found such a work to recommend where earlier editions proved too challenging. When his granddaughter, Virginia Randolph, responded to her fiancé, Nicholas Trist, regarding his struggles with an early edition of *Coke on Littleton,* she enclosed a note from her mother, Jefferson's daughter, who advised, "if you have not advanced too far in Coke to render it unimportant I shall send you the title of a book which Papa [her father] recommended to Francis [Eppes] as much the best he says it is as easy as Blackstone."[53] Two months later Jefferson wrote directly to Trist to make sure that he had obtained the correct edition, "Thomas's new arrangement of Coke Littleton," adding that it "is admirably executed. The whole matter of Coke & of Littleton is digested according to Blackstone's method, not omitting one word. . . . It is now unquestionably the elementary book to be first read by every student, and is as easy & more profound than Blackstone."[54]

Jefferson's reference to Blackstone implicitly acknowledged the value of the *Commentaries* in teaching law to beginners, even as he was warning against the seductive Tory dangers lurking within its pages. To his dismay, he found Virginia's "young brood of lawyers" to be a new generation of Tories under the sway of Blackstone's complacency.[55] For many years before the founding of the University, Jefferson had been recommending St. George Tucker's edition of the *Commentaries* when suggesting reading for students asking for guidance in the study of law. Tucker's *Commentaries* provided a republicanized version of the English edition of lectures Blackstone had written and published for his conservative Oxford audience.[56] For his intended republican readers in Virginia, Tucker inserted hundreds of footnotes and numerous appendices to steer them away from Blackstone's heresies. On its reissue more than two centuries later, it merited a book review by the distinguished legal scholar Robert Cover, who aptly described Tucker: "No other commentator of such pure Jeffersonian pedigree and persuasion ever wrote."[57]

Jefferson's opinion of Tucker illustrates how the label "Jeffersonian" was broad enough to paper over differences in the fragmented political culture of the early republic, and the two men had unbridgeable disagreements within their shared commitment to states' rights. Tucker's 1803 publication of his *Commentaries* included his well-known 1796 "Dissertation on Slavery," in which he had the courage to assail human chattel slavery in a manner that Jefferson could not or would not do.[58] That alone, however, had not sufficed to cause him to exclude it as the primary resource for beginners, and as late as 1814, Jefferson was still recommending Tucker's edition "as the last perfect Digest" of common law and equity.[59] Yet events in the 1820s troubled him enough to doubt its suitability for legal education, after the Missouri Crisis and a series of Supreme Court decisions that augured the consolidation of federal authority over the individual states. Altogether, these brought to the surface a steadily growing dread of an ascendant Supreme Court dominated by John Marshall, in whom he saw the malevolent influence of Blackstone. Such fears had fed Jefferson's misgivings about Tucker's views on the judicial power of the national government for many years. Tucker, for example, had a more expansive view of federal power under the Commerce Clause, and he believed in a strong judiciary with the authority to

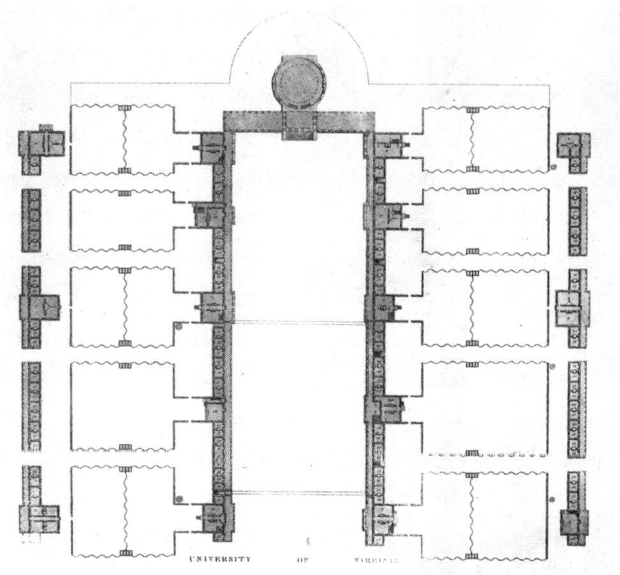

Thomas Jefferson's plan of the University of Virginia, 1825. (Albert and Shirley Small Special Collections Library, University of Virginia)

review legislation, a power that Jefferson opposed as unconstitutional.[60] Without comment, Jefferson stopped recommending Tucker's *Commentaries,* silently replacing it with Edward Christian's edition in 1822.[61] As classes were about to commence in 1825, he wrote to his bookseller to supply the texts he believed necessary to begin instruction and included Blackstone's *Commentaries,* but, he specified, "not Tucker's edition."[62] As far as can be inferred from the University's library's holdings in 1828, students attending lectures in law had access only to Christian's edition with its heavy emphasis on natural law and no antislavery essay.[63]

The First Law Professors

When the University of Virginia received its charter in 1819, the appointment of its law professor seemed imminent to many, but before that could be settled a frustrating process unfolded. Jefferson had initiated the search in 1817 when he contacted and hired Thomas Cooper, a political and religious radical who had studied law, medicine, and natural science and had taught at Dickinson College and the University of Pennsylvania. Jefferson, however, had not anticipated the depth of opposition to a radical such as Cooper, who sensed the distrust of his religious opinions and resigned before the University opened.[64] Jefferson's well-laid plan to move forward with a like-minded ally in the shaping of the University became instead a frustrating task that would take eight years and failed offers to ten other men before he finally recruited a young and relatively unknown lawyer, John Tayloe Lomax. Jefferson would discover that politics in academia could be paralytic, but his own insistence on constitutional orthodoxy also contributed. Francis Walker Gilmer, a trusted friend whom he had sent to England to recruit faculty, wrote on his return, as classes began without a professor of law, "The university has been very near its exit in the first few months of its birth. . . . Scarcely a thing has been done which I should approve, and half the utility of my labours in England has been marred, by Mr. J[efferson']s self-willed, & misguided mind."[65] As the search for the law professor dragged on, clouded by disagreement as to what type of background best qualified a candidate—judicial, legislative, or practical—the Board of Visitors was forced to meet and "to pay special attention to the principles of government which shall be inculcated . . . and for this purpose it may be necessary to point out specifically where these principles are to be found legitimately developed."[66]

The specifics of what to include or exclude from the Law School curriculum remained vague when Lomax arrived in Charlottesville on July 5, 1826, the day after Jefferson's death. The twenty-six students who had registered to study law met the following week, but their late start made fitting an entire session's material into the five remaining months difficult. When Lomax had a full session the next year, he still found it insufficient to include both academic and practical elements, and he was asked to report and explain why. In his report on the Law School in 1827 he admitted defensively, "As yet the professor of Law has not had time to enter upon one branch of the Duties which have been assigned to the Law School in the Law of Nature and Nations, Constitutional Law, etc." For that reason, it was necessary "for the present to devote all the attention of this professorship exclusively to that part of the instruction which regards municipal Law that which constitutes the ordinary business of the Courts of Virginia."[67]

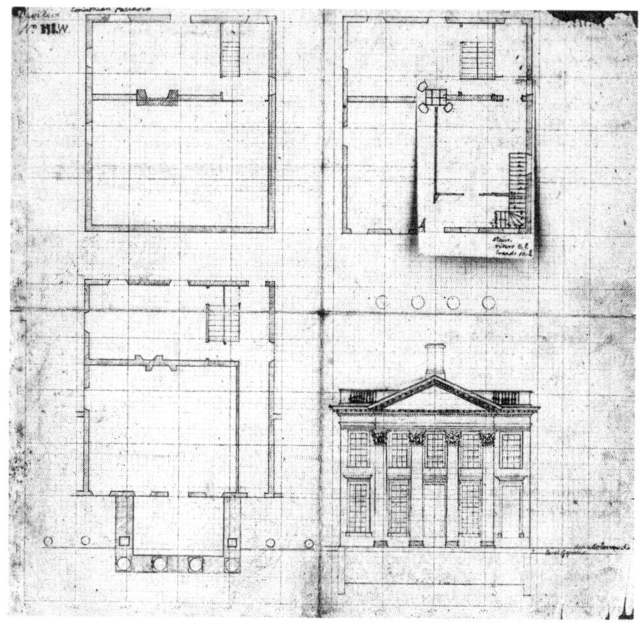

An architectural drawing by Thomas Jefferson of Pavilion III at the University of Virginia. When John Tayloe Lomax began lecturing as the University's first law professor, he lived and taught in Pavilion III. (Albert and Shirley Small Special Collections Library, University of Virginia)

Two years later, enough questions were still being raised about "the course of study intended to be pursued in the Law School," and Lomax once again had to explain what he was teaching in 1829. "It has been found necessary, however, to adapt the plan of study in some degree to the wishes and necessities of those who are desirous to read law for a profession," he conceded, and he proposed to offer practical instruction in one semester as other schools did, making a "first session an epitome of instruction in all the important subjects of municipal law." If a student wished to enroll for a second term, "he will have the principles, which he has been acquiring the first, more deeply inculcated and more extensively diversified in their application." The plan was a concession to students who sought a one-year program as a path to enter practice more quickly. Lomax nevertheless hoped that "the day is not very distant when his labours may be transferred to the higher" branches of law, but he probably did not expect it to happen while he taught at the University.[68] Fewer law students were willing to spend two or three years in study. "Their demand for the law is as for a trade," he complained, and "I found myself irresistibly compelled to labor for the satisfaction of this demand, or that the University would have no students of law."[69] In addition to student pressures, his salary was proving inadequate to the needs of his growing family. Offered a seat on the Circuit Superior Court of Law and Chancery, he resigned his professorship in 1830 to accept the post and establish his own private law school in Fredericksburg.[70]

Lomax was succeeded at the University by John Anthony Gardner Davis, who had moved his practice from Middlesex to pursue success in Charlottesville, where he married Jefferson's great-niece, spent a year studying at the University, and, with Thomas Walker Gilmer, established the Jeffersonian *Virginia Advocate* newspaper.[71] Davis introduced commercial law into the curriculum but otherwise organized his course around lectures that followed the familiar organization of Tucker's Blackstone, though with a caveat in his first lecture, recorded in a student notebook: "Blackstones treatise is admitted to be elementary & superficial; & not to be relied on to form a lawyer nor could any treatise equally concise. But is an [admir]able outline of the science. Mr. Jefferson attributed to Blackstone much of the heresy in politics that is prevalent. He is indeed a decided Monarchist; but this is an objection which lies against all Common Law writers for the lex prerogativa a part of the Common Law."[72] Davis relied on the republicanized edition of the Commentaries by St. George Tucker, who admitted his reliance on Christian's twelfth edition for notes "as appeared likely to be of use to an American Student" and acknowledged that Tucker had made "copious" use of them.[73] Davis added his own comments and noted those of others. John W. Stevenson's (Law 1834) student notebook from 1832 to 1833 is exemplary in its cross-referencing and inclusion of the comments made by other scholars criticizing or endorsing Blackstone. For example, Stevenson recorded Davis's comment made "in contradiction" of a point made by Blackstone, with citations to other authorities, and another that "Blackstone has imperfectly supplied the subject of Guardian & Ward."[74] Conversely, Stevenson quoted, "Blackstones exposition of the origin of the Common Law is certainly correct," noting "See Hales Hist Common Law, Chap IV—also most English historians & lawyers in confirmation of this."[75]

Davis struggled with natural law in his very first lecture, when he introduced the subject of master and servant, "to which in this state we must add slaves." He confronted it directly in principle: "Blackstone asserts that a state of slavery [is] contrary to reason & the principles of natural Law" and added, "This opinion I am not disposed to controvert." A solution eluded him as it had Jefferson, however, and Davis, too, evaded the question of emancipation as Jefferson had done. Dismissing the conventional legal, moral, and political defenses raised in the debate, he closely followed Jefferson on the practical dilemmas of emancipation and quoted, "In the language of Mr. Jefferson we had the wolf by the ear and to hold it or let it go would be attended with equal difficulty & danger." So much for convention, however, and Davis subtly slipped into his lecture a novel and lawyerly antislavery point. To counter the practical objection, Davis cited Kames's *Principles of Equity* to dismiss the equitable plea of "equal difficulty and danger" that stood in the way of emancipation: "The influence of public utility stops here, and never authorises a court of equity to enforce any positive act of injustice." Yet, notwithstanding the force of that argument, Davis, like Jefferson, equivocated on a solution and finally retreated to utility: "For if all owning slaves had been willing to yield them up without consideration what was to be done with them? When were they to be removed? And for them to live amongst us as free persons was entirely out of the question."[76]

Davis also served as chairman of the faculty—a thankless position that demanded he enforce discipline on Grounds. On the night of November 12, 1840, he rushed from his residence in Pavilion X, the new home of the law professor, to quiet two raucous students, one of whom shot and mortally wounded him. Shocked mourners eulogized the qualities sought in a "model lawyer" for a profession under sharp criticism for the "low, or base" motivations of that "diminutive animal called a *pettifogger*." One obituary commented hopefully, "It is thought, that once graduates of his law-school have taken their places at the Bar, the Profession, in Virginia, has breathed a more enlarged spirit, and a purer and a higher tone."[77]

The Board of Visitors filled the professorship of law on an interim basis, for approximately six months, with Richmond native Nathaniel Pope Howard, who lectured from Davis's class notes until Henry St. George Tucker agreed to accept the position.[78] Tucker solidified the place of natural law in the curriculum by announcing, “As we approach our *entré* upon the great theatre of life, it is important that we lay aside somewhat of the metaphysical subtleties of the schools” and follow natural law, which he defined as “that *rule of rectitude which is prescribed to us by the author of our being and pointed out by reason;* and which lies at the foundation of all wise and salutary systems of positive law.”[79] As it had been under Davis, the law curriculum was divided into two sessions, with the Junior (first-year) Class studying “the Elementary principles of municipal law; the Law of Nature and Nations; the science of Government; and constitutional law . . . guarding [the student] against latitudinarian constructions and the invasion of the reserved rights of the States,” while the Senior (second-year) Class was devoted to professional preparation on statute and common law.[80]

Tucker embodied the changes that had overtaken Virginia and the legal profession, and the contrast between his generation and his father’s epitomized the impact of economic decline and a retreat into a nostalgic reimagining of southern life and law. The elder Tucker had anticipated a Virginia moving away from dependence on agriculture and slavery and had divested himself of much of his human property.[81] The deepening sectional rift led him ultimately to succumb to the attraction of slavery, and he moved steadily away from many of the opinions he had expressed early in his career. His son Henry St. George did not have far to go to reach those conclusions, and he put Blackstone to good use as a template for the natural sanctity of property rights, not only in land but “of slaves as property.” Where his father had questioned the very notion of property in human beings, the son offered an editorial comment in his *Notes on Blackstone’s Commentaries:* “The student is referred to my appendix for a reading of the slave act in which a full view will attempt to be given of the laws relating to slaves in Virginia.”[82] The *Notes* did not avoid the subject of the enslaved as human chattel, and Tucker devoted numerous sections to the ways that Virginia law supplied rules and procedures for managing the property rights involved. Tucker, of course, gave obligatory praise to Blackstone’s *Commentaries,* which he recognized as “deservedly, if tritely, called a mine of learning.”[83]

Tucker’s *Lectures on Constitutional Law, for the Use of the Law Class at the University of Virginia,* which he read for his Junior course, presented a robust case for the southern position that repudiated the "political heresy" of "the United States as constituting *one people* instead of a confederacy of sovereign states . . . who retain their sovereignty, and all the rights of sovereignty which they have not expressly transferred to the federal government."[84] He opposed nullification, but he was so devoted to the protection of slave property that he opposed it on the grounds that it would be used by northern abolitionists. Tucker's *Lectures* posed for his students hypothetical questions about the autonomy of southern property holders, especially concerning the enslaved. If applied to fugitive enslaved persons, he asked, could federal courts issue restraining orders to effect "a suspension of vital laws, until the decision is promulgated as to their supposed validity" because of some "technical and quibbling objection"? If so, this would mean that "if the surrender of our runaway slaves, or of the negro stealers, who carry them off is evaded, against the plain words of the constitution, we must wait for redress" by a constitutional amendment. "And when may that be expected? *Ad Graecas Calendas!* Never! Never, at least, if the spirit of abolition and fanaticism are not checked in their rapid and alarming growth."[85] His *Lectures on Natural Law* complemented his defense of slavery by denying that the enslaved had any natural right to property in themselves, while he approvingly quoted Henry Clay that "the rights of the master over the slave" predated and were guaranteed by the Constitution.[86]

Tucker retired after four years at the University, weakened by a bout of paralysis that resulted in cognitive decline.[87] He left a legacy, however, out of proportion to the relatively short time he taught at the University. In a long teaching career that began at his proprietary law school in Winchester in 1824, Tucker developed lectures and published materials that elevated natural law to canonical status. When he arrived at the University in 1841, Tucker announced his credo in an *Introductory Lecture* that expressed in rousing military terms a message in which southern constitutional doctrine became a call to arms.[88] Although his paralysis weakened him and limited his duties, he had already seized the opportunity to address the student body with an emphatic statement of the primacy and power of "*natural* law." He cast his argument in unashamedly combative terms, much unlike the language of his father's genteel southern past and more fitted to a combative future. The students' legal education, he promised, would sustain them "on your entering upon this distinguished arena . . . from which you step at once upon the great theatre of life, with weapons," as he told them to "arm for the fight." He continued: "In our ample arsenals you will find weapons of your warfare. The armory of Lord Coke will furnish mail for your defence and the battle axe for assault." A "victory" would mean an education whose "legitimate fruits are a steadfast adherence to *things as they are.*"[89]

Tucker could not have chosen a credo farther from Thomas Jefferson's determination in founding the University than to assert that the purpose of education was to ensure "a steadfast adherence to *things as they are.*" In an ironic twist on his belief that "the earth belongs in usufruct to the living," the preservation of "things as they are" would repudiate the Rockfish Gap Report's Jeffersonian manifesto that "it cannot be but that each generation succeeding to the knowledge acquired by all those who preceded it, adding to it their own acquisitions & discoveries, and handing the mass down for successive & constant accumulation, must advance the knowledge & well-being of mankind."[90] The physical campus stood as an aspirational reminder of an objective that seemed, a quarter century after its founding, to exist only on paper, much as Central College had been when Jefferson and the commissioners met in that tavern in the Blue Ridge. For the University to fulfill those goals would require the realization of another Jeffersonian imperative, one that he set out in accepting an honorary degree from the president of Harvard in 1789: "It is the work to which the young men, whom you are forming, should lay their hands. We have spent the prime of our lives in procuring them the precious blessing of liberty. Let them spend theirs in shewing that it is the great parent of science and of virtue; and that a nation will be great in both always in proportion as it is free."[91]

Notes

1. "Rockfish Gap Report of the University of Virginia Commissioners," 4 August 1818, in James P. McClure and J. Jefferson Looney, eds., *The Papers of Thomas Jefferson, Digital Edition* (Charlottesville: University of Virginia Press, Rotunda, 2008–25), 13:210, https://rotunda.upress.virginia.edu/founders/TSJN-03-13-02-0197-0006. (The main series is hereafter cited as *PTJ,* and the Retirement Series as *PTJRS.* Note

that original spelling from quoted material has been preserved throughout this chapter.)

2. Thomas Jefferson to James Madison, 11 April 1818, *PTJRS,* 12:625, https://rotunda.upress.virginia.edu/founders/TSJN-03-12-02-0517. (Thomas Jefferson is hereafter cited as TJ.)
3. Frederick W. Page, "Our Library," *The Alumni Bulletin of the University of Virginia* 2, no. 3 (November 1895): 80.
4. TJ to José Corrêa da Serra, 24 October 1820, *PTJRS,* 16:367, https://rotunda.upress.virginia.edu/founders/TSJN-03-16-02-0298.
5. "Rockfish Gap Report," *PTJRS,* 13:214.
6. "Rockfish Gap Report," *PTJRS,* 13:212.
7. TJ to Joseph Priestley, 18 January 1800, *PTJ,* 31:320, https://rotunda.upress.virginia.edu/founders/TSJN-01-31-02-0275.
8. "Rockfish Gap Report," *PTJRS,* 13:210.
9. TJ to John Hartwell Cocke, 19 July 1817, *PTJRS,* 11:545, https://rotunda.upress.virginia.edu/founders/TSJN-03-11-02-0150.
10. Louis P. Nelson and Maurie D. McInnis, "Landscape of Slavery," in *Educated in Tyranny: Slavery at Thomas Jefferson's University,* ed. Maurie D. McInnis and Louis P. Nelson (Charlottesville: University of Virginia Press, 2019), 42–74. An incomplete list of persons enslaved at the University can be found in that book's dedication. The complex and neglected history of African Americans is a notable part of the ongoing digital project "Jefferson's University: The Early Life," which includes much information on enslaved individuals in this period, http://juel.iath.virginia.edu. The manner in which "Jefferson sought to instill his vision of the intelligent, and sometimes reluctant, enslaver" is the subject of Justene Hill Edwards's "Teaching the Laws of Slavery, 1826–1865" in the present volume.
11. TJ to John Page, 25 December 1762, *PTJ,* 1:5, https://rotunda.upress.virginia.edu/founders/TSJN-01-01-02-0002.
12. TJ, "Autobiography," in *Thomas Jefferson: Writings,* ed. Merrill Peterson (New York: Library of America, 1984), 4.
13. TJ, "Autobiography," 44.
14. TJ to Thomas Jefferson Randolph, 24 November 1808, Founders Online, National Archives, https://founders.archives.gov/documents/Jefferson/99-01-02-9151.
15. "79. A Bill for the More General Diffusion of Knowledge," 18 June 1779, *PTJ,* 2:527. The bill's fate is followed in an editorial note, 2:534–35, https://rotunda.upress.virginia.edu/founders/TSJN-01-02-02-0132-0004-0079.
16. TJ to George Wythe, 13 August 1786, *PTJ,* 10:244–45, https://rotunda.upress.virginia.edu/founders/TSJN-01-10-02-0162.
17. TJ to Charles Yancey, 6 January 1816, *PTJRS,* 9:331, https://rotunda.upress.virginia.edu/founders/TSJN-03-09-02-0209.
18. John Bernard, *Retrospections of America, 1797–1811* (New York: Harper & Brothers, 1887), 238.
19. Edward Coke, *The First Part of the Institutes of the Lawes of England; Or, a Commentarie upon Littleton* . . . (London: Printed for the Societie of Stationers, 1628) (hereafter cited as *Coke on Littleton*).
20. TJ to Madison, 17 February 1826, Founders Online, https://founders.archives.gov/documents/Madison/04-03-02-0712.
21. *Coke on Littleton,* Preface (n.p.).

22. The enduring "dilemma" this created can be followed through many studies. Useful overviews are Robert Stevens, *Law School: Legal Education in America from the 1850s to the 1980s* (Chapel Hill: University of North Carolina Press, 1983); and Alfred Zantzinger Reed's report to the Carnegie Foundation, *Training for the Public Profession of the Law . . .* (New York: Carnegie Foundation for the Advancement of Teaching, 1921).
23. TJ to Francis Eppes, 17 March 1793, *PTJ,* 25:396, https://rotunda.upress.virginia.edu/founders/TSJN-01-25-02-0357.
24. For Virginia's bar admission standards at that time, see Reed, *Training for the Public Profession,* 96–98.
25. TJ to William Wirt, 10 January 1808, Founders Online, https://founders.archives.gov/documents/Jefferson/99-01-02-7178. Popular discontent directed at lawyers is examined in detail by A. G. Roeber, *Faithful Magistrates and Republican Lawyers: Creators of Virginia Legal Culture, 1680–1810* (Chapel Hill: University of North Carolina Press, 1981).
26. TJ to Wythe, 1 March 1779, *PTJ,* 2:235, https://rotunda.upress.virginia.edu/founders/TSJN-01-02-02-0090.
27. John H. Langbein, "Blackstone, Litchfield, and Yale: The Founding of the Yale Law School," in *History of the Yale Law School: The Tercentennial Lectures,* ed. Anthony T. Kronman (New Haven, CT: Yale University Press, 2004), 21–32.
28. Timothy Dwight, *Travels in New-England and New-York* (New Haven, CT: S. Converse, 1822), 4:306.
29. William Blackstone, *Commentaries on the Laws of England,* 4 vols. (Oxford: Clarendon Press, 1765–69).
30. Blackstone, *Commentaries,* 1:5–7.
31. TJ to John Tyler, 17 June 1812, *PTJRS,* 5:136, https://rotunda.upress.virginia.edu/founders/TSJN-03-05-02-0112.
32. TJ to Thomas Cooper, 16 January 1814, *PTJRS,* 7:126–27, https://rotunda.upress.virginia.edu/founders/TSJN-03-07-02-0071.
33. TJ to Tyler, 26 May 1810, *PTJRS,* 2:420, https://rotunda.upress.virginia.edu/founders/TSJN-03-02-02-0365.
34. W. Hamilton Bryson, *Legal Education in Virginia, 1779–1979: A Biographical Approach* (Charlottesville: University Press of Virginia, 1982), 29–37, concisely evaluates this transitional period in Virginia. On the lasting impact of proprietary schools, see Craig Evan Klafter, "The Influence of Vocational Law Schools on the Origins of American Legal Thought, 1779–1829," *American Journal of Legal History* 37, no. 3 (July 1993): 307–31.
35. TJ to Wythe, 1 March 1779, *PTJ,* 2:235, https://rotunda.upress.virginia.edu/founders/TSJN-01-02-02-0090.
36. Bryson, *Legal Education in Virginia,* 592, 606.
37. Creed Taylor, *Journal of the Law-School, and of the Moot-Court Attached to It at Needham, in Virginia . . .* (Richmond, VA: J. & G. Cochran, 1822), v–vii.
38. "Rockfish Gap Report," *PTJRS,* 13:222.
39. Matthew Hale, *The History of the Common Law of England: And an Analysis of the Civil Part of the Law,* 6th ed., with additional notes and references . . . , ed. Charles Runnington (London: H. Butterworth, 1820), Preface (n.p.).
40. TJ, "Catalog of Books for the University of Virginia Library, 1825," MSS 38–747,

Albert and Shirley Small Special Collections Library, University of Virginia (hereafter cited as SSCL).

41. TJ to Cooper, 16 January 1814, *PTJRS,* 7:126, https://rotunda.upress.virginia.edu/founders/TSJN-03-07-02-0071.

42. TJ to Page, 25 December 1762, *PTJ,* 1:5, https://rotunda.upress.virginia.edu/founders/TSJN-01-01-02-0002.

43. TJ to Page, 25 December 1762, *PTJ,* 1:5.

44. *Coke on Littleton,* "Epilogus," 395. Harold J. Berman elucidates this process in "The Origins of Historical Jurisprudence: Coke, Selden, Hale," *Yale Law Journal* 103, no. 7 (May 1994): 1688–92.

45. TJ to John Garland Jefferson, 11 June 1790, *PTJ,* 16:480, https://rotunda.upress.virginia.edu/founders/TSJN-01-16-02-0278.

46. *Oxford English Dictionary* (Oxford: Oxford University Press, 2023), s.v. "perfection, v[erb]," "To bring to perfection, to perfect," https://doi.org/10.1093/OED/1188194386; see also Matthew Crow, *Thomas Jefferson, Legal History, and the Art of Recollection* (Cambridge: Cambridge University Press, 2017), 16; *Coke on Littleton,* "Of Frankalmoigne," 97b.

47. Page, "Our Library," 79.

48. Ashby v. White, 92 ER 126 (1703), commonplaced as entry no. 494 in *Jefferson's Legal Commonplace Book,* ed. David Thomas Konig and Michael P. Zuckert (Princeton, NJ: Princeton University Press, 2019), 210. On TJ's regard for Holt, see TJ to Peter Carr, 8 May 1791, *PTJ,* 20:378, https://rotunda.upress.virginia.edu/founders/TSJN-01-20-02-0118.

49. TJ to John Wayles Eppes, 10 June 1822, *PTJRS,* 18:446, https://rotunda.upress.virginia.edu/founders/TSJN-03-18-02-0389; John H. Thomas, *A Systematic Arrangement of Lord Coke's First Institute of the Laws of England, on the Plan of Sir Matthew Hale's Analysis; with the Annotations . . .* (London: S. Brooke, 1818). A first American edition, published in Philadelphia, appeared in 1827.

50. Hale, *History of the Common Law of England,* Preface (n.p.).

51. Berman, "Historical Jurisprudence," 1688–89, 1705, 1707.

52. TJ to Cummings, Hilliard & Co., 17 January 1825, Founders Online, https://founders.archives.gov/documents/Jefferson/98-01-02-4879.

53. Virginia Jefferson Randolph (Trist) to Nicholas P. Trist with Note from Martha Jefferson to Nicholas Trist, 28 April 1822, Nicholas Philip Trist Papers, Family Correspondence, Box 2, Trist, Virginia Jefferson Randolph (1821–23), MSS43232, Library of Congress.

54. TJ to Trist, 14 June 1822, *PTJRS,* 18:475, https://rotunda.upress.virginia.edu/founders/TSJN-03-18-02-0416. "Blackstone's method" followed that of Hale, which "was borrowed by William Blackstone with minimal modification and therefore provides the structure of Blackstone's *Commentaries.*" Alan Cromartie, "Hale, Sir Matthew (1609–1676)," *Oxford Dictionary of National Biography* (September 2004), https://doi.org/10.1093/ref:odnb/11905.

55. TJ to Madison, 17 February 1826, Founders Online, https://founders.archives.gov/documents/Madison/04-03-02-0712.

56. St. George Tucker, ed., *Blackstone's Commentaries: With Notes of Reference to the Constitution and Laws of the Federal Government of the United States; and of the Commonwealth of Virginia . . .* (Philadelphia: Birch and Small, 1803).

57. Robert M. Cover, review of *Blackstone's Commentaries*, ed. Henry St. George Tucker, *Columbia Law Review* 70, no. 8 (December 1970): 1475–76.
58. Tucker's "Dissertation on Slavery: With a Proposal for the Gradual Abolition of It, in the State of Virginia," appeared as "On the State of Slavery in Virginia," in Note H of vol. 1, part 2, 79–86, of his 1803 edition of the *Commentaries*.
59. TJ to John Minor, including an earlier letter to Bernard Moore, 30 August 1814, *PTJRS*, 7:627–28, https://rotunda.upress.virginia.edu/founders/TSJN-03-07-02-0455.
60. On Tucker's broad expansion of federal authority by the Commerce Clause, see David Thomas Konig, "St. George Tucker and the Limits of States' Rights Constitutionalism: Understanding the Federal Compact in the Early Republic," *William and Mary Law Review* 47, no. 4 (February 2006): 1279–341.
61. TJ to Francis Eppes, 9 April 1822, *PTJRS*, 18:334–35, https://rotunda.upress.virginia.edu/founders/TSJN-03-18-02-0291; William Blackstone, *Commentaries on the Laws of England . . .*, with notes and additions by Edward Christian, 12th ed. (London: Strahan and Woodfall, 1794).
62. TJ to Jacob Abbott Cummings, 17 January 1825, Founders Online, https://founders.archives.gov/documents/Jefferson/98-01-02-4879.
63. William Peden, ed., *1828 Catalogue of the Library of the University of Virginia* (Charlottesville: Printed for the Alderman Library of the University of Virginia, 1945).
64. Cooper to TJ, 24 April 1820, Founders Online, https://founders.archives.gov/documents/Jefferson/03-15-02-0522.
65. Francis Walker Gilmer to John Randolph of Roanoke, 25 May 1825, "Letters of Francis Walker Gilmer," *Tyler's Quarterly Historical and Genealogical Magazine* 6, no. 3 (January 1925): 197.
66. Minutes of the Board of Visitors of the University of Virginia, 4 March 1825, Founders Online, https://founders.archives.gov/documents/Madison/04-03-02-0487.
67. John Tayloe Lomax, "Report on the School of Law and the School of Modern Languages," 19 July 1827, MSS 11950, SSCL.
68. "University Intelligence," *Virginia Literary Museum and Journal of Belles Lettres, Arts, &c* 1, no. 8 (1829): 124–26.
69. Philip Alexander Bruce, *History of the University of Virginia, 1819–1919: The Lengthened Shadow of One Man* (New York: Macmillan, 1920), 2:103.
70. Bryson, *Legal Education in Virginia*, 362.
71. Bryson, *Legal Education in Virginia*, 181.
72. John W. Stevenson Student Notebook, 1 February 1832, Professor J. A. G. Davis Lectures, Student Notebooks, RG-32-400, Arthur J. Morris Law Library Special Collections, University of Virginia (hereafter cited as LLSC).
73. Tucker, *Commentaries*, vol. 1, "Advertisement" (n.p.).
74. John W. Stevenson Student Notebook, ("contradiction") 1 February 1832, ("imperfectly") 27 February 1832.
75. Stevenson Student Notebook, 5 February 1832.
76. Stevenson Student Notebook, 20 February 1834; see also Henry Home Kames, *Principles of Equity* (Edinburgh, UK: Printed for Bell & Bradfute, 1825).
77. Lucian Minor, *Discourse on the Life and Character of the Late John A. G. Davis, Professor of Law in the University of Virginia, Delivered before the Society of Alumni, June 29th, 1847* (Richmond, VA: Shepherd and Colin, 1847), 25–27, italics in the original.
78. Bryson, *Legal Education in Virginia*, 306.

79. Henry St. George Tucker, *A Few Lectures on Natural Law* (Charlottesville, VA: James Alexander, 1844), 2, italics in the original.
80. *Catalogue of the Officers and Students of the University of Virginia, Session of 1841–1842* (Charlottesville, VA: James Alexander, 1842), 15.
81. See Phillip Hamilton, *The Making and Unmaking of a Revolutionary Family: The Tuckers of Virginia, 1752–1830* (Charlottesville: University of Virginia Press, 2003).
82. Henry St. George Tucker, *Notes on Blackstone's Commentaries for the Use of Students* (Winchester, VA: Samuel H. Davis, 1826), 399, citing Revised Code, ch. 111.
83. Tucker, *Notes on Blackstone's Commentaries,* 3.
84. Henry St. George Tucker, *Lectures on Constitutional Law, for the Use of the Law Class of the University of Virginia* (Richmond, VA: Shepherd and Colin, 1843), 9–10, italics in the original.
85. Translation: "On the Greek calends," which did not exist. Tucker, *Lectures on Constitutional Law,* 196, italics in the original.
86. Tucker, *Few Lectures on Natural Law,* 182.
87. Alta Elizabeth Cassady, "Henry St. George Tucker, Legal Educator" (master's thesis, College of William & Mary, 1978), 21.
88. Henry St. George Tucker, *Introductory Lecture Delivered by the Professor of Law in the University of Virginia* (Charlottesville, VA: Magruder & Noel, 1841).
89. Tucker, *Introductory Lecture,* 3, 4, 8, 9, italics in the original.
90. TJ to Madison, 6 September 1789, *PTJ,* 15:392, https://rotunda.upress.virginia.edu/founders/TSJN-01-15-02-0375-0003; "Rockfish Gap Report," *PTJRS,* 13:213.
91. TJ to Joseph Willard, 24 March 1789, *PTJ,* 14:699, https://rotunda.upress.virginia.edu/founders/TSJN-01-14-02-0437.

Teaching the Laws of Slavery, 1826–1865

Justene Hill Edwards

IN THOMAS JEFFERSON'S famed *Notes on the State of Virginia,* published in 1785, he wrote of his complicated perspective on slavery. Jefferson recognized, and grappled with, his realization that slavery and mastery had the potential to alter the character of enslavers. "There must doubtless be an unhappy influence on the manners of our people produced by the existence of slavery among us," Jefferson opined.[1] "The whole commerce between master and slave is a perpetual exercise of the most boisterous passions, the most unremitting despotism on the one part, and degrading submissions on the other. Our children see this, and learn to imitate it."[2] The institution, shaped by the interactions between enslavers and the enslaved, engendered the most destructive parts of human nature: greed, laziness, and hedonism. He contended that the dangerous influence of slavery manifested not only in the lives of the enslaved, but also in the behavior of the enslaver.

Jefferson carried this equivocation about slavery, and the complexities inherent in the relationship between enslavers and the enslaved, into establishing the University of Virginia in 1819 and enrolling the first class of students in 1825. In founding a university where students would not only learn about natural sciences, philosophy, and literature, but also the legal tenets of statesmanship and mastery, Jefferson sought to instill his vision of the intelligent, and sometimes reluctant, enslaver in a new generation of students.

Jefferson's image of the erudite, begrudging, and benevolent enslaver was indirectly embedded in the curriculum *and* in student life in the early years of UVA. Students who enrolled at Jefferson's University would cultivate an appreciation of the liberal arts by taking classes in any of the original eight schools, including law.[3] Regardless of subject, students cultivated an understanding of slavery conveyed through the teachings of professors who often promoted their own proslavery agendas. Students also learned skills of mastery through their interactions with enslaved laborers who lived in, worked at, and maintained the University. The first students to matriculate at UVA entered the classroom, shared meals in dining halls called "Hotels," and walked around Grounds absorbing lessons on how to navigate a world in which they would hold people of African descent in bondage.[4]

Thomas Jefferson's legacy permeated almost every aspect of academic and social life on Grounds. Between the University's welcoming of the first students in March 1825 to the beginning of the Civil War in 1861, Jefferson loomed large on the small but growing campus. His position as a statesman, his perspective on democracy, and even his outlook on slavery, however fraught, shaped almost every aspect of the University. This influence included the introduction of legal education—and the effect of slavery and the experiences of the enslaved on the evolution of the Law School's curriculum.

UVA's early curriculum was filled with lessons on philosophy and political theory, and in courses on law and jurisprudence students gained a firm foundation of proslavery thought and how to preserve the institution indefinitely. Deeply entwined in the UVA Law curriculum were lessons in how to navigate the legal landscape of slavery in an increasingly slaveholding nation. All six antebellum law faculty members had connections to slavery, either through their own investments or family ties. Their relationships to slavery as an institution, from which they personally profited, inevitably shaped their perspectives on law and legal education. The law faculty used a specific curriculum and corresponding treatises, such as the popular *Commentaries on the Laws of England* by

Sir William Blackstone, to structure their teachings about slavery as a legal and just institution.[5] Students were ensconced in an environment where they were free to develop their personal opinions about slavery and slaveholding in America while they learned the practical and theoretical skills of practicing law.

The legal education that students received reflected the transformation of how the law faculty thought about slavery. From embracing a Jeffersonian perspective on bondage, the "necessary evil" outlook in the early republican period, to one that also saw slavery as a "positive good" in the Civil War era, faculty and students reflected the ways in which proslavery ideas developed in the nation, writ large.[6] The lectures, readings, and personal lives of the law faculty, and the class notes of early students, demonstrate that slavery was both a formal and informal aspect of academic life at UVA.

Historiographical conversations about the intersections between slavery and American higher education have become a fertile intellectual battleground. Historians and legal scholars have interrogated how the rise of the American university, as early as the seventeenth century, planted the seeds of proslavery thought.[7] Missing from these important interventions is the role of the student in understanding proslavery legal education in the nineteenth century, in particular the period of slavery's great expansion and contraction in American society between 1830 and the start of the Civil War. By considering law student notebooks, a clearer understanding emerges of the ways students absorbed law professors' teaching of proslavery legal thought in the classroom. According to Karen S. Beck, in the nineteenth century student notebooks were not simply ephemera.[8] Rather, students took notes to understand the law and legal tools and to create a reference source for use in their future legal careers. A necessary addendum is a more focused interrogation of how the growth and professionalization of legal education in the nineteenth century became intertwined with the history of American slavery.

Slavery and the Making of the Academical Village

At a Board of Visitors meeting on April 7, 1824, members discussed and approved the creation of a professor of law as one of the University's eight professorships. The man appointed to the position would be responsible for teaching "Common and Statute Law that of the chancery, the laws Feudal, civil, mercatorial, maritime and of Nature and Nations; and also the principles of government and political economy."[9] The ideal candidate would relinquish all other professional commitments—such as a judgeship or other elected office—and focus solely on instruction.

The following year the Board of Visitors held a meeting on March 4, 1825, just before the first students arrived, during which they approved the readings that would support the law curriculum. These men, notably Jefferson, were especially concerned with the political education that students would receive. To ensure the curriculum was compatible with the "principles of government" as articulated in and in the spirit of the Virginia and US constitutions, students would be required to read a specific list of texts.[10] In order to guide students in understanding "the general principles of liberty and the rights of man in nature and in society," the law professor would teach John Locke's "Essay Concerning the True Original Extent and End of Civil Government," Algernon Sidney's *Discourses on Government*, the Declaration of Independence, *The Federalist Papers*, George Washington's farewell address, and the 1799 Virginia resolution that nullified the 1798 federal Alien and Sedition Acts.[11] Each of these readings addressed issues that directly and indirectly invoked forms of bondage and its antitheses—slavery and slaveholding as well as freedom and liberty. From Locke's statements on freedom, writing, "The natural liberty of man is to be free from any superior power on earth," to the Virginia resolution that proposed that states had the right to reject federal law, the UVA law curriculum created an ideal pedagogical environment for law faculty to encourage the expansion of slavery in the United States.[12]

In addition to outlining the law curriculum's structure, the Board of Visitors, guided by Jefferson's stewardship, also defined how enslaved labor would, and would not, be used on Grounds. Its members decided on October 4, 1824, five months before the first class arrived, that students could not bring enslaved people with them (though faculty could). Bound up with other regulations, the board mandated: "No student shall, within the precincts of the University, introduce, keep or use any spirituous liquors or vinous liquors, keep or use weapons or arms of any kind, or gunpowder, keep a servant, horse or dog."[13] The board classified enslaved people with other forms of chattel and property, which communicated to students how members understood the role of the enslaved. These regulations did not keep students from finding ways to keep enslaved people close, either through violent coercion or ingenuity. Students might house the people they enslaved outside of Grounds or take on authoritarian and often violent relationships with people enslaved by UVA's hotelkeepers.[14]

Jefferson was unsure about the influence of slave ownership on students during their time at the University. In keeping with his perspective that slavery fed men's undesirable attributes—that of laziness and giving in to their "most boisterous passions"—the guideline that prohibited students from bringing enslaved persons to Grounds was meant to encourage industriousness and independence. But the board perhaps did not foresee the ways in which enslaved laborers would be forcefully integrated into the University community, and how their visibility on Grounds would collide with Jefferson's mission of educating a new generation of politicians and enslavers.[15]

The University's reliance on enslaved labor began on the first day of construction. The board decided early on that they would rely on the robust network of enslavers in Albemarle and neighboring counties for labor. For this reason, the University purchased only *one* enslaved person initially. In April 1819, as construction continued into its second year, Jefferson agreed to purchase an enslaved person for $125, to be owned by the University outright.[16] But the vast majority of enslaved men and women were rented or hired out from local enslavers willing to forego their bondspeople's labor for a specific period of time—a year for example—or to complete discrete projects.[17] In exchange, the enslaver would be compensated for the enslaved person's labor. As Louis P. Nelson and James D. W. Zehmer have considered, there were instances in which enslaved laborers could earn money for themselves through completing work that exceeded hirers' expectations.[18]

In March 1825, the first group of students began classes in what was then known as the University of Virginia in Charlottesville (originally Central College).[19] The inaugural class of students who arrived in Charlottesville in March 1825 lived alongside seven professors who taught in

Sketch of a University of Virginia student posing on the Lawn, dated 1853 and drawn by David Hunter Strother. (Albert and Shirley Small Special Collections Library, University of Virginia)

seven of the original eight schools: medicine, mathematics, chemistry, ancient languages, modern languages, natural philosophy, and moral philosophy.[20] A law professor had yet to be hired. Faculty and students were surrounded by enslaved women and men who were hired by the University and made responsible for maintaining the grounds on which they lived. These enslaved laborers were also witnessing the growth of liberal arts education in Virginia while living under a system of forced bondage. The education enslaved people received was through completing the necessary labor to ensure that a new generation of enslavers would learn the philosophies and analytical tools necessary to support their futures as enslavers.

The law professor would complement the growing list of faculty members who would make real Jefferson's vision of training the next generation of gentlemen fit to lead the new (slaveholding) republic. Jefferson, as David T. Konig explores in this volume, believed that for the faculty to have the maximum educational and social impact on the students, they needed to live on Grounds.[21] In this way, Jefferson's architectural priorities reflected this goal. Designed around what were called pavilions, the buildings that comprised Jefferson's Academical Village would house each of the University's planned ten schools, with classrooms on the ground level of each pavilion and faculty housing on the upper floors. The ten pavilions represented the Jeffersonian view that the faculty and students would live, work, and eat together, to build a vibrant intellectual community.[22]

The pavilions would also house the enslaved people owned by the University's faculty. Strategically designed to obscure the enslaved people's working and living spaces, the basements of the pavilions were structured to accommodate the kitchens in which the enslaved would work and the bedrooms in which they would live. Intended to cater to both the faculty and students, the pavilions were sites of learning. Faculty would use the spaces not only to teach their primary subjects but also to instruct students on how to navigate the domestic sphere of mastery over the enslaved.[23] Law classes were assigned to Pavilion III, which would also house the law professor. And, as with the other pavilions, Pavilion III came equipped to accommodate the new law professor's enslaved people, who were in many ways coerced to participate in the pedagogical project of teaching the first classes of UVA students how to think about slavery and mastery.

In a February 17, 1826, letter to James Madison, Jefferson detailed his goals for the University's first professor of law. He sought a "Law-Professor" who could teach students English common law as articulated in the works of Blackstone and Sir Edward Coke.[24] More specifically, he believed the University required a professor adept at teaching a combination of common law and American republican ideology to train a new crop of lawyers, jurists, and legislators. "It is in our Seminary that the Vestal flame is to be kept alive," he wrote. "If we are true and vigilant in our trust, within a dozen or 20 years, a majority of our own legislature, will be from our school," Jefferson argued, and "many disciples will have carried it's doctrines home with them to their several states, and have leavened thus the whole mass."[25] With this mission, to influence both the students and the legal philosophies that the students carried with them upon graduation, the University hired its first law professor: John Tayloe Lomax.

UVA's First Law Professor

Lomax arrived in Charlottesville in July 1826, ready to embark on a new phase of his career. He was returning to his native Virginia to take the professorship after spending his formative years in Maryland. Lomax graduated from St. John's College in Annapolis in 1797, having benefited from the largess of his uncle, John Tayloe III, a prominent planter and enslaver from Richmond County, Virginia. After graduation, Lomax spent four years in Annapolis reading legal theory and treatises. In 1801, he traveled back to Port Royal, Virginia, and set up a law practice. Following stints in Port Royal, Fredericksburg, and Menokin, where he honed his practice, he accepted UVA's offer to spearhead the University's School of Law.[26]

Lomax's attentiveness to the legal curriculum would be front and center when he accepted the professorship at UVA in 1826. While he largely employed the curriculum Jefferson and the Board of Visitors had devised, he added some selections of his own. He also approached his teaching of the law in as practical a manner as possible. Given the ongoing popularity of apprenticeship in America and the slow professionalization of law, Lomax recognized his students needed the intellectual tools to begin practicing law as soon as possible—whether they remained in the program one year or two and whether they graduated or not (at the time, a degree was not necessary to become a practicing attorney).[27]

In addition to teaching, Lomax served as faculty chairman during 1827–28 and served again from June 1830 to July 1831. In this position, he was responsible for adjudicating disputes that arose on Grounds, especially those that involved students. This role was particularly important for ensuring students learned a sense of decorum, a trait that enslavers such as Jefferson publicly espoused as a facet of benevolent mastery.[28] During Lomax's first year as chairman, he received complaints about a range of issues, from students wishing to withdraw from certain classes to buildings falling into disrepair. One of the more troublesome issues with which Lomax dealt was interactions between students and enslaved people. The young white men who matriculated to UVA during the University's first era sought to use their time in college to ascend the southern political power structure. As historian Alan S. Taylor has argued, "Young men attended college to claim a place in Virginia's governing class."[29] Lomax understood that he was responsible for ushering male students—who were born into wealth and privilege—through the educational and social gauntlet. This required him to recognize their broader political goals and reprimand the sometimes irreverent, immature, and violent behavior they exhibited. Lomax was a law professor in the classroom, but as faculty chairman he was a mediator, judge, and sometimes jury. Ultimately, Lomax's actions as faculty chairman represented the practical applications of the law he wished to imbue in his law students.

Lomax's position was even more important as he mediated instances of violence between students and enslaved laborers. One such incident occurred in June 1828. Warner W. Minor was the hotelkeeper of Hotel C during the 1827–28 school year. Minor sent a letter to Lomax detailing an incident of student misconduct toward an enslaved person. In it, he accused a student, T. J. Boyd, of hitting one of Minor's enslaved laborers in his dining room. After the faculty met to discuss the infraction, Lomax met privately with Boyd to discuss the incident. Boyd told Lomax that he was upset Minor had required him to move out of Hotel C. When the faculty affirmed Minor's decision, Boyd sent a note to Lomax asking that they reconsider. After considering the incident and Boyd's request, Lomax sent for Boyd and "inform[ed] him that altho' I would refer his request to the faculty if he insisted on it, my advice was that he should acquiesce." Boyd eventually "consented and merely expressed with that he should not appear to have been turned out of his house by Mr. Minor."[30]

Students and faculty cultivated a distinct perspective on the legal agency of enslaved people within the new republic. Through his role as a law professor, his position as faculty chairman, and his social duties as an enslaver, Lomax brought these distinct perspectives to his teachings of the law. For students, classroom lectures on Washington's farewell address and the Virginia Constitution were inevitably paired with everyday interactions with enslaved individuals. For example, in Washington's 1796 farewell address, students were reading Washington's meditation on federalism, republicanism, and the challenges of keeping a geographically diverse nation unified. Though not explicitly stated, Washington urged white men who would inherit the republic to look to one another, despite political and economic differences, for national strength. "While then every part of our country thus feels an immediate and particular interest in Union, all the parts combined cannot fail to find in the united mass of means and efforts greater strength, greater resource, proportionably greater security from external danger," students read in Washington's address.[31] One of the most prominent threats to union, and to the stability of the young republic, was the threat of rebellious bondspeople. At the time of their reading, the young men on Grounds would have read and gossiped about the successful overthrow of slavery in Haiti, previously St. Domingue.[32] This knowledge, combined with reading Washington's words in the context of law and union, would have shaped students' perspectives on mastery and influenced how they interacted with the enslaved people owned by faculty such as Lomax.

During his time at UVA, Lomax continued buying and selling enslaved people as he expanded his legal career. According to the 1830 Virginia personal property tax records, Lomax enslaved six people during his tenure living as a faculty member in Charlottesville.[33] He even advertised the public sale of a thirty-five-year-old "capable house servant" on July 9, 1830. Presumably, he was divesting himself of unnecessary property, including "various items of household & kitchen furniture" before he vacated Charlottesville and began his judicial appointment that same year.[34]

Neither his family's economic condition nor his faculty salary was enough to keep Lomax at UVA.[35] Instead of continuing his teaching career at the Law School, he decided to move to a position that allowed him to reach his financial goals more readily. In 1830, the Virginia General Assembly elected Lomax to serve as a judge on Virginia's Fifth Circuit. But he did not hang up his professorial robes in exchange for judicial ones. Lomax continued to teach law in Fredericksburg. In 1831, he put his entrepreneurial skills to good use by teaching law classes in the basement of his home, using the skills that he cultivated as a law professor at UVA.[36]

John A. G. Davis

With Lomax's exit in 1830, the Board of Visitors went in search of a new professor of law. They appointed a young, Virginia-raised lawyer named

NOTICE.

ON the 17th inst., in the afternoon, at the University, will be offered at Public Sale a capable HOUSE SERVANT about thirty-five years of age.

—ALSO—

Various articles of

HOUSEHOLD & KITCHEN FURNITURE.

Among which are included a Mahogany Sideboard, a China Press, Chairs, three Bureaus, a set of large Mahogany Dining Tables, and also various pieces of Tea and Table China—Two Milch Cows will also be sold. All purchases less than $5, will be paid in cash, a credit of six months will be allowed on all purchases amounting to more than $5—the purchaser giving bond with approved security.

JOHN TAYLOE LOMAX.

The privilege is reserved of retaining (if need be) the use of all or any of the furniture, until the 11th of August, when they will be delivered at the University in the same condition as when sold to the purchasers. J. T. L.

July 9—'30 2t

Newspaper advertisement posted by University of Virginia Law professor John Tayloe Lomax selling an enslaved person alongside pavilion furniture at a public sale at the University, 1830. (*Virginia Advocate*, July 9, 1830)

John A. G. Davis. Born to a family of enslavers in Middlesex County, Virginia, the twenty-eight-year-old Davis eagerly accepted the law professor position. Davis advocated for a strict interpretation of the US Constitution, honed by his own studies at the College of William & Mary and by law practice in Charlottesville that predated his appointment.[37]

Davis approached UVA's legal curriculum as Lomax had, with a distinct emphasis on Blackstone's *Commentaries* and practical skills. When referencing the common law on slavery, Blackstone contended, "I have formerly observed that pure and proper slavery does not, nay cannot, subsist in England; such I mean, whereby an absolute and unlimited power is given to the master over the life and fortune of the slave."[38] Blackstone continued, "It is repugnant to reason, and the principles of natural law, that such a state should subsist anywhere."[39] Blackstone even extended his argument to assert that England would not "endure the existence of slavery within this nation."[40] Law students were reading this 1765 treatise on English law and jurisprudence within a state increasingly dedicated to the preservation of slavery. It was from this perspective on Blackstone's legal theories where Davis diverged—and made his mark on the UVA law curriculum. By deploying Blackstone in a proslavery context, Davis ushered into UVA's curriculum a new way for students to defend against the rising tide of antislavery jurisprudence that had begun to creep into public discourse during the antebellum era.[41]

According to student notes, Davis taught Blackstone's *Commentaries* with a clear perspective on how to leverage his legal perspectives to support the legality of slavery in Virginia and the nation.[42] According to the 1838–39 lecture notes of George W. Blattermann (Law 1839), Davis argued that the United States inherited the peculiar institution and had little influence over adopting such a morally dubious practice. Instead of dealing with the morality of American slavery, Davis claimed the English introduced and brought enslaved Africans to the American colonies, thus exculpating enslavers of any responsibility as articulated by Blackstone. Blattermann wrote of Davis's interpretation, "When we became independent, (from which time only [should] we be held

Portrait of University of Virginia law professor John A. G. Davis. (Albert and Shirley Small Special Collections Library, University of Virginia)

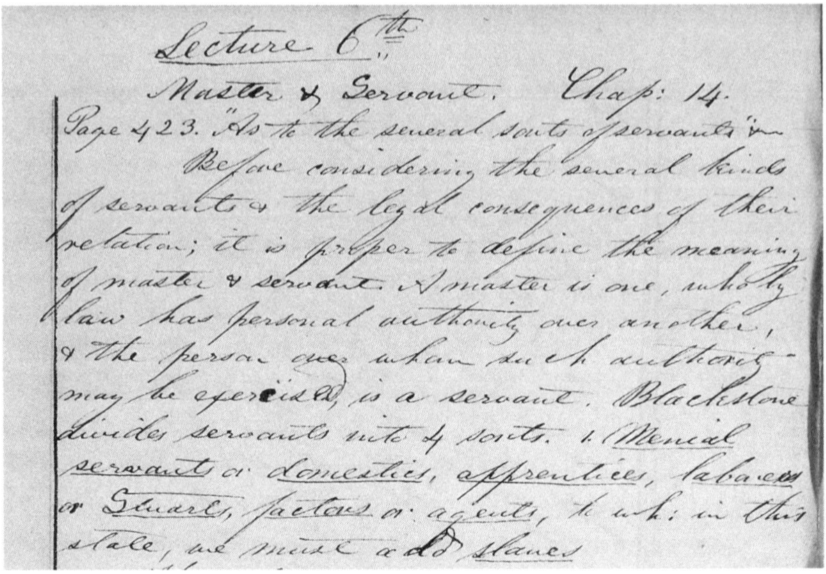

Lecture 6th

Master & Servant. Chap: 14.

Page 423. "As to the several sorts of servants" &c

Before considering the several kinds of servants & the legal consequences of their relation; it is proper to define the meaning of master & servant. A master is one, who by law has personal authority over another, & the person over whom such authority may be exercised, is a servant. Blackstone divides servants into 4 sorts. 1. Menial servants or domestics, apprentices, labourers or Stewards, factors or agents, to wh: in this state, we must add slaves

University of Virginia law student George W. Blatterman's (Law 1839) notebook. Here he recorded lecture notes titled "Master and Servant" from John A. G. Davis's course in 1839. (Albert and Shirley Small Special Collections Library, University of Virginia)

responsible for our institutions & civil policy) we found slavery established in this country."[43] By arguing that the United States, once independent from Britain, took a passive role in slavery and the slave trade, Davis championed a legal theory of slavery in which the institution could not have been easily destroyed because it was so entrenched in American society. Davis went so far as to argue that universal emancipation and the abolition of slavery was an impossibility under the common law. Blattermann wrote, "For, if all owning slaves had been willing to yield them up, without consideration; what was to be done with them? Where were they to be removed to?, and for them to live amongst us as free persons was entirely out of the question."[44] Davis, like Jefferson, could not imagine a world where white and free Black people peacefully coexisted.

Davis's teachings on the laws of slavery included discussions of the expansiveness and limitations of congressional power, including the legality of what became known as the Missouri Compromise and other federal laws. Davis urged his students to consider the relationship between federal authority, state power, and the growth of slavery in the United States. In the 1840–41 academic year, student Thomas H. Tutwiler (Law 1842) enrolled in Davis's course. In a lecture titled "Admission of States," Tutwiler recorded Davis as saying, "It was proposed to impose as a condition of her admission, a perpetual inhibition of slavery within her limits. We have now to examine neither the motives or the policy of such prohibition, but merely consider the power of Congress to impose it."[45] Davis analyzed the reach of federal authority instead of the role of slavery in the admissions of new states. Davis was encouraging students to consider this perspective, which formed the basis for a states' rights argument against the encroachment of federalism. And the relationship between slavery and federalism was only one of the ideas regarding laws of slavery that Davis discussed in the classroom.

As a student, Tutwiler was transcribing Davis's lessons on republicanism and its compatibility with slavery as a legal institution. Davis applied this lesson again to his discussion of the Missouri Compromise of 1820. But instead of simply reiterating his lesson on federal authority, Davis ushered students into a discussion of republicanism, a form of government wherein a population is governed by officials that they elect.[46] According to Tutwiler's notes, Davis stated, "Indeed the avowed purpose of the Missouri restriction was to abolish slavery in the new States."[47] Davis taught that the ultimate goal of the political compromise, which admitted Missouri as a slave state, Maine as a free state, and barred the spread of slavery to the Louisiana Territory north of the 36°30′ parallel, was not to stave off a legislative gridlock over slavery, but to abolish slavery writ large.[48] Davis then chipped away at arguments that suggested that slavery "was incompatible with a Republican form of Govt hence the right to impose the restriction on Missouri." He then contended, "The argument of course fails if it can be shown that slavery is consistent with a Republican Government." Davis concluded by arguing, "This is abundantly proved by the fact that all the States when they formed and adopted the Constitution held slaves."[49] Because the nation, with its republican structures and institutions, was created with states where slavery was legal, Davis constructed a legal narrative about republicanism and slavery that underscored their compatibility.

Slavery continued to be woven into Davis's teachings on the law throughout his tenure. The idea of the "just & mild" form of slavery that he believed existed in states such as Virginia was the compromise, according to Davis.[50] Echoing the arguments made by proslavery apologists such as Thomas R. Dew and South Carolinian James Henry Hammond, Davis proposed that slavery exerted an "injurious influence" on the nation's prosperity.[51] To keep the growing number of enslaved people from waging insurrection, Davis asserted that, as of late, enslaved persons were "more comfortable & happy than the lower classes of people, in any other country."[52] By recognizing the danger that enslaved people posed to political and social stability, Davis chose to teach his students legal maneuvers to substantiate slavery. The insurrection led by Nat Turner on August 21, 1831, undoubtedly shaped Davis's interpretations of slavery and mastery. In Southampton, Virginia, around 150 miles southeast of Charlottesville, Turner gathered a group of approximately sixty enslaved people to stage an insurrection. In the ensuing chaos, the group killed about fifty-five white people, and Turner was on the lam for about two months before being captured, tried, and hanged, as were eighteen other enslaved people. The event ignited fear among white Virginians and led to even more stringent laws controlling the lives and mobility of enslaved persons.[53]

Davis's teachings were also shaped by his own investments in slavery. Davis's father, Staige Davis, owned thirty-five people who worked on his Middlesex County, Virginia, plantation as of 1810.[54] When his father died in 1813, Davis inherited his estate, including these enslaved people.[55] According to the 1830 census, Davis owned seventeen bondspeople during his tenure at UVA, some of whom may have lived with him on Grounds and at Lewis Farm, his plantation in Charlottesville.[56] A year later, in December 1831, Davis, John A. Carr, the University's proctor, and Robert Maskell Patterson, who taught natural philosophy, purchased an enslaved man named Lewis Commodore for $580. Commodore worked as a bell ringer and attendant around the University and was considered to have been "a most valuable servant."[57] He was up for "public sale in Charlottesville" during the first week of December 1831. Davis, Carr, and Patterson believed that "to lose his service would be a real misfortune to the University."[58] Therefore, they resolved to purchase Commodore "for the use of the institution." The following year, the Board of Visitors agreed to reimburse the three men and take on the deed to Commodore's life.[59]

Like Lomax, Davis also served as faculty chairman, a position that required him to mediate disputes involving faculty and students. During his three-year tenure (1835–37 and 1839–40) in the position, he had the responsibility of showing students what composed mastery looked like in practice. On December 9, 1835, Davis was called to intervene in a dispute between a student, William W. Harris, and Mrs. Sarah Carter Gray, the hotelkeeper of Hotel E. According to Gray, Harris struck one of her servants. The other students who witnessed the events confirmed Gray's accusation, that Harris had "behaved with great impropriety." Though the students also argued that the servant "was impertinent to him," Davis wrote, "but not to such a degree however as to excuse his rudeness & violence."[60] In his role as the faculty chairman, Davis decided to refer the event to the faculty for adjudication to decide Harris's fate. Davis was compelled to make an example of Harris, to demonstrate to the wider student body the practice of mastery over servants and slaves. He was demonstrating for UVA students how to move through the world as a master and as an enslaver.

Davis's tenure as UVA's law professor came to a quick and violent end in 1840. On the evening of November 12, 1840, Davis intervened in what he believed was a dispute outside of his campus residence in Pavilion X. Students William A. Kincaid (Law 1843) and Joseph G. Semmes were parading around Grounds, wearing masks, and carrying pistols. As Davis exited Pavilion X and confronted the students, Semmes discharged his gun, fatally shooting Davis. He died two days later of a gunshot wound to the abdomen.[61] The Board of Visitors hired Nathaniel Pope Howard a mere two weeks after Davis's death. On a one-year contract, Howard's tenure did not last long enough the make a lasting impact on the University or law curriculum.[62]

Henry St. George Tucker

In the wake of Davis's death and the short-term appointment of Howard, the Board of Visitors needed to fill the professor of law position quickly. They found their candidate in Henry St. George Tucker in 1841, son of the famed St. George Tucker of William & Mary. Tucker had an esteemed political and legal career before accepting his post at UVA. He had served in the US House of Representatives, the Virginia state senate, and as a superior court judge. Educated at the College of William & Mary, Tucker spent the time between his political positions in private practice around Winchester, Virginia. To supplement his income during his years as a judge, he opened his own law school in 1824, known as the Winchester Law School. Similar to the curriculum of UVA, Tucker relied on Blackstone's *Commentaries* as the textbook from which he formed his lectures.[63]

When he arrived in Charlottesville in 1841, Tucker brought with him a wealth of legal experience and a distinct perspective on slavery. He hailed from a prominent enslaving family in Virginia. Prior to his acceptance of the UVA law professorship, Tucker enslaved forty-six Black persons. He expected to maintain two residences in Charlottesville: one in Pavilion X, his residence on Grounds, and another property in Charlottesville to accommodate his household and the people he enslaved.[64]

Though Tucker was born to a family whose investments in slavery made them both wealthy and influential, he was also influenced by the political ideals of his father, St. George Tucker, whose conflicting views on slavery largely mirrored Jefferson's. In 1796, the elder Tucker had published *A Dissertation on Slavery: With a Proposal for the Gradual Abolition of It, in the State of Virginia*, a treatise on the benefits of gradual emancipation for the growing population of Black people in the new nation. Asserting that an event like the revolution in St. Domingue could readily take place in the United States, the elder Tucker argued that gradual emancipation would quell the specter of violent rebellion among Virginia's enslaved population. He appealed to members of the Virginia General Assembly, even sending a copy of the 106-page treatise to Thomas Jefferson. No political movement occurred in terms of legislative consideration, and neither did Tucker divest himself of his investments in his enslaved property after the publication and circulation of his tract. Nevertheless, St. George Tucker's *Dissertation on Slavery* thrust the conversation about abolition and colonization into Virginia's political discourse. By the end of the antebellum era, Tucker's *Dissertation* was the only effort to end slavery through an act of the Virginia General Assembly.[65] Despite his father's public pronouncements about slavery and abolition, Henry St. George Tucker maintained his ownership of enslaved people until his death in 1848.

His investments in slavery and enslaved people aligned with his perspective on the law, especially the legal foundations for states' rights. Tucker did not shroud his support for the autonomy of states to protect slavery. He even went so far as to articulate his legal perspective on states' rights in the official description of his law course. Tucker wrote that the goal of his course was to "lay before the student the most able dissertations on both sides of the great constitutional questions which have arisen in our country; to impress upon his mind the inestimable value of the union on the one hand, and the vital importance of preserving the rights of the States on the other." But Tucker admitted that the discussion would not be nonpartisan. He sought to instill in his pupils arguments for the political and legal strength of state autonomy. He wanted students to be equipped to defend "against latitudinarian constructions and the invasion of the reserved rights of the States, while the disorganizing principles which lead to convulsion and disunion are earnestly discarded and industriously controverted."[66] Tucker did not shy away from states' rights political ideology in his law courses. His proslavery legal and political ideologies infiltrated his teachings on American law.[67]

Tucker's time at UVA ended in 1845, when he resigned due to his poor health.[68] His legacy at UVA was shaped by his staunch proslavery and states' rights perspectives. As faculty chairman from 1842 to 1844, Tucker presided over the introduction of the Honor Code to govern exam taking.[69] The Honor Code would be student driven, meaning that students were made responsible for ensuring that their classmates complied with its policies. In his law courses, Tucker furnished students with an arsenal of legal tools to defend against the onslaught of antislavery legal arguments—which continued to come during the next decade.

John B. Minor and James P. Holcombe

When Tucker resigned, the Board of Visitors decided to appoint John Barbee Minor as professor of law. Known for his rigor among his students, Minor began his fifty-year teaching career at UVA in 1845, as the national conversation about slavery and the future of the institution dominated the public sphere.[70] With the introduction of Texas and Florida into the federal union as slave states and the issue of slavery's future splintering political parties in the 1840s, Minor pushed legal education at UVA in an even more proslavery direction.

Minor's guiding legal principle involved belief in the idea that slavery was a necessary evil.[71] Following the perspectives of thinkers such as Jefferson himself, the necessary evil argument for slavery was undergoing a dramatic shift. Minor believed that slavery was necessary for maintaining the stability of the new nation. Minor was also part of a growing contingent of slavery apologists who believed that slavery was a positive good for the enslaved. No longer were white Americans ashamed of their investments in slavery. They began to freely accept and support the enslavement of people of African descent.[72]

As Randall N. Flaherty notes in this volume, Minor brought this perspective into the classroom.[73] Though he taught many of the same texts as his predecessors, including Blackstone's *Commentaries* and Vattel's *Law of Nations,* Minor's legal perspective was one of a proslavery apologist.[74] A diligent student of Virginia's slave statutes, Minor supported controversial legislative acts such as the Fugitive Slave Act of 1850.[75] Its passage proved to be a pivotal moment, not just for Minor as an enslaver and professor, but for the nation writ large. The law unilaterally protected enslavers' property rights, and in the process, it threatened the safety and security of free Blacks. The law also reflected a proslavery legal understanding of American jurisprudence and the role of the federal government in protecting enslavers' economic rights to recoup their enslaved property.[76]

Minor gave yearly lectures on the legal history of slavery in Virginia. But his teachings on slavery and American law held, at its intellectual core, the idea that Virginians had been unwilling participants in the English project of slavery and colonization. According to law student James M. Hanger (Law 1856), in an 1854 lecture Minor began by stating that slave trading in Virginia began, in earnest, with tobacco cultivation. Hanger wrote, "The slave trade having been thus begun it was encouraged by the raising of tobacco."[77] Minor suggested that Virginia's planters and enslavers adapted to the economic conditions of commerce in the Atlantic world by embracing slavery as a form of labor organization. His proposal, of colonists' acquiescence, continued by introducing to students the 1620 arrival of African slaves from a Dutch trading ship and interrogating how Blackstone defined slavery and the legal status of enslaved versus indentured laborers.[78]

And when Minor addressed the political conflagration between American colonists and British lawmakers in the 1760s and early 1770s, he highlighted how taxation and slave importation policies were factors in the outbreak of the Revolutionary War. Minor argued that Virginia's slaveholders did, in fact, hold antislavery beliefs and sentiments—even going so far as to contend that lawmakers passed antislavery legislation in the late 1770s. Hanger wrote, "The first use Va made of her independence was in (Oct 1778) (See 9 Hen. Statute at Large 471) to pass an act prohibiting the importation of slaves, with a penalty upon the importer of 1000 lbs of tobaco [*sic*] for each slave imported & freedom to the slave."[79] Minor went so far as to declare, "This was the first antislave trade movement in the world."[80] Though Minor made a triumphant call to his students that Virginia had enacted the "first antislave trade movement," the law did not limit slavery, nor did it prevent enslavers from bringing enslaved people into the colony and state. Hanger notes, of Minor's lecture, that at the outbreak of the American Revolution, Virginians were afraid of "those negroes to rise in arms against us."[81] Minor then connected the legislative history of slave importation bans at the state level to national bans at the federal level, suggesting that Virginia was in the vanguard of newly created states that reevaluated their legal and economic relationship to the slave trade—but not to slavery as an institution.

In his teachings and in his personal life, Minor underscored the importance of the master/slave relationship. As an enslaver himself, Minor believed in the supremacy of slavery as a legal institution. In his personal notes on the laws that governed enslaved people as gifts, for example, Minor was adamant that property rights of enslavers be protected when enslaved people and their children were bequeathed as gifts after an enslaver's death.[82] Minor's legal teaching echoed his personal tendencies regarding slavery. According to the 1850 census, he enslaved six people who resided in Charlottesville during his first years as law professor. Ten years later the number rose to ten, which suggests that as his career in academia progressed, so too did his investments in slavery.[83]

Minor's academic investments in slavery were perhaps best reflected in an October 26, 1856, lecture entitled "Slavery in Relation to the Federal

Government." Minor's student James L. Hubard (Law 1857) wrote that Minor discussed the ways in which the Constitution protected slavery, slaveholders' property rights, and the master/slave relationship.[84] In fact, according to Hubard's notes, Minor believed that northern states were willing and eager to use federal authority to abolish slavery entirely. He argued, "The jealousy of the Northern states became aroused, and many of their delegates favored giving Congress the power to legislate on slavery."[85] Yet, despite the long history of slavery in Virginia, Minor continued to weave his beliefs about slavery in the legal education that he was delivering to students, especially during the antebellum era.

While Minor became a stalwart fixture at the University, the Board of Visitors decided in 1851 to add another professor to expand the University's strength in legal education. They appointed James Philemon Holcombe (College 1839), who became known as the most adamant defender of slavery at UVA.[86] By the time Holcombe joined Minor at the Law School, he was writing and giving public lectures in defense of slavery. One of his most prominent public speeches occurred before the Virginia State Agricultural Society in 1858. The title of his lecture, "Is Slavery Consistent with Natural Law?," offered a legal and philosophical defense of the enslavement of people of African descent. "African Slavery in the United States is consistent with Natural Law," he argued, "because if all the bonds of public authority were suddenly dissolved . . . it would be our right and duty to reduce the negro to subjection."[87] Holcombe believed it was white Americans' right to enslave and subjugate people of African descent. His belief in a natural racial hierarchy of people undergirded his broader understanding and teaching. But it is worth noting, as Peter C. Myers contends, that during the antebellum and Civil War eras, abolitionists such as Frederick Douglass also used the ideology of natural law to advocate for the morality of antislavery and abolitionism. Though these natural law ideologies did not infiltrate Minor's legal curriculum, natural law as a racial philosophy became a popular proslavery and antislavery tool.[88]

Holcombe did not hesitate to integrate his proslavery thoughts into his law lectures. In a lecture on constitutional and governmental law, for example, Holcombe guided students through a hypothetical defense of slavery if debating someone from a free northern state or from Britain.

He also lectured on the legislative authority of slave states to augment their population by counting the number of enslaved people.[89] These legal ideas, designed to support the permanence and expansion of slavery through legal and constitutional mechanisms, formed a visible facet of the legal curriculum under Holcombe and Minor.[90]

UVA students in the antebellum era learned about the practical applications of law not only through their lectures and discussions, but also through their interactions with the enslaved laborers who served them, cleaned classrooms, washed their clothes, and in general ensured that the University continued to function. The legal education that UVA students received was filtered through their interactions with the hundreds of enslaved laborers who worked in the shadows.

During the outbreak of the Civil War, Holcombe resigned to run for Virginia's Secession Convention, a position to which he was elected.[91] Minor stayed behind during the wartime conflict, continuing to teach his proslavery legal perspective to students who remained on Grounds. Minor also kept a wartime diary of the ebbs and flows of Confederate and Union soldiers in Charlottesville in the early 1860s as he agonized over the future of the nation—and the future of slavery in it.[92]

The Civil War would put the law faculty's theories to the test. If secession was a legal and righteous cause, if slavery was bound to forever shape interactions between white and Black people, or if people of African descent were to wedge themselves into the body politic, then the war would be the litmus test. Though the war's end did not stop the law faculty teaching about race and slavery, surely the end of slavery as an institution shaped the environment in which they taught their legal ideas. Ultimately, slavery, as a legal concept and as a real institution, influenced the ways in which the legal curriculum evolved at the University of Virginia. But as slavery died its slow and agonizing death, the tethers of these concepts continued to pervade the curriculum in seen and unseen ways.

Notes

1. Thomas Jefferson, *Notes on the State of Virginia* (Paris: printed by the author, 1785), 298. (Thomas Jefferson is hereafter cited as TJ.)

2. TJ, *Notes on the State of Virginia, 298.*
3. The eight original schools were "Antient languages, Modern languages, Mathematics, Natural philosophy, Natural history, Anatomy and Medicine, moral philosophy, and Law." See University of Virginia Board of Visitors Minute Book, 1817–1828, 7 April 1824, RG-1/1/1.381, Albert and Shirley Small Special Collections Library, University of Virginia (hereafter cited as SSCL).
4. For more on the history of slavery at the University of Virginia, see Maurie D. McInnis and Louis P. Nelson, eds., *Educated in Tyranny: Slavery at Thomas Jefferson's University* (Charlottesville: University of Virginia Press, 2019); Jennifer Oast, *Institutional Slavery: Slaveholding Churches, Schools, Colleges, and Businesses in Virginia, 1680–1860* (Cambridge: Cambridge University Press, 2016), 174–89; Alan Taylor, *Thomas Jefferson's Education* (New York: W. W. Norton, 2019).
5. For more on the selection of early texts for the Law School, see David T. Konig, "Jeffersonian Foundations of Legal Education in Virginia, 1779–1845," in this volume.
6. McInnis and Nelson, *Educated in Tyranny,* 122–23. See also Elizabeth R. Varon, "The Civil War and Reconstruction, 1861–1877," in this volume.
7. Alfred L. Brophy, *University, Court, and Slave: Pro-Slavery Thought in Southern Colleges and Courts and the Coming of Civil War* (New York: Oxford University Press, 2016); Leslie M. Harris, James T. Campbell, and Alfred L. Brophy, eds., *Slavery and the University: Histories and Legacies* (Athens: University of Georgia Press, 2019); Taylor, *Thomas Jefferson's Education;* Craig Steven Wilder, *Ebony and Ivy: Race, Slavery, and the Troubled History of America's Universities* (New York: Bloomsbury, 2013).
8. Karen S. Beck, "One Step at a Time: The Research Value of Law Student Notebooks," *Law Library Journal* 91, no. 1 (Winter 1999): 36.
9. University of Virginia Board of Visitors Minute Book, 1817–1828, 7 April 1824.
10. University of Virginia Board of Visitors Minute Book, 1817–1828, 4 March 1825.
11. University of Virginia Board of Visitors Minute Book, 1817–1828, 4 March 1825.
12. For a discussion of John Locke's proslavery ideologies, see, for example, Brad Hinshelwood, "The Carolinian Context of John Locke's Theory of Slavery," *Political Theory* 41, no. 4 (August 2013): 562–90; Jennifer Welchman, "Locke on Slavery and Inalienable Rights," *Canadian Journal of Philosophy* 25, no. 1 (March 1995): 67–81. For analysis of the 1799 Virginia Resolution, see Douglas Bradburn, "A Clamor in the Public Mind: Opposition to the Alien and Sedition Acts," *William and Mary Quarterly* 65, no. 3 (July 2008): 565–600; K. R. Constantine Gutzman, "The Virginia and Kentucky Resolutions Reconsidered: 'An Appeal to the Real Laws of Our Country,'" *Journal of Southern History* 66, no. 3 (August 2000): 473–96.
13. University of Virginia Board of Visitors Minute Book, 1817–1828, 4 October 1824.
14. McInnis and Nelson, *Educated in Tyranny,* 94–103.
15. In July 1840, the Board of Visitors expanded on the rule that forbade students from bringing enslaved people on Grounds. Even students who lived off campus were forbidden from bringing enslaved people with them. This shows Jefferson's influence, even after his death. See University of Virginia Board of Visitors Minute Book, 1817–1828, 4 July 1840.
16. Brendan Wolf, "Slavery at the University of Virginia," *Encyclopedia Virginia,* Virginia Humanities, https://encyclopediavirginia.org/entries/slavery-at-the-university-of-virginia/.
17. For a discussion of slave hiring, see Jonathan D. Martin, *Divided Mastery: Slave Hiring in the American South* (Cambridge, MA: Harvard University Press, 2004); John J.

Zaborney, *Slaves for Hire: Renting Enslaved Laborers in Antebellum Virginia* (Baton Rouge: Louisiana State University Press, 2012).

18. Louis P. Nelson and James Zehmer, "Slavery and Construction," in McInnis and Nelson, *Educated in Tyranny*, 27–41.
19. TJ to Charles Yancey, 6 January 1816, Founders Online, National Archives, https://founders.archives.gov/documents/Jefferson/03-09-02-0209.
20. *Catalogue of the Officers and Students of the University of Virginia, Marth 7th, 1825–December 15th, 1825* (Charlottesville, VA: Chronicle Steam Book Printing House, 1880), 4.
21. Konig, "Jeffersonian Foundations of Legal Education," in this volume.
22. John G. Waite Associates, Architects, and University of Virginia, *Pavilion IX: University of Virginia, Historic Structure Report* (Albany, NY: John G. Waite Associates, Architects, 2010), 15–16, https://officearchitect.virginia.edu/sites/officearchitect/files/2020-12/Pavilion_IX_HistoricStructureReport.pdf.
23. "Pavilion III," Slavery & the UVA School of Law: A History, LLSC, https://slavery.law.virginia.edu/people-places/places/pavillion-iii.
24. TJ to James Madison, 17 February 1826, Founders Online, https://founders.archives.gov/documents/Jefferson/98-01-02-5912.
25. TJ to Madison, 17 February 1826.
26. "Lomax, John Tayloe," in *Appleton's Cyclopedia of American Biography*, ed. James Grant Wilson and John Fiske (New York: D. Appleton, 1888), 4:8; David Brown and Thane H. Harpole, "Menokin," *Encyclopedia Virginia*, https://encyclopediavirginia.org/entries/menokin/. According to David T. Konig, Lomax was not Jefferson's first choice as law professor. See Konig, "Jeffersonian Foundations of Legal Education," in this volume, for more on the search for the Law School's first professor.
27. "Overview of the Legal Curriculum, 1826–1865," Slavery & the UVA School of Law: A History, LLSC, https://slavery.law.virginia.edu/teaching/curriculum.
28. On benevolent mastery, see Elizabeth Fox-Genovese and Eugene D. Genovese, *The Mind of the Master Class: History and Faith in the Southern Slaveholders' Worldview* (Cambridge: Cambridge University Press, 2005); Eugene D. Genovese, *Roll, Jordan, Roll: The World the Slaves Made* (New York: Pantheon, 1974); Jeffrey Robert Young, *Domesticating Slavery: The Master Class in Georgia and South Carolina, 1670–1837* (Chapel Hill: University of North Carolina Press, 2005).
29. Taylor, *Thomas Jefferson's Education*, 81.
30. Journals of the Chairman of the Faculty, 1827–1864, 25–30 June 1828, 1:13, RG-19/1/2.041, SSCL.
31. George Washington, *An Address to the People of the United States* (New Castle, DE: Samuel & Johnson Adams, 1796), 8.
32. For a discussion of the rebellion on St. Domingue, see Laurent Dubois, *Avengers of the New World: The Story of the Haitian Revolution* (Cambridge, MA: Belknap Press, 2004); C. L. R. James, *The Black Jacobins: Toussaint L'Ouverture and the San Domingo Revolution* (New York: Vintage Books, 1989).
33. "John Tayloe Lomax, 1826–1830," Slavery & the UVA School of Law: A History, LLSC, https://slavery.law.virginia.edu/people-places/faculty/lomax.
34. Notice, *Virginia Advocate*, 9 July 1830.
35. W. Hamilton Bryson, "The History of Legal Education in Virginia," *University of Richmond Law Review* 14, no. 1 (1979): 180.
36. Bryson, "History of Legal Education in Virginia," 180–81; W. Hamilton Bryson, *Legal*

Education in Virginia, 1779–1979: A Biographical Approach (Charlottesville: University Press of Virginia, 1982), 362.

37. Bryson, *Legal Education in Virginia,* 181–83.
38. William Blackstone, *Commentaries on the Laws of England,* 4 vols. (Oxford: Clarendon Press, 1765–69), 1:411.
39. Blackstone, *Commentaries on the Laws of England,* 1:411.
40. Blackstone, *Commentaries on the Laws of England,* 1:412.
41. See Kate Masur, *Until Justice Be Done: America's First Civil Rights Movement, From the Revolution to Reconstruction* (New York: W. W. Norton, 2021).
42. For analyses on Blackstone and how jurists used *Commentaries* to support their defense of slavery, see Albert W. Alschuler, "Rediscovering Blackstone," *University of Pennsylvania Law Review* 145, no. 1 (November 1996): 1–55; Travis Glasson, "'Baptism Doth Not Bestow Freedom': Missionary Anglicanism, Slavery, and the Yorke-Talbot Opinion, 1701–30," *William and Mary Quarterly* 67, no. 2 (April 2010): 279–318; Thomas D. Morris, *Southern Slavery and the Law, 1619–1860* (Chapel Hill: University of North Carolina Press, 1996).
43. George W. Blattermann Student Notebook, 1838–39, n.d., 66, Professor J. A. G. Davis Lectures, Student Notebooks, RG-32-400, Arthur J. Morris Law Library Special Collections, University of Virginia (hereafter cited as LLSC).
44. Blattermann Student Notebook, 1838–39, n.d., 66.
45. Thomas H. Tutwiler Student Notebook, 1840–41, n.d., 181, Professor J. A. G. Davis Lectures, Thomas Tutwiler Notes, 1840, MSS 7343, SSCL.
46. See Alexander Hamilton, John Jay, and James Madison, *The Federalist: A Commentary on the Constitution of the United States: A Collection of Essays* (Philadelphia: J. B. Lippincott, 1864), 434–40.
47. Tutwiler Student Notebook, 1840–41, 183.
48. John Craig Hammond, "President, Planter, Politician: James Monroe, the Missouri Crisis, and the Politics of Slavery," *Journal of American History* 105, no. 4 (March 2019): 843–67.
49. Tutwiler Student Notebook, 1840–41, 183–84.
50. Blattermann Student Notebook, 1838–39, n.d., 67.
51. Harris, Campbell, and Brophy, *Slavery and the University,* 63–66.
52. Blattermann Student Notebook, 1838–39, n.d., 67.
53. Patrick H. Breen, *The Land Shall Be Deluged in Blood: A New History of the Nat Turner Revolt* (New York: Oxford University Press, 2016); Vanessa M. Holden, *Surviving Southampton: African American Women and Resistance in Nat Turner's Community* (Urbana: University of Illinois Press, 2021); Christopher L. Tomlins, *In the Matter of Nat Turner: A Speculative History* (Princeton, NJ: Princeton University Press, 2020).
54. 1810 US Census, Urbanna, Middlesex County, Virginia, Roll 69:43.
55. "John Anthony Gardner Davis, 1830–1840," Our History: Former Faculty, Arthur J. Morris Law Library, University of Virginia, https://libguides.law.virginia.edu/faculty/davis.
56. "John Anthony Gardner Davis"; "The Farm," National Register of Historic Places, National Park Service, US Department of Interior, https://www.dhr.virginia.gov/wp-content/uploads/2018/04/104-0002_The_Farm_1995_Final_Nomination.pdf.
57. University of Virginia Board of Visitors Minute Book, 1829–1956, 18 July 1832, vol. 2, 1829–37, RG-1/1/1.382, SSCL; Journals of the Chairman of the Faculty, 20 July 1831–20 July 1832, 31 December 1831, 3:62.

58. Journals of the Chairman of the Faculty, 31 December 1831, 3:62.
59. University of Virginia Board of Visitors Minute Book, 1829–1956, 18 July 1832.
60. Journals of the Chairman of the Faculty, 7 September 1835–10 August 1836, 9 December 1835, 6:25.
61. Robert F. Haggard, "John A. G. Davis (1802–1840)," *Encyclopedia Virginia*, https://encyclopediavirginia.org/entries/davis-john-a-g-1802-1840/.
62. "Nathaniel Pope Howard," Our History: Former Faculty, Arthur J. Morris Law Library, University of Virginia, https://libguides.law.virginia.edu/faculty/nphoward.
63. Bryson, "History of Legal Education in Virginia," 179.
64. "Henry St. George Tucker, 1841–1845," Slavery & the UVA School of Law: A History, LLSC, https://slavery.law.virginia.edu/people-places/faculty/tucker; Philip Alexander Bruce, *History of the University of Virginia, 1819–1919: The Lengthened Shadow of One Man* (New York: Macmillan, 1920), 3:66.
65. St. George Tucker, *A Dissertation on Slavery: With a Proposal for the Gradual Abolition of It, in the State of Virginia* (Philadelphia: Printed for Mathew Carey, 1796); Phillip Hamilton, "Revolutionary Principles and Family Loyalties: Slavery's Transformation in the St. George Tucker Household of Early National Virginia," *William and Mary Quarterly* 55, no. 4 (October 1998): 531–56; Don Riddick, "The Second Most Powerful Pen in Early Virginia: St. George Tucker," *Journal of Southern Legal History* 4 (1995–96): 72; Samantha Seeley, *Race, Removal, and the Right to Remain: Migration and the Making of the United States* (Chapel Hill: University of North Carolina Press, 2021), 194; St. George Tucker to TJ, 2 August 1797, Founders Online, https://founders.archives.gov/documents/Jefferson/01-29-02-0388.
66. *Catalogue of the Officers and Students of the University of Virginia, Session of 1841–42* (Charlottesville, VA: James Alexander, 1842), 15.
67. Henry St. George Tucker, *Lectures on Constitutional Law: For the Use of the Law Class at the University of Virginia* (Richmond, VA: Printed by Shepherd and Colin, 1843).
68. Bryson, "History of Legal Education in Virginia," 186.
69. University of Virginia Faculty Minutes, vols. 1–19, 1825–1970, 4 July 1842, RG-19/1/1.461, SSCL.
70. Bryson, "History of Legal Education in Virginia," 186–87. For more on Minor's tenure at the Law School, see Randall N. Flaherty, "John B. Minor and the Science of Legal Education, 1845–1895," in this volume.
71. "John Barbee Minor, 1845–1895," Our History: Former Faculty, Arthur J. Morris Law Library, University of Virginia, https://libguides.law.virginia.edu/faculty/j-minor.
72. For a discussion of the necessary evil and positive good argument of American slavery, see Lacy K. Ford, *Deliver Us from Evil: The Slavery Question in the Old South* (New York: Oxford University Press, 2009).
73. See Flaherty, "John B. Minor and the Science of Legal Education," in this volume, for an analysis of Minor's perspective on teaching law and the legal defense of slavery.
74. *Catalogue of the Officers and Students of the University of Virginia, Session of 1845–46* (Philadelphia: C. Sherman, 1846), 23–24.
75. "John Barbee Minor, 1845–1895."
76. Brophy, *University, Court, and Slave*, 159–81.
77. James Marshall Hanger Student Notebook, Notes on Blackstone, 1853–54, n.d., Lecture 11th, 1854, 37, RG-32-400, LLSC. For a study of the history of tobacco cultivation in Virginia, see Allan Kulikoff, *Tobacco and Slaves: The Development of Southern

Cultures in the Chesapeake, 1680–1800 (Chapel Hill: University of North Carolina Press, 1986).

78. Hanger Student Notebook, n.d., Lecture 11th, 1854, 37.

79. Hanger Student Notebook, n.d., Lecture 11th, 1854, 38. See also Virginia Assembly, "Bill to Prevent the Importation of Slaves, &c., [16 June 1777]," Founders Online, https://founders.archives.gov/documents/Jefferson/01-02-02-0019. For a discussion of Virginia's temporary slave importation ban, see Gary J. Kornblith, *Slavery and Sectional Strife in the Early American Republic, 1776–1821* (Lanham, MD: Rowman & Littlefield, 2009), 16–17.

80. Hanger Student Notebook, n.d., Lecture 11th, 1854, 38. For a history of the abolitionist movement that foregrounds the actions and experiences of enslaved people, see Manisha Sinha, *The Slaves' Cause: A History of Abolition* (New Haven, CT: Yale University Press, 2016).

81. Hanger Student Notebook, n.d., Lecture 11th, 1854, 38.

82. John B. Minor Diary, vol. 2, 1843–73, 16 May 1855, 278–79, 284–89, John B. Minor Papers, MSS 3114, SSCL.

83. "John Barbee Minor, 1845–1895."

84. For a discussion of the Constitution as a proslavery and antislavery document, see David Waldstreicher, *Slavery's Constitution: From Revolution to Ratification* (New York: Farrar, Straus and Giroux, 2009); Sean Wilentz, *No Property in Man: Slavery and Antislavery at the Nation's Founding* (Cambridge, MA: Harvard University Press, 2018).

85. James L. Hubard Student Notebook, 28 October 1856, Professor John B. Minor's Junior Law Class, University of Virginia Student Notebooks, RG-22/1/1.002, SSCL.

86. Holcombe's history suggests that his proslavery bona fides emerged despite his family's antislavery ones. Born in Virginia to parents who owned enslaved people and a small plantation, Holcombe was a child when his parents decided to divest themselves of slavery. They moved from Lynchburg, freed their fifteen enslaved people, took their sons, and moved to the free state of Indiana. See "James P. Holcombe, 1851–1861," Our History: Former Faculty, Arthur J. Morris Law Library, University of Virginia, https://libguides.law.virginia.edu/faculty/holcombe.

87. James P. Holcombe, *An Address Delivered before the Seventh Annual Meeting of the Virginia State Agricultural Society, November 4th, 1858* (Richmond, VA: MacFarlane and Fergusson, 1858), 2.

88. Peter C. Myers, "Seed-Time and Harvest-Time: Natural Law and Rational Hopefulness in Frederick Douglass's *Life and Times*," *Journal of African American History* 99, no. 1–2 (Winter-Spring 2014): 56–70.

89. George R. Calvert Student Notebook, 1856–57, n.p., n.d., Professor Holcombe's Lectures, University of Virginia Student Notebooks, RG-22/1/1.841, SSCL.

90. For more on Holcombe, Minor, and the Law School during the Civil War and Reconstruction, see Varon, "Civil War and Reconstruction," in this volume.

91. "James P. Holcombe, 1851–1861."

92. Minor Diary, "Speculations," 353–73.

John B. Minor and the Science of Legal Education, 1845–1895

Randall N. Flaherty

IN PROFESSOR JOHN BARBEE MINOR'S classroom at the University of Virginia, Minor taught his students a map of the law. In this role as law teacher and legal geographer, Minor took direct inspiration from Sir William Blackstone on how a law professor in the age of legal science should teach: "He should consider his course as a general map of the law, marking out the shape of the country, its connexions and boundaries, its greater divisions and principle cities." The role of the law teacher, Blackstone expounded, was to trace the contours of law's foundational principles.[1] During Minor's tenure as head of the UVA law program from 1845 until his death in 1895, the law curriculum reflected Minor's understanding that it was the primary role, and indeed benefit, of an academic law program to teach law as a science, through which the instructor laid out a structured, hierarchical outline of the principles of the common law. In this way, law's established principles could be organized and classified, much like biology, moving from general to specific. Structural clarity enabled reason. Once properly digested, students could use these principles to deduce legal truth and the correct application of law in specific cases. UVA was Minor's laboratory for teaching this process of legal science.

Legal science carried a variety of definitions in this era, but it held distinct meaning for Minor and his peers. Law was a science, they argued, because its principles could be induced through observation of human experience, classified, and then used to form case-specific conclusions through deductive reasoning.[2] As David T. Konig writes in this volume, Thomas Jefferson founded the UVA curriculum, including the law curriculum, with these scientific aims in mind, where analysis, reason, and classification existed as pathways to acquiring knowledge.[3] Legal science and liberal arts, both central to UVA's early curriculum, were legacies of the enlightenment and were emerging in this period as alternatives to classical or religious teaching and as new justifications for university education, including academic law programs. As with so much of UVA, Minor represented an adaptation from the ways of Jefferson: the science of Minor's legal curriculum was less about experiment and more about classifying legal truths.[4]

Like geometry or math, legal science could be proven. Minor taught his students that the evidence for legal reasoning came from human experience, starting with history but carrying into the present. Minor emphasized Anglo-Saxon and English history in solidifying custom and common law. Since the map of law was a product of society and its

Photograph of Professor John B. Minor (Law 1834), ca. 1859. (Albert and Shirley Small Special Collections Library, University of Virginia)

necessities, Minor embraced the liberal arts structure at UVA that allowed for broad humanistic studies. He valued the social modeling and mentorship that the Academical Village fostered for students. While law students rushed to copy down Minor's lectures in class, they bore witness in and out of the classroom to custom being justified through practice, most especially the University's reliance on enslaved laborers for its essential operations. Law and society were irrevocably linked.

Minor's teaching methods became the foundation for the culture and reputation of the UVA School of Law over the course of his fifty-year tenure. By the time of his death in 1895, the network of Law School alumni that had trained with Minor referred to themselves as the "John B. Men."[5] It was his reputation as a teacher that brought distinction to the Law School, particularly in the South. His methods were famous for being steady and unchanging. Consequently, Minor's emphasis on legal science and its established principles and customs embedded the UVA Law School curriculum with a deep conservatism. By Minor's death, his entrenched teaching methods were decidedly of an earlier time, and they left in place at the Law School a curriculum that resisted the empirical and analytical styles of the emerging case method in legal education.

A Lawyer in Training and Practice

Before arriving at UVA as law professor in 1845, Minor was already a man of Virginia and an apostle of Jeffersonian thinking as it related to legal education. Born in 1813 in Louisa County, just east of UVA, Minor grew up as one of nine children on a family property devoted primarily to agriculture. The Minors were sustained by and profited off the labor of the people they enslaved, a practice that Minor continued as an adult.[6] Minor's father, Lancelot, had no formal law training but did serve locally in a variety of legal and business roles, such as trustee or executor for estates.[7] In 1822, Minor's older brother Lucian attended the law program at William & Mary. By the time Minor contemplated his own collegiate career in 1831, Lucian was engaged in private practice.[8]

In January 1832, Minor enrolled at UVA at age eighteen. It had not been his first choice: Minor had spent a semester at Kenyon College in Ohio before walking back to Virginia in time for spring lectures at UVA.[9]

Settling into the University, Minor embraced the liberal arts approach and took classes in the schools of law, mathematics, chemistry, ancient languages (Greek and Latin), and modern languages (French, Spanish, German, and Anglo-Saxon) from 1832 to 1834.[10] He eventually graduated from the schools of chemistry (1833) and law (1834).[11] UVA referred to all of its schools and their classes as "branches of science," separate from religious instruction or the more ad hoc learning through apprenticeship.[12] In the law program, Minor studied under Professor John Anthony Gardner Davis, who methodically wrote out his daily lectures and taught with a particular focus on government and a strict interpretation of the US Constitution.[13]

Minor resided in UVA's Academical Village, where he became a de facto member of the Davis family. Lucian arranged for Minor to tutor Davis's three sons and live with the Davises in their Pavilion III home. Davis wrote to Minor that they would "add you to the number of our family, and shall be glad of your company."[14] The omnipresent labor of enslaved people to operate the hotels and the households of the professors, including the Davises, made real for Minor UVA's distinctive overlap of domesticity, legal education, and enslavement. For the 1832–33 session, Minor lived in West Lawn Room 7, immediately adjacent to Pavilion III.[15] His back window looked out over the backyards, including Pavilion III's detached kitchen. That spring Minor complained to the UVA faculty chairman "of being greatly annoyed by hogs under his window."[16] These yards were busy spaces for gardening, washing, cooking, and raising livestock, all of which would have been carried out by enslaved individuals.

After graduating from the law program in 1834, Minor entered private practice with brother Lucian. That winter he married Martha Macon Davis, the sister of Professor Davis, an introduction likely made in Pavilion III.[17] Lawyering exhausted him.[18] Minor's cases forced him to travel throughout central Virginia. Much like Jefferson, Minor rued the haphazard approach to practicing law he witnessed. Minor believed in the promise of academic legal education for bringing order to this chaos and, critically, for creating lawyers who would safeguard and spread republicanism. On May 7, 1845, Minor wrote to his wife from Orange County that the work of court "lingers beyond my patience."[19] That same week, Minor learned there would be a vacancy in the law professorship at UVA.[20] He had remained close to UVA after graduation. In 1844, after moving his practice to Charlottesville, he accepted an invitation from the UVA law students to preside over their moot court.[21] In 1845, he served as acting president of the University's new Society of Alumni.[22] Minor immediately put his name forward as an applicant for the law chair.

Lucian Minor counseled his brother to leverage his UVA ties in his application. With potential recommenders, Lucian advised Minor to amplify his scientific approach, which he had learned at UVA: "you were [a UVA] law graduate—that you were familiar with Mr. Davis's course—that you have for 2 sessions, or one & a half, conducted the moot court—that your studies of law since you began practice have been considerably methodical, & aimed to digest its principles as much as possible into scientific forms."[23] Minor learned that the Board of Visitors (BOV) was considering his candidacy against at least seven others, most of whom were Virginia judges.[24] Lucian assured Minor that his familiarity with UVA would carry the day: "your great fitness arises in a good degree from you having been a student at the University, & knowing the *genius loci* so well. So you need set up for *being* the *genius loci.*"[25] After the BOV's first choice declined, Minor became their unanimous selection.[26] Minor heard this news on July 30 and immediately wrote to his father: "I take to my pen to announce to you, first of all persons in the world . . . my appointment to the chair of law in the University."[27]

Teaching Law

Minor was only thirty-two when he took up the law professorship in the fall of 1845. By this time, law classes, like most disciplines at the University, had moved out of the law professor's Pavilion classroom and into the Rotunda. Law classes met in the eastern, oval-shaped classroom on the first floor of the Rotunda, with benches and desks for students and a blackboard for the professor.[28] On October 6, Minor gave his inaugural lecture, likely in this space, to all twenty-five law students.[29] Minor's inaugural talk set the theme for his fifty-year UVA career. Lawyers steadied society by adhering to established legal principles and ancient rights, he stated. As champions of historical constitutional liberties, lawyers enabled societal progress. They tamped down disruptive chaos through reasoned and systematic work. They protected society amid the opposing "pitiless storms" of popular vengeance or tyrannical leadership. Minor stated that it was "the whole professional training of lawyers" that empowered and enabled this guardianship, an explicit reminder of the exclusive academic space this group inhabited. But the lawyer that Minor idealized nonetheless knew society around him: the "distinctions of social right and wrong, between what men in society may, must or must not do, are the subjects of their daily investigation."[30]

Indeed, in Minor's law program, broader society as he and his students perceived it was always close because the Law School was embedded within UVA's liberal arts structure. The law curriculum catered both to aspiring lawyers, who required a rigorous explication of the law, and to academic students who sought general legal knowledge for a career outside of law. Minor continued this flexible, dual nature of the law curriculum from his predecessors. The Law School would still be divided between a Junior and Senior class. The Junior Class would study theories of government, the law of nations, and municipal law and would appeal to any UVA student seeking legal knowledge as part of their "general" or "liberal professional" education. This course met Tuesday, Thursday, and Saturday in the proscribed time for law under the University Enactments, which scheduled core classes for each school to avoid overlap and to enable interdisciplinary studies. Meanwhile, the Senior Class met Monday, Wednesday, and Friday and catered to students looking to study law as a profession. It covered common and statute law, equity, and maritime and commercial law. For this Senior Class, Minor continued and presided over the Law School moot court.[31]

The University degree structure was similarly accommodating. Just as in other UVA schools, law students who did not seek the full Bachelor of Law degree could earn a certificate of proficiency in constitutional law or government.[32] To graduate with a Bachelor of Law degree, a student had to demonstrate knowledge of the full law program by passing midterm and final exams in both the Junior and Senior classes and then a graduation exam on the full curriculum. Most UVA Law School students throughout Minor's tenure did not choose that track toward graduation, but high graduation rates were never Minor's goal in this liberal arts environment. Common practice among students newly arrived at UVA and

Sketch of John B. Minor leading a University of Virginia Moot Court competition. *Corks and Curls,* vol. 1, 1888. (University of Virginia Libraries)

considering legal studies was to meet with Minor at his Pavilion X office and discuss whether they intended to graduate.[33] The duality of the program allowed Minor to keep a rigorous system in place for the future lawyers, while not excluding a more general audience, who would come away with valuable "elementary attainments." Minor wrote approvingly of this system in 1855: "The standard required is high, and the result is to diminish the no. of grads . . . in proportion to the entire no. of law students considerably."[34] Making explicit contrast to Harvard's LLB residency requirement, Minor praised the UVA policy that made graduation dependent on "stringent examination" rather than length of residence.[35]

UVA faculty administered the University Enactments that governed these operations, including class schedules and graduation requirements. Faculty governance in lieu of a university president was a Jeffersonian policy, and Minor revered UVA's implementation of republican self-government.[36] In particular, Minor praised and vehemently fought to preserve the University's financial structure through which each professor received a set attendance fee from each of his students on top of a uniform annual salary. To Minor, and to Jefferson, who imported this financial framework from William & Mary, this method united individual faculty interests with that of the University: the more students who enrolled in a class, the more a faculty member earned. Successful as this policy was for Minor, it bred friction at UVA. In 1865, before the BOV implemented an 1875 salary cap, Minor was the highest paid professor at the University, making up to six times the salary of others due to student fees. It worked in Minor's favor, and it was not lost on his academic and medical school colleagues, that Minor benefited from the steady demand for legal training and that the manner in which he taught law–through recitation of a highly structured and largely static schema—could accommodate large and lucrative class enrollments.[37]

For all student audiences, Minor believed that teaching law as a science was the best pedagogical method. Law existed as a set of foundational principles derived from human experience, he argued. Classifying these principles into an organized schema enabled scientific legal reasoning: a learned student could use these principles to deduce the correct application of law in a specific scenario. This was law's scientific method. Michael H. Hoeflich writes that this prevailing form of legal science was not the empirical, experimental legal science of the case method used later in the nineteenth century, but a paradigm of deductive reasoning akin to the mathematical and natural sciences.[38] Minor and his contemporaries believed that this method of classification was particularly important for understanding the common law, which would otherwise be a nebulous body of precedent and custom. To Minor and his contemporaries, Blackstone's *Commentaries* revealed how organizing common law principles into a rational scheme enabled learning and reasoning, and Minor used that "incomparable" work to structure his own lessons on the common law throughout his career.[39]

Beyond UVA, these legal science methods were core to developing and justifying academic law programs as they emerged throughout the United States in this period. They structured American legal publications such as Joseph Story's many treatises, as well as Story's design of the Harvard legal curriculum.[40] Theodore W. Dwight, a founding member of the Columbia University Law School when it opened in 1858, pondered: "It seems to be a wise and natural method in the study of other sciences to obtain an accurate outline before crowding the mind with details. Why not in law?"[41] Dwight's pedagogical method mirrored Minor's throughout their parallel careers. Dwight grounded his "Columbia method" in the logical organization of legal principles and drew inspiration from the "scientific" system of "great principles" in Roman civil code. Dwight believed that Blackstone was successful in making sense of the common law in his *Commentaries* because he borrowed the structured arrangement of Justinian's *Institutes*.[42] Law had a logic; legal truth was knowable using the map of legal principles.

Minor's classroom practice reflected his dedication to teaching scientifically through the textbook and lecture method that had become standard in American legal pedagogy by this time.[43] Each class began with Minor examining students on the content and readings from the previous lecture, as required under University rules, in Minor's didactic, yet authoritarian, style. According to James C. Lamb (Law 1879), these daily tests were "in the conversational style, based on the pupil's answers to questions on the text of the lesson previously assigned for study, the questions being skillfully framed to test the knowledge of the pupil, and usually capable of a categorical answer."[44] Richard Thomas Walker Duke Jr. (Law 1874) recalled that Minor "quizzed a great deal & used question and answer as a vehicle of continued dissertation upon the subject under discussion."[45] Minor valued these tests as a means to expose confusion and help students further digest legal principles through verbal recitation. In his first year of teaching, these daily examinations filled sixty to seventy minutes of most ninety-minute class sessions in both the Junior and Senior law classes.[46] His written examinations at the middle and end of each session, similarly, were places for recitation, not debate. He asked students to recall rules, such as "Explain the consideration necessary to support an executory contract," or to define and compare concepts, such as "Explain fully what distinguishes chancery from common law jurisdiction."[47]

As Minor shifted from quiz to lecture each day, the focus shifted to Minor as the expositor and authority on law. Students arriving at class found the blackboard filled with a detailed, hierarchical outline of the day's lesson. Leading principles comprised the outline's main headings. Indented underneath, in a specific format of numbered and lettered subheadings, Minor outlined subsidiary concepts and finished with cites to case law, commentaries, and statutory modifications. This pedagogy was "tabular analysis" or "analytical arrangement" in the tradition of Matthew Bacon's *Abridgement.* For assigned readings, Minor selected specific editions that incorporated this structured, classified arrangement of legal concepts, such as J. H. Thomas's edition of Coke's *Institutes* and Joseph Chitty on contracts.[48] To Minor, this teaching method revealed quickly to a student's eye that law was made up of an ordered set of principles, and the hierarchical format enabled knowledge retention: "the Student will find such summaries . . . afford important aids to memory in recalling the leading principles of complex subjects, the relations of whose parts are often very imperfectly understood until they are exhibited in this, or in some similar compact form."[49]

Minor used this outline method for his entire fifty-year career at UVA. John W. Daniel, who attended Minor's class in 1866 and later became a US senator, reflected on this "topographical map" of law Minor would paint for his students: "His pupils see the law in looking at his analysis on a blackboard or on the printed page as you will see on such a cast the outlines of boundaries and the courses of streams, and realize the relative importance of the main principles and their ramifications and exceptions, as they would realize the proportionate elevation of mountains and plains and valleys."[50] The process engendered copious notetaking. In 1857, Minor sought a publisher for his criminal law lectures. He usually wrote this outline out on the blackboard, he told the publisher, but he and the students were "getting tired of the labour." Minor hoped the printed version, with its tabular form and margins for handwritten annotations, would provide a useful alternative.[51] Later in his career, Minor selected students to chalk his outline on the blackboard before class.[52]

Minor's lectures built off his blackboard outline. In addition to his own legal knowledge, Minor drew on textbooks to formulate his daily outline and his subsequent lectures, which often followed the pages of an assigned reading. According to the Law School catalog, the lecture's goal was to "supply what is deficient, and explain what is obscure in the text, and to induce a thorough practical comprehension of the subject under consideration."[53] Minor's students thought of him as a master lecturer and expositor of legal rules. He used repetition for clarity. He modulated his voice. His passion for the law drew students' attention. "In the lecture-room," Lamb recalled, Minor "was supreme."[54] He had no patience for disobedience. Minor kept strict order and could lose his temper with a wrath of "lightning & thunder."[55] Misbehaving students were brought "immediately to the stand to be questioned on the lesson." After lecture concluded, Minor encouraged his students to continue their studies at home by rewriting the day's notes or abstracting ideas from readings to prepare for the next lecture.[56]

The Logic of the Law

Minor's curriculum mapped out legal principles from general to specific. He wrote in 1850, "You may consider the science of law as having its object the development of the principles, which ought to control and regulate the conduct of states as between each other, the conduct of governments towards their subjects, and the conduct of citizens of the same state amongst themselves."[57] Explicating these three classes of law, from the broad scope of international law, to constitutional law, to the specifics of municipal law, framed the curricular structure of Minor's law program. The Junior Class followed this trajectory from international to municipal, and then the Senior Class dove deeper into legal procedure with long sections on pleading and property. In both classes, Minor showed connections and distinctions between international or English law and law in the United States, especially in Virginia. Particularly in his Senior Class, Minor's state code references were exclusively to Virginia. This was a deliberate pedagogical choice, not evidence of parochialism, Minor argued: "It is essentially immaterial whether [the student] learns the statute law of one State or another, provided he learns it *thoroughly.* When he has become perfectly master of the general statutes of any one State, a very short time—a few weeks at farthest—will suffice to acquaint him with the corresponding statutes of any other State."[58] Overall, this curricular structure enabled the study of legal theory and practice, Minor believed. Theory was the bedrock of practice. It gave reason and logic to legal procedure.

Sitting in his first Junior Class on October 6, 1846, John S. Henshaw (Law 1847) took notes as Minor began with a lecture on the history of the law of nations. Drawing on the preface to Emmerich de Vattel's *Law of*

Nations, Minor presented an origins timeline for this foundational legal framework: Rome fell, Christianity spread in Europe, the feudal and aristocratic system gave order to society, and, consequently, Hugo Grotius wrote a law of nations in the seventeenth century. Samuel von Puffendorf improved on Grotius, then Vattel improved on Puffendorf, and now, in the UVA Law School classroom, Henshaw and his classmates would join this conversation.[59] Assigning roughly forty pages of reading per class, Minor methodically outlined Vattel's *Law of Nations* with his students over the next two months, moving through the general principles of nations, commerce, property, treaties, and war. Understanding these "preliminary principles" of international law and their historical origins should ground American legal education, Minor believed, even if they did not constitute the everyday concerns of a practicing lawyer.[60] Making connections from Vattel's international framing to the local, Minor noted where legal principles outlined by Vattel had been modified in Virginia, such as property ownership by noncitizens.[61]

After two months of Vattel, Henshaw noted on November 12 that the Junior Class had moved to a new segment on government. Just as in Davis's class, Minor did not use a textbook for these lectures and relied instead on his own notes, possibly drawn from Davis's lectures.[62] Minor began again with fundamental principles. He referenced the Virginia Declaration of Rights and the Declaration of Independence as containing "truths too familiar to be proved," including that "all men are created equal," that "all power is originally vested in the people," and that "government ought to be instituted for the common benefit & protection." The American Revolution, Minor suggested, had rescued these maxims from oblivion, and they were now "impregnable." Nonetheless, they were worth studying because the process of translating these great principles into the details of government were much debated.[63]

Minor's discussion of government over the next month moved from general forms to the structure of government in the United States and Virginia.[64] He argued that government had its origins in human necessity to maintain patriarchal order in the earliest families and in society's consent to sacrifice just enough individual independence to a public authority in order to promote the "happiness and welfare of the community."[65] Minor claimed there need not be unanimous concurrence in this process. Rather, the majority would decide, and the rest should acquiesce.[66] Transitioning into constitutional law, Minor taught primarily with the *Federalist* and James Madison's report on the 1799 Virginia Resolutions, both required by the BOV.[67] Henshaw was enthusiastic to reach the end of the *Federalist* after three weeks, writing "Conclusion! Conclusion!!" in his notebook.[68]

Minor and the Junior Class finally transitioned to municipal law, a topic that filled the remainder of the term. Minor relied on Blackstone's *Commentaries* as the organizing framework. Following Blackstone's outline of British law, Minor moved through definitions of the common law and statute law and then into rights concerning persons. He covered property, personal liberty, and private relations such as master and servant. He moved next to civil actions, including divorce, probate, prize cases, and equity, and finally on to public wrongs, with a detailed look at criminal law.[69] Municipal law was not pure theory. Just as he did with Vattel's *Law of Nations,* Minor stated legal principles from Blackstone and then explained how the rule was practiced or applied in the United States and Virginia, especially if there was divergence. Some divergence occurred on a high level. Henshaw noted Minor on property, for example: "The inviolability of private property is certainly a principle of the English law—but guaranteed only by the general genius of her institution. In US the same principles prevail but guaranteed by the constitutions both of the federal government & those of the states."[70] But much of the lecture focused on minute principles in Virginia law. On the role of sheriffs, for example: "The treatment of prisoners is very carefully provided for by our law. The jailor is to see that they [are] provided with sufficient clothing bedding & fire &c & clothing will often be provided by the county court especially in the case of slaves who have run away."[71] Minor concluded these discussions with string cites to cases, reports, treatises, or other legal authorities.

Building on the Junior Class introduction to "elementary principles" of municipal law, the Senior Class went further into legal procedure. The annual UVA catalog outlined the goals of the course: "The subjects studied by the Senior Class are the Common and Statute Law, the Principles of Equity, and Maritime and Commercial Law."[72] Minor returned Thomas's edition of Coke's *Institutes* to the foremost text of the class. Under Henry

St. George Tucker's curriculum, Coke had only been a text of "occasional examination."[73] The course was designed to prepare these future lawyers for pleadings and procedural paperwork. When Isaac H. Carrington (Law 1847) sat down in the first session of Minor's Senior Class in fall 1847, he found himself, much like Henshaw, listening to a history of law, specifically a history of the English common law. Discussing English yearbooks, Magna Carta, and the earliest treatise writers such as Bracton and Glanville was critical, Minor argued, because this history showed the gradual creation of a system of law through analytical arrangement. Littleton wrote a treatise on land tenure, Coke used that foundation to arrange his own work, Lord Hale and William Blackstone followed, and then J. H. Thomas "admirably rearranged" Coke's work in the 1820s, thus making it the "preferred" edition in Minor's class. Law grew more scientific, more reasoned over time, Minor lectured: "Reason, according to Coke, is the life of the law. That is, an artificial perfection of law reason gotten by long study." Because law existed in a rational arrangement, studying it scientifically was best. "Lord Coke's course of study particularly recommended," Carrington noted in his student notebook. "Elements should always be mastered first."[74]

Minor centered property in the Senior Class curriculum. For the first half of the session, from October to January, the class worked through Coke's second volume on real property, dealing first with estates. In each class, Minor offered detailed expositions of Virginia legal rules related to inheritance, tenancy, frauds of conveyances, mortgages, law of descents, and deeds, among others, often starting with a reference to their history. Carrington filled his first notebook before the Senior Class was even done with property and Coke's *Institutes.*[75] For the remainder of the term, the Senior Class moved through pleading, contracts, securities, executors and administrators, and equity pleading.[76] By 1849, Minor also offered a supplementary class for Senior students with a focus on equity. The textbook was *Introduction to Equity Jurisprudence* by James P. Holcombe, an 1839 UVA alumnus.[77]

The focus on common law in the early UVA Law School curriculum for both the Junior and Senior classes reflected Minor's legal expertise in that area, and curricular expansion during Minor's fifty-year career would come from the few additions of new faculty members. In 1851, Holcombe told Minor that he was eager to teach law at his alma mater. Minor saw this as an opportunity to add depth to the UVA Law School curriculum in Holcombe's areas of expertise, especially equity and mercantile law, to which Minor often gave short shrift. He and Holcombe planned to add an Intermediate Class and co-teach all courses. Minor would teach common law topics, while Holcombe would teach equity, mercantile law, and civil law. The Senior law class would see the biggest expansion into equity, mercantile law, securities, civil law, and the exposition of leading cases. This change was critical for the usefulness and reputation of UVA, Minor believed, since the University would train the future leaders of state and federal government.[78]

Holcombe's subsequent hiring in 1851 was one of the few additions to the law faculty during Minor's tenure at UVA. After teaching as an adjunct under the plan that he and Minor had devised, Holcombe was appointed a full professor in 1854.[79] Starting in 1856, Minor and Holcombe divided the Law Department into two schools, each with Junior and Senior classes. Minor taught the Department of Common and Statute Law, while Holcombe taught the Department of Equity, Mercantile, International and Constitutional Law, and Government, Etc. Department titles reflected their areas of teaching. This structure would remain in place, with only slight modifications to the assigned readings, until Minor's last year at UVA. When Holcombe left the Law School in 1861 to join the Confederate Congress, as Elizabeth R. Varon outlines in this volume, Minor was again the sole member of UVA's law faculty, and he taught both departments through the Civil War.[80] In 1866, Stephen O. Southall (Law 1841) joined the faculty and took over Holcombe's department, leaving the reading and curriculum intact until his death in 1885. James Gilmore immediately took over and remained in place, also with no significant changes, through Minor's death in 1895.[81]

Other than the division of the Law Department into its two schools in 1856, the curriculum of the law program changed very little through Minor's tenure, except to become more entrenched around John Minor. In the 1870s, Minor began using his lithographed lecture notes and his own publications as assigned readings in his classes. The curriculum expanded slightly at the end of Minor's life with the addition of new faculty, and members of Minor's family filled these new positions. In 1890, an aging Minor hired his son John B. Minor Jr. (Law 1890) as an assistant. Minor Jr. remained an instructor of law until 1893, when he was replaced by his brother, Raleigh C. Minor (Law 1890). That same year, Minor's Department of Common and Statute Law divided into two parts, a split that would be formalized in 1894 with Part Two becoming a third school within the law program. Minor continued to lecture on property and pleading. To teach Part Two, and then the law program's third school, William Minor Lile (Law 1882), Minor's grandnephew, joined the faculty in 1893 as professor of common and statute law, mercantile, and criminal law. He would later become the first Law School dean from 1904 to 1932. Lile's classes in these early years focused on corporate law and personal property. His primary readings were Minor's *Institutes* and Minor's *Synopsis of Criminal Law.*[82]

The Experience of the Law

In 1854, the Annex opened on the north side of the UVA Rotunda, and Minor's law class moved into this new academic space. He taught on the ground floor, in the largest of the Annex's new classrooms.[83] The law books had their own nook in the Rotunda library and would eventually move to the Annex into a small room across from the law lecture hall, a shift that reflected the law program's growing distinction as a professional school at UVA and within the nation.[84] In 1850, the UVA Law School was the only program that *Hunt's Merchants' Magazine* of New York was aware of in the South, despite the existence of academic programs in various other southern states.[85] UVA remained the "alma mater of Virginia statesmen" and the preeminent university in the South, a position of prominence that would take on new height with the approaching Civil War.[86] Despite this growth, the curricular structure remained the same, as it would for the rest of Minor's tenure: two years of law study were recommended but not required for graduation, and the Junior/Senior division still enabled the law program to serve a variety of students at UVA. In 1854, ninety-eight students took law classes at UVA, a third of which also took classes in other UVA schools.[87] When Minor lectured, his classroom became a dedicated law space. When class ended, students navigated hallways filled with students from other schools. They crisscrossed the Lawn to meals or the library. The law program was embedded in the Academical Village and the liberal arts world of UVA.

Observations and knowledge about broader society provided critical data on law's reasons, and Minor understood the law program's immersion in legal science and liberal arts as one of the key benefits of an academic legal education. Students could understand law more fully by studying humanity, and vice versa. Minor argued for the general benefit of obtaining some degree of legal knowledge for doctors, clergy, legislators, engineers, and others of the "learned professions" outside of law.[88] Within the legal community, he regretted the view that "no knowledge of anything outside of the law is needful, neither language, nor science, nor literature, nor history; nay, that within the precincts of the law itself, nothing is worthy of attention but what is actually and directly demanded in the daily practice of the *trade* of an attorney."[89] In a letter to a prospective law student in 1846, Minor wrote specifically on the importance of studying history, particularly English and Anglo-Saxon history. One could not understand a society "without a knowledge of that society's history," Minor wrote, and this was "emphatically" true for the common law, whose maxims and rules "owe their introduction & long observance,

The Rotunda Annex, shown here in the 1890s, housed John B. Minor's law classes, which were held on the ground floor in the largest classroom. (University of Virginia Libraries)

to successive exigencies of society."[90] The idealization of Anglo-Saxon society as an origin of the common law worked particularly well as a pedagogical tool in the white male intellectual community that UVA built and that tied its own history to Anglo-Saxon roots. As David Konig writes, UVA students looked to history in their lessons and in their library to validate the present.[91] Studying the historical origins of law with a lens fine-tuned on the Anglo-American experience became a self-fulfilling exercise. Studying their own history, their own legal philosophies, and their own patriarchal societies confirmed for law students the continued validity and timelessness of these principles.[92] The common law they learned from Minor and experienced in action at UVA served these students well. The laws made sense. They were reasonable.

The distinctive residential landscape of UVA—its melding of academic and domestic space—bore out Minor's constant classroom emphasis on the importance of human experience to establishing common law principles. This lesson was made most clear in his teachings on slavery, for which he perpetuated the claim of his Law School faculty predecessors of slavery as a necessary evil and added new emphasis on the institution as a positive good for the Black population, as Justene Hill Edwards discusses.[93] Henshaw noted Minor's argument to the Junior Class on the topic of master and servant in 1847: "Slavery in Va is justified by necessity," and the condition of the enslaved population in the United States was better than the condition of the free Black population.[94] Indeed, as law students took these notes in their Rotunda classroom, which was cleaned and kept warm by Lewis Commodore and other enslaved people, enslavement touched every facet of their lives at the University and visibly kept the Academical Village operating.[95] Meanwhile, as the Senior Class learned from Minor about how state law allowed the bondage of enslaved people to be sold, mortgaged, inherited, or hired, they also learned from him that these legal rules came from custom, and that custom meant reason: "Nothing contrary to reason can be law," he lectured.[96] Examples of legal slavery existed all around the law students, particularly on this residential campus. Through the powerful alignment of the lived experience and classroom lessons, the Academical Village normalized Black enslavement as necessary legal custom.

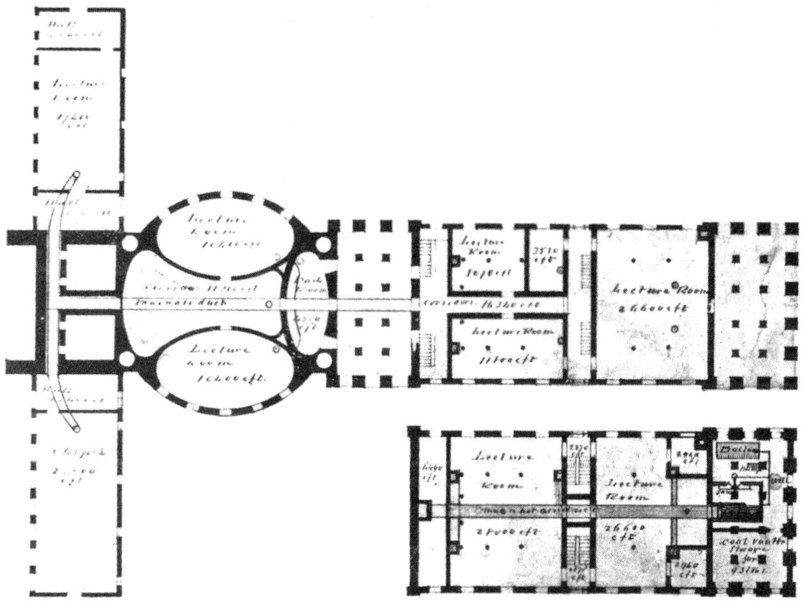

Floor plan of the ground level of UVA's Rotunda and Rotunda Annex, 1859. (Winterthur Museum)

Minor valued the opportunity that UVA's residential structure offered his male students to learn about society and the expectations it had for them. Living together on the Lawn, without the intervening authority of a college president, was a great educational advantage, Minor wrote, primarily through "the cultivation of friendly social relations between the students and the Professors and their families. Not only does such intercourse contribute eminently to order and mutual kindly sympathy, but it affords important aid in educating the moral faculties, as well as in cultivating the understanding."[97] Minor embraced his role as mentor and advised students and alumni with a "fatherly interest."[98] As Laura F. Edwards writes, Minor's home in Pavilion X became a de facto extension of the law classroom.[99] To students, "his home was ever open," recalled an alumnus.[100] Minor was a devout Christian and took on religious mentorship with zeal. He believed that divine law paralleled and complemented the human-made common law.[101] A student recalled: "he probably never lost an opportunity to press on his pupils in private . . . the claims of personal religion." Minor held a Sunday Bible class for law students in their regular lecture room until his final year of life, when he held this class in his Pavilion X office.[102]

George L. Christian (Law 1865) never forgot the mentorship he received from Minor. Christian had fought in the Confederate army for three years before losing one of his feet and the heel of the other in battle. Christian arrived at UVA in the fall of 1864 determined to study law and devoted thoroughly to the Confederate cause: in both pursuits he found a dedicated ally in Minor. At Minor's insistence, Christian's introductory interview turned into a two-night stay at Minor's Pavilion X home. "Indeed, if I had been his own son, he could not have been more kind to me than he was," Christian recalled.[103] There, Christian likely would have seen Minor's private office and interacted with the people that Minor enslaved. He met Minor's children; Minor introduced Christian to his daughter Mary as a "brave soldier in Lee's Army who had been shot in battle in defense of his country."[104] Eventually Christian rented a room with William C. Holmes (Law 1865), a fellow law student and wounded veteran who had lost a hand. Christian purchased the bondage of an enslaved "crippled" woman to cook for them, and Minor lent the two men a wash basin. In the classroom, the work of the law curriculum carried on. Minor lectured twice daily in his usual style to diminished classes populated with wounded Confederate veterans and men too young for service. Holmes helped Christian walk to class; Christian took notes for Holmes.[105]

Minor's Legacy

Minor was resolute in continuing to teach law in his structured, historical way until his passing in 1895. He died just days after reaching the fiftieth anniversary of his hiring at UVA, and he was beloved. The marble bust of Minor presented to the University by Law School alumni in honor of his fifty years of teaching carried an apt inscription under Minor's name: "He taught the law and the reason thereof." By this time, Minor had trained roughly six thousand students, many of whom would go on to serve in positions of significance in Virginia, the American South, and the federal government.[106] In 1895, the law program was one of the largest schools at UVA and comprised a quarter of the University student body.[107] The Law

School was considered the preeminent school for legal training in the American South and Southwest. Minor's methods and standards built a large following of loyal "John B. Men" alumni. At his jubilee anniversary event in June 1895, BOV member R. G. H. Kean (Law 1853) voiced a consensus across the UVA Law School community: "That Prof. Minor, in the fifty years of his work in the Law School of the University, has exerted, and still indirectly exerts, *a wider influence for good upon society in the United States than any man who has lived in this generation.*"[108] At Minor's death shortly thereafter, the accolades continued. "He stamped his personality on the jurisprudence and legal ethics of his country," the Virginia Court of Appeals resolved, and "he let reason reign in all of his actions."[109] The northern press focused more on his regional prominence. The *Chicago Tribune* referred to him as "one of the most distinguished jurists of the South."[110]

Praise for Minor's teaching methods at the close of his career often came as a defense against changes in academic legal education. Minor had steeped his curriculum in prominent texts such as Blackstone and Vattel and in the science of law of which they were a part. Those methods had once been the sign of a nationally premier academic law program. In the 1870s, Christopher Columbus Langdell at Harvard had introduced the case method into legal training, which steadily spread through academic legal curricula. As Hoeflich writes, the case method was deductive, just like Minor's legal science, and was similarly based on the idea that law was fundamentally a set of principles. The critical difference from Minor's methods, however, was in how one derived those principles. Whereas Minor looked to history for the origins of set legal maxims, often using treatises and social observation, Langdell's case method looked to the data in appellate cases to deduce these principles. Rather than Minor's steady exposition of legal rules through lecture and quizzing, Langdell utilized the Socratic method to introduce investigation and experimentation into the classroom.[111] Langdell would change his conclusions in class "in light of new suggestions," something that was foreign both to Minor's teaching methods and his understanding of law.[112] As Anne M. Coughlin writes, the use of the case method in this period paralleled and reinforced initiatives to professionalize legal education, particularly those pushed by the nascent American Bar Association.[113] Minor's methods were growing out of step with the larger context of American legal education, a process that both endeared him to his followers and limited his relevance to American legal education beyond the South.[114]

Minor's *Institutes* typified this dynamic. In 1875, Minor published the first two volumes of what would eventually be his four-volume *Institutes of Common and Statute Law,* an outline of legal rules and accompanying commentary that he modeled on Blackstone's *Commentaries.* The goal, Minor wrote, was to present "in print what the author had been accustomed, for many years, annually to exhibit on the blackboard: that is, a mere tabular analysis of part of his course of instruction in the Law Department of the University of Virginia."[115] This published outline of law would supplement his oral lectures, just as the blackboard outline had. Minor took pains with the printer to continue his specific indentation system, which would have been familiar to "those who for the last thirty years have pursued their legal studies at the University of Virginia."[116] Minor's long career had convinced him of the utility of this analytical method for teaching "the science of law."[117] As the case method began to spread through legal curricula in these same years, Minor's *Institutes*

John B. Minor in his Pavilion X office on the East Lawn, ca. 1890s. (Albert and Shirley Small Special Collections Library, University of Virginia)

set in print his ode to teaching law in the former ways of legal science, through a structured, set outline of legal rules. It became the central assigned reading in the UVA Law School curriculum and a standard reference text for southern lawyers. In law journals, however, reviews were mixed for reasons that belied changes in legal education. The book's outline form was "complicated and mysterious," said one.[118] The *Albany Law Journal* cut to the core of the difference between Minor and the new era of legal science. Its review thanked Minor for undertaking such a task but called it hopeless: "The law is too Protean to be fixed."[119]

Minor's map of the law, however, was more fixed than not. If there was undiscovered territory, it was in the far corners of oblivion, and he did not explore it, even if social changes demanded it. At Minor's death, tributes abounded for his contributions to UVA and to the legal community, particularly through his famed "analytical" teaching methods.[120] "It would be impossible to say how much Mr. Minor has contributed to the clearness and accuracy of the general legal mind, especially in Virginia and the South, by the mere use of this logical and scientific arrangement of his matter," Lamb wrote in the *Virginia Law Register.* But even as former students praised Minor's methods, they saw the rigidness he bred into the UVA Law School curriculum through his unflinching devotion to teaching common law as "the historical source and basis of nearly all our jurisprudence."[121] Students recalled his in-class "wrath" and "unrelenting hostilities" over changes to the common law, such as homestead debt exemptions, code pleading, and especially married women's property acts, as Laura Edwards discusses.[122] As Elizabeth R. Varon writes, Minor retained his discussion of slavery in his postbellum *Institutes* simply by making it historical, writing "the continuance of slavery *was* justified in Virginia" and citing Thomas Dew on the "disastrous effects of emancipation."[123]

Minor, nonetheless, had created an experience and a tradition. Even as Duke faulted Minor for teaching in the "age of the mammoth," Duke valued the lifelong friendships he had forged with classmates such as Thomas Nelson Page (Law 1874), and he praised Minor "as the greatest teacher I ever knew."[124] In contrast to places like Columbia, where the passing or expulsion of the old guard from the law faculty led to an embrace of the case method and the new legal science, Minor's imprint remained strong at UVA for decades, especially through enduring familial ties.[125] In 1954, Law School Dean Frederick D. G. Ribble (Law 1921), himself a Minor descendent, published Minor's regular farewell address to the Senior Class, which Minor's son Raleigh Minor, also on the Law School faculty, had continued to give after Minor's death. Ribble noted Minor's persistent influence in the legal community, writing, "His Institutes have been standard authority for many years and are still quoted, particularly in the realm of Real Property." Minor's address called on his Senior Class students to devote themselves to the hard and honest labor of systematically studying law, particularly as guardians of society's morals. Ribble believed the address still encapsulated the Law School: "In my judgement it is the best verbal expression of the spirit of the Law School—a spirit which holds today as it did in the days of the author."[126]

Notes

1. William Blackstone, *Commentaries on the Laws of England: In Four Books, With an Analysis of the Work* [. . .] (New York: W. E. Dean, 1851), 1:20–21.
2. William P. LaPiana, *Logic and Experience: The Origin of Modern Legal Education* (New York: Oxford University Press, 1994), 29.
3. See David T. Konig, "Jeffersonian Foundations of Legal Education in Virginia, 1779–1845," in this volume. See also Johann N. Neem, "From 'Ancients and Axioms' to 'Every Branch of Science': Thomas Jefferson's Philosophy of Liberal Education," in *The Founding of Thomas Jefferson's University,* ed. John A. Ragosta, Peter S. Onuf, and Andrew J. O'Shaughnessy (Charlottesville: University of Virginia Press, 2019), 306–24.
4. Neem, "From 'Ancients and Axioms,'" 319–20.
5. "Minor Hall," *University of Virginia Magazine,* n.s., 45, no. 5 (February 1902): 304.
6. The 1820 census lists fourteen enslaved people as part of Lancelot Minor's household and notes that the household was primarily engaged in agriculture; see US Census, 1820, Louisa County, VA, 471. For nine siblings, see John B. Minor Jr., *The Minor Family of Virginia* (Lynchburg, VA: J. P. Bell, 1923), 21–22. (John B. Minor is hereafter cited as JBM.)
7. See Thomas Jefferson to Lancelot Minor, 19 February 1812, Founders Online, National Archives, https://founders.archives.gov/documents/Jefferson/03-04-02-0396. For Minor noting the importance of his father's training in enabling him to become the new law chair at UVA, see JBM to Lancelot Minor, 31 July 1845, Papers of the Minor and Wilson Family, MSS 3750 (hereafter cited as MWP), Albert and Shirley Small Special Collections Library, University of Virginia (hereafter cited as SSCL).
8. W. Hamilton Bryson, *Legal Education in Virginia, 1779–1979: A Biographical Approach* (Charlottesville: University Press of Virginia, 1982), 435–37.
9. Bryson, *Legal Education in Virginia,* 417.
10. "University of Virginia," *Richmond Enquirer,* 3 August 1832; "University of Virginia,"

Richmond Enquirer, 5 August 1834. Minor had ambitions to earn a newly established master's degree, which required a student to graduate from the schools of Antient Languages, Mathematics, Natural Philosophy, Chemistry, and Moral Philosophy. *Catalogue of the Officers and Students of the University of Virginia, Session of 1832–33* (Charlottesville, VA: D. Deans, 1833), 25 (hereafter cited as *UVA Catalogue*).

11. University of Virginia Faculty Minutes, vols. 1–19, 1825–1970, 19 July 1833, 12 July 1834, RG–19/1/1.461, SSCL. See also Henry Reck, "John Barbee Minor: The Early Years," *Magazine of Albemarle County History* 12 (1953): 24–38.
12. University of Virginia, *Enactments Relating to the Constitution and Government of the University of Virginia* (Charlottesville, VA: Cary, Watson, 1831), 3.
13. Lucian Minor, *Discourse on the Life and Character of the Late John A. G. Davis, Professor of Law in the University of Virginia, Delivered before the Society of Alumni, June 29th, 1847* (Richmond, VA: Shepard and Colin, 1847), 16.
14. J. A. G. Davis to JBM, 17 December 1831, MWP.
15. See *UVA Catalogue 1832–33*, 10–11; and map: Peter Maverick, Plan of the University of Virginia, 1825, 6552-a, RG–30/1/8.381, SSCL.
16. Journals of the Chairman of the Faculty, 1827–1864, 11 May 1833, 4:69, RG–19/1/2.041, SSCL.
17. Bryson, *Legal Education in Virginia*, 417–19.
18. JBM to William Blackford, 28 May 1845, Blackford Family Papers, 1742–2003, Southern Historical Collection, Wilson Library, University of North Carolina (cited hereafter as BFP).
19. JBM to Martha Minor, 7 May 1845, MWP.
20. William Blackford to JBM, 2 May 1845, MWP.
21. John Saunders, J. R. Tucker, and John T. Thornton to JBM, 4 January 1844, MWP; Recollection by J. R. Tucker, printed in *Report of the Eighth Annual Meeting of the Virginia State Bar Association* (Richmond, VA: Williams, 1896), 20.
22. *Richmond (VA) Daily Whig*, 24 July 1845.
23. Lucian Minor to JBM, 7 June 1845, MWP.
24. JBM to William Blackford, 11 July 1845, BFP.
25. Lucian Minor to JBM, 7 June 1845, MWP.
26. On July 4, 1845, the Board of Visitors (hereafter cited as BOV) appointed lawyer and former congressman John M. Patton as law professor, but he declined. University of Virginia BOV, Minute Books, 1829–1956, 4 July 1845, vol. 3 1837–55, RG–1/1/1.382, SSCL (hereafter cited as BOV Minutes).
27. Joseph Cabell to JBM, 29 July 1845, and JBM to Lancelot Minor, 30 July 1845, MWP.
28. BOV Minutes, 21 July 1830; JBM, "Historical Sketches of Virginia, Literary Institutions of the State, University of Virginia," *Old Dominion* 4, no. 6 (15 June 1870): 331.
29. Four additional students joined later in the session, bringing the total to twenty-nine. "School of Law Monthly Class Report, for Month Ending 1st November 1845," MWP.
30. "Inaugural Lecture," October 1845, Papers of John B. Minor, MSS-79-8, Arthur J. Morris Law Library Special Collections, University of Virginia (hereafter cited as LLSC).
31. *UVA Catalogue 1845–46*, 23–24; University of Virginia, *Enactments Relating to the Constitution and Government of the University of Virginia* (Philadelphia: C. Sherman, 1838), 26.
32. *UVA Catalogue 1845–46*, 27.
33. Enoch Faw Diary, 1857, MSS 4897, SSCL.

34. JBM to Charles Colby, 19 May 1855, JBM Letterbook, John B. Minor Papers, 1843–1892, MSS 3114, SSCL (cited hereafter as JBMP).
35. JBM to Henry Randall, 9 August 1851, JBMP.
36. JBM, "Historical Sketches of Virginia, Literary Institutions of the State, University of Virginia," *Old Dominion* 4, no. 4 (15 April 1870): 202.
37. JBM, "Historical Sketches of Virginia,", 199; Philip Alexander Bruce, *History of the University of Virginia, 1819–1919,* vol. 4 (New York: Macmillan, 1921), 42–48.
38. M. H. Hoeflich, "Law & Geometry: Legal Science from Leibniz to Langdell," *American Journal of Legal History* 30, no. 2 (April 1986): 96–101. William LaPiana also argues that legal science was widespread in the antebellum period. LaPiana, *Logic and Experience,* esp. 29–54.
39. John B. Minor, *Institutes of Common and Statute Law* (Richmond, VA: Whittet & Shepperson, 1875), 1:vii.
40. For the incorporation of legal science thinking into American legal curricula and treatises, see Steve Sheppard, "An Introductory History of Law in the Lecture Hall," in *The History of Legal Education in the United States: Commentaries and Primary Sources,* ed. Steve Sheppard (Pasadena, CA: Salem Press, 1999), 1:17–22. For Story and Harvard, see Daniel R. Coquillette and Bruce A. Kimball, *On the Battlefield of Merit: Harvard Law School, the First Century* (Cambridge, MA: Harvard University Press, 2015), 173.
41. Theodore W. Dwight, "Columbia College Law School, New York" in *Green Bag* 1, no. 4 (April 1889): 147.
42. Dwight, "Columbia College Law School," 147–48. See also George C. Austin, "The Dwight Method of Legal Instruction," *Law Quarterly Review* 9, no. 2 (April 1893): 171–78.
43. For the instructional method at Harvard and its widespread use, see Coquillette and Kimball, *On the Battlefield of Merit,* 167.
44. James C. Lamb, "John B. Minor," *Virginia Law Register* 1, no. 7 (November 1895): 478.
45. Richard Thomas Walker Duke Jr., "Recollections," 1899–1926, vol. 3, 108–9, MSS 9521-o, SSCL.
46. "School of Law, Monthly Class Report for the Month Ending 1st November 1845," MWP.
47. Final Examination, Senior Class, 1852; Examination for Degrees, 1846, MWP.
48. Matthew Bacon, *A New Abridgment of the Law* (London: A. Strahan, 1832); Isaac H. Carrington Student Notebook, 1 October 1846, Professor John B. Minor's Senior Law Class, Student Notebooks, RG-32-400, LLSC; J. H. Thomas, *A Systematic Arrangement of Lord Coke's First Institute of the Laws of England: On the Plan of Sir Matthew Hale's Analysis,* 3 vols. (Philadelphia: Robert H. Small, 1827). Joseph Chitty, *A Practical Treatise on the Law of Contracts . . .* (Springfield, MA: G. and C. Merriam, 1844). For Minor's statement on tabular analysis and how he came to use it in his teaching, see preface to John B. Minor, *A Synopsis on The Laws of Crime and Punishments in Virginia: For the Use of the Students of Law in the University of Virginia,* 2nd ed. (Richmond, VA: M. W. Hazlewood, 1869), 3.
49. JBM, *Synopsis on the Laws of Crime and Punishments,* 3. For analytical arrangement, see JBM, preface to Minor, *Institutes of Common and Statute Law,* 1:v.
50. John Warwick Daniel, "John B. Minor," *Speeches and Orations of John Warwick Daniel,* comp. Edward M. Daniel (Lynchburg, VA: J. P. Bell, 1911), 586. Daniel represented Virginia in the US Senate from 1887 to 1910; see William Bland Whitley, "John War-

wick Daniel (1842–1910)," *Encyclopedia Virginia,* Virginia Humanities, https://perma.cc/78X6-P5FP.

51. JBM to Messrs. Smith, English & Co., 28 January 1857, JBMP. The published notes became the first edition of Minor's *A Synopsis on the Laws of Crime and Punishments* (Philadelphia: William S. Young, 1858).
52. Duke, "Recollections," 3:113–14.
53. *UVA Catalogue 1845–46,* 24.
54. Lamb, "John B. Minor," 478. John W. Daniel said in 1895, at an event commemorating Minor's career: "To this analytical plan he added his oral lectures, as if a painter were to come along and turn the map into a picture." Daniel, "John B. Minor," 586.
55. Duke, "Recollections," 3:108.
56. Enoch Faw Diary, 6 October 1857 and 8 October 1857.
57. JBM to William Wirt Henry, 7 August 1850, printed in W. Hamilton Bryson, *Essays on Legal Education in Nineteenth Century Virginia* (Buffalo, NY: William S. Hein, 1998), 153.
58. *UVA Catalogue 1845–46,* 23; JBM, preface to Minor, *Institutes of Common and Statute Law,* 1:vi.
59. J. S. Henshaw Student Notebook, 6 October 1846, Professor John B. Minor's Junior Law Class, Student Notebooks, RG-32-400, LLSC.
60. James A. Latane Student Notebook, 4–9 October 1851, Professor John B. Minor's Junior Law Class, Papers of the Latané and Related Waring, Allen, Temple, Roane, and Dix Families, 1650–1898, Box 3, MSS 6490, SSCL; Minor's full list of lecture topics and readings was listed in the University's 1849 annual report. "Report of the Rector and Visitors of the University of Virginia, 1849," in *Governor's Message and Annual Reports of the Public Officers of the State* . . . (Richmond, VA: William F. Ritchie, 1849), 57–60 (cited hereafter as *Annual Report 1849*).
61. Henshaw Student Notebook, 17 October 1846.
62. *Annual Report 1849,* 60; Henshaw Student Notebook, 12 November 1846.
63. Henshaw Student Notebook, 12 November 1846.
64. Henshaw Student Notebook, 12 November 1846; *Annual Report 1849,* 60–61; Latane Student Notebook, 11–14 October 1851.
65. Henshaw Student Notebook, 12 November 1846.
66. Henshaw Student Notebook, 17 November 1846, 12 November 1846, and 14 November 1846.
67. BOV Minutes, 4 March 1825.
68. Henshaw Student Notebook, n.d., December 1846.
69. *Annual Report 1849,* 57–59.
70. Henshaw Student Notebook, 19 January 1847.
71. Henshaw Student Notebook, 17 January 1847.
72. *UVA Catalogue 1845–46,* 23–24.
73. *UVA Catalogue 1844–45,* 17; *UVA Catalogue 1845–46,* 23.
74. Carrington Student Notebook, 1 October 1847.
75. Carrington Student Notebook, n.d., 144.
76. *Annual Report 1849,* 54–56.
77. *Annual Report 1849,* 57; James P. Holcombe, *Introduction to Equity Jurisprudence, on the Basis of Story's Commentaries, with Notes and References, to English and American Cases, Adapted to the Use of Students* (Cincinnati, OH: Derby, Bradley, 1846).

78. JBM to Joseph Cabell, 7 May 1851, and JBM to JL Bell, 18 May 1851, JBMP.
79. *UVA Catalogue 1851–52,* 27–28; *UVA Catalogue 1854–55,* 25–26.
80. See Elizabeth R. Varon, "The Civil War and Reconstruction, 1861–1877," in this volume.
81. *UVA Catalogue 1866–67,* 34; *UVA Catalogue 1885–86,* 41.
82. *UVA Catalogue 1890–91,* 26; *UVA Catalogue 1893–94,* 40–41. For more on the Law School under William Minor Lile, see G. Edward White, "Poised between a Regional and a National Law School, 1920–1960," in this volume.
83. Duke, "Recollections," 3:107; Montgomery C. Meigs, "University of Virginia, Plans of Public Rooms with Proposed Arrangement for Heating Them," 16 February 1859, Papers and Plans, 1856–1892, Manuscript Collection, Folio 16, Winterthur Library, Winterthur, DE.
84. "The Law Library," *Alumni Bulletin* 1, no. 3 (November 1894): 88.
85. "Law Schools in the South and West," *Hunt's Merchants' Magazine and Commercial Review* 23, no. 4 (October 1850): 475.
86. *Richmond Daily Times,* 11 February 1851; "Southern Collegiate Institutions," *New Orleans Weekly Delta,* 8 April 1850.
87. *UVA Catalogue 1854–55,* 7–15.
88. JBM, *Institutes of Common and Statute Law* (1876), 1:2–9.
89. JBM, *Institutes of Common and Statute Law* (1876), 1:19, italics in the original.
90. JBM to A. A. Clayton, 21 December 1846, JBMP.
91. See Konig, "Jeffersonian Foundations of Legal Education in Virginia, 1779–1845," in this volume.
92. Dorothy Ross, "Historical Consciousness in Nineteenth-Century America." *American Historical Review* 89, no. 4 (October 1984): 909–28.
93. See Justene Hill Edwards, "Teaching the Laws of Slavery, 1826–1861," in this volume.
94. Henshaw Student Notebook, 28 January 1847.
95. President's Commission on Slavery and the University, *Report to President Teresa A. Sullivan* (2018), 34.
96. Carrington Student Notebook, 1 October 1847.
97. JBM, "Historical Sketches of Virginia," 205.
98. Daniel, "John B. Minor," 585.
99. See Laura F. Edwards, "Coverture and Virginia Law Professors: The Nineteenth Century," in this volume.
100. Lamb, "John. B. Minor," 482.
101. Latane Student Notebook, 1851, 4.
102. Lamb, "John. B. Minor," 482.
103. George L. Christian, "Reminiscences and a Contrast," *Alumni Bulletin* 2, no. 2 (April 1909): 197.
104. Christian, "Reminiscences and a Contrast," 197.
105. Christian, "Reminiscences and a Contrast," 198–99, 201.
106. Lamb, "John. B. Minor," 479. See list of alumni at 1916 event honoring UVA and Minor, including Supreme Court Justice James McReynolds and US Attorney General Thomas Watt Gregory (both Law 1884). "U. of V. Alumni Dine," *Washington Post,* 13 May 1916.
107. *UVA Catalogue 1894–95,* xx.
108. R. G. H. Kean, "Prof. John B. Minor's Jubilee," *Virginia Law Register* 1, no. 3 (July 1895): 235; italics in the original.

109. "In Memory of Prof. Minor," *Washington Post,* 2 August 1895.
110. "Church and Clergy," *Chicago Daily Tribune,* 4 August 1895.
111. Hoeflich, "Law & Geometry," 119–20.
112. William Schofield, "Christopher Columbus Langdell," *American Law Register (1898–1907)* 55, no. 5 (May 1907): 276.
113. See Anne M. Coughlin, "'This Mob of Men': The Road to Coeducation at the University of Virginia School of Law, 1870–1923," in this volume.
114. Griffith Ogden Ellis, "Some Defects in Our Present System of Legal Education," *American Lawyer* 4, no. 10 (October 1896): 452–53.
115. JBM, *Institutes of Common and Statute Law* (1876), 1:v, vii.
116. JBM, *Institutes of Common and Statute Law* (1876), 1:v, vii
117. JBM, *Institutes of Common and Statute Law* (1876), 1:v–vi.
118. "Book Notices," *American Law Review* 13, no. 4 (July 1879): 735–36.
119. "New Books and New Editions," *Albany Law Journal* 19 (3 May 1879): 363.
120. Lamb, "John B. Minor," 473–84. A shortened version also appeared in *Virginia Magazine of History and Biography* 3, no. 3 (January 1896): 295–97. See tributes to JBM at the Virginia State Bar Association annual meetings in 1895 and 1896. *Report of the Seventh Annual Meeting of the Virginia State Bar Association* (Richmond, VA: Williams, 1895), 40–44; *Report of the Eighth Annual Meeting,* 18–23, 49–65 (Lamb's tribute).
121. Lamb, "John B. Minor," 479.
122. Lamb, "John B. Minor," 480; Duke, "Recollections," 3:109–10; Edwards, "Coverture and Virginia Law Professors," in this volume.
123. Varon, "Civil War and Reconstruction," italics added; JBM, *Institutes of Common and Statute Law* (1876), 1:163, 171.
124. Duke, "Recollections," 3:109, 112; R. T. W. Duke Jr., "Remarks of Judge R. T. W. Duke, Jr.," in *Report of the Eighth Annual Meeting of the Virginia State Bar Association,* 22.
125. For the importance of decanal appointments in shifting law school practices around the case method, see Sheppard, *History of Legal Education,* 1:21, 33.
126. "The Farewell Address of John B. Minor to His Graduating Classes," foreword by F. D. G. Ribble, *Alabama Lawyer* 15, no. 3 (July 1954): 327–33.

The Civil War and Reconstruction, 1861–1877

Elizabeth R. Varon

IN MARCH 1864, at the outset of the Civil War's third bloody year, a faculty committee consisting of law professor John Barbee Minor (Law 1834), chemistry professor Socrates Maupin (Grad 1833), and literature and history professor George Frederick Holmes promulgated a report on the current condition and future promise of the University of Virginia. The report, which was adopted by the rest of the faculty, opened on a note of optimism—reflecting "upon the present condition & future prospects of the University," the committee expressed "the hope that the institution may be successfully kept alive during the war, and be prepared at its close to commence a new career of vigorous usefulness." As the report delved deeper into the "future prospects" of the University, however, its authors struck notes of caution and wariness. Little more could be accomplished during the war itself than merely "to keep the institution in being," they wrote. And even the advent of peace would pose daunting challenges: "It cannot be doubted that in the languor and inaptitude for literary pursuits likely to follow the war, in the total want of adequate preparation on the part of the youth of the Country, & of good schools where such preparation can be had, [and] in the dilapidated fortunes of a vast proportion of our countrymen . . . this institution will encounter obstacles & difficulties in its revival which can be surmounted only by the utmost zeal, and by steady & indefatigable industry on the part of the instructors."[1]

Minor, who had, in 1864, already led the UVA Law School for two decades, foresaw some of the dangers and destruction posed by southern secession. But he had also, along with his fellow UVA faculty members, played a crucial role in priming the pump for war. To a significant degree, the UVA Law School faced a crisis of its own making during the war years. Minor would emerge from the war defiantly determined to restore the prospects of the Law School, the primacy of Virginia within the Union, and the racial caste system.

"A Necessary Revolution"

The secession of Virginia in April 1861 plunged Minor's beloved Law School into crisis. As UVA students flocked to the secessionist banner (more than five hundred of the University's six hundred 1861 enrollees would serve in the Confederate army), the Law School was emptied out, with only nine students matriculating for the 1861–62 term. Minor's rigorous, distinctive program of legal education—balancing the scholarly study of foundational texts such as Blackstone and Vattel with moot court argumentation—continued despite the paucity of students (enrollment would drop to five in 1862–63). But dashed was Minor's conceit that he and his faculty could remain, as lofty guardians of civic virtue, above the political fray. He had long committed himself to the ethos of his predecessor in the UVA law professorship, Henry St. George Tucker. These men sought to impress upon students both "the inestimable value of the union on one hand, and the vital importance of preserving the rights of the states on the other," by juxtaposing texts such as James Madison's essays in the *Federalist Papers* and his defense of state sovereignty in the *Virginia Report of 1799–1800*. But the growing power and fury of Virginia's secession movement ominously tilted the scales away from Unionism and confounded Minor's balancing act.[2]

During the secession crisis, Minor was an archetypal "conditional Unionist," or "reluctant Confederate"—labels that modern scholars use to describe those in the Upper South who initially preached caution but eventually swung into the secessionist column. Unlike diehard "unconditional" Unionists (those who never accepted secession), conditional Unionists were willing for their states to remain in the Union on the condition that the newly elected president, Abraham Lincoln, and his Republican Party make some concessions to the slaveholding states and refrain from any acts of federal "coercion." Unionists of both types shared a profound foreboding that disunion would be a cataclysmic catastrophe. They felt betrayed and victimized by what they saw as the forces of extremism—New England abolitionism and South Carolina secessionism—and believed that Virginia, as the ancient "mother of all states," should play a role as mediator in the sectional conflict. Steeped in a tradition of proslavery Unionism, they warned that a civil war would destroy slavery in its wake. Thus Minor himself lamented, in family letters in late 1860, "the wicked madness which would plunge us into the vortex of civil war," and hoped that Virginia would "interpose a calm, earnest and dignified mediation worthy of her character."[3]

During Virginia's secession convention, lasting from February to April 1861, Unionist delegates (of both the conditional and diehard types) initially outnumbered so-called immediate secessionists, who wanted Virginia to join the new Confederacy formed by Deep South states. But over the course of the convention, against the backdrop of events such as Lincoln's inaugural address, failed peace negotiations, the fall of Fort Sumter, and Lincoln's call for troops to resist the insurrection, secessionists gained the upper hand in the convention, luring conditional Unionists to their side by casting disunion as a positive good and promising that if civil war came, the slave South would triumph and prosper. The time for compromise was over, they insisted, and it was degrading for Virginia to beg for peace—instead it should reprise its role of 1776 and lead the new revolution. Secessionists offered two justifications for their movement: some emphasized the constitutionality of secession as a legal remedy, while others invoked the natural inalienable right to oppose tyranny and cast secession as an extralegal revolutionary resort. Minor, watching the convention debates from afar, clearly preferred the second argument. He had little affinity for states' rights theorizing and worried that secession would bring "the premature destruction of Slavery." But after Lincoln's April 15 call for troops, which was widely interpreted by conditional Unionists as an act of coercion, Minor embraced secession. On April 17, 1861, Virginia's convention passed a secession ordinance by a tally of eighty-eight to fifty-five. Minor, in the subsequent ratification referendum, "voted heartily for the ordinance, not indeed as an act of secession (the whole doctrine touching [which] I thought unwise & unwarranted by the history, text, or spirit of the Constitution), but as a necessary revolution."[4]

Historians seeking to explain how and why conditional Unionists proved so susceptible to secessionist appeals have emphasized the shared assumptions of both camps—that abolitionism posed an existential threat to the South, that the "Black Republican" president Lincoln had no right to interfere with slavery, and that secession was a justifiable last resort should Lincoln and the northern population prove themselves to be "hostile and uncompromising," as Minor put it. Minor, like many other erstwhile Unionists in his milieu, cast Lincoln's call for troops as the turning point in Virginia's debates—the moment that forced the forbearing, cautious Commonwealth to side with its "sister" southern states, rather than join the invaders. But such a view, while conveniently painting Virginians as victims, occluded the ways that they had stoked the fires of secession.[5]

Faculty and students at UVA Law had played a key role in building the case for the cultural, social, economic, and political incompatibility of the free-labor North and slave-labor South. UVA professors such as Albert T. Bledsoe—a minister, lawyer, mathematics professor, and future Confederate assistant secretary of war—churned out lectures and tracts in the late 1850s defending slavery, portraying it as a "positive good," and insisting that "blacks have been elevated and improved by their servitude in this country." Minor's right-hand man on the Law School faculty, Professor James P. Holcombe (College 1839), whom Minor brought on board in 1851 to teach equity and commercial law, was every bit as rabid a defender of slavery as Bledsoe, insisting in an 1858 address that white southerners had a natural duty to "reduce the negro to subjection." The legal historian Alfred L. Brophy regards Holcombe as exemplifying the trends in southern higher education in the antebellum era, as the academy became a key site for "the generation and dissemination of pro-slavery thought," and the South "turned from talking about the importance of slavery to considering it axiomatic that slavery was a blessing and constitutionally protected." The jurisprudence of men such as Holcombe, Brophy explains, "denied universal truths of equality in favor of calibration of rights according to station in society," on the assumption that "people are inherently unequal and that some are better fit for slavery than freedom." "Our rights are not those that we would have in a natural state," Holcombe explained to students in his Junior law class lectures, "but they are relative, they depend on our condition in society."[6]

As Justene Hill Edwards notes in this volume, Minor instructed students in the defense of slavery—promoting both its "permanence and expansion," as Hill Edwards puts it—in his Law School lectures. His classes provided glosses on texts such as Blackstone and on William Waller Hening's *Statutes at Large* (a compendium of Virginia laws, including its slave codes, dating back to the colonial era) by insisting, as student notes from Minor's October 26, 1860, Junior Class lecture spell out, that "slavery [was] justified by the necessities of society; we could not possibly get along, or exist as a society if slaves were emancipated."

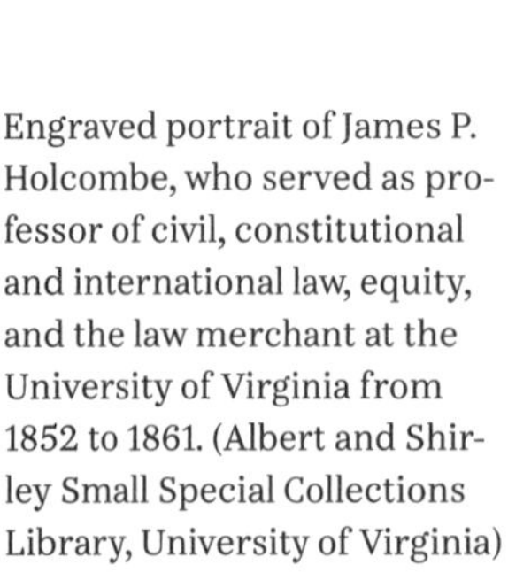

Engraved portrait of James P. Holcombe, who served as professor of civil, constitutional and international law, equity, and the law merchant at the University of Virginia from 1852 to 1861. (Albert and Shirley Small Special Collections Library, University of Virginia)

Those "necessities," Minor illustrated in a variety of lectures on slavery, property, citizenship, contracts, the Constitution, and federalism, were manifold. The necessities included property rights and personal profit: he lectured to students, for example, on the protocol for selling enslaved persons, observing that "in case of slaves and work cattle there must be at least a month's notice." The necessities also included social control: Minor took note, in an 1860 lecture, of the Virginia law granting "the privilege to a master of punishing his slave even maliciously if done in private." And they included sectional comity: Minor credited the concessions to slaveholding interests in the Constitution (such as the three-fifths compromise and slave trade clause) as having "happily adjusted" the "bad feeling between the advocates and opponents of slavery in the national convention." Well before Virginians decided on political separation from the Union, the state's leading educators framed enslavement as a constitutional right that must be protected from the "jealousy of the northern states," as Minor put it.[7]

Some of those educators openly promoted secession as the only means to preserve slavery in the event of Lincoln's election. At UVA, there was no more ardent secessionist than the Law School's Holcombe. Unlike Minor, who refrained from overtly addressing the secession debates in his lectures, Holcombe showed no such restraint. As revealed by the student notebooks of Philip Pendleton Barbour (Law 1861)—who took Holcombe's Junior law course in the winter of 1860–61, as seven Deep South states left the Union and formed the Confederacy—Holcombe used his lectern as a bully pulpit to build support for Virginia's secession. Holcombe endorsed John C. Calhoun's constitutional theories that cast the Union as a compact between sovereign states and that reserved for individual states the constitutional right to undo the compact, should other states betray its terms. In a typical secessionist argument, Holcombe pointed to northern defiance of the 1850 Fugitive Slave Law as a major breach of contract. This Calhounian political philosophy emphasized the danger, in democracies, that majorities would ride roughshod over minorities (by which Calhoun, and Holcombe, meant outnumbered southern enslavers). Holcombe spelled out for his students exactly what the fledgling Confederacy stood for, noting that while the US Constitution had eschewed the use of the term "slaves," in the new southern version "the term 'slaves'" was "used on all occasions." While the US Constitution had not explicitly guaranteed the right to enslave people, the Confederate constitution stipulated that no law could be passed denying the "right of property in negro slaves." Holcombe also took to the hustings as a politician to preach to Albemarle County's voters. In a public speech on January 2, 1860, he seethed that "the election of a Black Republican President" was an "act of aggression on the right of property in slaves" and that the North was intent on "converting African slaves into freemen, by converting Southern freemen into slaves."[8]

UVA students were a captive audience for men such as Holcombe but also influenced them in turn. As the historians Peter S. Carmichael and Alfred Brophy have shown, southern campuses—and UVA in particular—were hotbeds of secessionism in 1860–61. Students were steeped not only in proslavery ideology but also in tales of Virginia's heroic founders, laments about the state's lost primacy in the Union, and visions of a return to glory in a Confederacy that would protect their right to own enslaved persons. Well before Virginia's convention voted to secede, UVA's student body rallied around the Confederate flag, figuratively and literally. On March 16, 1861, zealous students hung the rebel flag from the Rotunda to the dismay of some older professors who were still in the conditional Unionist camp. Four days later, Holcombe, who had resigned his seat on the faculty to represent Albemarle County in Virginia's secession convention, gave a stem-winding speech to his fellow delegates there in which he declared, "African slavery constitutes the wisest and most beneficent adjustment possible of the relations between the two races, and that it is to be cherished and defended to the last extremity." Virginia, which had in its glory days in the early republic "been accustomed to lay down the rule for the construction of the Constitution, and to fix the principles of public policy," could no longer do so in a Union of free states, under the "iron hand of oppression." It could only restore its leadership role within a "splendid Confederacy, homogeneous in its feelings and its interests—a Confederacy that will change the moral sentiment of the world in reference to slavery." Holcombe's speech "made him the idol of the inflamed students who marched on Richmond in mid-April demanding an end to the older generation's procrastinations," as the historians William W. Freehling and Craig M. Simpson have explained.[9]

The Storm of War

Holcombe would go on to serve in the Confederate Congress and never return to his law professorship. Minor, by contrast, would stay rooted in Charlottesville, trying to preserve the Law School amid the storm of war. He threw himself into the Confederate cause, serving in 1863 as an organizer of a local volunteer defense association called the "Albemarle Minute Men." He summoned his neighbors to arms by invoking the "repeated raids of the enemy, enticing away negroes, carrying off horses and wagons, destroying cattle, provisions and crops, dragging citizens into captivity, and beggaring families." Minor clung to the hope that slavery could survive the war. He continued to rent, buy, and sell enslaved persons, offering "several valuable negroes" for sale as the executor of his late brother Charles's estate in 1862 and selling an enslaved man named Philip, who had frequently attempted to escape, in July 1863. But he could not keep the tide of emancipation at bay—when the Union army approached Charlottesville near the end of the war, "multitudes of servants went off with them," including a man named Henry whom Minor had enslaved. "Poor misguided creatures!" Minor wrote in his diary, reflecting his persistent anti-abolitionism and his inability to fathom the determined desire of the enslaved for freedom.[10]

As the Confederacy's fortunes waned in 1864–65, Minor lamented the war's destructiveness but doubled down on his view that the state of Virginia was an innocent victim in the drama of war. Reflecting in July of 1864 on the "rupture of the late Union," Minor recapitulated the argument that secessionist and abolition demagogues were to blame for the war and that Virginia's "conciliatory bearing" during the secession crisis, "wholly free from bluster & menace," was met with contempt by the Lincoln administration. He attributed to the North's leaders "that mysterious prostration of understanding, & blindness of heart, which can only be regarded as a judgment of God on whom He would destroy." Looking back over three years of war, Minor wrote unrepentantly in 1864, "Nothing that has since occurred has tended to modify my convictions of the madness & wickedness of the act of secession by the cotton States, or of the necessity, for her own sake, that Virginia, having exhausted all the resources of compromise & conciliation, should at length associate herself with them."[11]

This sense of Virginia's blamelessness pervaded Minor's interpretation of Confederate surrender. When the Union army approached Charlottesville in early March 1865, Minor waved the white flag, as part of a delegation requesting that the Yankees spare the University and the town. The fact that the request was granted did little to blunt Minor's bitterness at the impending defeat of Lee's army. On April 3, 1865—less than a week before Grant's triumph at Appomattox—Minor wrote in his diary, "My idea is to prosecute the war for independence as long as it may be done with hope, in the judgment of our military leaders, or rather of our leader, Gen. Lee." As the historian Gary W. Gallagher has explained, Lee and his army were the focal point of Confederate nationalism; Confederates' confidence in Lee was "almost unlimited," as Minor himself put it. In the same diary passage, Minor laid out the stakes of continued resistance to "Yankee domination." A Union victory would not only bring "loss & suffering" to the white population but also "moral ruin" to the "poor negro." Since Black individuals were "doomed apparently to a hopeless inferiority," Minor opined in April 1865, committed as ever to proslavery cant, the "best that can befall them is domestic bondage to a community softened by the influences of a Christian humanity."[12]

Minor regarded Lee's surrender on April 9 as an ignominious "scene of humiliation." With "no rational hope of independence" remaining, he contemplated taking an oath of allegiance to the United States. He decided that he would "defer it as long as possible," in part because he resented the oath's clause requiring the taker to "abide by & support all acts of Congress enacted during the rebellion touching slavery." Minor finally took the oath on May 18, 1865, although it was "repugnant" to him, as part of his newly forming commitment to a restoration of the Union on the South's terms. Like Lee himself, Minor accepted surrender and rejected the prospect of continued guerrilla warfare because they hoped that the peace could bring to Virginia and the South "a greater and more paramount influence than formerly," to quote Minor, within

AMNESTY OATH.

Office of Provost Marshal,

Charlottesville, Va., May 18th 1865.

I, John B. Minor do solemnly swear, in the presence of Almighty God, that I will henceforth faithfully support, protect and defend the Constitution of the United States, and the Union of the States thereunder; that I will in like manner abide by and faithfully support all Acts of Congress passed during the existing rebellion with reference to slaves, so long and so far as not repealed, modified or held void by Congress, or by decision of the Supreme Court; and that I will in like manner abide and faithfully support all Proclamations of the President made during the existing rebellion, having reference to slaves, so long so far as not modified or declared void by decision of the Supreme Court—So Help me God.

Sworn and subscribed to, before me

this 18th day of May 1865.

John B. Minor

Provost Marshal.

Formal Amnesty Oath signed by John B. Minor and witnessed by a provost marshal, May 18, 1865. (Arthur J. Morris Law Library Special Collections, University of Virginia)

the US government. Some measure of conciliation was necessary, both men reckoned, to restore Virginia's standing in the Union and hasten its return to the councils of state.[13]

Reconstruction and Restoration

This vision of Virginia's postwar political restoration shaped Minor's effort to revive the Law School. Minor remained the only law professor for the 1865–66 session, but he avidly promoted the Law School—sending circulars advertising it throughout the South—and the numbers of students began to tick back up, with a class of 67 matriculating that year (out of a total number of 323 students at the University). The following year, the University hired Stephen Osbourne Southall (Law 1841) as a second law professor (to fill Holcombe's former role), while enrollment surged to 121. This was a recognition, as Holcombe's initial hire had been, that however exalted Minor's reputation as a legal scholar and mentor, Virginia could not fully compete with law schools such as Harvard—which had multiple professors and a more varied legal curriculum—unless it too

Law Class of 1868–69 on the steps of the UVA Rotunda with Professor John B. Minor seated in front. (Albert and Shirley Small Special Collections Library, University of Virginia)

grew and cultivated a national reputation. Such ambitions notwithstanding, UVA Law's teachings continued to be unmistakably sectional. Southall's inaugural address, delivered to law students in 1866, paid homage to the professors who had come before him, praising the "subtle analysis" of Tucker and the "sparkling elocution of Holcombe." Southall painted a grim picture of the "fearful portents" on the horizon—of the "horrors of anarchy and despotism" brought on by Confederate defeat. He clung to the hope, he told the students, that "fanaticism must finally spend its rage, and cease to bellow through the regions of the North," but he also asked them to be at the ready, "waiting the proper time and occasion to enlist under the banners of conservatism and to retrieve the fortunes of a desolated land."[14]

The curriculum, with regard to course of study and assigned texts, remained largely the same as before the war, but the context had changed dramatically. Virginia was debating Reconstruction, with some conservatives arguing that they should reject and defy Congress's new protocols, in its March 1867 Reconstruction Acts, for readmission into the Union, while others argued that Virginia should offer some measured compliance—just enough to exert control over the process. Minor was in the second camp, writing in an April 1867 letter that Virginia should participate in congressional Reconstruction "with as little unmanly repining as possible," in the "full confidence" that white citizens, who outnumbered Black citizens in the state, would be able to "gain control of the Colored vote." While Radical Republicans made headway in Virginia's constitutional convention of 1867–68, conservatives would gain the upper hand by 1869, by accepting (in theory) Black suffrage on the condition that former Confederates not be disfranchised. Conservatives proceeded to suppress and undermine Black voting in the 1870s through measures such as poll taxes, as well as violence and intimidation, driving down the number of Black voters and officeholders.[15]

Against this backdrop of a conservative resurgence, Minor trained a new generation of lawyers, jurists, and politicians. With slavery having been abolished by the Thirteenth Amendment (1865) and Virginia's old slave codes no longer applicable, Minor adjusted—minimally—his teaching of the subject. He turned his Junior Class lectures on the specifics of Virginia's slave codes into a history lesson, prefacing his reflections with "it was held from an early period" and other such references to the past. But if the laws themselves had changed, underlying attitudes had not. Telling students in 1866 that "our right to slaves grew out of a political necessity," Minor then revealed how proslavery ideology had survived the death of slavery. Acknowledging that Virginia's colonial laws were harsh, he added: "But we must consider that in 1669 the negroes were perfectly wild & barbarous & the most stringent and seemingly cruel methods of punishment were essential to the security of the masters life, hence in 1669 it was [held] that if a master beat a slave to death when the slave attempted to resist he should not be accused of felony." The advent of congressional Reconstruction did nothing to change Minor's tune—in the 1868 version of this lecture he was still defending the "introduction and perpetuation" of slavery as a "political & social necessity." And he was still insisting that "some very severe and hard laws were enacted regarding the subject of slaves yet they were founded on substantial grounds," and offering as an example a master's right to beat his own enslaved persons.[16]

Minor tried in the postwar period to extend the reach of the Law School and make it accessible to more white southern men. Virginia Law had catered to wealthy families who could afford to send their sons to law school, if only briefly. After the Civil War, there was an uptick in students who needed to delay payment of enrollment fees. Minor sought to ease the financial burden on such students by waiving their fees until after graduation, so that they could defer tuition payments until they were earning a living. In 1870 he debuted a new summer law course that was, in part, a response to students who desired legal training with him without enrolling in a degree program (although it was entirely separate from the Law School itself). He would preside over the summer school until his death in 1895.[17]

Minor increasingly used his own texts in his pedagogy, including his *Synopsis of Criminal Law* and his massive four-volume *Institutes of Common and Statute Law,* which was published over the course of two decades starting in the 1870s. The *Institutes,* dedicated to Minor's "former and present pupils," were culled from Minor's lecture notes and thus represent the broad public promulgation of material that had only been accessible to his students until that time. In volume one of the *Institutes,* on the "rights which relate to the person," Minor rephrased but did not repudiate his long-standing defense of slavery. "When slaves constitute a considerable part of the population of a State," he declared, "the continuance of the institution may, and generally will become a necessity, because more injury would result to the body politic from its precipitate abolition than from its maintenance." Minor discoursed on the "*aggressive fanaticism*" of abolitionists, the "*disastrous results of emancipation,*" and the glories of African colonization (the movement to deport freed Black persons to Africa), citing such sources as Thomas Dew, an influential proslavery ideologue and former William & Mary president, who had died in 1846. Minor, in short, clung long after emancipation to the "necessary evil" defense of slavery: the Jeffersonian-era doctrine that held that whatever lamentable effects slavery had on society's morals, state-sponsored abolition would be worse.[18]

In repurposing these views, Minor was not simply stuck in the past. Instead, he was contributing to the framing of a powerful new ideology, the creed of the Lost Cause, that undergirded the anti-Black legal proscription and extralegal violence of the Jim Crow era. According to the Lost Cause creed, Confederates were blameless; congressional Reconstruction was a tragedy; and reunion should be premised on white southern home rule and on the North's willingness to share the moral high ground with ex-Confederates. The essence of the Lost Cause was that the Civil War was not lost and could yet be won by new forms of racial segregation. Minor was not, by the standards of his social milieu, a sectional extremist. After the war, as before, he carefully positioned himself as a respectable moderate, opposed to the passionate demands of radicals on the left and right and committed to deliberation, compromise, and gradualism. But just as his prewar defense of slavery had primed the pump for secession, his critique of abolitionism and of Reconstruction now set the stage for Jim Crow.[19]

Minor had a more visible public profile than before the war and found an outlet for his agenda, beyond the University, in the Educational Association of Virginia (EAV). The EAV was a professional society for educators that counted among its prominent members former Confederate leaders, including Robert E. Lee and Lee's former aide-de-camp, Charles S. Venable (Law 1846). As their 1866 annual meeting, held in Charlottesville, resolved, the EAV's purpose was to "restore the confidence and respect once enjoyed by Virginia," before it had been stripped by the war of "one-third of her territory, and two-thirds of her capital." Only the "education of the sons of Virginia" could restore its lost primacy and "veneration." Through the EAV and other avenues, Minor supported what he considered to be gradual, moderate progress—and he did so to keep the prospect of transformative change at bay. He joined with William Henry Ruffner, for example, in promoting the establishment of (segregated) public schools in Virginia but broke with Ruffner over soliciting federal aid for those schools. Minor opposed such aid on the grounds that he did not want "the fingers of Congress thrust into our affairs," and he warned that Virginians should not "sell [their] birthright," as he wrote to Ruffner, "to unite . . . with barbaric negroes." Minor avidly promoted the education of white women through female academies but also pointedly rejected married women's property rights. In his lectures and published *Institutes,* he derided Virginia's 1877 married women's property act (which removed some of the legal disabilities of coverture) as "full of evil omen to the domestic peace of the families of the Commonwealth," in that it would "abolish virtually the husband's leadership of the family."[20]

Legacies

Some of the ways that Minor's teachings influenced his students are exemplified by the careers of Richard Thomas Walker (R. T. W.) Duke Sr. and his son R. T. W. Duke Jr., who both attended the Law School (Sr. in 1849–50 and Jr. in 1873–74). The Dukes illustrate how UVA was an incubator for Jim Crow proscription, just as it had been an incubator for proslavery ideology and secessionism. The elder Duke launched a successful career as a lawyer and embraced the Confederacy and the Lost Cause. He served in the Confederate army as a colonel and, after the war, in the US Congress, where he protested against extending citizenship rights to African Americans. The younger Duke, who idolized his father, attended UVA during Reconstruction and then embarked on his own legal career, serving as judge of the Corporation (circuit) Court and as the Commonwealth's attorney for Albemarle County in the early twentieth century. During his time at UVA, Duke Jr. imbibed Lost Cause apologetics through Southall's lectures, which, Duke's lecture notes reveal, attributed prewar sectional strife to "jealousy" on the part of the North; decried the "principle of unlimited submission to the general Govt" that had been foisted on the defeated South; and cited the Virginia and Kentucky resolutions in support of state sovereignty.[21]

R. T. W. Duke Jr. became an influential mouthpiece in Virginia for white supremacist grievance and dogma. His extensive private memoirs and abundant public speeches glorified slavery in the Old South; expressed his implacable loathing of northerners, Lincoln, and the Republican Party; and derided the Union soldiers and Freedmen's Bureau officials who were stationed in Charlottesville after the war to facilitate the transition between slavery and freedom.

The younger Duke deemed congressional Reconstruction, with its centerpiece of Black voting, "the worst crime in the history of civilization." The purpose of Reconstruction, Duke insisted, was to place the South "under the heel of the negro"; he trafficked, in other words, in the Lost Cause myth of Reconstruction as a "tragic era" of "black rule"—a myth that flies in the face of the fact that even at the height of congressional Reconstruction, Black individuals were underrepresented in southern politics. In Duke's world view, formerly enslaved persons had no place whatsoever in Virginia politics. He rejoiced in the overthrow of Reconstruction by ex-Confederates and sought to prevent the return of Black citizens to political life. He campaigned, for example, against the Readjuster movement, which tried to fuse disgruntled white farmers and marginalized Black voters in Virginia into a new coalition. Duke's politics went together with his Confederate memorialization activities. He became a popular speaker on the Confederate circuit and at Democratic Party events in Virginia in the early twentieth century and used both settings to hurl blame at the North and cast the Confederacy as faultless. For example, at a tribute to the Confederate dead at Richmond's Oakwood Cemetery in May 1908, Duke defended the "deathless memory of an immortal cause," proclaiming that "slavery was right and emancipation a wrong and a robbery." "Truth is truth" and "must be fearlessly told," he cried out, adding, "Let it hurt who it may." Even as he rode the lecture circuit as an unreconstructed rebel, R. T. W. Duke Jr. himself remained very active and visible in University affairs, as an officer in the alumni society and as a mentor and employer for UVA Law students.[22]

Duke's long career as a Lost Cause warrior secured him a conspicuous place in the inaugural ceremonies of the Stonewall Jackson and Robert E. Lee monuments in Charlottesville in the early 1920s. Jurists such as Duke made ideal marshals and orators at Confederate memorial events, as they could cloak the proceedings in the authority of the state. Duke appeared before audiences at Confederate events as "the Judge"—a man who represented the legal regime of Jim Crow. On October 19, 1921, the day of the Jackson statue dedication, Duke "presided over the exercises of the unveiling" and accepted the Jackson statue, a gift from local philanthropist Paul Goodloe McIntire, who studied at the University in 1878–79, on Charlottesville's behalf. Among the other Law School alumni who participated in the program of events was E. Lee Trinkle (Law 1898), the Democratic nominee for governor, who proclaimed, on an unmistakably political note, that Virginia would be "careful that the evil days of reconstruction shall not return." At the May 21, 1924, Lee unveiling, Duke participated in a massive procession that snaked its way through Charlottesville to the new Lee Park downtown. After "the multitude assembled about the statue," Duke was the first man they heard from, as he assumed his role as the "presiding officer" of the day's events, welcoming a series of speakers who made the case that Robert E. Lee, a "Victor over Defeat," represented "the moral greatness of the Old South."[23]

Duke's career not only reveals the racial animus at the heart of the Lost Cause creed—it also reflects UVA's central role in promulgating Lost Cause propaganda. Prominent Lost Cause spokesmen included the influential writer Thomas Nelson Page, who studied at UVA Law in 1873–74 and whose wildly popular poems, stories, and novels "promoted the image of an Old South replete with gracious aristocrats and loyal servants," and William & Mary president Lyon Gardiner Tyler, who studied at UVA Law in 1875–76 and made it a major theme of his public life to critique the late President Abraham Lincoln and glorify the Confederacy. In 1920 Tyler wrote and published the pamphlet *A Confederate Catechism,* a compendium of Lost Cause talking points. On the causes of the war, Tyler

The Stonewall Jackson monument dedication in 1921 in Charlottesville. (Albert and Shirley Small Special Collections Library, University of Virginia)

declaimed that "it was not slavery, but the vindictive, intemperate anti-slavery movement that was at the bottom of all the troubles." And on slavery itself, he added, "the Southerners took the negro as a barbarian and cannibal, civilized him, supported him, clothed him, and turned him into a devout Christian."[24]

UVA Law alumni literally translated racist attitudes into racist laws in their roles as members of the Virginia General Assembly and as leaders of the state Democratic Party. The Confederate veteran John W. Daniel (Law 1866) of Lynchburg, Virginia, who studied law at UVA right after the war, "indulged his passion for oratory by memorializing the Confederate war effort and speaking out against Reconstruction" and became an influential conservative voice in the Virginia legislature. As a delegate to the Virginia Constitutional Convention of 1901–2, he served on the suffrage committee tasked with eliminating the vestiges of Black voting, and he supported poll taxes and other measures of voter suppression enshrined in the 1902 state constitution. J. Taylor Ellyson, who studied law at UVA from 1867 to 1869, was chairman of the Virginia Democratic Party at the time of the 1901–2 constitutional convention and promoted the disfranchisement clauses, proclaiming that they would "forever remove the negro as a factor in our political affairs." The incoming Democratic governor Andrew Jackson Montague (Law 1885), another UVA Law alumnus, crowed that the law would "effectually exclude the idle, shiftless and illiterate of the negro race from the suffrage." Through figures such as these, UVA Law lent its institutional prestige to the Lost Cause creed and to Jim Crow legal repression.[25]

As part of their segregationist agenda, the historian W. Fitzhugh Brundage has observed, southern whites "ensured that public spaces conspicuously excluded any recognition of the recalled past of blacks." One could never glean, from R. T. W. Duke Jr.'s version of the past, or from John B. Minor's, that Black individuals had outnumbered whites in Albemarle County during the Civil War era, or that Black persons experienced the Union army's arrival in the city in March 1865 as a moment of liberation, or that more than 250 Black men born in Albemarle County fought in the Union army. One could not glean that the Black delegates to Virginia's 1867–68 Constitutional Convention, among them the Union veteran James T. S. Taylor of Albemarle County, had enshrined the principle of human equality in the new charter by paraphrasing Jefferson's "all men are created equal" language, imbuing that language with a universalist meaning.[26] In protest against the Lost Cause, African Americans in the Jim Crow era elaborated their own Civil War memory tradition, celebrating milestones such as the Thirteenth Amendment with a focus on the righteousness of the Union war, of emancipation, and of Black Union soldiers. African Americans found their own champions, who directly confronted both the rhetoric and policies of men such as Duke. A leading spokesman for Black Virginians in this era was John R. Mitchell Jr., editor of the most influential Black newspaper in the state, the *Richmond Planet*. Mitchell was as popular among Black persons in Charlottesville as Duke was among whites. In a May 1890 editorial on the Lee monument unveiling in Richmond—entitled "What It Means"—Mitchell lamented that Confederate memorialization "fosters in this Republic, the spirit of Rebellion and will ultimately result in handing down . . . a legacy of treason and blood."[27]

The Lost Cause creed sought to distort the South's complex history. But that history could not be easily swept away. Amid the abundant evidence of the persistent provincialism and regionalism of the UVA Law School, there were signs of its potential national profile and reputation. One such sign was the prominence of a small but influential number of former Law School students who sided with the Union, not the Confederacy, during the Civil War and went on to play notable roles in politics and jurisprudence, in places other than Virginia. Those men included James Patterson Sterrett, a Pennsylvania native who studied law at UVA in 1847 and was admitted to the bar in 1848 in both Pennsylvania and Virginia. Sterrett made a name for himself practicing law in Pittsburgh, winning election as a judge in Alleghany County in 1862. An ardent Unionist during the Civil War, Sterrett maintained that the "patriotism of the loyal masses of the North and West" proved "the capacity of our people for self-government." His record and reputation as an "able jurist and a clear, close, logical reasoner" helped him rise through the ranks to a seat on the Pennsylvania Supreme Court in 1877 and then to the chief justice position in 1893. Another such example is Ohioan John A. Hunter, who studied law at UVA in 1857. After practicing as a lawyer in Ohio and Missouri and then doing a brief stint as a Union Army officer during the war, Hunter worked as an internal revenue collector and attorney, eventually earning an appointment as chief justice of the Supreme Court of the Utah Territory in 1879. He served on the bench for a time with fellow UVA Law Unionist Jacob S. Boreman, who studied at the Law School in 1855 and was an associate justice. The two men courted some opposition from Mormons through their strong stand against polygamy.[28]

Some of those who studied under John Minor at UVA Law steered even farther away from the path he prescribed. Charles Philip Redmond of New Jersey, who attended UVA in 1858–59 after studying at Princeton, practiced law briefly in Iowa before joining the Union Army there in 1861. He eventually settled in Little Rock, Arkansas, and in September 1864 President Abraham Lincoln appointed him as the district attorney for eastern Arkansas. A self-described Radical Republican, Redmond went on to hold positions as a clerk and then judge in Arkansas, where he championed Reconstruction measures. In a scene counter to Minor's postwar teachings at UVA, Redmond led, in 1867, a reading of the Declaration of Independence at a political meeting of Arkansas freed people. Joseph Rundle of Baltimore, Maryland, who studied law briefly at UVA in 1856–57, served in the Union Army during the war and then joined with some fellow Maryland veterans in condemning President Andrew Johnson's permissive policies and supporting Congress's more stringent Reconstruction program. These Union veterans rejected the Confederate apologetics of the Lost Cause creed and proclaimed themselves still "ready and willing to resist a revolutionary overthrow of the Republican Government of the United States."[29]

In keeping with the Lost Cause image of a solidly Confederate South, the University of Virginia did nothing during Minor's tenure as Law School head to celebrate or even acknowledge that some of his students leveraged their UVA Law educations for causes other than Virginia's political supremacy. Instead, long after the Civil War, the University of Virginia chose again and again to valorize its Confederate alumni and play up its own role and self-image as a bastion of conservative southern values. "Fate denied them victory but crowned them with glorious immortality." So read the inscription on the bronze statue, erected on UVA's campus in 1893, honoring Confederate soldiers who had died in Charlottesville's hospitals. The address that day was given by former Confederate soldier Robert Augustus Stiles, who studied Law at UVA in 1865–66. Minor's own tenure as leader of the Law School was commemorated for its sectional, not national, significance. "Surely no man has held over any section a wider or more potent influence than he has exercised over the bench and bar of the South," future dean of the Law School William Minor Lile (Law 1882) declared upon Minor's death in 1895. It would take a new century to begin to reorient UVA Law toward the future and toward national ambitions.[30]

Notes

1. John B. Minor Diary (vol. 2, 1843–73), 14 March 1864, 340–41, John B. Minor Papers, MSS 3114, Albert and Shirley Small Special Collections Library, University of Virginia (hereafter cited as SSCL).
2. Ervin L. Jordan, *Charlottesville and the University of Virginia in the Civil War* (Lynchburg, VA: H. E. Howard, 1988), 23; *Catalogue of the Officers and Students of the University of Virginia, Session of 1865–66 (with Catalogues of Sessions 1851 to 1865, Prefixed)* (Richmond, VA: Chas. H. Wynne, 1866), 7–8; *Catalogue of the Officers and Students of the University of Virginia, Session of 1844–45* (Philadelphia: C. Sherman, 1845), 17; Holly Beth Fitzsimmons, "The Law and the Reason Thereof: John B. Minor and Legal Education at the University of Virginia, 1845–1895" (master's thesis, University of Virginia, 1976), 2, 17, 27, 45. For more on John B. Minor, see Randall N. Flaherty, "John B. Minor and the Science of Legal Education, 1845–1895," in this volume.
3. L. Minor Blackford, "The Great John B. Minor and His Cousin Mary Face the War: Correspondence between the Professor of Law and the Lynchburg Blackfords, 1860–1864," *Virginia Magazine of History and Biography* 61, no. 4 (October 1953): 440–41.
4. On Virginia secession see William A. Link, *Roots of Secession: Slavery and Politics in Antebellum Virginia* (Chapel Hill: University of North Carolina Press, 2003); William W. Freehling and Craig M. Simpson, eds., *Showdown in Virginia: The 1861 Convention and the Fate of the Union* (Charlottesville: University of Virginia Press, 2010); Shearer Bowman Davis, *At the Precipice: Americans North and South during the Secession Crisis* (Chapel Hill: University of North Carolina Press, 2014), 14–15; "destruction of slavery," qtd. in Blackford, "Great John B. Minor," 446; Minor Diary, "Speculations," 28 July 1864, 358, 372.
5. Minor Diary, "Speculations," 353, 363, 365.
6. Alfred L. Brophy, *University, Court, and Slave: Pro-Slavery Thought in Southern Colleges and Courts and the Coming of the Civil War* (Oxford: Oxford University Press, 2016), 280, 294; Bledsoe as quoted in Elizabeth R. Varon, *Disunion!: The Coming of the American Civil War, 1789–1859* (Chapel Hill: University of North Carolina Press, 2008), 290; W. Hamilton Bryson, *Legal Education in Virginia, 1779–1979: A Biographical Approach* (Charlottesville: University Press of Virginia, 1982), 291–92; James P. Holcombe, *An Address Delivered before the Seventh Annual Meeting of the Virginia*

State Agricultural Society, November 4th, 1858 (Richmond, VA: MacFarlane and Fergusson, 1858), 4; Philip Pendleton Barbour Student Notebook, opening lecture, [n.p., n.d.], Professor James P. Holcombe's Junior Law Class, University of Virginia Student Notebooks, RG-22/1/1.841, SSCL.

7. See Justene Hill Edwards, "Teaching the Laws of Slavery, 1826–1865," in this volume; James L. Hubard Student Notebook, 26 October 1860, 11 January 1857, 26 October 1860, and 28 October 1856, Professor John B. Minor's Junior Law Class, University of Virginia Student Notebooks, RG-22/1/1.002, SSCL. The Minor quote comes from Hubard's notes and is also rendered in Upshur Quinby's notes for 26 October 1860. Quinby recalled that Minor told the class that slavery was "an inexorable political necessity" in the South. Quinby's notes for Minor's 29 and 31 October lecture further echo Hubard's. Upshur Quinby Student Notebook, 26, 29, and 31 October 1860, Professor John B. Minor's Junior Law class, Papers of the Quinby, Teackle, and Upshur Families of Somerset County, Maryland, and Accomack and Northampton Counties, Virginia, MSS 2338, 2338-a, 2338-b, MSS 2871, SSCL.
8. Barbour Student Notebook, 1 and 23 November 1860, 4 and 21 December 1860, and "The Constitution of the Confederate States"; James P. Holcombe, *The Election of a Black Republican President an Overt Act of Aggression on the Right of Property in Slaves: The South Urged to Adopt Concerted Action for Future Safety* (Richmond, VA: Chas. H. Wynne, 1860), 9, 12; "Speech of Professor Holcombe before the People of Albemarle," *Richmond Whig*, 28 January 1860.
9. Peter S. Carmichael, *The Last Generation: Young Virginians in Peace, War, and Reunion* (Chapel Hill: University of North Carolina Press, 2005); Brophy, *University, Court, and Slave*, 281–83; Hahna Cho, "The Flag of the Confederacy Flies Atop the Rotunda," Jefferson's University: The Early Life Project, https://perma.cc/LQ23-7H52 (hereafter cited as JUEL); Freehling and Simpson, "James Holcombe's Secessionist Speech, March 20" in *Showdown in Virginia*, 62, 63, 68, 72.
10. Bryson, *Legal Education in Virginia*, 293; John B. Minor, "To the Men of Albemarle: [. . .]," broadside, 28 June 1863, SSCL; Notice, *Richmond Enquirer*, 12 June 1863; Notice, *Richmond Daily Dispatch*, 15 April 1862; 1860 US Census, Albemarle County, VA, St. Anne's Parish; Tax List, 27 February 1863, Papers of the Minor and Wilson Families, MSS 1052, MSS 3750, MSS 38-602, SSCL; R. Turk to John B. Minor, 22 August 1863, JUEL, http://juel.iath.virginia.edu/resources; Minor Diary, 6 March 1865, 384.
11. Minor Diary, "Speculations," 353–73.
12. Minor Diary, 3 March 1865, 3 April 1865, 378, 387–88; Gary W. Gallagher, *Becoming Confederates: Paths to a New National Loyalty* (Athens: University of Georgia Press, 2013).
13. Minor Diary, 10, 13, 28 April 1865 and 18 May 1865, 391–96, 412–13, 422–23; Gallagher, *Becoming Confederates*, 29–30.
14. *Catalogue of the Officers and Students of the University of Virginia, Forty-Third Session—1866–67* (Richmond, VA: Richmond Med. Journal, 1867), 19; Marsha Trimble, "Attending the Lectures of Law: A Perspective on the 19th-Century Law School Experience," *UVA Lawyer* 20, no. 2 (Spring 1996): 42–47; Stephen O. Southall, *Inaugural Address, Delivered to the Law Class of the University of Virginia* (Richmond, VA: Enquirer, 1867), 5, 11–12.
15. Editorial, *Richmond Daily Dispatch*, 5 October 1866; Fitzsimmons, "Law and the Reason Thereof," 39; John B. Minor to S. D. Cabanis, 3 April 1867, Papers of John B. Minor, MSS 3114, SSCL.

16. John M. White Student Notebook, Lecture 13, 1866, Professor John B. Minor's Junior Law Class, University of Virginia Student Notebooks, RG–22/31, SSCL; William M. McAllister Student Notebook, 6 November 1868, Professor John B. Minor's Junior Law Class, Student Notebooks, RG–32–400, Arthur J. Morris Law Library Special Collections, University of Virginia.
17. Trimble, "Attending the Lectures of Law," 42–47; *Catalogue of the Officers and Students of the University of Virginia, Forty-Seventh Session—1870–71* (Charlottesville, VA: Chronicle Printing and Stationery House, 1871), 63.
18. *Catalogue of the Officers and Students of the University of Virginia, 1870–71,* 50; Fitzsimmons, "Law and the Reason Thereof," 24; John B. Minor, *Institutes of Common and Statute Law,* vol. 1, *The Rights Which Relate to the Person* (Richmond, VA: Whittet & Sheperson, 1875), 159, 168, italics in the original. See also David Thomas Konig, "Jeffersonian Foundations of Legal Education in Virginia, 1779–1845," in this volume.
19. Elizabeth R. Varon, "UVA and the History of Race: The Lost Cause through Judge Duke's Eyes," *UVA Today,* 4 September 2019, https://perma.cc/W8CC-ZHNE.
20. "Convention of the Educational Association of Virginia," *Richmond Daily Dispatch,* 19 July 1866; "Address to the Parents and the Public of Virginia," *Richmond Daily Dispatch,* 12 March 1867; Walter J. Fraser Jr., "William Henry Ruffner and the Establishment of Virginia's Public School System, 1870–1874," *Virginia Magazine of History and Biography* 79, no. 3 (July 1971): 262, 272; Notice, *Richmond Whig,* 11 July 1856; John B. Minor, *Institutes of Common and Statute Law,* 2nd ed., 3:83, 85. For more on women's property rights of the period and how these rights were taught at the Law School, see Laura F. Edwards, "Coverture and Virginia Law Professors: The Nineteenth Century," in this volume.
21. R. T. W. Duke Jr. Student Notebook, 18 March 1873 and 10 May 1873, Professor Stephen O. Southall's Junior Law Class, University of Virginia Student Notebooks, RG–22/31, SSCL; Varon, "UVA and the History of Race"; "Death of Editor-in-Chief: Judge R. T. W. Duke, Jr.," *Virginia Law Register* 11, no. 12 (April 1926): 757–60; Michael Peter Charles Smith, "Richard Thomas Walker Duke (1853–1926)," *Dictionary of Virginia Biography,* Library of Virginia, https://perma.cc/XDZ6-TV95.
22. R. T. W. Duke Jr., "Recollections," 1899–1926, 1:17–26, 216–17; 2:34–35, 46–51; 4:73–78, 136–37, MSS 9521–o, SSCL.
23. *Proceedings of the Thirty-Fourth Annual Meeting of the Grand Camp Confederate Veterans Department of Virginia* (Petersburg, VA: Frank A. Owen, 1922); "To Unveil Statue of 'Stonewall' Jackson during Reunion in Charlottesville," *Staunton News Leader,* 22 September 1921; "The Stonewall Jackson Monument," *University of Virginia Alumni News* 10, no. 3 (September 1921): 327; "Aftermath of Big Reunion," *Charlottesville Daily Progress,* 21 October 1921; "The Jackson Monument at Charlottesville, Va.," *Confederate Veteran* 30 (February 1922): 44; John S. Patton, ed., *Proceedings of the 37th Annual Reunion of the Virginia Division of the Grand Camp U. C. V.* (1924), 5–6, 13–15, 20–21, 39–41; Brendan Wolfe, "History Writ Aright," *Brendan Wolfe,* http://brendanwolfe.com/lee-monument/; "Lee Statue Is Unveiled," *Charlottesville Daily Progress,* 21 May 1924.
24. Caroline E. Janney, "The Lost Cause," *Encyclopedia Virginia,* Virginia Humanities, https://perma.cc/8SJG-4BSJ; Taylor S. Hagood, "Thomas Nelson Page (1853–1922)," *Encyclopedia Virginia,* https://perma.cc/DT5P-J8KS; Lyon Gardiner Tyler, *A Confederate Catechism: The War of 1861–1865* (1920), 2, 8.

25. William Bland Whitley, "John Warwick Daniel (1842–1910)," *Encyclopedia Virginia*, https://perma.cc/78X6-P5FP; "James Taylor Ellyson (20 May 1847–18 March 1919)," *Dictionary of Virginia Biography*, https://perma.cc/4ZH8-2244; J. Taylor Ellyson, John Goode, and Andrew Jackson Montague, "No White Man to Lose His Vote in Virginia," broadside, 1901.
26. W. Fitzhugh Brundage, *The Southern Past: A Clash of Race and Memory* (Cambridge, MA: Belknap Press, 2005), 6–10; Elizabeth R. Varon, "'Oppression at the Hands of the Rebels,' Part One: Virginia Unionists Petition Congress," *Black Virginians in Blue* (blog), John L. Nau III Center for Civil War History, 5 March 2025, University of Virginia, https://naucenter.as.virginia.edu/blog-page/oppression-hands-rebels-part-one-virginia-unionists-petition-congress.
27. On African American soldiers from Charlottesville, see William W. Wurtz, "A Word on Methods: Recovering the Stories of Black Virginians in the Union Army," *Black Virginians in Blue* (blog), John L. Nau III Center for Civil War History, 3 January 2017, https://naucenter.as.virginia.edu/blog-page/word-methods-recovering-stories-black-virginians-union-army; John R. Mitchell Jr., "What It Means," *Richmond Planet*, 31 May 1890. On Mitchell's popularity in Charlottesville, see "Editor Mitchell in Charlottesville," *Richmond Planet*, 13 June 1896, and Editorial, *Richmond Planet*, 16 August 1902.
28. "James Patterson Sterrett," *UVA Unionists*, John L. Nau III Center for Civil War History, https://perma.cc/PHS4-JHWW; "John A. Hunter," *UVA Unionists*, John L. Nau III Center for Civil War History, https://perma.cc/6L9G-FDS2; "Jacob Smith Boreman," *UVA Unionists*, John L. Nau III Center for Civil War History, https://perma.cc/D6LT-T33P.
29. "Charles Philip Redmond," *UVA Unionists*, John L. Nau III Center for Civil War History, https://perma.cc/LR59-4SRM; "Joseph Rundle Jr.," *UVA Unionists*, John L. Nau III Center for Civil War History, https://perma.cc/ZE7F-8MSY.
30. Robert Stiles, *Address at the Dedication of the Monument to the Confederate Dead, University of Virginia, June 7, 1893* (Richmond, VA: Taylor & Taylor, 1893), 1; *Catalogue of the Officers and Students of the University of Virginia, 1865–66*, 18. Lile as quoted in Fitzsimmons, "Law and the Reason Thereof," 47–48.

Coverture and Virginia Law Professors

THE NINETEENTH CENTURY

Laura F. Edwards

IN 1852, the eldest daughter of University of Virginia law professor John Barbee Minor identified herself on the fly leaf of her diary in big, bold script. The volume belonged to "Mary L. Minor" of the "University of Virginia." The place of residence might seem odd, given that Mary was an eleven-year-old girl with no prospect of ever attending the University. But that was where Mary lived, down the Lawn from the Rotunda in Pavilion X, with her father, her stepmother, enslaved workers, a few students, and an always changing, but ever-present, cast of relatives. Students at Virginia Law came and went. But Mary stayed. She arrived in 1845 when her father took up his post there and left in 1895 when he died.[1]

Mary's tenure at the University spanned a period marked by dramatic changes in legal education. When she and her family arrived in 1845, Pavilion X was the University's designated residence for the law professor. The integration of the domestic with the professional had defined legal training for centuries, with students studying and living in the homes of their instructors in an apprenticeship system. Law schools in the United States between the Revolution and the Civil War kept that model, with professors teaching a handful of students, often in their residences, sometimes as freestanding enterprises, and sometimes in conjunction with universities. In that context, all the women, free and enslaved, who lived in the household played a role in legal education. They tended to the physical needs of students—although the heavy labor was done by enslaved women in states that sanctioned slavery and by hired servants in states that did not—while the wives and daughters of law professors trained aspiring young lawyers in the social skills necessary to succeed. Some even married law students, including Mary's half-sister Susan Colston Minor Wilson. By the time Mary's father died in 1895, however, much of that had changed. The slow, steady creep of professionalization had separated legal education from daily life and from women, a change that culminated in 1911 when the Law School moved to Minor Hall, a new building away from the Lawn named in honor of Mary's father.[2]

The separation of the professional from the domestic at UVA Law was related to broader changes that reshaped the legal status of women over the course of the nineteenth century. In the first half of the century, women fell into different legal categories based on considerations other than their gender: the laws of slavery shaped the legal status of women who were held in bondage; racial restrictions constricted free Black women; coverture limited married women's rights to own property, contract, or act legally in their own names. While coverture did not apply to unmarried women, other laws denied them the vote and limited their participation in public governance. By the end of the nineteenth century, however, coverture's restrictions extended outward to affect all women, regardless of race or marital status, and even limited the effects

Undated photo of Susan Colston Minor (seated), Martha "Mattie" Macon Minor (standing, left), and Nannie Jacqueline Minor (standing, right): John B. Minor's daughters. (Albert and Shirley Small Special Collections Library, University of Virginia)

of reforms, particularly married women's property acts. Race still mattered enormously in determining women's legal status. While slavery was abolished, Jim Crow laws reinstated old barriers and created new ones. But, regardless of race, all women experienced legal limitations because of their status as women.[3]

Three of the UVA Law School's first professors—John A. G. (J. A. G.) Davis (1830–40), Henry St. George Tucker (1841–45), and John B. Minor (1845–95)—played instrumental roles in this transformation. Like legal professionals elsewhere in the nineteenth century, they embraced and taught the rigid definition of coverture elaborated by Sir William Blackstone and wrote it into their legal treatises. This version of coverture then jumped from treatises into statutes, appellate decisions, and legal practice, replacing the more fluid set of principles that had once defined married women's legal status. The implications spread to unmarried women, whose economic prospects were based on the possibility that they would marry and be subject to coverture. By the end of the century, UVA Law School professors, like legal professionals elsewhere, extended this form of coverture further, using it as a description of female nature: all women needed the kinds of legal protections associated with coverture.[4]

The Restrictions of Coverture

The restrictions associated with coverture have maintained an aura of timelessness, despite efforts to situate them in historical context. In scholarly literature and popular accounts, coverture's legal tentacles reach out from somewhere in the depths of a misty past to keep all married women legally ensnared until the extension of rights cut those bonds. There is some truth to that characterization. In general, coverture "covered" a wife's legal identity with that of her husband, transferring legal control over her property to him and negating her other rights, including the right to contract and to prosecute legal matters in her own name. Those restrictions also had strong cultural resonance in the early modern period, meshing as they did with deeply held assumptions about women's inherent inferiority and their need for male protection.[5]

The application of coverture's restrictions, however, has varied widely over time and space. In eighteenth- and early nineteenth-century Virginia, the restrictions existed alongside other legal principles, some associated with coverture, that allowed married women to possess property and act legally in their own names. There was reason for that flexibility: rigid readings of coverture's restrictions imperiled a patriarchal order that maintained familial interests over generations, often through female relatives, and that elevated the interests of families over creditors. Longstanding, widely accepted legal principles in Anglo-American law treated property as a collective asset to which all family members—through the generations—had claims. While patriarchal in its basic logic, this view of property included women; property regularly passed through women to keep it in the family line. The claims of families, moreover, took precedence over those of creditors. Coverture's restrictions failed to account for those strategies and the familial relationships they privileged. Married women were not just wives; they were also mothers, daughters, sisters, aunts, and grandmothers, as well as community members. All those other relationships came with their own legal implications. Many married women could and did manage their own affairs and those of their children and extended families. Many more found themselves thrust into that situation because their husbands could not. Turning resources that families needed into the property of individual husbands and their creditors seemed not just unwise, but downright wrong to many Virginians.[6]

That was why so many Virginians worked around the limitations of coverture. Consider the long life of entail, which kept property in the family line by giving heirs use rights, limiting their ability to sell or mortgage property, and shielding it from the claims of creditors. Virginia abolished entail in 1776, touting it as a democratic reform to keep land from amassing in the hands of the privileged few. But entail was not just used by the wealthy. It was one of many legal practices that protected family property, shielding it from creditors so that it could be passed through the generations. The 1776 statute turned entailed property into fee simple property, making it the individual possession of whoever held it at that time. If lodged in married women's names, it transferred to their husbands, passing out of their families' hands.[7]

The prohibition of entail, however, did not eliminate the concept of familial property that underlay it, and Virginians kept trying to preserve those principles in practice. In 1837, J. A. G. Davis published *An Exposition of the Principles Which Distinguish Estates Tail from Other Limitations,* based on lectures on that topic. The need for an entire treatise on entail might seem unnecessary. But entail's prohibition generated a new set of legal questions about families' efforts to pass property through the generations and protect it from creditors in ways that were like entail, although not named as such. In his lecture notes at Virginia Law in 1838, student George W. Blattermann (Law 1839) wrote that "the whole time allotted for this lecture" on entail "cd [*sic*] be easily occupied . . . in explaining the distinction" between entail and other kinds of estates.[8]

Separate estates, which also accommodated conceptions of family property, became popular after entail's prohibition. While coverture resided in common law, the logic of separate estates derived from another body of law known as equity. In equity, a married woman could maintain property through the creation of a separate legal entity in the form of a trust and make the trust the owner of the property. A trustee then managed the property—the separate estate—for the married woman. The terms of the trust determined the extent of a woman's control, and the involvement of trustees varied widely. Separate estates occupied considerable space in the lectures and treatises of UVA law professors, suggesting their importance in legal practice. Robert T. Hubard's (Law 1861) notebook from John Minor's 1861 Junior law class has several pages devoted to separate estates. Hubard noted that a separate estate given to a married woman was to be "enjoyed in common," by which he meant the woman's husband and children could use the property and income from it, but it was "held to be one indivisible estate" in trust for the married woman. After jotting down an example of this principle, Hubard observed that the intent was obvious: to protect family property from the husband's debts. The principles were widely known outside professional legal circles as well. As cases in the Virginia Supreme Court of Appeals suggest, it did not require great wealth or legal acumen to insert the language necessary to establish a separate estate in ordinary documents, including deeds, wills, and marriage settlements.[9]

Long-standing principles associated with coverture allowed married women access to family property in other ways as well. By locating such extensive authority in husbands, coverture gave them the power to will property to their wives and other female relatives. Wives also acted under the legal authority of their husbands. Wives, for instance, did not have to obtain their husbands' permission when trading for "necessaries." Seizing on that opening, wives and merchants applied very generous definitions, which meant that married women made their own decisions about the use of family property all the time.[10] Similarly, married women also acted as their husbands' legal agents, which created space for women to manage their households' property. John Minor referred to that kind of slippage in a letter requesting advice about a case involving a legal contract made with a married woman. "It is to me a novel case," he wrote, because "abundant authority exists showing that a *feme covert* [a married woman] cannot contract, or be sued as a *feme sole* [an unmarried woman]." And yet, that is exactly what had happened. It was not always easy to tell when a wife was acting on her own and when she was acting on behalf of her husband.[11]

Married women also ran businesses in their own names, using customary practices that acquired legal force in common law through use, overriding coverture's restrictions. The rules varied from state to state and even within states. In some places, married women had to register with local authorities to trade in their own names. In other places, married women could acquire the status of independent traders through practice. As long as they kept their businesses separate from their husbands, they could operate separately from their husbands. The records of R. G. Dun and Company, a credit reporting firm set up in the 1840s, have numerous instances of married women in Virginia running their own businesses, based on established practice that acquired legal force.[12]

Teaching Coverture at Virginia Law

Conceptions of property that emphasized the entire family's claims continued into the late nineteenth century, as did acceptance of married women's control, if not outright ownership, of certain kinds of property. But legal education, written expressions of law, and legal practice, particularly at the appellate level, moved in a very different direction over the nineteenth century, elevating the restrictions associated with coverture and even extending them.

Like other legal professionals in the new republic, UVA's first law professors rushed to fill a perceived void: the absence of a clearly defined body of law in the new republic. In so doing, they drew heavily on Sir William Blackstone's influential *Commentaries on the Laws of England,* quoting extensively or simply duplicating the volumes and then providing commentary. Blackstone remained required reading at UVA Law throughout the antebellum period. Student notebooks reflect the centrality of Blackstone to the curriculum, with large sections of notes generally following the organization of his *Commentaries.* As John Minor explained in the introduction to the first volume of his influential *Institutes of Common and Statute Law,* published in 1875, his "scheme . . . was to follow in general the outlines of . . . [Blackstone's] incomparable Commentaries." Minor's *Institutes* were based on lectures, delivered by J. A. G. Davis, that he had heard as a student and then elaborated upon when he took over as UVA Law professor.[13]

When it came to coverture, Blackstone consolidated its restrictions into a statement that described married women's legal status in all contexts. Blackstone's version, in which coverture suspended "the very being or legal existence of the woman . . . during the marriage," downplayed other elements of coverture and competing principles. It was innovation disguised as tradition, as historian Holly Brewer has argued. Selecting from among conflicting principles, Blackstone fashioned a new synthesis that elevated the restrictions of coverture over other practices in common law and even within coverture that allowed women to control property. Narrowing the legal prerogatives of wives, this new version of coverture forced married women to work through their husbands in all economic matters. His definition not only undercut wives' connections outside their households but also characterized husbands' authority as an unconditional right they held as individuals, rather than a privilege exercised for the public good. Then he wrapped it all up in the mantle of timelessness, portraying his newly restrictive version of coverture as the way it had always been.[14]

The transformation of women's legal status was part of a larger effort to professionalize and streamline law, making it more friendly to commercial interests. Although UVA Law School professors were concerned with women's interests, at least as they defined them, the strict definition of coverture they taught aided that effort. This version of coverture created a uniform definition of married women's status that was less subject to regional variation and local interpretations. It also concentrated authority over family property in the person of the husband, rather than diffusing it through families and over generations. The more rigid conceptions of coverture that gained ground in the nineteenth century turned family property into the individual possession of husbands and fathers, elevating not only their claims but also those of their creditors over the interests of wives and children.[15]

Virginia Law professors assigned treatises with this conception of coverture, elaborated on it in their lectures, and then drew on those lectures as the basis for their own treatises. Minor's *Institutes of Common and Statute Law* were based in the lectures he had been giving for decades. "Lecture 34th," wrote law student Phillip B. Hiden (Law 1866) in 1866: "Nature & origin of property. It is of divine origin. Read 2 Black 1st Chap." Minor's students learned that property was closely aligned with marriage: together, they "consolidated the fundamental groundwork of all society." The 1861 notebook of Robert Hubard revealed the nature of

Main Grounds at the University of Virginia with Pavilion X, home of the Davis and Minor families, in foreground, ca. 1890s. (Albert and Shirley Small Special Collections Library, University of Virginia)

that relationship in his notes on the buying and selling of real estate. That right extended to everyone, except: "(1) Those wanting understanding, e.g. idiots, lunatics & infants: (2) Those wanting freedom of will, married persons & those under duress, whether of threats or imprisonment, (3) Those who have no real title to the land." The claims of wives to family property were akin to those who had none at all.[16]

Over time, coverture's property restrictions elbowed out other, less limiting elements traditionally associated with coverture, and Minor's teachings helped cement this transition in Virginia. The handling of paraphernalia—clothing, jewelry, and other similar items that had considerable value then—is representative. Minor turned paraphernalia into the husband's property in a way that emphasized wives' diminishing claims on family property generally. As he explained in his *Institutes,* the term referred only to "apparel and ornaments" that were "given [to a wife] *by her husband.*" As such, "*paraphernalia* are the property of the husband; and if he chooses to dispose of them in his lifetime, he is at liberty to do so." A wife could claim apparel given to her by third parties. But anything that a husband "gave" to his wife belonged to him and his creditors, except necessary apparel. Of course, in Minor's restrictive reading of coverture, everything a wife produced belonged to her husband, so even items she produced herself were "given" to her by her husband.[17]

Minor's insistence on a particular version of common law as the default body of law for the state of Virginia extended his restrictive view of coverture. Treatises published earlier in the nineteenth century made it clear that coverture's restrictions applied within common law, a body of law that existed alongside other bodies of law, particularly equity. Even then, common law also made room for customary practices that modified or even conflicted with coverture's restrictions and were not recorded in writing. While narrowing common law, pushing the importance of customary practice outside its bounds, Minor also elevated common law over other sources of law as the primary body of law for the state of Virginia. Common law was *the* law to Minor. He even used the two terms—law and common law—interchangeably. Statutes, equity, and customary practices were subordinate, working around the edges, modifying common law, although Minor accepted those modifications grudgingly. He had to discuss equitable principles because they were impossible to ignore in Virginia legal practice. But he refused to acknowledge their place within the body of Virginia law, omitting them from the title of his treatise even as they appear all over its pages. Nor did the importance of other common law principles, including the place of custom, appear in his treatises. In so doing, he elevated a restrictive view of coverture as the only option, turning it into the definition of married women's legal status generally. As he wrote in the second volume of his *Institutes* (1877), "A Married Woman has, *in law, no Separate Existence.* She is *one with her husband,* and in law her existence is merged in his, so far as concerns relations of business and property." Further, a "Married Woman is *under the constraint of her Husband.* It is true in fact, as it is in law, that a married woman, in matters of business and property, in which both are concerned, seldom persistently maintains an opinion and will adverse to her husband. His influence is ultimately absolutely controlling, to which if she opposes any resistance at all, it is a vain one; and if occasional exceptions are exhibited, they serve only to make the general rule more noticeable."[18]

Married women's subordination in common law, moreover, reflected the natural order of things. Referencing Colossians 3, Minor wrote that a wife's marriage vows to her husband had legal force as "divine precept": "'Wives, submit yourselves unto your own husbands, as it is fit in the Lord.'" The text echoed notes students took of his lectures, where religion and law were aligned when it came to women's relationships to their husbands. The passages reflected Minor's own religious leanings, which carried over into his legal teachings. Minor's earlier teachings on "Husband & Wife" in the 1840s began with the ecclesiastical courts in England and moved from there to common law. In later life, he taught a Sunday Bible class for students.[19]

Whatever diluted the legal principles of coverture in common law also threatened society at large. Minor opposed Virginia's married women's property acts, passed in the 1870s, for that reason: they imported equitable principles into the ambit of common law, undermining the common law logic that supported husbands' authority by allowing married women to own certain kinds of property in their own names. Equity, at least, remained separate from common law and did not allow women to own property outright. Married women's property acts altered the very nature of coverture, creating two legal agents when there should have been one: the husband. Such acts, he wrote, "abolish virtually the husband's headship of the family, contrary to the common law, to common reason, to the Scriptures, and the fruitful experience for many centuries of the race from which we spring." More than that, they "introduce causes of domestic strife and division, by creating diverse and sometimes conflicting interests in husband and wife; it incurs the danger of family factions and feuds." Family discord then led "to that deplorable result, a house divided against itself," a none-too-subtle reference to the recent Civil War.[20]

Minor was anticipating disaster in 1877 after Virginia passed its married women's property acts. It was the last state to do so. The first had been adopted in the 1830s and had produced neither marital nor social dissolution. By the 1870s, moreover, the legal subordination of wives to their husbands had become so entrenched in Virginia that legal mechanisms allowing them greater control of property could not dislodge it. In fact, Minor had it backward: equity did not change common law; it was the other way around. Over the course of the nineteenth century, the restrictive principles associated with coverture in common law bled into the legal handling of separate estates in equity. Virginia's Supreme Court of Appeals did give women more control over the property in their separate estates. At the same time, these decisions left husbands' common law authority over wives undisturbed, which made it easier for husbands and their creditors to access property that was, in theory, beyond their control. The court also left restrictions in place that limited the ability of women with property in separate estates to access credit and, hence, manage their property.[21]

Married women's property acts did not overturn coverture either. The early acts generally gave women control over only certain kinds of property: what they brought into marriage or acquired afterward through inheritance or gift. Such measures were not new. Entail, marriage settlements, separate estates, and other legal arrangements had accomplished similar ends. In fact, early married women's property acts affirmed established conceptions of property as a familial possession by providing another way to put assets in married women's names and out of creditors' reach. Virginia's first act, passed in 1875, was a badly framed debt relief measure: it protected married women's property from their husbands' creditors without specifying that married women could own property. While the 1877 act corrected that omission, allowing married women to own property that they brought into marriage or acquired through inheritance or gift, it did not change legal practice in the state that much. Basically, it created another way to establish a separate estate, a fact reflected in the name given to those claims: "statutory separate estates."[22]

Like acts in other states, Virginia's 1875 statute worked around the edges of coverture but left it intact. It did not allow women to claim their wages, the value of anything they produced while married, or a share in the family's property. Nor did it extinguish coverture's other restrictions on married women's legal agency, including the right to contract in her own name. The next round of acts, which were first passed in other states beginning in the 1860s, did allow married women to keep their wages. Virginia included that provision in 1886, but only for work done outside the household. Not until 1900 did the Virginia legislature allow married women to contract in their own names, just like unmarried women. Still, because coverture gave husbands ownership of family property, married women could not claim the value of anything they produced within their households or even anything they purchased for their households out of their wages or separate estates. They had to keep their property apart from the family finances to maintain a claim to it. If they paid the mortgage, the house still belonged to their husbands and could be claimed by his creditors. If they bought goods for their families' use, those things belonged to their husbands and could be claimed by his creditors. If they used their property for their families on a regular basis, the courts interpreted that pattern as an ongoing transfer to the husband, and they lost claim to it all.[23]

Married women's property acts also helped solidify a long-standing connection between women's property and fraud. The consolidation of property in the name of the husband elevated creditors' claims over those of family members, including wives. By extension, alternative efforts to keep property in the hands of families and shield it from creditors became fraud. That so many of those efforts to bypass coverture put resources in the hands of married women linked all women's property ownership with fraud. The issues run through Minor's diary. After working through notes on wives' inability to buy or sell real estate, he turned to the various means of defrauding creditors by conveying real estate to those legally unable to buy and sell it, namely wives and children, scrawling furiously about the rights that husbands acquired in their wives' property at marriage. Later, he was back to fraud, namely instances in which husbands made gifts to their wives to avoid creditors. The equation was clear: women with property signaled the possibility of fraud.[24]

In case after case in Virginia's appellate court, creditors accused those indebted to them of transferring property to their female relatives to defraud them. In one sense, that was entirely accurate. One point of legal arrangements that put property in married women's hands was to prioritize the interests of families, particularly those of women whose property rights could be extinguished by coverture, over those of creditors. Married women's property acts moved the logic of separate estates into the ambit of common law, while stripping these arrangements of the equitable principles that protected married women's property from creditors. The discussion surrounding homestead laws, which were passed around the same time as married women's property acts in Virginia, was explicit on this score: they were seen as measures akin to welfare, providing wives a claim to family property that they otherwise lost through coverture and needed to carry on their lives. What was a legitimate means of shielding family property in one area of the law became fraud in the context of other legal principles that elevated the claims of creditors over those of families. Bottom line: when women had property, it always had the whiff of something fraudulent designed to undercut the claims of creditors.[25]

That link then undermined all women's relationship to property and placed them at an economic disadvantage. When men presented themselves to creditors, it was presumed that they had the full array of rights necessary to own and control property, which meant that they could assume legal responsibility for its management. That was not the case with women because their legal capacity depended on their marital status, which could be difficult to determine and could change suddenly. The results limited the economic options of married women, who could not claim family property and whose ability to borrow against their own property was limited. Not only did the legal order promoted by UVA Law

School professors make women's property suspect, but it also made property ownership for them utterly different than it was for men.[26]

Those principles did little to protect women. The new version created deeply gendered structural inequalities that have made it difficult for all women to manage property and accumulate wealth. For individual women, even unmarried white women from privileged families, the result was uncertainty and, often, impoverishment. Such was the fate of wives and daughters of the UVA law professors who wrote a rigid definition of coverture into their state's legal system.

Mary Jane Terrell Davis lived on the edge after her husband, J. A. G. Davis, was shot and killed in a student riot in 1840. According to family lore, the carriages that bore Davis's body to the cemetery stopped on the way back to carry Mary Jane and her children away from their residence, which was part of the Law School. The story's don't-let-the-door-hit-you-on-the-way-out quality underscored the structural realities of the situation. Like her husband, Mary Jane Davis had worked for the University, taking care of the law students who studied in her home. Some also boarded there. But the University's legal relationship was to her husband, not to her, and she received no compensation for, or even recognition of, the labor she had provided. Fortunately, Mary Jane's husband had owned a house nearby, so the family had a place to live. But they did not have much else. Davis's talents did not extend to finances, and his estate was encumbered and uncertain given the claims of creditors, which were numerous. With mounting debts and few assets, Mary Jane Davis scraped by, sharing her home with the families of relatives to spread out expenses, taking charity from one of her husband's former students, accepting help from her eldest son, and running a girls' school. She did all that without ever owning any of the family property, even though she was no longer under the restrictions of coverture. In his will, her husband had only given her use of the property and for only as long as she did not remarry. Even then, he gave creditors first crack at the family property. That was the first provision of his will, although it was largely unnecessary given the legal principles that he had helped embed in Virginia law.[27]

The wife and daughters of John Minor met a similar fate. Minor also elevated his creditors over his family, a point that he made clear in the first provision in his will, "that all my just debts . . . be promptly paid." He gave the bulk of what remained to his wife and two unmarried daughters: "I lament more than I can express the small provision which I have been unable to make for my dear family. They will remember however the losses I have sustained." Minor's language reflects the legal principles he taught his whole life: the family property belonged to him; he supported his wife and daughters with it. Yet his wife and daughters had worked all their lives for the University of Virginia, just as Mary Jane Davis had. They had helped amass the property that was now being willed back to them, as if it were a gift. The estate was not enough to support them, even then. After Minor's death, his widow Ellen Temple Hill Minor made ends meet by scrimping here, saving there, and contributing to the household budget through various means. Mary Minor, who helped her stepmother run

Nannie Minor, daughter of John B. Minor, ca. 1899. (Albert and Shirley Small Special Collections Library, University of Virginia)

Ca. 1890s photograph taken on the front porch of Pavilion X featuring Mildred Henderson, likely a domestic worker, in foreground and members of the Minor family in the background, presumably Mary L. Minor and Nannie Minor, daughters of John B. Minor. (Albert and Shirley Small Special Collections Library, University of Virginia)

the household her entire life, pooled resources with her younger half-sister Susan at the end of her life. Susan's husband, also a lawyer, died and left her only debts. So, she moved in with Mary, providing household labor to her aging sister in exchange for a place to live. The other unmarried daughter, Nannie, was the most secure. That was because she had left her father's household long before his death to create a career of her own as a nurse and social worker in Richmond. In his will, Minor left his law library to his sons, as if his daughters had no need for his law books. But, if anything, they needed more knowledge of the law than their brothers did to survive in their daily lives.[28]

Notes

This essay would not have been possible without the contributions of Meggan F. Cashwell and Addison R. Patrick. We were working on this piece in the middle of the pandemic, which limited my research possibilities to what I could pull up on my computer. Meggan and Addison supplied everything else, answering my questions and following leads in the archives in Virginia about the legal principles of coverture and the women who were caught up in them, particularly the women in families of the UVA law professors.

Much of what we found is not included here because of space constraints. But all that background informs the analysis, which looks much different than it would have without all their work. Thank you also to Meggan, Addison, and Randall N. Flaherty for their editorial insights. Thank you as well to Justene Hill Edwards and David Thomas Konig, whose thoughts also strengthened the piece.

1. Mary L. Minor Diary, 1852, Papers of the Minor and Wilson Family, MSS 38–602, Albert and Shirley Small Special Collections Library, University of Virginia (hereafter cited as SSCL). For more on John B. Minor's tenure at Virginia Law, see Randall N. Flaherty, "John B. Minor and the Science of Legal Education, 1845–1895," and Elizabeth R. Varon, "The Civil War and Reconstruction, 1861–1877," both in this volume.
2. For legal education, see James P. Ambuske and Randall Flaherty, "Reading Law in the Early Republic: Legal Education in the Age of Jefferson," in *The Founding of Thomas Jefferson's University,* ed. John A. Ragosta, Peter S. Onuf, and Andrew J. O'Shaughnessy (Charlottesville: University of Virginia Press, 2019), 224–57; Hugh MacGill and R. Kent Newmyer, "Legal Education and Legal Thought, 1790–1920," in *The Cambridge History of Law in America,* ed. Michael Grossberg and Christopher Tomlins (New York: Cambridge University Press, 2008), 2:36–67. See also David Thomas Konig, "Jeffersonian Foundations of Legal Education in Virginia, 1779–1845," in this volume.
3. For more on the laws of slavery, see Justene Hill Edwards, "Teaching the Laws of Slavery, 1826–1865," in this volume.
4. For Blackstone's version of coverture and its influence, see Holly Brewer, "The Transformation of Domestic Law," in *The Cambridge History of Law in America,* 1:288–323; Laura F. Edwards, "The Legal World of Elizabeth Bagby's Commonplace Book: Federalism, Women, and Governance," *Journal of the Civil War Era* 9, no. 4 (December 2019): 504–23.
5. This version of coverture is most closely associated with Sir William Blackstone, *Commentaries on the Laws of England* (London, 1765–69; reprint, Chicago: University of Chicago Press, 1979), 1:421–33. Mary R. Beard, *Woman as Force in History* (New York: Macmillan, 1946), questioned the emphasis on common law and its restrictions in the 1940s. For more recent discussions, see Brewer, "Transformation of Domestic Law"; Sara T. Damiano, *To Her Credit: Women, Finance, and the Law in Eighteenth-Century New England Cities* (Baltimore: Johns Hopkins University Press, 2021); Edwards, "Legal World of Elizabeth Bagby's Commonplace Book"; Joan R. Gundersen and Gwen Victor Gampel, "Married Women's Legal Status in Eighteenth-Century New York and Virginia," *William and Mary Quarterly* 39, no. 1 (January 1982): 114–34; Ellen Hartigan-O'Connor, *The Ties That Buy: Women and Commerce in Revolutionary America* (Philadelphia: University of Pennsylvania Press, 2009); Reva B. Siegel, "'The Rule of Love': Wife Beating as Prerogative and Privacy," *Yale Law Journal* 105, no. 8 (June 1996): 2117–207; Linda L. Sturtz, *Within Her Power: Propertied Women in Colonial Virginia* (New York: Routledge, 2002).
6. For these conceptions of property, see Gregory S. Alexander, *Commodity and Propriety: Competing Visions of Property in American Legal Thought, 1776-1970* (Chicago: University of Chicago Press, 1997); Claire Priest, *Credit Nation: Property Laws and Institutions in Early America* (Princeton, NJ: Princeton University Press, 2021); Carol M. Rose, "Property as Wealth, Property as Propriety," *Nomos* 33 (1991): 223–47.
7. For entail, see Holly Brewer, "Entailing Aristocracy in Colonial Virginia: 'Ancient

Feudal Restraints' and Revolutionary Reform," *William and Mary Quarterly* 54, no. 2 (April 1997): 307–46; Priest, *Credit Nation,* 128–45; Claire Priest, "The End of Entail: Information, Institutions, and Slavery in the American Revolutionary Period," *Law and History Review* 33, no. 2 (May 2015): 277–319.

8. For an example of Davis's lectures, see John W. Stevenson Student Notebook, 15 March 1834, Professor J. A. G. Davis Lectures, Student Notebooks, RG-32-400, Arthur J. Morris Law Library Special Collections, University of Virginia (hereafter cited as LLSC). J. A. G. Davis, *An Exposition of the Principles Which Distinguish Estates Tail from Other Limitations* (Charlottesville, VA: Tompkins & Noel, 1837); George W. Blattermann Student Notebook, 1838–39, n.d., 139–40, Professor J. A. G. Davis Lectures, Student Notebooks, RG-32-400, LLSC; John B. Minor Diary (vol. 2, 1843–73), n.d., 306–26, MSS 3114, SSCL; John B. Minor, *Institutes of Common and Statute Law* (Richmond, VA: printed by the author, 1877), 2:85–86. Also see Deane v. Hansford, February 1838, 36 Va. 98, 9 Leigh 253; Pryor v. Duncan, 1 April 1849, 47 Va. 27; Nowlin v. Winfree, 19 January 1852, 49 Va. 346; Camp v. Cleary, 19 January 1882, 76 Va. 140.
9. Robert Thruston Hubard Student Notebook, 1861, 15 April 1861, Professor John B. Minor's Junior Law Class, Notebook of Law Lectures, 1861–66, MSS 5624, SSCL; Suzanne Lebsock, *The Free Women of Petersburg: Status and Culture in a Southern Town, 1784–1860* (New York: W. W. Norton, 1984), 54–86.
10. For necessaries generally, see James Kent, *Commentaries on American Law* (New York: O. Halsted, 1827), 2:123–26; Tapping Reeve, *The Law of Baron and Femme, of Parent and Child, of Guardian and Ward, of Master and Servant,* [. . .] (New Haven, CT: Oliver Steele, 1816), 79–85; Reeve, *Law of Baron and Femme,* 3rd ed. (Albany, NY: Gould, 1862), 156–66; St. George Tucker, ed., *Blackstone's Commentaries: With Notes of Reference to the Constitution and Laws of the United States; and of the Commonwealth of Virginia,* vol. 1, pt. 2 (Philadelphia: William Young Birch and Abraham Small, 1803), 442. See also Laura F. Edwards, *Only the Clothes on Her Back: Clothing and the Hidden History of Power in the Nineteenth-Century United States* (New York: Oxford University Press, 2022), 21–38.
11. Ann E. Tucker to John B. Minor, 3 July 1845; John B. Minor to Hon. Lucas Thompson, 14 February 1845; John B. Minor Papers, all in Anne Firor Scott, Martin Paul Schipper, and Mary Susan Ker, eds., *Southern Women and Their Families in the 19th Century: Papers and Diaries* (Bethesda, MD: University Publications of America, 1991), microfilm, Ser. G:pt. 2, reel 28.
12. See Edwards, *Only the Clothes on Her Back,* 233–55. In 1867, Virginia's appeals court affirmed long-standing practice: Penn v. Whitehead, 26 June 1867, 58 Va. 503; see also Virginia, 1840–95, R. G. Dun & Company credit report volumes, MSS 791 D987, Baker Library Special Collections and Archives, Harvard Business School.
13. Tucker, *Blackstone's Commentaries;* Minor, *Institutes of Common and Statute Law* (1875), quote from 1:vii. Blackstone moved into magistrates' manuals slowly, although the influence was evident by the 1830s. See Laura F. Edwards, "The Material Conditions of Dependency: The Hidden History of Free Women's Control of Property in the Early Nineteenth-Century South," in *Signposts: New Directions in Southern Legal History,* ed. Sally E. Hadden and Patricia Hagler Minter (Athens: University of Georgia Press, 2013), 171–92. On required texts for UVA Law, see *A Catalogue of the Officers and Students of the University of Virginia for the Eighth Session, 1831–1832* (Charlottesville: Chronicle Steam Book Printing House, 1880) and catalogues for subsequent sessions through 1888; "JUEL Resources," Jefferson's University: The

Early Life Project, http://juel.iath.virginia.edu/resources; University of Virginia, *Law Department Announcements, 1892–1893* (1892), and announcements for years 1895–1923.

14. Quote from Blackstone, *Commentaries on the Laws of England,* 1:430.
15. Efforts to streamline law and make it more favorable to commercial interests had been ongoing. For classic statements, see James Willard Hurst, *Law and the Conditions of Freedom in the Nineteenth-Century United States* (Madison: University of Wisconsin Press, 1956); Morton J. Horwitz, *The Transformation of American Law, 1780–1860* (Cambridge, MA: Harvard University Press, 1977). For the interposition of lawyers and legal procedure in that transformation, see, for instance, Cornelia Hughes Dayton, *Women before the Bar: Gender, Law, and Society in Connecticut, 1639–1789* (Chapel Hill: University of North Carolina Press, 1995); Kellen Richard Funk, "The Lawyers' Code: The Transformation of American Legal Practice, 1828–1938" (PhD diss., Princeton University, 2018); Bruce H. Mann, *Neighbors and Strangers: Law and Community in Early Connecticut* (Chapel Hill: University of North Carolina Press, 1987); MacGill and Newmyer, "Legal Education and Legal Thought."
16. Phillip B. Hiden Student Notebook 2, 1866, n.d., 49, Professor John B. Minor's Notes on Common and Statute Law, Student Notebooks, RG-32-400, LLSC; Hubard Student Notebook, 28 January 1861.
17. Tucker, *Blackstone's Commentaries,* 2:435; Minor, *Institutes of Common and Statute Law* (1876), 1:301–2, italics in the original.
18. Minor, *Institutes of Common and Statute Law* (1877), 2:576, italics in the original.
19. Minor, *Institutes of Common and Statute Law* (1876), 1:285; John S. Henshaw Student Notebook, 22 February 1847, Professor John B. Minor's Junior Law Class, Student Notebooks, RG-32-400, LLSC; James C. Lamb, "John B. Minor," *Virginia Law Register* 1, no. 7 (November 1895): 482.
20. Minor, *Institutes of Common and Statute Law* (1895), 3:85; Sarah Frances Ketchum, "Married Women's Property Law in Nineteenth-Century Virginia" (master's thesis, University of Virginia, 1985), 47.
21. For the protections in equity, see Bernie D. Jones, "Revisiting the Married Women's Property Acts: Recapturing Protection in the Face of Equality," *American University Journal of Gender, Social Policy & the Law* 22, no. 1 (2013): 91–147.
22. For married women's property acts in Virginia, see Cynthia Gianakos, "Virginia and the Married Women's Property Acts" (master's thesis, University of Virginia, 1982); Ketchum, "Married Women's Property Law."
23. Married Women's Property Act, 1875, *Acts and Joint Resolutions of the General Assembly of the State of Virginia, at the Session of 1874–5* (Richmond: R. F. Walker, Supt. Public Printing, 1875), 442–43; Ketchum, "Married Women's Property Law," for the acts generally and for the 1900 act.
24. John B. Minor Diary (vol. 2, 1843–73), var. dates 1855–60, 278–79, 284–89, 306–22, 323–26, John B. Minor Papers, MSS 3114, SSCL. Also see Edwards, *Only the Clothes on Her Back,* 212–78.
25. Alison D. Morantz, "There's No Place Like Home: Homestead Exemption and Judicial Constructions of Family in Nineteenth-Century America," *Law and History Review* 24, no. 2 (Summer 2006): 245–95.
26. Women's inability to contract in their own names was extended from separate estates in equity to statutory separate estates; see Darnall v. Smith's Adm'r, 25 November 1875, 67 Va. 878.

27. Lucy Minor Davis Reminiscences, 5–6, Papers of the Fishburne Family, MSS 6355-c, SSCL; John Gardner Davis Will, 18 July 1839, Will Book 14, 108, Albemarle County Circuit Court, Clerk's Office (hereafter cited as ACCC).
28. John B. Minor Will, 21 February 1895, Will Book 30, 249–50, ACCC. Agreement between Mary L. Minor and Susan C. Wilson, 12 January 1901, in Mary L. Minor and Susan C. M. Wilson Financial and Legal Records, in Scott, Schipper, and Ker, *Southern Women and Their Families,* reels 35, 36, and 57; Mary L. Minor Will, 24 April 1902, Will Book 31, 420, ACCC.

“This Mob of Men”

THE ROAD TO COEDUCATION AT THE UNIVERSITY OF VIRGINIA SCHOOL OF LAW, 1870–1923

Anne M. Coughlin

ON JUNE 3, 1921, William Minor Lile, the dean of the Law School at the University of Virginia, welcomed a gathering of alumni to the proceedings celebrating the University’s centennial. With the opening words of his salutation—“Gentlemen of the Law School”—Lile made it plain that he had crafted his remarks for an audience consisting only of white men.[1] To be sure, the assemblage must have included some people who were neither “men”—they were women—nor “gentle”—they were Black. As Laura F. Edwards explains, throughout the nineteenth century, the Law School relied heavily for its success on the attentive presence and unpaid labor of many women, “free and enslaved.” The women who lived and worked in faculty pavilion homes in the Academical Village supplied a whole range of material and emotional support to the young men who were studying to be Virginia lawyers. By the opening decades of the twentieth century, however, the physical separation of home and business increasingly had taken hold, reinforcing the Victorian ideology that assigned women to the former and men to the latter. In 1911, for example, law professors began teaching their classes in Minor Hall, a new building constructed specifically for the Law School outside of the Academical Village.[2] Still, it is fair to suppose that, on that “sultry summer afternoon,” some white women stepped away from their household cares and joined the professional convocation as guests of Law faculty, Law students, and

Law alumni.[3] Moreover, since the gentle hosts could not possibly have pulled off a four-day festival without the assistance of dozens of servants, many Black people—formerly enslaved persons and their descendants—must have been within Lile's earshot, too. But no woman or person of color who was present on that day was one of those to whom Lile extended his "right royal welcome."[4] In that gathering, only the "sons of the Law School" mattered.[5] Women and Black people did not.

If there were any doubts, Lile explicitly acknowledged what he suspected must be on at least some of his sons' minds on that June day, namely, that this "happy" all-male "family reunion" was destined to be the last of its kind.[6] Lile wrapped up his preliminary comments with a prediction: "No daughters have as yet graced the family circle, but they are well on the way."[7] The prophecy took little foresight. At the time that Lile offered it, three white women had completed their first year of law studies at the University of Virginia. Just two years later, one of these women, Elizabeth Nelson Tompkins (Law 1923), would become the first woman to graduate from the Law School. During her second year, Tompkins took the Virginia bar exam and passed it with a perfect score. Rather

Photograph of Dean William Minor Lile (Law 1882), ca. 1920s. (Arthur J. Morris Law Library Special Collections, University of Virginia)

than leaving the Law School and entering private practice immediately upon passing the bar, as her classmate Rose May Davis did—and as some of her male classmates presumably did too—Tompkins instead chose to stick it out and complete her degree.[8]

Though Lile could foresee the coming of women—indeed, they had arrived—his rhetoric reveals that he did not then imagine that Black students would someday be included in the Law School's class reunions. In Lile's mind's eye, his future daughters would be "'fair Portias.'"[9] The fact that this reference was, at best, tongue-in-cheek suggests that of the two meanings of the word "fair"—a just or impartial character or a light or blonde appearance—Lile had the second one in the forefront of his mind.[10] He could not but have believed that, like his Law School sons, all his future daughters would be white. How could they be otherwise? After all, on the second day of the centennial exercises, the audience had been treated to a speech by the rector of the University commemorating the "military genius and personal bravery" of the University's sons who fought on behalf of the Confederacy "at Chancellorsville and Gettysburg."[11] Moreover, "shortly before the Centennial Celebration, there was shown on the moving-picture screen in Virginia and other states a series of important events and noteworthy scenes in the history of the University," including a performance that depicted "making the Confederate flag."[12] As the rector exclaimed, the boys who had "died in the defense of their homes," as well as the gentlemen who honored them that day, were bound by the "ties of blood" and "of race."[13] They had been shaped by "the soul of the South and the traditions of the University of Virginia."[14] Clearly, for the University's leaders, therefore, the decision to allow less than a handful of white women to join "that mystical body of Virginians" did not portend the admission of Blacks.[15]

After alluding to what was to be an important theme of his speech—the interesting development now familiarly known as "coeducation"—Lile offered a sketch of the history of the Law School, its current condition, and his aspirations for its future trajectory. In the main, his narrative dovetails with the received wisdom about the genealogy of legal training in the United States, which culminated in the rise of private and public law schools as the dominant, indeed all but exclusive, pathway to the bar. At the same time, his observations enrich and complicate the standard account. According to that account, the proprietary law schools of the late eighteenth century ultimately were absorbed into and replaced by college and university programs, and of those programs, Harvard Law School would emerge as the standard of excellence in all things pedagogical, which everyone else imitated. However, the University of Virginia Law School, which opened its doors in 1826, was not a descendant of the proprietary model, but an alternative to it.[16]

On that auspicious day in June 1921, Lile did not hesitate to criticize one of the developments taking place in Cambridge, namely, the emergence of the "so-called Case Method" for teaching law, for which Harvard Law School Dean Christopher Columbus Langdell is given the lion's share of the credit.[17] Lile acknowledged that his contemporaries at other law programs faulted his law school for being "old fogyish, and out of date," for sticking with "the old fashioned text-book and lecture system."[18] And he conceded that there were good things to say on behalf of Langdell's case method of instruction. The case method was a good way to cultivate a law "student's reasoning faculties."[19] The method also generated "lively debate[s]," in which professors and students—or, at least, the students who were tapped to "participate"—might devote "an entire lecture hour" to ventilating such fine points as "whether the key to a man's shop is personalty [*sic*] or realty and therefore the subject or not the subject of larceny."[20] The case method's attractions notwithstanding, Lile was quick to praise UVA's decision to stick with its own way of doing things in the classroom. Unlike UVA's traditional text-and-lecture approach, the Harvard method was slow and inefficient, leaving gaps in the students' understanding of the numerous cases that professors lacked time to cover in their Socratic debates, and neglecting altogether that "large part of the body of the law" that consisted of conventional rules, "which are to be mastered only by memorizing them."[21] The wisdom of the Law School's "deliberate choice" to retain its "conservative" pedagogy was "abundantly sustained by the results."[22] Of the "5571 degrees conferred by" the University since its founding, "2051 have been degrees from the Law School—or 37% of the total."[23] Moreover, when they went out into the profession, Lile observed, Virginia Law's men served in "high positions . . . throughout the country" and consistently proved themselves to be "accomplished, well-rounded, high-minded and efficient lawyers."[24]

By contrast, Lile spoke grudgingly—even regretfully—about the Law School's decision to begin admitting women into its "sacred precincts."[25] The secondary literature on women's education reveals that Lile was far from alone in lamenting the arrival of women in his classrooms. The leaders of many of the most venerated law programs in the country "unleashed venomous response[s]" to the burgeoning movement to educate women on the same basis as men.[26] Yet, the precise objections offered by Lile and his Virginia contemporaries move us to try to grasp the import and intensity of the feelings that motivated so many University administrators, alumni, faculty, students, and friends to denounce coeducation. At this distance it can be difficult to credit those passionate objections, for many of them were explicitly rooted in a "science" of sex differences that has been thoroughly debunked.[27] Bad science notwithstanding, the opponents of coeducation were convinced that the experiment would be a social and economic catastrophe. By "open[ing] the doors of Jefferson's masculine University to women," the opponents reckoned, UVA would contribute to the unravelling of the entire social order and the destruction of their beloved way of life. At stake in the campaign was nothing less than the domestic "soul of the South."[28]

A History of Apprenticeship

As Lile recounted with understandable pride, the University of Virginia was home to one of the first formal law programs in the country, offering aspiring lawyers the opportunity to learn the law in classrooms with professors rather than in apprenticeships with established members of the bar. Thomas Jefferson's "main purpose in establishing a chair of law in the State University was to afford facilities for legal training, superior to the office method," Dean Lile recounted.[29] Jefferson recommended that law students, like all other undergraduates, should receive a broad education, one that was more academic than practical. In addition to enrolling in general university courses, they were to study a large selection of texts on law, legislation, constitutions, and political philosophy, which would prepare them for careers as statesmen, legislators, and judges as well as practicing lawyers. Moreover, Lile acknowledged that, when prescribing the legal course of instruction, Jefferson also was determined that his Law School's curriculum would convey to law students "sound" (Whiggish) "political principles."[30]

Unlike the UVA Law School, most of the other early law programs built quite directly on the apprenticeship model. The first and by far the most famous proprietary program was the Litchfield Law School, which was founded in Connecticut in 1784 by Tapping Reeve, a well-respected and well-connected practitioner to whom young men from across the country sought to apprentice themselves.[31] At some point, Reeve must have noticed that it would be more efficient, not to mention more lucrative, to take on a group of apprentices and train them together. Thus, the law classroom—as distinct from the law office—began to emerge as a site for educating future members of the bar. For his Litchfield lectures, Reeve is said to have read the content of "written notes that were meant to be copied verbatim" by his students, stopping occasionally to offer explanations, illustrations, and case citations.[32] Impressed by the financial success of the Litchfield venture, colleges and universities followed suit and began creating their own law programs or acquiring existing proprietary schools along with their instructors (usually, their owners) and (best of all) their students.[33]

By the time of UVA's centennial, as Lile remarked, the "standard law schools," which included Harvard, had begun to overhaul and professionalize their programs. At the University of Virginia, law still was an undergraduate degree, but by 1921 applicants needed one year of college courses and to have earned a high school diploma.[34] On top of their enhanced entrance requirements, law schools were beginning to converge on a broader and more demanding curriculum, according to which studying "'principles before practice [was] the true watchword.'"[35] For example, in academic year 1909–10, UVA Law adopted a new course of study, which took three years for law students to complete.[36] Most schools expected that their students would continue to spend part of their time working in law offices, but this practical training was merely part of a formal academic program in which students also attended a "series of expository lectures, supplemented by examinations, quizzes, and moots."[37] Nineteenth-century law schools began requiring their students to take written examinations rather than being allowed to self-report their progress on their way to earning a diploma.[38] Written exams had at least a couple of merits: in addition to reassuring college officials that their law graduates possessed the knowledge necessary to represent clients in basic legal matters, they also established that the students could read and write.[39]

All but taken for granted today, these innovations were dramatic and contentious in their time. As Lile remarked, contemporary lawyers themselves tended to reject proposals to reform legal education or to increase the requirements for admission to the bar. According to Lile, unlike their "medical friends," many lawyers "los[t] no opportunity of blocking efforts within the profession to raise legal standards" on the ground that the reforms would have had the effect of excluding them "from the Law School, and from the bar" of which they fancied themselves to be "a shining ornament."[40] However, starting in the middle of the nineteenth century, there was a "resurgence of interest in [an] upgraded bar," and "law was beginning once more to be seen as a learned profession."[41] Ultimately, lawyers and other opponents could not withstand those progressive forces, and enhanced curricular, pedagogical, and professional standards became the order of the day.

Women Lawyers

When in 1890 she set out to answer the question of "how many women there are in the law," Lelia J. Robinson, who would become the first woman admitted to the Massachusetts bar, encountered a number of obstacles.[42] First, she would have to persuade at least some of her readers, if not her publisher, that women lawyers in fact existed. At that time, the "popular idea" was that the woman lawyer, no less than a "sea-serpent," was a mythical creature, with "the one . . . about as real as the other."[43] Second, since the available data were fragmentary and unreliable, Robinson found herself forced to create a "somewhat extended system of correspondence" that she hoped would allow her to name all of the women who had "studied law to the point of a degree or of admission to the bar, as well as the number of actual practitioners."[44] Third, she acknowledged that her mode of inquiry was fallible for a number of reasons, including the fact that "many addresses have been lost, especially by means of the somewhat inconvenient custom of changing a woman's name at marriage."[45] Finally, Robinson pointed out that it was difficult to locate women lawyers who had taken a break from practice in order to care for their children or manage other domestic obligations. Apparently, for some respondents, these women no longer should be counted as lawyers at all, a judgment that Robinson herself rejected. In Robinson's opinion, just "as we do not cease to regard as a lawyer the politician who spends his days at Washington in his country's service, so neither should the woman who has temporarily or even permanently abandoned the office and the courtroom for the platform or the nursery, thereby lose recognition as a lawyer."[46]

At the time that Robinson was attempting to document the prevalence—indeed, the very existence—of women lawyers, the legal profession was undergoing more than one important transition. There were few law schools then in existence, and only a small number of law programs were willing to entertain women's applications for admission. One of the first law departments to do so was Washington University in St. Louis, which opened its doors to a woman named Lemma Barkaloo in 1869.[47] However, as Robinson remarked in her report, "the Law Department of the University of Virginia," like the vast majority of "Southern schools," did not at the time she was writing "admit women as students."[48] In this regard, UVA Law could pride itself for being in good company since many other "prominent law schools," including the northeast elites—Harvard, Columbia, and Yale—also barred women from admission.[49]

In those turbulent years, women who for any reason could not—or who did not want to—secure a law school seat could and did seek to become lawyers in the conventional way still followed by many of their male peers—that is, by serving as apprentices to established practitioners. Some of the women included in Robinson's survey followed that route, reading law in the offices of their husbands, fathers, or other male family members, and those same women often practiced as associates of their male kin once they obtained their law licenses.[50] While it may have been more comfortable and less expensive for women to study law in the offices of their male family members than to venture away from home to join a law school program, the fact that a woman had completed a legal apprenticeship was no guarantee that she would be granted a license to practice law. The gatekeepers to the bar—judges, court personnel, bar officials, and legislators—were men, and many of them were no more inclined to welcome women into their fold than were law school administrators and faculty members. For example, Belva A. Lockwood, the first woman admitted to the United States Supreme Court Bar, gained her place there in 1879 only "after securing the passage of an Act of Congress providing for the admission of women to this the highest court in the Country."[51] Despite her professional recognition and success in the District of Columbia, Lockwood's efforts to gain admission to the Virginia bar went nowhere. Although Virginia had reciprocity agreements that allowed all licensed attorneys to practice in the Commonwealth, and Lockwood was licensed in other states as well as in the District of Columbia, in 1893 the Supreme Court of Appeals of Virginia denied her petition for admission. She sought leave to file a petition for mandamus in the case in the United States Supreme Court, but that court rejected her petition too, saying that it was for the Virginia courts to decide whether a Virginia statute providing for admission to the bar of a "person" with a law license was "confined to males, and whether women are admitted to practice law in that Commonwealth."[52]

As for why women should be denied access to a legal education and to the practice of law, opponents put forward a host of shifting objections. During this period, prominent medical experts opined that not just law school but all forms of higher education had the potential to destroy women's health and, ultimately, the health of the entire human race.[53] The reproductive function imposed on adolescent girls physiological demands that deprived them of the physical and mental "power" required for "the tasks of the school."[54] Managed improperly, the education of women amounted to a "slow suicide," leading to weakness, disease, madness, sterility, and death.[55] Though the catamenial function might be mysterious, its disruption in young women by educating them on the same basis as men induced a "host of ills . . . known to the physicians and the sufferers as amenorrhea, menorrhagia, dysmenorrhea, hysteria, anemia, chorea, and the like."[56] Many observers were quick to offer anecdotal evidence of the alleged lethal impacts of education on women. For example, Lemma Barkaloo, the first woman to study law at Washington University in St. Louis, died of typhoid fever before she could finish her degree. As Virginia Drachman explains, opponents of women's education attributed Barkaloo's death to "over-mental exertion."[57] Thus, whether or not women possessed the intellectual capacity for higher education—and more than one reputable commentator was convinced that, because of their smaller brains, women did not—men of science used their training to amplify well-worn cultural reasons for denying women access to colleges and universities. As a leading physician put it, women's periodical physical organization "limits her power, and reveals her divinely-appointed tasks," which were "widely different" from those of men.[58]

Just as physicians asserted that higher education "unsexed" women's bodies, other observers claimed that higher education—and especially coeducation—would have the effect of "unsexing" their personalities, temperaments, and characters. In the late nineteenth century, a majority of UVA's faculty and Board of Visitors agreed that coeducation would have a pernicious impact on young women, with devastating consequences for southern society. Put bluntly, coeducation would transform women into men. One UVA professor believed, for example, that women admitted to the University "would become familiar, boisterous, bold in manners, often rudely aggressive, and ambitiously competitive with men, thus producing, in general, a type of womanhood from which we devoutly pray to be spared."[59] Prominent faculty members openly chastised the women who sought coeducation for their willingness "to give up their delicacy and refinement, their modest, demure and bashful, blushing bearing to assume the bold and brusque manners of a less accomplished and less polished sex."[60] University officials believed that they had a solemn obligation to protect those women—as well as the University and southern civilization—from themselves. At the same time—and, presumably, as important—the presence of women students would destroy UVA's ability to "inculcate manliness and men's high ideals" in the boys for whom the University was founded. UVA's "history, its traditions, its system of government are all founded on the teaching of men and the association of men with men."[61] Women should not be permitted to evict men from valuable seats in University classes, especially when their presence on Grounds would distract their male classmates from the academic training and extracurricular activities essential to their formation as proper men.

Likewise, those who opposed legal training for women voiced a range of objections, some overlapping with, and others distinct from, the reasons why women should not be admitted to a university education at all. During his centennial remarks, Dean Lile alluded to some of the standard objections to women's education. For one thing, he feared that women law students would prove to be "a disturbing element in our peculiarly and traditional virile surroundings."[62] Lile implied that average women—whom he dismissed at "airyfairy Lillians"—lacked the intellectual talent and discipline to complete the rigorous course of law studies.[63] Lile confirmed too that he and his colleagues did not believe "the law a fit profession for the mothers of the coming generations."[64] Though he did not elaborate this last objection, Lile surely had in mind one of the most prominent explanations for why law—as opposed to other professions—was an especially ruinous occupation for women. Exposure to the courtroom's nasty cases, indecent facts, sharp practices, and combative adversaries—not to mention brutish clients—would rob women of the virtuous character that was associated with an innocent and chaste femininity. The societal implications were frightening: polluted by contact with such worldly matters, women would fall from their exalted positions—they would be thrust out of the sacred domestic sphere that they were formed to occupy—with devastating consequences for the men and children whose virtue nature had entrusted to their wives and mothers. As one state court judge proclaimed in the late nineteenth century, "To expose women to the brutal, repulsive, and obscene events of courtroom life . . . would shock men's reverence for womanhood and relax the public's sense of decency."[65] Many nineteenth-century judges just could not find it in the law—or themselves—to permit women to pursue such a destructive path. Courtrooms were, and always had been, masculine spaces where women must not be allowed to tread.

Virginia Drachman argues that the state and institutional actors who opposed women's access to the bar had another "greater concern" about the emergence of women lawyers, and it is one to which Lile glancingly referred in his centennial address. Many judges were reluctant to endorse arguments in favor of women's admission to the practice of law that could also be understood to support "the volatile issue of suffrage for women."[66] That is, in the late nineteenth century, "judges feared that admitting women to practice law would entitle them to vote."[67] In its (in)famous decision rejecting Myra C. Bradwell's application for a "license as an attorney at law," the Illinois Supreme Court relied explicitly and heavily on this line of reasoning.[68] Under the applicable Illinois attorney licensing statute, the only express requirement for admission to the bar was that the applicant obtain "a certificate from the court of some county of his good moral character," a requirement that Bradwell had satisfied.[69] Moreover, a provision of the Illinois code offered a basic canon of construction that appeared on its face to support Bradwell's substantive position: "whenever any person is referred to in the statute by words importing the masculine gender, females, as well as males, shall be deemed to be included."[70] Still, the Illinois Supreme Court reasoned that a decision in Bradwell's favor would not be "a matter of mere judicial discretion," but "an act of judicial usurpation, deserving of the gravest censure."[71] At the time that the licensing statute was enacted, the belief "that God designed the sexes to occupy different spheres of action, and that it belonged to men to make, apply and execute the laws, was regarded as an almost axiomatic truth."[72] A decision to grant Bradwell a law license "would mean that, in the opinion of this tribunal, every civil office in this State may be filled by women."[73] Crucially, such a decision also would imply that women should be granted "[a] direct participation in the affairs of government, in even the most elementary form, namely, the right of suffrage."[74] These things the court was "not yet prepared to hold."[75]

Of course, at the time that Lile offered his centennial reflections to the sons of the Law School, women had gained the right to vote. In Lile's telling, this notable development was the reason why UVA Law had allowed the three "fair Portias" to enter its masculine grounds. The Law School took this regrettable step, Lile remarked, "for the same reason that the gods gave the frogs a king—they clamored (I dare not say croaked) for it so vociferously. Voters as they now are (the women, not the frogs), their insistence and persistence—their crying aloud night and day without surcease—their strident threats of forcing their way in by the legislative door, and therefore on their own terms—convinced us that discretion was the better part of valor. We surrendered on very honorable terms, magnanimously dictated by ourselves."[76] About eighteen months later, Lile expressed optimism that the "frogs" had been appeased by the Law

School's strategic decision to admit a token number of women. In his annual report to the University president in January 1923, Lile reassured senior administrators that "there has been no addition to the list of women students in the Law School, since the entrance of these two [remaining women candidates] in 1920–1921. It appears, therefore, that the clamor for the admission of women to the Law School, so vociferous two years ago, was largely *vox et praeterea nil* [voice and nothing more]."[77] However, little did Lile know.

Coordinate versus Coeducation

In Lile's centennial reflections, listeners could detect the convergence of the movement for coeducation with the push for more stringent standards for admission to law schools and to the bar. In his remarks, Lile characterized the presence of women in the first-year law class as a thoroughly regrettable development, one in which the University and the Law School had acquiesced but which they emphatically did not celebrate.[78] Lile himself did not endorse the move, for he did not believe that law was a "fit profession" for women.[79] But he took some comfort in the fact that female applicants were required to satisfy more demanding entrance requirements than their male counterparts. "To exclude the airyfairy Lilians as a disturbing element in our peculiarly and traditionally virile surroundings," Lile reported, women could secure admission to the Law School only if they were "twenty years of age and the holder of a baccalaureate degree—or else twenty-two years of age and having completed two years of standard college work."[80] In (virtually) the next breath, but without adverting to the heightened entrance requirements for women that he had just praised, Lile asserted that the Law School had been doing a "disastrous" disservice to the (virile?) young men whom it had been admitting "fresh from the high schools," and he insisted that it was high time to cease doing so.[81] Lile lamented, "The result ha[d] been the veritable slaughter of the innocents," with many of the high school graduates flunking out at the beginning of their law school careers.[82] Thus, Lile predicted without a hint of irony or self-awareness, the Law School was likely to adopt for its intended male applicants the entrance standards "exacted by the best professional and pedagogical thought of

Stills from the University of Virginia's 1921 centennial film *Shadow of the Founder*, which featured historical reenactments of scenes from the University's first century, published in a 1922 booklet. *The Centennial of the University of Virginia*, 1922.

the country," to wit, "the requirement of a baccalaureate degree."[83] Of course, this was the same—or, rather, slightly more stringent—entrance criterion that he had just lauded for its effect in depressing the number of eligible women students by weeding out the coeds whose unserious presence would disrupt the success of the young men who were forced to study at their sides.

Over the years, numerous observers have explained that leaders at the Law School—just as Lile recounted in his parable of the frogs—agreed to admit women at the time that they did as a preemptive arrangement that would prevent the General Assembly from forcing coeducation upon the Law School or, what was considered to be far worse still, on the University as a whole.[84] Women had obtained the right to vote in 1920, and the men of the University of Virginia had reason to fear that they would exercise their political clout to secure equal access to public higher education or at least to more than the token access that individual University administrators might be persuaded or pressured to allow. Starting in the 1870s, different coalitions of progressive Virginians had argued that it was in the public interest to allow the Commonwealth's white daughters to attend colleges and universities. These groups put forward competing reasons for educating women. The earliest proponents argued "that the development of good public elementary and secondary schools in Virginia depended on good programs of higher education for Virginia's teachers, the majority of whom were women."[85] Others argued that the Commonwealth owed all women, not just those who were training to be teachers, access to the same educational resources that it offered to men. And they proposed competing programs. Virginia should allow women to be educated in existing university classrooms and facilities alongside men, or Virginia should establish separate colleges and normal schools for women that would offer them educational training coordinate to that for men.[86]

Mary Cooke-Branch Munford, a suffragette from Richmond, led the state's coordinate college league. Sparked by the rise of women high school graduates after Virginia established a statewide system for public education in 1870, the coordinate college movement formalized its legislative agenda in 1910. Munford began corresponding with UVA President Edwin Alderman, who supported the idea of a coordinate system, while rejecting proposals that called for any form of coeducation to take place on or near the University's Grounds. She wrote to President Woodrow Wilson, who attended the UVA Law School during the 1879–80 session, to ask him to endorse her cause. Starting in 1910, Munford's league took bills to the Virginia legislature during every biennial session through 1918 arguing for the establishment of a coordinate college. Sitting in the audience at these sessions, listening to Munford's movement play out in the state legislature, was Elizabeth Tompkins, a Westhampton College student with aspirations for a career in law.[87] In three of those terms, the bills passed the Virginia Senate, but not the House of Delegates. As the movement gained traction, UVA alumni increasingly spoke out against the creation of a coordinate college. In addition to their desire to preserve UVA's traditional role in educating Virginia gentlemen, alumni argued that it would be unfair to allocate state moneys to coordinate education—the available resources for the higher education of Virginians would be better spent on increasing literacy and public education in the state's rural areas.[88]

The year 1918 proved to be a breakthrough year for Munford's movement. World War I pushed the state's focus abroad, rather than on local issues. Critically that year, the College of William & Mary decided to coeducate its undergraduate school. In 1920, the passage of the Nineteenth Amendment extended suffrage to women. Now that women were able to express their views at the ballot box, holdouts to the coordinate and coeducation plans considered whether Virginia would stay ahead of the resulting changes they saw in women's access to higher education, or lag behind.[89] The coordinate college movement was quelled in the face of new energy behind a movement to admit white women to UVA's graduate schools, which passed the UVA Board of Visitors in 1920.[90] In fall 1920, the first three women enrolled in UVA's law program. Elizabeth Tompkins, who had observed the coeducation and coordinate college debates firsthand, was one. Joining Tompkins were Rose May Davis and Catherine "Kate" R. Lipop Graves (Law 1923). By the time of the University's centennial, therefore, UVA had adopted limited coeducation—the admission of women to graduate programs—in an effort to appease the Munford crowd and stall, perhaps forever, the move to throw open to women all seats at UVA.

The First Woman Law Graduate

Less than two months before Lile acknowledged in his centennial address that the Law School had admitted three women to its "sacred precincts," one of those women, Elizabeth Tompkins, wrote a letter to her father in which she proposed dropping out of UVA Law and continuing her studies at the "Richmond College night School of Law."[91] At the time,

Rose May Davis, center, one of the first three women to attend UVA Law, at her doctoral graduation from Duke University, ca. 1929. Davis was also the first woman to earn a doctoral degree from Duke. (Duke University Archives)

Tompkins had successfully completed her first year of law studies, and there was every reason to believe that she would continue to earn solid, and even excellent, marks. Yet, as she told her father, she was twenty-three years old "and a thinking individual," and she was convinced that she would be far better off in Richmond than in Charlottesville.

From all appearances, Tompkins was well positioned to make prudent assessments about where she would find professional success and personal happiness. After graduating from an all-girls high school in Richmond, Tompkins received her BA in 1919, with high honors, from Westhampton College, which also was located in Richmond. When asked many years later in an interview by Westhampton undergraduates "what attracted" her to the school, Tompkins gave two reasons: Westhampton "was good scholastically," and she "could afford it." In the end, she emphasized, "money" was "the deciding factor" in her decision to study in-state rather than to "go off" to one of the "northern colleges," such as

1919 The Tower Page 173

Elizabeth N. Tompkins
Richmond, Va.

VIRGINIA RANDOLPH ELLETT SCHOOL

Nickname: "Tommy."

Hobby: Competition with M. Laws in wearing loud hose.

Chances for Matrimony: "The more I see of men, the better I like horses."

Ambition: To be a corporation lawyer.

Chief Charm: Genuineness.

Likely to Be: A professional woman.

"*'Tis better to have bluffed and passed, than never to have passed at all*"

All great people have their peculiarities; and this Senior's peculiarity is that she is possessed of more than usual intelligence. If you don't believe this, please explain how she can carry more classes than she needs, be history assistant, business manager of the Annual, work in archives, be a bacteriologist at Medical College, and still have time to go to the movies and play cards. Also "Tommy" has demonstrated her ability to think and act quickly in an emergency, for who has not seen her "awkwardly gallop" down the hockey field in a wild attempt to rescue the ball from Fanny G. However, with her knowledge of business affairs, coupled with an indomitable determination to become a corporation lawyer of note, we predict a prosperous career for her.

Elizabeth N. Tompkins's (Law 1923) page in her undergraduate yearbook, 1919. (Boatwright Memorial Library, University of Richmond)

Bryn Mawr, for which she was "otherwise eligible." Reflecting back on that important decision, Tompkins declared that she had not "a regret in the world."[92] There are good reasons to credit that assertion. When Tompkins—whose nickname was "Tommy"—arrived at Westhampton, she made it known that her ambition was to "to be a corporation lawyer."[93] To say the least, this was a remarkable aspiration for a young woman at that time. Although higher education was beginning to open to women, the legal profession was thought to be a particularly unsuitable occupation for them. Guardians of the bar, including men who ran UVA Law School, openly derided women who wanted to join them. Not surprisingly, most of the women who sought to attend colleges and universities claimed to have their sights set not on lawyering, but on teaching or nursing. If that were not enough, the specific professional character whom Tompkins aimed to become—the "corporation lawyer"—had just begun to appear in legal circles at the beginning of the twentieth century.[94] The character would come to dominate elite legal practice, but it was a role that men were just then beginning to try on for size. From our vantage point, therefore, it is astonishing that Tompkins not only harbored an ambition to practice what she called "corporation" law, but that she used her Westhampton yearbook profile to announce the ambition to those in her circle.

Seemingly as remarkable, after she graduated from Westhampton, Tompkins moved from Richmond to New York City to attend Columbia University, where she received her MA. This move, too, must have been part of her strategy to become one of the first women admitted to study law at the University of Virginia. In an interview she gave at Westhampton in 1975, Tompkins suggested that she pursued the prestigious master's degree because it would enhance her chances of admission to UVA Law School.[95] In the interview, Tompkins mentioned that she was "intellectually alert as to what was going on" in the world around her, but she denied being interested in what her interviewer called "the feminist movement to get the Nineteenth Amendment pass[ed]." Indeed, Tompkins said, she remembered the movement for women's suffrage "not at all." By contrast, she did recall Munford's "movement to make the University of Virginia coordinate." She had followed that campaign closely, even to the point of attending "all the meetings, the committee meetings" devoted to it. In those circles, it is likely that Tompkins got wind of the Law School's decision that in 1920 it would begin admitting women who were able to satisfy restrictive admission criteria. Since she received her BA from Westhampton in 1919, she faced what we would call a "gap year." While no contemporaneous texts reveal why Tompkins decided to devote that precious year to obtaining her MA, her reflections in the Westhampton interview suggest that she decided to earn the MA less for its own sake than for its value in securing her a seat at UVA Law School. In the interview, she confessed with some chagrin that she did not remember what she "wrote her [MA] thesis on." But when asked whether she faced a "very difficult fight to be admitted" to "law school as a woman," she responded: "No, not at all. No question. You see, I have a BA from Westhampton and an MA from Columbia." Thus, despite her stated determination to avoid the financial burden of an out-of-state education, she spent a year studying at Columbia to burnish her resume, to gain a credential that exceeded those that UVA Law planned to demand from women applicants and that would guarantee her admission there.

Tompkins's 1921 letter to her father, Samuel W. Tompkins, was loving, lengthy, and candid, so candid that it's plain she never intended for it to be read by anyone but her parents. Samuel Tompkins himself had practiced law at a Richmond firm, W. D. Tompkins and Company, where his uncle was a senior partner. Like other first-year law students, including those who are enrolled at the Law School today, Tompkins must have enjoyed peppering her letter with legal terms of art, which were deployed to persuade her father to endorse the "conditions precedent" for her "well considered plans." In support of her "side of this proposition," Tompkins made a number of claims, including her estimation that the Richmond law program's reputation was "getting to be nothing to be snipped at." For one thing, the Richmond dean was "considered good by all." She also pointed to evidence that the Richmond program offered effective training that would set her up well for practicing law in Virginia. Notably, UVA Law itself employed one of the Richmond faculty members to coach its students "for the State Bar," while another Richmond law professor actually "ma[de] out the State Bar Exams, the very things [Tompkins was] turning Heaven and earth to pass." On the "vital question of expenses," she did not mince words, telling her father, "You are no young man, and a thousand dollars a year is an enormous amount to be taken out of a moderate family." If she moved back to Richmond, she was confident that she would be able to pay her own way. She would save money by boarding at "Cousin Sallie's." Then, by taking classes at night, she would be free during the day to work in a law office where she could both earn the money to pay for her tuition and gain practical knowledge that had "to be learned sooner or later."[96]

In her letter, moreover, Tompkins made it clear that she dreaded the prospect of returning to Charlottesville for her second year. When it came to the quality of her law courses at UVA and how they might compare to the offerings at Richmond, she said, "there is one excellent Law professor at this school, Mr. [Charles A.] Graves," with whom she had already enjoyed the privilege of taking "the two big subjects: Contracts and Torts." For most of the other professors she cared "not a rap either as men or as teachers," judging them to be no better than the instructors one would find "in any prep school." Even worse, one of her professors, George B. Eager, was an "old devil," and she confided in her father that she felt "this helpless, hopeless feeling at the mention of any classes he

Law professor Charles A. Graves teaching in Minor Hall, staged for *Shadow of the Founder,* a film celebrating UVA's centennial, spring 1921. (Albert and Shirley Small Special Collections Library, University of Virginia)

teaches." Since she had studied harder for Eager's class than for any others, she had "no regrets and no reproaches to make upon" herself, but she felt on his exams that she was "butting up on this invisible wall, which is as inevitable as the Rock of Gibraltar."[97] Clearly, she believed that her classroom experiences at Richmond would be no worse, and might be far better, than what she could expect if she were to tough it out for two more years at UVA.

But it was about her male classmates that Tompkins had the harshest things to say. These portions of her letter are especially vivid, and for Tompkins's professional descendants, they describe experiences that are painful to contemplate and to remember. The passages are angry, a tone that is striking, coming as it does from an author who fully appreciated the magnitude of what she would achieve were she to be "the first woman" to graduate from UVA Law School. Moreover, Tompkins's regret—and, presumably, her frustration and disappointment—at the thought of forgoing that honor was compounded by the knowledge that she also would be thwarting the expectations of her father, whose own "dream" had been to study at UVA Law. "For that reason above all else," Tompkins told her father, "I would adore to be able to turn over to you my LLB, the first one given to a woman from the University of Virginia Law School." Yet, Tompkins included in her letter depictions of Virginia Law men that are so disagreeable that one wonders whether she believed that her father might conclude that it was going to be too personally costly for her to secure "the honor of being the first woman" along with "the pleasure" it would give to him.[98]

Early in the letter, she acknowledged that she felt isolated at UVA Law, and she identified some of the ways that her solitude made it difficult for her to thrive academically. Her description conveys, too, how lonely she must have felt in the Law School, all but cut off from the companionship she had enjoyed in her all-women's high school and all-women's undergraduate college. The passage highlights the value of student-on-student interactions and conversations in the legal educational experience, not to mention the importance of kind friendships to the individual student's personal happiness and flourishing. In this portion of the letter, Tompkins reassured her father that, while she hoped that he would bless her plan, she would follow his advice if he counseled her to remain in

Exterior of Minor Hall in 1921, home of the Law School from 1911 to 1932, with students walking to classes. (Albert and Shirley Small Special Collections Library, University of Virginia)

Charlottesville. She wrote, "If you can show better views and arguments on your side for returning here next winter, then I am perfectly willing. I don't care personally a straw for I have learned to get along without the girls, and this mob of men are so many ants in a hill. But the way I feel is this, I have been here nearly a year now, and outside of class I have never heard a word of Law discussed or mentioned. There has been and there is no one to argue with when I leave class at noon. I have no Law afterwards. I can only dig it by reading and understanding only probably one half at that. The boys at practically every fraternity have a roundtable and discuss Law every night for an hour. Of that, I know nothing."[99]

Tompkins's experience of isolation was a common one among "the first generation of women in America to attend law school."[100] These pioneers were transforming women's place in society, but to do so they had to "give up the comforts of female friendship and to interact in a community without women."[101] Still, there were other women—Lelia Robinson included—who reported having far more positive experiences when they integrated law programs. Though Robinson was "the only woman among 150 male classmates" at Boston University Law School in 1881, she appears to have recalled her law school days fondly, even going so far as to say that "'I was not permitted to realize or remember the fact that I was the only woman in a large school of men. I was simply a student like the rest.'"[102] In later years, Tompkins too had somewhat kinder things to say about the men among whom she studied law. Still her praise was less than effusive. As she put it in an interview with the *Virginia Law Weekly* in 1980, "It took them one semester to find out that I was not after a husband and another semester to find out that I could do the work. After that everything was fine."[103]

In a passage in the penultimate paragraph of her 1921 letter to her father, Tompkins's tone is darker still. Again, she went out of her way to emphasize that she understood the significance of her quest to be "the first woman," but she explained: "I am writing you all this because I worry so over it all that I am not capable of judging fairly as a disinterested party, and perhaps you can. Consider it from all sides, and let's see what is best to be done. Again, I want you to know that personally it makes no difference to me where I am. In eight months, I think I have gained the respect of the boys, or as many of them as are gentlemen. They are beginning to know that I am not after them, and that they have nothing that I want; and they pay me no mind; and I don't notice them. In fact, if they did but know it, this mob of crawling humanity has destroyed any liking I might have once had for men, and they are now more repulsive than snakes that crawl in the grass. This town is just what my idea of H___ will be, and they are the devil in men's clothing." As in the prior passage, Tompkins insisted that it made no difference to her "personally" where she completed her law studies.[104] If ever there were an example of "protesting too much," this passage would seem to fit the bill perfectly. The rhetoric that Tompkins employed, describing her male peers as ants, snakes, and devils, referring to the hell that was her life in Charlottesville—all of these verbal gestures belie her claim that she would not care—and care deeply—if her father advised her that she should remain at UVA.

Presumably, Dean Lile would have professed to be surprised by Tompkins's negative assessment of her male classmates' demeanor and behavior. Likewise, it's fair to suppose that he would have been disconcerted to learn that in a letter she wrote to her parents in 1923 she referred to him as "that ugly old scoundrel."[105] In his annual report to UVA's president in 1921, Lile declared that the admission of women was the "most important change in the organization of the Law School" in its history.[106] Once again, however, his tone was tongue-in-cheek as he referred to the "radical departure from the traditional policies of the University" that brought "these new and strange beings" to Grounds.[107] He even went so far as to identify the three women law students by their names—Rose May Davis, Elizabeth Tompkins, and Kate Lipop—on the ground that "perhaps they are entitled to be immortalized by naming them in this report."[108] Lile reassured President Alderman that "there has been no perceptible protest against the presence of these three on the part of the male students—and I hope and believe that the experience of these three young women in our midst has not been for them a trying or unhappy one. I made occasion, at the very beginning, to appeal in their behalf to the chivalry of the young gentlemen of the several classes, and the response has been all that could be desired."[109] Although Tompkins did not describe the precise behaviors committed by her "repulsive" classmates, Fanny Graves Crenshaw, who was one of Tompkins's professors at Westhampton, offered this observation during an interview on her notable students: "We had Elizabeth Tompkins, who was the first girl in the law school at the University of Virginia, and she was the kind of person who suffered because the boys just tortured them. I think that there was one other girl. All of the law students would be on the front steps when they arrived, and they applauded them. If they were called on in class, they applauded them. They did everything they could to worry them."[110] That description leaves readers to worry: What would the Virginia men have done to their women classmates had Lile not appealed to their chivalry? What was his tone when making that appeal, and how did that tone condition its content? How could the dean of the Law School not know exactly what his "sons" were up to on the "front steps" of his school and in its classrooms? Surely, he did know, and it may well be that the men's "repulsive," even cruel, behavior was all that he did expect, if not desire, from them.

We have no record of what Samuel Tompkins advised his daughter to do upon hearing that she proposed leaving her seat at UVA to complete her law studies in Richmond. In the end, Elizabeth Tompkins remained in Charlottesville, and her male classmates neither worried nor tortured her into dropping out of UVA. In the photograph of the class of 1923, of

UVA Law Class of 1923 outside of Minor Hall. Elizabeth N. Tompkins stands in the front row of students, behind Professor Charles A. Graves. (Arthur J. Morris Law Library Special Collections, University of Virginia)

which she was a member, she occupies a prominent position—her expression all but inscrutable—standing in the middle of the second row, directly behind the all-male faculty and surrounded by that mob of male classmates. Of that class, Dean Lile said in his diary, "We had 71 graduates of the Law School this session, made up of an unusually fine body of *men,* with one exception—that of our first *woman* graduate. The exception applies to her sex and not to her capacity, for she is an unusually capable person and stood near the very top of her class."[111] Despite her high class ranking and Lile's evident admiration for her, Tompkins at first had trouble securing employment. After graduation, she clerked for two years in the Charlottesville law office of Duke, Duke & Gentry, but, in December 1924, she wrote to Lile, imploring him to help her find new employment in a law office.[112] In a later diary entry, Lile would mention with pride—and no little weariness—his diligent efforts to give "advice and comfort" to the "deserving but often desperate" graduate who "is deeply disturbed as to what is to happen to him when the thrill of graduating is over, and he finds himself facing the real world instead of the artificial one in which he has spent his college life." Most of these "youngsters" sought "letters of testimonial" from their dean, and he made it "a rule never to deny a proper testimonial to a student who deserves it, and never to give one to a student who does not."[113] In his letter responding to Tompkins's plea for help in getting placed, Lile said only that he knew "of no opening in a law office which you could hope to secure at this time." As for why her cause was likely to be hopeless, Lile did not suggest that she was incompetent or undeserving. Nor did he suggest that her law school experience had artificially blinded her to the exigencies the real world would impose on her. Rather, he expressed his "fear that the ancient prejudice against women as legal practitioners is going to make it difficult for you to secure a desirable office position except with some friend who knows and appreciates your qualities and qualifications." But he made no offer to help her overcome that prejudice by interceding on her behalf with his friends and acquaintances in the bar. Instead, he recommended that she "be bold enough to go to Richmond and open a law office on your 'own hook.' You would, of course be handicapped on account of your sex and the before mentioned prejudice, and business might be slow in coming, but I believe that in the long run you could make an eminent success out of the experiment."[114]

Tompkins ultimately did practice in a law office. The first woman to graduate from UVA Law School, Tompkins eventually went into private practice in Richmond, and she served in a number of public service positions as well, including as the commissioner of accounts for Hanover County, commissioner in chancery for circuit courts in Hanover and Richmond, and in various leadership roles at the University of Richmond.[115] She remained in close contact with her female professors and mentors at Westhampton College, taking no little satisfaction in the legal support she was able to give to them and their families over the years.[116] Tompkins practiced law until the age of eighty-one, and when she died two years later, she had fulfilled two of her undergraduate yearbook's predictions. Her classmates had declared her "Likely to Be: A professional woman." As for what her "Chances for Matrimony" might be, her classmates offered a quote from Tompkins herself, saying "The more I see of men, the better I like horses."[117] Elizabeth Tompkins was eminently a professional woman: she worked as a lawyer for more than half a century, and she never married.

Notes

1. John Calvin Metcalf, ed., *The Centennial of the University of Virginia, 1819–1921: The Proceedings of the Centenary Celebration, May 31 to June 3, 1921* (New York: G. P. Putnam's Sons, 1922), 149 (hereafter cited as *Centennial Proceedings*).
2. See Laura F. Edwards, "Coverture and Virginia Law Professors: The Nineteenth Century," in this volume.
3. *Centennial Proceedings*, 149; see, e.g., William Minor Lile, *The Diary of a Dean: Excerpts from the Private Journal of William Minor Lile*, ed. Kristen H. Jensen and Taylor Fitchett (Charlottesville: University of Virginia Law Library, 2011), 67. Centennial guests included women relatives of alumni, former professors, and visiting dignitaries.
4. *Centennial Proceedings*, 150.
5. *Centennial Proceedings*, 149, 150, 152. In one of his diary entries, Lile estimated that "some 1,500 or more alumni returned for the occasion." See Lile, *Diary of a Dean*, 67.
6. *Centennial Proceedings*, 149, 150.
7. *Centennial Proceedings*, 150.
8. Arthur J. Morris Law Library Special Collections, University of Virginia (hereafter cited as LLSC), *100 Years of Coeducation at UVA Law* (unpublished booklet, 2022), 9, https://issuu.com/uvalawschool/docs/2020_centennial_brochure_v9.
9. *Centennial Proceedings*, 150.
10. See Noah Webster, *Webster's New International Dictionary of the English Language: With a Reference History of the World: Based on the International Dictionary of 1890 and 1900*, ed. William Torey Harris and F. Sturges Allen (New York: G. & C. Merriman, 1920), 784. Certainly, Shakespeare had both meanings in mind when he described the attributes of his "fair Portia," one of the protagonists of *The Merchant of Venice*.
11. *Centennial Proceedings*, 51–52.
12. *Centennial Proceedings*, vii, 57.
13. *Centennial Proceedings*, 52.
14. *Centennial Proceedings*.
15. *Centennial Proceedings*.
16. See Charles R. McManis, "The History of First Century American Legal Education: A Revisionist Perspective," *Washington University Law Quarterly* 59, no. 3 (1981): 597–659.
17. *Centennial Proceedings*, 158. See McManis, "The History of First Century American Legal Education," 598–99, 631–37, on Langdell and the impact of his method on legal education.
18. *Centennial Proceedings*, 157–58.
19. *Centennial Proceedings*, 158.
20. *Centennial Proceedings*.
21. *Centennial Proceedings*, 158–59.
22. *Centennial Proceedings*.

23. *Centennial Proceedings*, 156.
24. *Centennial Proceedings*, 159. For the eventual adoption of the case method at UVA Law, see G. Edward White, "Poised between a Regional and a National Law School, 1920–1960," in this volume.
25. *Centennial Proceedings*, 156.
26. Virginia G. Drachman, *Sisters in Law: Women Lawyers in Modern American History* (Cambridge, MA: Harvard University Press, 1998), 42.
27. As Justice Ruth Bader Ginsburg noted in her opinion for the court in United States v. Virginia, 518 U.S. 515 (1996), in the eighteenth century Dr. Edward H. Clarke of Harvard Medical School was the most influential physician who opined on the dangers of higher education for women, 536n9.
28. *Centennial Proceedings*, 156, 52.
29. *Centennial Proceedings*, 152.
30. *Centennial Proceedings*, 152–53. On Jefferson's plan for and the early history of UVA Law School, see David T. Konig, "Jeffersonian Foundations of Legal Education in Virginia, 1779–1845," in this volume.
31. See McManis, "History of First Century American Legal Education," 618n133.
32. See William P. LaPiana, *Logic and Experience: The Origin of Modern American Legal Education* (New York: Oxford University Press, 1994), 49.
33. See Robert Stevens, *Law School: Legal Education in America from the 1850s to the 1980s* (Chapel Hill: University of North Carolina Press, 1983), 73–91.
34. *Centennial Proceedings*, 156.
35. Stevens, *Law School*, 23.
36. *Centennial Proceedings*, 155.
37. Stevens, *Law School*, 24.
38. See Peggy Cooper Davis and Elizabeth Ehrenfest Steinglass, "A Dialogue about Socratic Teaching," *New York University Review of Law & Social Change* 23, no. 2 (1997): 261; William Epstein, "The Classical Tradition of Dialectics and American Legal Education," *Journal of Legal Education* 31, no. 3–5 (1982): 399.
39. See Brainerd Currie, "The Materials of Law Study," *Journal of Legal Education* 3, no. 3 (Spring 1951): 331, 368–72.
40. *Centennial Proceedings*, 157 (some internal quotation marks omitted).
41. Stevens, *Law School*, 10.
42. Lelia J. Robinson, "Women Lawyers in the United States," *Green Bag* 2, no. 1 (January 1890): 10.
43. Robinson, "Women Lawyers in the United States."
44. Robinson, "Women Lawyers in the United States," 10–11.
45. Robinson, "Women Lawyers in the United States," 11.
46. Robinson, "Women Lawyers in the United States," 10.
47. Drachman, *Sisters in Law*, 37.
48. Robinson, "Women Lawyers in the United States," 11–12.
49. Robinson, "Women Lawyers in the United States," 12.
50. Robinson, "Women Lawyers in the United States."
51. Robinson, "Women Lawyers in the United States," 27.
52. In re Lockwood, 154 U.S. 116, 118 (1894).
53. One of the leading texts of the day on the physiological dangers of education for women was Edward H. Clarke, *Sex in Education, or, a Fair Chance for the Girls* (Boston, MA: James R. Osgood, 1873).

54. Clarke, *Sex in Education*, 54.
55. Clarke, *Sex in Education*, 64.
56. Clarke, *Sex in Education*, 48.
57. Drachman, *Sisters in Law*, 38n5. According to Robinson, though Barkaloo did not receive her law degree, "she was admitted to the bar of the Supreme Court of Missouri in March, 1870," and she "was the first woman in this country to try a case in court." See Robinson, "Women Lawyers," 13. Presumably, Barkaloo took and passed the Missouri bar exam after completing less than the full roster of law courses at Washington University.
58. Clarke, *Sex in Education*, 13.
59. Mary E. Whitney and Rebecca S. Wilburn, *Women and the University* (Charlottesville: University Press of Virginia, 1969), 31 (quoting UVA Professor Noah F. Davis).
60. Whitney and Wilburn, *Women and the University*, 31–32.
61. Whitney and Wilburn, *Women and the University*, 59.
62. *Centennial Proceedings*, 156.
63. *Centennial Proceedings*.
64. *Centennial Proceedings*.
65. In re Goodell, 39 Wis. 232 (1875).
66. Drachman, *Sisters in Law*, 22.
67. Drachman, *Sisters in Law*, 21.
68. In re Bradwell, 55 Ill. 535 (1869).
69. In re Bradwell, 55 Ill. 535 (1869) at 538.
70. In re Bradwell, 55 Ill. 535 (1869) at 541.
71. In re Bradwell, 55 Ill. 535 (1869).
72. In re Bradwell, 55 Ill. 535 (1869) at 539.
73. In re Bradwell, 55 Ill. 535 (1869) at 540.
74. In re Bradwell, 55 Ill. 535 (1869) at 539.
75. In re Bradwell, 55 Ill. 535 (1869) at 540.
76. *Centennial Proceedings*, 156.
77. Dean's Annual Report, 1 January 1923, Deans' Papers, RG–32-100-78, LLSC.
78. *Centennial Proceedings*, 156.
79. *Centennial Proceedings*.
80. *Centennial Proceedings*.
81. *Centennial Proceedings*, 157.
82. *Centennial Proceedings*.
83. *Centennial Proceedings*, 156.
84. Phyllis Leffler, "Mr. Jefferson's University: Women in the Village!," *Virginia Magazine of History and Biography* 115, no. 1 (2007): 56–107.
85. Whitney and Wilburn, *Women and the University*, 6.
86. Whitney and Wilburn, *Women and the University*, 9.
87. Elizabeth Nelson Tompkins, interview by Suzanne Ivey and Jacqueline Lassiter Wilkins, 25 March 1975, interview transcript, Westhampton College Oral Histories, University of Richmond Libraries' Digital Collections, https://richmond.access.preservica.com/uncategorized/SO_d04f313f-c5a5-4216-8091-bb6b12a25584/.
88. For Munford and the coordinate college movement, including support from Alderman and Wilson, see Walter Russell Bowie, *Sunrise in the South: The Life of Mary-Cooke Branch Munford* (Richmond, VA: William Byrd Press, 1942), 102–22, 127–43. See also Anne Hobson Freeman, "Mary Munford's Fight for a College for Women

Co-ordinate with the University of Virginia," *Virginia Magazine of History and Biography* 78, no. 4 (October 1970): 481–91.

89. Bowie, *Sunrise in the South,* 143–44.
90. University of Virginia Board of Visitor Minute Books, 1829–1956, 12 January 1920, vol. 9 1915–1928, RG–1/1/1.382, Albert and Shirley Small Special Collections Library, University of Virginia.
91. Elizabeth Nelson Tompkins to Samuel W. Tompkins, 22 April 1921, Inventory of the Papers of Elizabeth N. Tompkins, MSS-97-4, LLSC.
92. Tompkins, interview by Ivey and Wilkins.
93. Westhampton College, *The Tower, 1919,* University of Richmond Libraries' Digital Collections, https://richmond.access.preservica.com/uncategorized/SO_e9660e3e-fa38-46b2-a274-f85e21be40f7/.
94. Jerold S. Auerbach, *Unequal Justice: Lawyers and Social Change in Modern America* (New York: Oxford University Press, 1976), 34–36.; Westhampton College, *The Tower, 1919.*
95. Tompkins interview by Ivey and Wilkins.
96. Tompkins to Samuel W. Tompkins, 22 April 1921.
97. Tompkins to Samuel W. Tompkins, 22 April 1921.
98. Tompkins to Samuel W. Tompkins, 22 April 1921.
99. Tompkins to Samuel W. Tompkins, 22 April 1921.
100. Drachman, *Sisters in Law,* 50.
101. Drachman, *Sisters in Law.*
102. Drachman, *Sisters in Law,* 53–54.
103. Jane Roush, "Early Women Law Graduates Recall Study in Male World," *Virginia Law Weekly,* 11 April 1980.
104. Tompkins to Samuel W. Tompkins, 22 April 1921.
105. Tompkins to Samuel W. and Sarah N. Tompkins, 18 February 1923, LLSC.
106. Dean's Annual Report, 1 January 1921, LLSC.
107. Dean's Annual Report, 1 January 1921.
108. Dean's Annual Report, 1 January 1921.
109. Dean's Annual Report, 1 January 1921.
110. Fanny G. Crenshaw, interview by Jacqueline Lassiter Wilkins and Suzanne Ivey, March 1973, transcript, Westhampton College Oral Histories, University of Richmond Libraries' Digital Collections, https://richmond.access.preservica.com/uncategorized/SO_8c2c5c68-a717-485e-b523-cef93c258a1d/.
111. Lile, *Diary of a Dean,* 70–72.
112. Roush, "Early Women Law Graduates Recall Study in Male World"; William Minor Lile to Tompkins, 4 December 1924, LLSC.
113. Lile, *Diary of a Dean,* 115.
114. Lile to Tompkins, 4 December 1924.
115. "Tompkins," *Richmond Times-Dispatch,* 28 June 1981.
116. Tompkins, interview by Ivey and Wilkins.
117. Westhampton College, *The Tower, 1919.*

Poised between a Regional and a National Law School, 1920–1960

G. Edward White

FROM UVA LAW'S first years, faculty and administrators believed that the school's preeminence in the American South gave it a place of prominence nationally. Not until the 1960s, nearly 140 years after its founding, did the school's distinctively "southern" and "Virginian" atmosphere seem irreparably at odds with its aspirations to national prominence in the minds of Law School leadership. In the four decades after 1920, the Law School acknowledged modernizing trends in the national landscape of legal education but did not rush to adopt them. The Law School was slow to hire faculty members who were not its own graduates or residents of southern states and slow to expand the number of non-southern applicants it admitted to the student body. It was even slow to embrace the case method of teaching and to require a college degree as a prerequisite for admission. That reluctance to shed its regional character was quite self-conscious: leaders of the school believed that its reputation as the leading law school in the South and its national visibility were closely connected.[1]

At the 1921 Centennial Celebration of the University of Virginia, Dean William Minor Lile (Law 1882), who had been teaching at the UVA School of Law since 1893 and serving as its first dean since 1904, devoted a portion of his remarks to the state of the Law School and to a defense of "the old fashioned text-book and lecture system" of teaching employed at UVA

Law. Lile noted that "most of the other law schools of the country" were now "thoroughly wedded to the so-called Case System," so that Virginia "[found] ourselves almost in a class by ourselves," and "[were] thought of, and not infrequently referred to by our contemporaries, as old-fogyish, and out of date." Nonetheless, Lile pointed out, Virginia "[had] held to our own methods—not from ignorance of the virtues of the other system, but from deliberate choice."[2]

Lile went on to make a brief defense of UVA Law's approach, which he described as a combination of the use of lectures and textbooks in classes supplemented by cases. Lile believed the case method did not give students sufficient familiarity with "a knowledge of fundamental legal principles." He thought it was important that law students learn those rules, "just as [they] must learn and remember the letters of the alphabet or the rules of Latin syntax."[3]

Although Lile conceded that "the reasoning qualities of our graduates" were "possibly not quite so highly . . . developed . . . as under the other system," he felt that an exclusive emphasis on the analysis of particular cases left gaps in students' knowledge. The case method used appellate opinions on legal subjects and intensive analysis of those opinions in classes, with the instructor acting as "the leader and interlocutor . . . of a sort of debating society."[4] Faculty such as Lile at UVA Law, however, continued to subject their students to daily oral tests and periodic written examinations in which students were asked to regurgitate rules, practices that went back to the first years of the Law School. The result was, Lile thought, that "our men go out into the profession not only with excellent reasoning powers, but fully equipped with a knowledge of fundamental legal principles."[5]

At the University's one hundredth birthday, the case method of instruction had become prevalent in American legal education. Credited to Harvard Law professor Christopher Columbus Langdell, who became dean of that institution in 1870, the case method had spread by the early twentieth century to Columbia, the University of Chicago, Northwestern, the University of Pennsylvania, and eventually Yale. In Langdell's version, students were taught to extract fundamental legal principles from cases he selected for his casebooks. But in the hands of more deft instructors, such as legal educators James Barr Ames and William A. Keener at

Law School dean William Minor Lile teaching in Minor Hall, spring 1921, in a still from UVA's centennial film, *Shadow of the Founder.* (Albert and Shirley Small Special Collections Library, University of Virginia)

Harvard, a Socratic style of exchange in classes became predominant. Ames, Keener, and others encouraged students to concentrate less on memorizing legal rules than in advancing arguments for one or another doctrinal positions.[6] Lile was signaling in his 1921 address that he, and the Law School, were unconvinced of the value of Socratic instruction.

That same year, Armistead M. Dobie, who had first joined the UVA Law faculty in 1907 after earning his LLB from the Law School in 1904, was taking leave to pursue an SJD (doctor of juridical science) degree at Harvard Law.[7] Dobie returned to the UVA Law School in 1922 an enthusiast for the case method. In 1931, Lile reported to University president Edwin A. Alderman that Dobie was utilizing casebooks in nearly all his courses—Sales, Code Pleading, Wills, Federal Procedure, and Legal History. Only in the last course did Dobie rely on what Lile called a "quasi-text book."[8] Lile recognized Dobie as a capable teacher and scholar and predicted accurately in 1924 that Dobie eventually would succeed him as dean. But he did not care personally for Dobie. In a journal entry he described Dobie as having an "objectionable personality—pompous, noisy, opinionated, and out of sympathy with our methods." Dobie's experience in visiting and studying at Harvard had "led him to ape Harvard methods and policies." Dobie also lacked, Lile believed, "sympathy for our traditional methods required for the executive head of this Law School."[9]

Lile retained his affection for the traditional approach to instruction, but as the Law School faculty expanded in the 1930s, most of his colleagues adopted the use of casebooks and some version of Socratic teaching. In the same 1931 report, Lile signaled that the older ways of teaching law were fading away. Younger faculty were ushering in a new era of legal pedagogy at UVA Law. As retiring dean, Lile assured Alderman that although he lamented this change, he would not stand in the way: "If, however, my younger colleagues believe, as they seem to believe, the newer and more popular system desirable, and their work as teachers of better quality than under former methods, I am not disposed to enter an official protest."[10] Of the seven faculty at the Law School, five were teaching exclusively from casebooks or taught casebooks with "parallel readings." Even Lile did not eschew casebooks altogether. In his courses—Legal Bibliography, Equity Procedure, and Negotiable Paper—he employed "text—largely his own." In two classes, Equity Jurisprudence and

Clark Hall, home of the Law School from 1932 to 1974, ca. 1940. (Arthur J. Morris Law Library Special Collections, University of Virginia)

Legal Ethics, he utilized a "combination."[11] By the mid-1930s, UVA Law faculty had overwhelmingly adopted the case method, and courses featured "oral discussion in the class-room of cases contained in standard case-books."[12]

When Dobie succeeded Lile as dean in 1932, UVA Law was beginning to respond to modernizing trends in the legal academy and profession. A little more than a decade before, in 1920, the Law School and other professional schools at UVA had conceded to admitting white women, after the passage of the Nineteenth Amendment and growing demands from the coordinate college movement.[13] In so doing, it was following in the footsteps of top-tier law schools such as Pennsylvania (1881) and Yale (1918).[14] As law schools dramatically expanded over the course of the mid-twentieth century, UVA Law continued to cater primarily to Virginians and residents of other southern states in the composition of its faculty and student body, while simultaneously seeking greater visibility as a national law school.

Poised between Region and Nation

While UVA Law balanced the dual pressures of attempting to maintain its established role as the leading southern law school and seeking to increase its national visibility, American legal education was undergoing a transformation. In the decades between 1920 and 1960, several factors served to alter the character of the American legal academy. The first was the disappearance of proprietary law schools, which had functioned in the nineteenth century as alternatives to schools affiliated with universities. Those schools were commonly established by local practitioners who gave the lectures, sometimes hiring additional faculty to supplement the process.[15] As American universities emerged and expanded in the late nineteenth and early twentieth centuries, adding undergraduate and graduate programs in the arts and sciences, they found it economically desirable to establish law schools. The case method made large faculty-student ratios possible, enabling law schools to amass higher tuition revenues without having to add many faculty members.[16] Universities concluded that merging with proprietary law schools would be financially advantageous. The result was that in many cities in which proprietary law schools had been established, a university in that city would seek to merge with the proprietary school.[17]

The folding in of law schools under the umbrella of universities proved so attractive financially that virtually all state universities that came into existence in the nineteenth century established law schools late in that century or early in the twentieth. The result was that the legal academy significantly expanded during those years. As a consequence, American law schools, traditionally regarded as undergraduate institutions, became post-undergraduate institutions as they added college attendance requirements as criteria for admission.[18] UVA Law bucked this trend. By the late 1930s, the school was nearly unique among law schools of comparable visibility in not insisting that its applicants had graduated from college.[19] In 1947, representatives from the Columbia, Harvard, and Yale faculties proposed developing a test to aid law schools in their admissions processes. This test would become the Law School Admission Test (LSAT).[20] UVA Law professor Emerson G. Spies was on the committee that helped develop the LSAT, which the Law School began requiring for applicants in 1948.[21] The LSAT was slow to be widely adopted, but by the 1960s was used by most law schools that aspired to national visibility.[22]

Additionally, the emergence and expansion of law schools as post-undergraduate institutions led to a marked stratification of the American legal academy. As more law schools emerged and the American Bar Association (ABA) accreditation process became more ubiquitous, a hierarchy of schools developed. At the bottom of that hierarchy were schools that had not received accreditation, which tended to be based on the number of faculty, faculty-student ratios, the quality of the school's library, and bar qualification rates. In the 1930s and 1940s, many law schools in the South were not accredited. That number diminished in the 1950s but still accounted for about 40 percent of schools in the region.[23]

The next rung on the hierarchy was occupied by schools that were considered "local," both in the composition of their student body and faculty and in their curricular emphasis. Such schools tended to feature courses on state law and procedure, and their graduates overwhelmingly practiced in the cities and states where they were located. Faculty in such schools tended to have heavy teaching loads and produce minimal scholarship, and many faculty members continued to practice law in addition to their teaching.[24]

The next rung included many state law schools. Although those schools encouraged their faculty to produce scholarship and offered courses with a "national" as well as a local emphasis, their student bodies were typically drawn from persons who lived in the requisite states and anticipated practicing there after graduation. The finances of such schools were heavily dependent on their tuition revenues, although they received some support from the states in which they were located. By the 1950s, many state law schools had ambitions of developing national reputations: they sought to create incentives for faculty to forego practicing law or consulting in order to concentrate on scholarship. In the 1950s, it became relatively common for faculty who had begun their careers at state schools to move to higher-prestige institutions, most of them in the private sector, if their scholarship became well regarded.[25]

At the top of the status hierarchy in the 1950s was a group of law schools, virtually all of them private institutions, which had in common an affiliation with a high-prestige university, a competitive admissions process, the successful placement of their graduates with law firms in diverse cities, the regular production of scholarship by their faculties, and in many cases ample endowments. Private institutions such as Harvard, Yale, and Columbia led the way in their fundraising and were thus able to pay high salaries to faculty and to compete with other schools to retain visible scholars. Although some state law schools, such as the University of California at Berkeley, Michigan, and Virginia, were commonly regarded as being in the top tier of American law schools by the 1950s, state schools were disadvantaged with respect to their fundraising, needing to rely on support from state legislatures, which was not invariably generous, and lacking well-established private endowments.[26] UVA Law's eventual rise to national stature was not immediate; there were local interests at play and institutional barriers to overcome. Nationalization was an intentional choice—one that would take balancing state interests with the aspirations of faculty and administrators who desired to see the school take its place among peer elite institutions in the South and North.

Regional Identity

The Law School that Lile shepherded in the 1920s was discernibly a regional institution, servicing primarily Virginia. Its eleven faculty members during this period, including Lile, were all from the American South, save Leslie H. Buckler, who was from England. Eight of them held law degrees from UVA. Six were from Virginia.[27] Lile needed no convincing about the "southern" identity of UVA Law and the connection of that identity to leadership in the region. In his 1921 dean's report, Lile had referred to "several Southern Law Schools" that "are considerably ahead of us in the matter of entrance requirements." Lile desired for the school to "lead and not follow."[28] He also described Duke and the University of North Carolina (UNC), two schools with ambitious admissions policies, as "menaces to our supremacy."[29]

UVA Law was in fact one of the most prominent law schools in the South and among the few with national aspirations. A 1938 article concluded that until 1913, "with the exception of the University of Virginia, there was no law school in the South that had been generally recognized as a first class law school."[30] In 1923, the ABA had begun the process of accrediting law schools, and eight schools in the South received accreditation: Virginia, UNC Chapel Hill, Emory, Texas, George Washington, Washington & Lee, Oklahoma, and West Virginia.[31] As other law schools emerged in southern states, Virginia needed, its administrators felt, to redouble its efforts to attract students from other southern states, lest its reputation degenerate to "local" status.[32]

The attractiveness of UVA Law to state residents and southern students was obvious in its enrollment statistics. Of the 296 students who enrolled in the Law School for the 1920–21 academic year, 179 were Virginians and 87 were from other southern states, meaning that only 29 came from states outside the South (one additional student was from Puerto Rico). Three of those students were women. By 1932, when Dobie succeeded Lile as dean, the composition of faculty and students had not significantly altered. Of the seven faculty members, five held law degrees from UVA—Dobie, Hardy C. Dillard (Law 1927), George B. Eager Jr. (Law 1910), Charles P. Nash (Law 1925), and Frederick D. G. Ribble (Law 1921). The other two faculty members, Buckler and Garrard Glenn, held law degrees from Maryland and Columbia, respectively.[33] The composition of the student body had changed somewhat. In the 1931–32 academic year, 257 students enrolled: 136 from Virginia, 61 from other southern states, and 58 from non-southern states (two additional students were considered international at the time). Only one—Marion Boyd Crockett Watson (Law 1932)—was a woman. At the onset of Dobie's deanship in 1932, enrollment was essentially identical to the prior year.[34]

As the decade of the 1920s opened, UVA Law seemed slightly out of touch with the trends in schools aspiring toward "national" reputations. Certain private law schools in this period, each of them affiliated with prestigious universities, made a determined effort to establish themselves as "national" institutions, drawing faculty and students from all regions and demonstrating their high academic standards and consequent prestige within the legal profession. Examples were Harvard, Yale, Columbia, Pennsylvania, Chicago, and Northwestern. All featured demanding admissions standards, sequenced curricula, rigorous examinations in courses, class rankings based on grades, and the cultivation of relationships between themselves and law firms in urban centers, all of which helped shift legal education to a post-undergraduate pursuit. These schools also adopted the case method and subsidized the production of scholarship by faculty. All had student-edited law journals that served as outlets for faculty publications and opportunities for their members to engage in the assessment and editing of scholarship. Membership in those journals was based on high grades and class rankings and was regarded as a credential for entrance into the legal profession.[35]

At the opening of the 1920s, alternatively, UVA Law could hardly have been called a post-undergraduate institution. More in line with legal instruction at American colleges and universities in the nineteenth century, attending law school at UVA was comparable to choosing a major. As of fall 1920, male students could be admitted to the Law School if they were eighteen years of age, had a certificate of good character, and had completed four years of high school (or the equivalent) as well as one year of college.[36] In 1922, a minimum of two years of college was required. Later, certain undergraduate course offerings were treated as prerequisites for admission.[37] It was not until 1939 that the Law School mandated at least three years of college attendance.[38]

Origins of UVA Law students by enrollment, 1919–1961

YEAR	VIRGINIA	OTHER SOUTHERN STATES	NON-SOUTHERN U.S. STATES	INTERNATIONAL	TOTAL
1919–1920	N/A	N/A	N/A	N/A	N/A
1920–1921	179	87	29	1 (Puerto Rico)	296
1921–1922	182	92	35	1 (Puerto Rico)	310
1922–1923	143	77	25	1 (Puerto Rico)	246
1923–1924	120	84	28	1	233
1924–1925	114	87	25	1	227
1925–1926	142	95	25	0	262
1926–1927	137	87	34	3	261
1927–1928	140	76	49	4 (2 Puerto Rico)	269
1928–1929	139	95	50	4 (3 Puerto Rico)	288
1929–1930	164	98	49	3 (2 Puerto Rico, 1 Hawaii)	314
1930–1931	146	90	53	2 (1 Puerto Rico, 1 Hawaii)	290
1931–1932	136	61	58	2 (1 Canal Zone, 1 Hawaii)	257
1932–1933	130	65	62	0	257
1933–1934	147	61	57	1 (Puerto Rico)	266
1934–1935	159	66	78	0	303
1935–1936	174	71	77	3 (2 Puerto Rico)	325
1936–1937	171	77	88	2 (1 Puerto Rico)	338
1937–1938	171	87	107	2 (1 Puerto Rico)	367
1938–1939	162	101	128	4 (Puerto Rico)	395
1939–1940	139	101	147	4 (3 Puerto Rico)	391
1940–1941	108	90	144	6 (1 Alaska, 1 Hawaii, 1 Puerto Rico)	348
1941–1942	71	60	100	4 (2 Puerto Rico)	235
1942–1943	30	13	36	1 (Puerto Rico)	80
1943–1944	24	14	24	0	62
1944–1945	29	16	15	0	60
1945–1946	65	60	34	2	161

YEAR	VIRGINIA	OTHER SOUTHERN STATES	NON-SOUTHERN U.S. STATES	INTERNATIONAL	TOTAL
1946–1947	241	234	170	7 (4 Puerto Rico)	652
1947–1948	267	256	223	14 (7 Puerto Rico, 1 AK, 1 HI)	760
1948–1949	194	149	194	6 (5 Puerto Rico)	543
1949–1950	221	151	177	7 (2 Puerto Rico, 2 HI)	556
1950–1951	222	112	178	3 (1 HI, 1 VI)	515
1951–1952	158	74	139	15 (3 HI, 1 Puerto Rico)	386
1952–1953	140	68	142	2	352
1953–1954	154	58	127	3 (1 Puerto Rico)	342
1954–1955	155	71	160	4 (1 Puerto Rico)	390
1955–1956	163	80	194	4 (1 Puerto Rico)	441
1956–1957	178	98	208	5	489
1957–1958	163	108	222	1	494
1958–1959	166	122	212	1	501
1959–1960	179	130	239	3 (1 Puerto Rico)	551
1960–1961	188	150	235	5 (1 Puerto Rico)	578

UVA Law was nonetheless seeking to increase its national visibility during this time. Indeed, the decline in the number of students from 1921 to 1932 was likely attributable to its efforts to increase admission requirements and thereby keep pace with national law schools. Lile himself was a proponent of professionalizing the law curriculum. He did not approve of what would now be called interdisciplinary subjects being taught in the Law School. Lile wanted an emphasis on "purely legal topics," by which he meant subjects that had practical utility to members of the legal profession.[39] That trend continued until the late 1930s, when courses such as Comparative Law, International Law and Relations, and Legal Philosophy began to be offered.[40]

Beginning with the hiring of Glenn from Columbia Law School in 1927,

UVA Law made a conscious effort to attract faculty and lecturers whose roots were in the South but who had studied or practiced law elsewhere. Other examples included William H. White, hired in 1936, a native Virginian who had received an SJD degree from George Washington University; Dillard, a native of Louisiana who had attended West Point and practiced in New York after being hired as an acting professor at UVA Law in 1927; and Ribble, who after graduating from the Law School and being appointed as an instructor the same year, had taken leave to pursue LLM (master of laws) and SJD degrees from Columbia in 1932 and 1937, respectively.[41]

By the 1940s, Virginia was appointing faculty members who had no previous contact with the Law School or the South. Examples were Emerson G. Spies, a resident of New York and graduate of Oxford, appointed in 1946; Laurens H. Rhinelander, a resident of Massachusetts and a graduate of Harvard, appointed in 1948; and Charles O. Gregory, a 1926 graduate of Yale who had practiced in New York for two years before joining

UVA Law Faculty, 1948. (Arthur J. Morris Law Library Special Collections, University of Virginia)

the University of Wisconsin faculty in 1928 and the University of Chicago faculty in 1930. Gregory's appointment in 1949 was particularly significant because he had a national reputation in the field of labor law and was the coauthor of one of the leading casebooks on torts.[42] Gregory's hiring signaled that UVA Law was regarded as an attractive option for faculty members from the nation's leading law schools.

As these incoming faculty members increasingly adopted the case method by the 1930s, the curriculum shifted—albeit slowly—to adapt what various deans' reports called the "mass methods of instruction."[43] Under the textbook, lecture, and quiz method employed for much of the Law School's early history, and championed by Lile throughout his deanship, large numbers of students could be taught by a single faculty member because the purpose of instruction was to present students with legal principles that they were expected to memorize and regurgitate.[44] The case method's emphasis on analyzing legal issues had the advantage, even Lile recognized, of improving the "reasoning faculties" of students.[45]

But the case method's emphasis on the close analysis of cases through a dialogue between instructors and students meant that much class time would be spent on conversations between a professor and one student in which other students did not participate. Even as late as the 1960s, Dean Ribble expressed concern that the case method's focus on dialogue could result in a conversation between the instructor and "one student for a half an hour with the rest of the students listening in." Although that might produce "a brilliant display and a fine demonstration, informative and inspiring," it resulted in low participation. The case method's emphasis on appellate opinions, often decided many years prior, only added to the issue, as it left little room for new discoveries.[46] Beginning in the 1930s, faculty tried to remedy this defect through the introduction of courses emphasizing statutes and administrative regulations, the use of extrajudicial sources such as the restatements of common law subjects, and the employment of courses along "historical and sociological lines."[47]

As faculty and deans worried that the case method would not provide enough attention to every student, they found other ways to respond to a growing demand for "individualization of legal education," as Ribble described it in 1941.[48] In 1938, the Law School initiated "sectionalization" of required courses in the first year, so that beginning students had opportunities for small classes.[49] In addition, practical legal skills became a core part of the curriculum in the 1940s in supplementary sessions with faculty members and small groups of students.[50] By 1950, the law student board established an annual "reading guide" calling students' attention to books from which they could learn basic skills or be exposed to extra-judicial materials influencing the development of the law. At the same time, an Introduction to Law course became required for first-year students. Multiple instructors taught the course in small sections.[51] In 1953, Buckler enlarged the goals of the class to include "education in the recognition of a legal problem, in the use of law books and other materials, and in the writing of memoranda and briefs."[52] A few years later, the Introduction course was folded into the required first-year Procedure course.[53]

Throughout his annual reports in the 1950s, Ribble continued to emphasize the need for individualized legal education. One significant factor in the strength of the faculty was their "constant and ready association with students," which began in the first year despite large class sizes. The Introduction to Law course offered opportunity for individualized instruction, but it was not until the third year that faculty and student interaction reached "its greatest effectiveness" via seminars and meetings between faculty and students. Given the time-consuming nature of individual meetings, faculty could not devote as much effort to publishing. But, as Ribble acknowledged, UVA Law's tradition was "to put the student ahead of the printed page, where there may be any conflict of interest." This "splendid tradition" of affording students "ready access to [their] professors" remained intact, as did comparatively large teaching loads for faculty, with all faculty expected to teach two courses each semester.[54] Even the arrangement of faculty offices in Clark Hall, the Law School's home since 1932, facilitated that access: many faculty offices were located on the first and second floors of the Law Library, where students regularly studied, and had windows on their doors making it clear when faculty were occupying them.

Student Body

As the composition of the Law School faculty took a gradual turn toward regional diversity in the 1930s and 1940s, the student body followed suit.

The years between 1933 and 1940 brought a steady increase both in the number of students from other southern states and non-southern states. The numbers of students from Virginia did not consistently decline in that time interval, and the size of the Law School student body increased every year between 1933 and 1940, reaching a high of 395 by the 1938–39 academic year.[55]

UVA Law, because of its prestige and relatively low cost, was an attractive option for residents of northern states. During the 1927–28 academic year, Virginia charged $250 for tuition and fees in comparison to Harvard, Yale, Columbia, and Pennsylvania, which charged $300 or more (the equivalent of over $5,100 today). At the time, no northern states had a full-time, accredited state law school, and Maine, New Hampshire, New Jersey, and Vermont had no accredited law schools.[56]

But the rising number of northern students distressed the Law School. In Dean Dobie's annual report in 1932, he addressed the issue, laying out enrollment figures showing that "exactly one-half of our students are from Virginia. The next three states furnishing the largest number of students are . . . New Jersey, New York, and Pennsylvania." Dobie was concerned that UVA Law was not attracting enough southern students. He assured UVA President John L. Newcomb that he would take up the matter: "To this problem I am giving due thought with the hope that means may be found for correcting this situation."[57] Almost two years later, Dobie noted that although a little over half of UVA Law students were in-state, the next largest group of students were from New York.[58] Beginning in 1934–35, the Law School cautiously started allowing some transfer credit, which invited a larger pool of applicants. In 1938, acting dean Ribble remarked that accepting transfer courses did not mean UVA Law would become a haven for "cast-offs," particularly for students who had failed at Harvard.[59]

Dobie's and Ribble's fears about the diminishing number of students from southern states at UVA Law, especially considering economic and educational trends that were driving more northern and fewer southern students to contemplate applying to the Law School in the 1930s, were a testament to UVA Law's established identity as a leader in the South. In 1929, after attending the annual meeting of the ABA, Ribble conveyed to Dean Lile his impressions that the "University of Virginia has ever had a high reputation among the Law Schools of the Nation and particularly the reputation of being a leader in the South." Ribble pointed out that some southern law schools, such as UNC, had recently increased their prominence, adding that "[their] growth is a forceful reminder of our own obligation of constant development to maintain and strengthen a position of useful importance which we may have long looked upon as being held by prescriptive right." Complacency could result in a "loss of national prestige and the condition of being simply a good local school."[60]

Competition from Duke and UNC needed a vigorous response, Ribble and Lile felt, because there was a vast difference between being the leading law school in a region and, as most other state law schools were, a local institution. A rise in student applications to UVA Law from areas outside the South was a signal of its national reputation, and if such students returned to their home regions to practice law after graduation, their doing so perpetuated that reputation and made it more likely that UVA Law would continue to attract applicants from those areas. Thus, when southern applicants declined in the 1930s, both Dobie and Ribble regarded the trend as potentially jeopardizing UVA Law's regional leadership. If students from North Carolina chose to enroll at UNC or Duke rather than UVA Law, they were suggesting there was no loss in prestige in doing so.

War Times and a New Era of Legal Education

As the Law School became more regionally diversified into the 1940s, it was confronted, along with other American institutions of higher education, with a deteriorating international situation, highlighted by aggressive invasions by the fascist regimes of Germany, Italy, and Japan; the outbreak of World War II in Europe; and, late in 1941, the entrance of the United States into the war. It was clear that a large American fighting force needed to be assembled in the wake of the United States declaring war against Japan and the Axis powers, and that such a force would be drawn largely from men of an age typically associated with entering law school. It was also evident that war-related offices of the federal government would be rapidly expanding, creating opportunities for Law School faculty over the age of combat eligibility to join the war effort.[61]

World War II would bring drastic change to life and learning at UVA Law. The war's effect on the size of the Law School faculty and student body was both immediate and remarkable. By 1943 the faculty was reduced to five members. A year later, acting dean White noted that student enrollment needed to be capped at 100–125, lest the quality of admitted students decline.[62] A total of 161 students matriculated in the 1945–46 academic year, 65 of them from Virginia and 60 from other southern states. Several innovations reflected the impact of wartime. The college requirement was reduced to two years, with military training being regarded as the equivalent of a third year if the dean felt it had provided sufficient "maturity" and training.[63] Altering the requirement allowed men who had entered the military in the middle of college to consider going directly to law school when discharged from the service.

Another wartime concession involved the acceleration of required time to obtain a law degree. Beginning in July 1942, the Law School offered instruction in the summer, making it possible for students to complete the program in two years by enrolling for eight consecutive terms.[64] This "accelerated" schedule of instruction consisted of four semesters of approximately three months each in a calendar year. That program, initially conceived as allowing men with service obligations to complete law school more quickly, was made available to all students and remained in place until 1949.[65]

UVA Law's most decisive change occasioned by the war was its curriculum. With a smaller faculty, the ability of instructors to teach required courses was reduced. The Law School abandoned required courses after the first year, making the last two years entirely composed of electives that catered to the expertise of the remaining faculty. This was already "customary practice among the better law schools in the United States."[66] The atmosphere at Virginia during the war years was one in which legal education was fitted around the imperatives of war. In 1942, the US Army began a School of Military Government at UVA—the first of its kind—for the purpose of training military officers.[67] Nearly ten years later, in 1951, the Judge Advocate General's (JAG) School moved to Clark

Hall upon the Law School's invitation (many law schools had invited the JAG School, including Harvard and Yale) for the purpose of training regular, reserve, and national guard officers in "military law."[68]

The entire Law School had to make wartime concessions, but for the Law Library, it became an opportunity for growth and a chance to bring its holdings up to national standards with increased funding and a staff that had the time to direct their attention to cataloging. The Law Library had been a source of concern to Law School administrators for some time. In 1938, acting dean Ribble noted that a "good library is a necessity for a good law school," but the Law Library was "barely within the minimum requirement" demanded by the Association of American Law Schools (AALS). In fact, the AALS had threatened suspension should its collection of statutes diminish.[69] The stature of the Law Library rapidly changed with the hiring of Frances Farmer, senior cataloguer and executive secretary, in 1942. Farmer was a 1933 graduate of T. C. Williams Law School in Richmond and had become law librarian there in 1938. In 1945 Farmer was appointed as the UVA Law School's law librarian. By the 1950s, relying largely on support from the alumni association, she had increased the catalogued volumes in the library to over one hundred thousand. In 1963, Farmer became UVA Law's first female law professor.[70]

The war had another, more indirect effect: it would serve as a catalyst for change in the Law School's orientation among other law schools in the nation. The continued expansion of the federal government during the war, the growing involvement of Law School faculty with war-related offices in the government, and the international experience of students and faculty involved with the war effort were signals of the greater involvement of American law schools with national and international affairs. After the war, the Law School's curricular emphasis on public law subjects continued, along with the addition of "practical" courses such as Office Practice and Taxation.[71]

After the war, Ribble's attitude toward balancing state and national interests had not changed even while enrollment skyrocketed. "To be a good law school for Virginia," Ribble wrote in his 1953 annual report, "[the institution] must be a national school. Otherwise, the best Virginians would go elsewhere, and the remainder gather in an isolated concentration on local law. Over the years, the effect would be a strong tendency towards a provincial and narrow law administration." But Ribble added that UVA Law occupied a central place in serving the state and nation. He felt the best way to underscore that service was to list the large numbers of Law School alumni occupying "places . . . in the state's legal system." Those included Governor John S. Battle (Law 1913); Attorney General J. Lindsay Almond Jr. (Law 1923); two justices on the Virginia Supreme Court of Appeals; seventeen circuit court judges; and eleven judges on city courts. The president and vice president of the Virginia State Bar and five of the seven members of that organization's executive committee were alumni, as well. In addition, an alumnus was the president of the Virginia Bar Association, as were five of the six members of that group's executive committee.[72]

In the postwar years student numbers dramatically increased. By the 1946–47 academic year, enrollment rose to a then unprecedented high

UVA Law Librarian Frances Farmer, Professor Hardy Cross Dillard (Law 1927), and Dean F. D. G. Ribble (Law 1921) review a collection of nineteenth-century French law books gifted to the UVA Law Library, 1963 (Arthur J. Morris Law Library Special Collections, University of Virginia)

Virginia Law Review student staff, including Margaret Gordon Seiler (Law 1951), a member of the *VLR* Board, ca. 1951. (Arthur J. Morris Law Library Special Collections, University of Virginia)

of 652 students, with the number of students from areas other than Virginia or the South increasing from 34 to 170. While the war opened many doors for women generally, female enrollment at UVA Law did not witness a drastic or immediate postwar shift. Ten women enrolled in 1945; by 1950, there were 18.[73] This postwar pattern remained roughly consistent through 1960–61. Total enrollment remained relatively high, although never exceeding the 760 students who matriculated in 1947–48. By 1960–61, it was clear that UVA Law was an institution peopled by more students from non-southern states than students from Virginia, and vastly more non-southern students than ever before.[74]

It was within a national context of civil rights activism, as well as key developments in the broader landscape of legal education, that the first Black students, led in 1950 by Gregory H. Swanson, enrolled at the Law School. In 1944, UVA Law resolved to start a graduate program to enhance its national prestige, commissioning faculty member Glenn, a "scholar and writer of national repute," to administer the program and affording him two months to study existing graduate programs at Columbia,

Harvard, and Yale.[75] Six years later Swanson, a Virginia lawyer who held a law degree from Howard University, would become the first African American student admitted to UVA and UVA Law after he sued for admission to this newly established LLM program and won his case. Swanson's legal team included famed civil rights attorneys Oliver W. Hill and Spottswood W. Robinson, along with Thurgood Marshall of the NAACP. The Law School faculty supported Swanson's entry, but the UVA Board of Visitors denied his application, prompting Swanson's lawsuit. That same year, racial integration in law programs was growing as a condition for national stature. At the 1950 annual meeting of the AALS, a group from Yale advocated for member schools to be excluded from the association if they rejected qualified applicants based on race. In 1951, the AALS determined it would not issue a mandate but rather encourage "equality of opportunity in legal education without discrimination or segregation on the ground of race or color." Dean Ribble chaired the 1956 Committee on Racial Discrimination to foster conversations around the topic of discrimination between the AALS and noncompliant law schools. The AALS later reprimanded law schools for rejecting viable Black applicants. The move to integrate the Law School also became a part of its growing national character and reflected the administration's desire to align with federal law—not change the culture of the school itself.[76] Black enrollment at UVA Law in the wake of Swanson's matriculation would not witness a noticeable increase for a few decades.[77]

By and large, the Law School maintained its homogeneity through the 1950s. Its faculty still comprised primarily Virginia graduates, and every dean was a southerner and a graduate of the Law School. Lile, Dobie, Ribble, and Dillard, who succeeded Ribble as dean in 1963, were all graduates of UVA Law, with Dobie and Ribble being Virginia natives and Lile and Dillard natives of Alabama and Louisiana, respectively. Its first non-Virginian dean, Monrad G. Paulsen, would succeed Dillard in 1968, ushering in a new era.[78]

By 1960, UVA Law was not too far removed from the place it had occupied in 1920: a school with a very strong regional presence that had looked to capitalize on that regional preeminence and its "southernness" to anchor its considerable national reputation. As it increasingly attracted students in the four decades after 1920 who aspired to practice

Interior of the UVA Law Library in Clark Hall, undated. (Arthur J. Morris Law Library Special Collections, University of Virginia)

law at firms in large cities outside the state, most prominently in New York, Washington, and Atlanta, it also remained a distinctly "southern" institution, featuring a majority of UVA Law graduates and residents of southern states on its faculty and a distinct majority of residents of Virginia and other southern states in its student body. It was also a conspicuously white and male institution, with no female or Black faculty members, and a nominal representation of female and Black students. Elaine R. Jones became the first Black woman to graduate from the Law School in 1970. By that time, she was the ninth Black student to graduate from UVA Law. Female matriculation rates drastically lagged behind those of men, with four female graduates in the 1960 class.[79]

As other law schools opened in the American South, administrators at the University of Virginia felt they needed to increase their efforts to recruit students from across the southern states, so that the school would not be seen as merely a local institution. The hope of those who shepherded the Law School in those four decades was that Virginia would simultaneously remain nationally visible and retain its own distinctive atmosphere, an atmosphere produced by the regional homogeneity of its student body and faculty. It was a hope that had largely been realized as the 1960s opened. Developments throughout American legal education and American culture in succeeding decades would flip this dynamic and collectively serve to diminish the "southernness" of the Law School as a way toward enhancing its national reputation.

Notes

1. Dean's Annual Report, 11 January 1930, 11, Deans' Papers, RG–32-100-78, Arthur J. Morris Law Library Special Collections, University of Virginia (hereafter cited as LLSC; the Dean's Annual Reports are hereafter cited as *DAR*). My thanks to the Special Collections staff at UVA Law for their help in identifying and gathering sources for this chapter.
2. John Calvin Metcalf, ed., *The Centennial of the University of Virginia, 1819–1921: The Proceedings of the Centenary Celebration, May 31 to June 3, 1921* (New York: G. P. Putnam's Sons, 1922), 157–58.
3. Metcalf, *Centennial of the University of Virginia,* 159.
4. Metcalf, *Centennial of the University of Virginia,* 158–59.
5. Metcalf, *Centennial of the University of Virginia,* 159.
6. G. Edward White, *Law in American History,* vol. 2, *From Reconstruction through the 1920s* (New York: Oxford University Press, 2016), 329–32.
7. "Armistead Mason Dobie, 1907–1939," Our History: Former Faculty, Arthur J. Morris Law Library, University of Virginia, https://perma.cc/F7FP-P5RJ.
8. *DAR,* 10 January 1931, 3.
9. William Minor Lile Journal (vol. 8, 1922–1926), 3 June 1924, Journals of William Minor Lile, MSS-89-1, LLSC.
10. *DAR,* 10 January 1931, 3.
11. *DAR,* 10 January 1931, 4.
12. University of Virginia, *Department of Law: Announcements 1934–1935,* University of Virginia Record, n.s., vol. 20, no. 3 (Charlottesville: University of Virginia, 1934), 7 (bulletin series hereafter cited as *LSR* for *Law School Record;* in 1953 the bulletin title changed to *School of Law: Announcements*).
13. LLSC, *100 Years of Coeducation at UVA Law* (unpublished booklet, 2022), 10, https://perma.cc/NZR6-GCCC. See also Anne M. Coughlin, "'This Mob of Men': The Road to Coeducation at the University of Virginia School of Law, 1870–1923," in this volume.
14. For statistics on female enrollment in American law schools, see "History," New York Women's Bar Association, https://perma.cc/2JRN-4XU4.
15. G. Edward White, *Law in American History,* vol. 1, *From the Colonial Years through the Civil War* (New York: Oxford University Press, 2012), 282–83.
16. White, *Law in American History,* 2:317.
17. Robert Stevens, *Law School: Legal Education in America from the 1850s to the 1980s* (Chapel Hill: University of North Carolina Press, 1983), 77–81.
18. Stevens, *Law School, 78–81.*
19. American Bar Association, *Annual Review of Legal Education for 1938* (Chicago: Section of Legal Education and Admissions to the Bar of the American Bar Association, 1939), 10–30 (American Bar Association hereafter cited as ABA).

20. William P. Lapiana, "Merit and Diversity: The Origins of the Law School Admissions Test," in *Before the Paper Chase: The Scholarship of Law School Preparation and Admissions,* ed. Tim Alan Garrison and Frank Guliuzza (Durham, NC: Carolina Academic Press, 2012), 67–70.
21. *DAR,* 20 January 1950, 10; *LSR,* 1948, 12.
22. By 1969, the ABA recommended that all approved law schools use the LSAT as part of the admissions process. See ABA, *Standards of the American Bar Association for Legal Education: Factors Bearing on the Approval of Law Schools by the American Bar Association* (Chicago: Section of Legal Education and Admissions to the Bar of the ABA, 1969), 11. See also Stevens, *Law School,* 221n38.
23. ABA, *Law Schools and Bar Admission Requirements in the United States: 1959 Review of Legal Education* (Chicago: Section of Legal Education and Admissions to the Bar of the ABA, 1959).
24. White, *Law in American History,* 2:342–43.
25. Olufunmilayo B. Arewa, Andrew P. Morriss, and William D. Henderson, "Enduring Hierarchies in American Legal Education," *Indiana Law Journal* 89, no. 3 (Summer 2014): 954–60.
26. Stevens, *Law School,* 206. See also Harry W. Jones, "Local Law Schools vs. National Law Schools: A Comparison of Concepts, Functions, and Opportunities," *Journal of Legal Education* 10, no. 3 (1958): 281–93.
27. The eleven Law School professors were William Minor Lile (1893–1932), Raleigh Colston Minor (1893–1923), Charles Alfred Graves (1899–1927), Armistead Mason Dobie (1907–39), George Boardman Eager Jr. (1911–42), Frederick Deane Goodwin Ribble (1921–66), Harold Hopkins Neff (1924–27), Hardy Cross Dillard (1927–70), Charles Patterson Nash (1927–67), Garrard Glenn (1928–49), and Leslie Hepburn Buckler (1919–56). See "UVA Law Faculty through History," Our History: Former Faculty, Arthur J. Morris Law Library, University of Virginia, https://libguides.law.virginia.edu/faculty.
28. *DAR,* 1 January 1921, 6.
29. *DAR,* 25 January 1927, 6.
30. Herschell Whitfield Arant, "A Survey of Legal Education in the South," *Tennessee Law Review* 15, no. 3 (April 1938): 179. Also quoted in Christina Leanne Farrell, "Southern Identity, National Prestige: The University of Virginia Law School and the Dilemma of Dual Identity, 1920–1940" (master's thesis, University of Virginia, 2006), 15.
31. A total of forty-one schools received accreditation in 1923. "List of ABA-Approved Law Schools," ABA, https://www.americanbar.org/groups/legal_education/resources/aba_approved_law_schools/in_alphabetical_order/. See also Alfred Zantzinger Reed, *Present-Day Law Schools in the United States and Canada* (Boston: D. B. Updike, Merrymount Press, 1928), 405–513.
32. *DAR,* 11 January 1930, 11.
33. See "UVA Law Faculty through History," for individual professors' biographical details.
34. Statistics are pulled from each *LSR* for the period. At the time, statistics on women were not included in the catalogue, but the dean sometimes mentioned female students in his report. Crockett Watson became the first woman to serve on the editorial board of the *Virginia Law Review.* LLSC, *100 Years of Coeducation,* 10.
35. White, *Law in American History,* 2:339–41.

36. *LSR,* 1920, 5. On women's admission requirements, see LLSC, *100 Years of Coeducation,* 8.
37. *LSR,* 1928, 5–6.
38. *DAR,* 20 January 1940, 2.
39. *DAR,* 11 January 1930, 16.
40. *DAR,* 20 January 1939, 5–7.
41. For biographies of former faculty, see "UVA Law Faculty through History."
42. "UVA Law Faculty through History." On Gregory, see Calvin Woodard, "Charles O. Gregory," *Virginia Law Review* 74, no. 1 (February 1988): 3–10.
43. *DAR,* 20 January 1938, 5.
44. *LSR,* 1922, 7–8.
45. Metcalf, *Centennial of the University of Virginia,* 158.
46. *DAR,* 1 February 1961, 63.
47. *DAR,* 10 January 1929, 7.
48. *DAR,* 18 January 1941, 9.
49. *DAR,* 20 January 1938, 5.
50. *DAR,* 18 January 1941, 8–9.
51. *DAR,* 20 January 1950, 31–33.
52. *DAR,* 20 December 1953, 17–18.
53. *DAR,* 1 February 1959, 32–33.
54. *DAR,* 20 January 1952, 9–13.
55. Statistics are pulled from the *LSR* for the years noted.
56. Reed, *Present-Day Law Schools,* 405–513, esp. 419, 453, 472, 491, 505.
57. *DAR,* 7 December 1932, 2.
58. *DAR,* 10 January 1935, 1.
59. *DAR,* 20 January 1938, 4–5.
60. *DAR,* 11 January 1930, 11.
61. Dean Ribble and Professors John Ritchie III, Dillard, Nash, William Barron, Edmund G. Belsheim, and Richard M. Welling served the war effort but not on active duty. See *DAR,* 19 January 1943, 4; *DAR,* 20 January 1944, 2.
62. *DAR,* 20 January 1944, 13.
63. In addition, students coming to law school from the military were permitted to enter at the beginning of the second or third term instead of the first. *DAR,* 20 January 1944, 5.
64. *LSR,* 1943, 2.
65. *LSR,* 1948, 2.
66. *DAR,* 19 January 1942, 5.
67. Rebecca Patterson, "Revisiting a School of Military Government: How Reanimating a World War II–Era Institution Could Professionalize Military Nation Building," *Kauffman Foundation Research Series: Expeditionary Economics* 3 (June 2011): 7, https://perma.cc/8S8F-YY6A.
68. *DAR,* 20 January 1952, 17; *LSR,* 1952, 12.
69. *DAR,* 20 January 1938,11.
70. LLSC, *100 Years of Coeducation,* 11; University of Virginia Board of Visitors Official Minutes, 1957–64, 7 June 1963, Box 4, RG-1/1/1.385, SSCL.
71. *DAR,* 20 January 1946, 5–6.
72. *DAR,* 20 January 1953, 2.
73. *LSR,* 1947, 71; *LSR,* 1945, 42–44; *LSR,* 1950, 52–61.

74. *LSR,* 1961, 76–77.

75. *DAR,* 20 January 1944, 10–11.

76. "Segregation & the Association of American Law Schools," University of Richmond Race & Racism Project, https://memory.richmond.edu/exhibits/show/modlin/law; Robert A. Leflar, "Legal Education: Desegregation in Law Schools," *American Bar Association Journal* 43, no. 2 (February 1957): 145–49; Maurice T. Van Hecke, "Racial Desegregation in the Law Schools," *Journal of Legal Education* 9, no. 3 (1957): 283–89.

77. Eric Williamson, "The Long Walk: What Life Was Like for Gregory Swanson, the Lawyer Who Integrated UVA," *UVA Lawyer* 42, no. 2 (Spring 2018): 36–40. In 1958, John F. Merchant became the first African American to graduate from the Law School. For more on Swanson and Merchant, see Risa Goluboff, Randall N. Flaherty, and Biruktawit M. Assefa, "Gregory H. Swanson and the Integration of the University of Virginia School of Law," in this volume.

78. See "UVA Law Faculty through History."

79. LLSC, *100 Years of Coeducation,* 13; *LSR,* 1961, 57–59. For more on Elaine Jones, see Claudrena Harold, "We Demand: Student Advocates for Curricular Change, 1960–1980," in this volume.

Constitutional Law at the University of Virginia

BETWEEN STATE CONSTITUTIONAL BOOKENDS, 1902–1971

A. E. Dick Howard and Catherine A. Ward

TWICE IN the twentieth century, Virginians acquired new constitutions—in 1902 and in 1971. The distance traveled between the racist and reactionary 1902 document and the progressive 1971 constitution is vast. But in the making of each of them, lawyers educated at the University of Virginia School of Law played a central role.

With the end of Reconstruction, conservative leaders in the former Confederate states set out to roll back the gains that formerly enslaved persons had made after the Civil War. In their quest to restore the old order, the "redeemers" could not restore slavery. But the revisionists sought to strip Black citizens of the franchise through such devices as the poll tax and restrictive registration devices.[1] Virginia joined the parade when, in 1901, delegates gathered in Richmond for a convention to write a new constitution for the Commonwealth.

John Barbee Minor (Law 1834) taught at the Law School from 1845 to 1895—the longest tenure of any UVA Law professor in that century. After the Civil War, Minor continued to defend slavery, saw emancipation as a disaster, and condemned Reconstruction as an unmitigated evil. Through his teaching and writing, Minor wholeheartedly embraced the notion of the Lost Cause—a belief that, although the South had lost the war, it could rise again through excluding African Americans from any role in the political community. Generations of Minor's students went on to have leading roles in Virginia's public life, including the General Assembly, the Democratic Party, and the constitutional convention of 1901–2.[2]

Virginia's 1901–1902 Constitutional Convention

In 1901, delegates gathered in Richmond for a convention to write a new state constitution.[3] Of the convention's 101 members, 34 had studied law at the University of Virginia.[4] Those UVA alumni were prominent in the Commonwealth's political and professional life and were among the most vocal and influential delegates at the convention. The 1901–2 delegates knew exactly what they wanted: white supremacy. Alfred Thom (Law 1876), of Norfolk, made it clear that being white was being destined to rule: "The Anglo-Saxon represents the very aristocracy of the races."[5] The path to white supremacy entailed the removal of Black voters from Virginia politics. Eppa Hunton Jr. (Law 1877), representing Fauquier County, saw Black suffrage as the problem: "I assert that the horror of negro suffrage to the people of Virginia has brought shame upon the white people of Virginia."[6]

In confronting the question of public education, delegates viewed spending money to educate Black persons as both wasteful and harmful. Brunswick County delegate Robert R. Turnbull (Law 1871), declaring the evils of educating Black individuals, said that education had made them vagabonds: "We have . . . unfitted them for what God Almighty intended them to be and . . . they are too proud to work on the farm and unfit for anything else."[7]

The men at the 1901–2 convention had ample precedents at hand. Reconstruction had come to an end. "Redeemed" governments had wrested control of southern states' governments from "carpetbaggers" who had been empowered by Radical Republicans in Congress. Mississippi led the way. Its 1890 constitution was imitated by other southern states, including Virginia.[8] These constitutions used a variety of devices to achieve disenfranchisement of Black citizens: the poll tax, literacy tests, understanding clauses, and grandfather clauses.[9]

The convention delegates in Virginia had little reason to worry that the United States Supreme Court would stand in their way. That tribunal had rejected a challenge to Mississippi's 1890 constitution. Justice Joseph

McKenna, writing for a unanimous court, ruled that Mississippi's constitution was neutral on its face; it did not matter that those who administered the state's laws might use them to discriminate.[10]

Unwilling to take the chance that the existing electorate (many of whom would be excluded from the franchise) might not approve the proposed constitution, the convention simply promulgated it. It took effect without a vote of the people.[11] Its framers' predictions about the franchise proved accurate. After 1902, fewer than 5 percent of all registered voters were Black, whereas in 1867 almost half had been Black.[12] Poor whites, as well, were disqualified in large numbers.[13] Virginia lived under the shadow of the 1902 constitution for the next half century. A smaller proportion of Virginians voted during the first half of the twentieth century than in any other state in the country or, indeed, any country in the world that had, or claimed to have, a representative democracy.[14]

Constitutional Law at UVA

The UVA Law alumni who attended the constitutional convention had received a thorough education in constitutional law and how to preserve states' rights. The study of constitutional law had always been central to the Law School's curriculum through readings and lectures, even though there was no dedicated course until much later. Describing the 1844–45 curriculum, Professor Henry St. George Tucker cited Blackstone's and Kent's commentaries as the basis for the study of constitutional law. Tucker stressed the great political issues of the day, including the rights of the states:

> In the arrangement of the political part of this course, the Professor's object has been to lay before the student the most able dissertations on both sides of the great constitutional questions which have arisen in our country; to impress upon his mind the inestimable value of the union on the one hand, and the vital importance of preserving the rights of the States on the other; thus guarding him against latitudinarian constructions and the invasion of the reserved rights of the States, while the disorganizing principles which lead to convulsion and disunion are earnestly discarded and industriously controverted.[15]

At the turn of the century, rarely did American law schools require students to take courses in constitutional law.[16] As the century opened, a course at UVA Law entitled Theory of Government; Constitutional Law; International Law occupied a place in the first-year curriculum. Professor Raleigh C. Minor (Law 1890), son of John B. Minor, taught this course and variations of it for the next two decades.[17] The class, meeting twice a week, used the third edition of Thomas M. Cooley's *Principles of Constitutional Law* (1891), as well as George B. Davis's *Elements of International Law* (1900) and Raleigh Minor's notes. Cooley's text was key, as it focused on settled principles, rather than theory, presenting "succinctly the general principles of constitutional law, whether they pertain to the federal system, or to the state system, or to both."[18]

By 1910, Minor's course had become simply Constitutional Law, meeting three times a week. International Law had morphed into its own elective course. An additional course, Constitution and Code of Virginia, appeared in the catalog for the first time. All were taught by Minor.[19] Between 1910 and 1920, his students used the third edition of Henry C. Black's *Handbook of American Constitutional Law* as their text.[20] In contrast to today's casebooks, Black's work resembles an encyclopedia of

Law professor Raleigh C. Minor teaching a law class in Minor Hall for the film *Shadow of the Founder,* spring 1921. (Albert and Shirley Small Special Collections Library, University of Virginia)

constitutional law "stated in the form of a series of brief rules, or propositions, numbered consecutively throughout the book . . . explained, amplified, and illustrated in the subsidiary text."[21]

The coverage in Black's textbook illustrates the way later Supreme Court cases transformed the study of constitutional law. Civil liberties, which make up so much of modern constitutional law courses, are assigned a single chapter in Black. That chapter, the longest in the book (at just over one hundred pages), covers the Bill of Rights, due process, and equal protection. Where a modern course might take several weeks to cover equal protection, that topic received only fifteen pages in Black. Similarly, due process was given thirty pages.[22] Other topics included in Black's coverage, such as search and seizure and freedom of expression, have long since been taught at UVA (as elsewhere) in separate courses.[23]

Raleigh Minor stepped down in 1922 due to his declining health (he died the following year). Frederick D. G. Ribble began teaching constitutional law at UVA. In 1921, the same year he graduated from the Law School, Ribble joined the faculty, becoming, at age twenty-three, its youngest member. Virtually any students who studied law at UVA between 1924 and 1964 found themselves in Ribble's classroom.

As one of his colleagues later noted, Ribble was known as a "master of the Socratic Method."[24] His classes challenged students to seek their own conclusions. Indeed, many of Ribble's students found his views enigmatic, with questions often left lingering in the air. Students in his constitutional law class encountered a heavy dose of commerce clause jurisprudence. This is hardly surprising when one considers that Ribble, on a fellowship at Columbia University, wrote a thesis on the commerce power under the direction of Noel T. Dowling, which resulted in the publication, in 1937, of Ribble's *State and National Power over Commerce.*[25]

While many other American law schools had adopted Harvard's case method in the late nineteenth century, Virginia still maintained a textbook and lecture approach.[26] Armistead M. Dobie (Law 1904), a UVA graduate who also studied at Harvard, introduced the case method to the Law School in the early 1920s. Ribble and younger faculty, including Hardy Cross Dillard (Law 1927), followed suit. But the transition took time and encountered some resistance at first. In 1930, when a hybrid method persisted at the Law School—allowing professors to choose their

Professor F. D. G. Ribble teaching a law class in Clark Hall, 1936. (Arthur J. Morris Law Library Special Collections, University of Virginia)

own pedagogical method—Ribble used a casebook for his constitutional law class in combination with "parallel readings."[27] By the mid-1930s, the case method dominated.

A perusal of the casebooks Ribble used over the years illustrates how the world of constitutional law changed during his tenure. An early casebook assigned by Ribble was the 1925 edition of Lawrence Evans's *Leading Cases on American Constitutional Law.*[28] Evans discussed due process and equal protection at greater length than do the earlier works of Cooley and Black (he gives both topics a separate chapter). Even so, Evans gave less space to due process (70 pages) or equal protection (90 pages) than to the commerce clause (220 pages), the police power (190 pages), or taxation (120 pages).

By the 1940s, Ribble had begun using Noel Dowling's *Cases on Constitutional Law.*[29] Ribble relied on this casebook and its successors through the rest of his teaching career. In the preface to his 1937 edition, Dowling had three goals for his casebook. First, he sought to "build a course in American Constitutional Law on the . . . theme of the regulatory power of government, national and state."[30] Regulatory power had been a core concern of constitutional law courses and casebooks for decades. A glance at student notebooks from Ribble's courses confirms this emphasis. Everard H. Smith Jr.'s (Law 1948) student notes from 1948 discuss the Supreme Court's jurisdiction, judicial review, delegation of legislative powers, administrative agencies, powers of Congress, and powers of the states as affected by the delegation of powers to the national government.[31] Dowling's second and third goals were to reexamine the doctrines of recent cases and to focus on procedural questions.[32] The last point reflected the author's concern with a practical dimension of teaching constitutional law—the "lawyer's job" in constitutional litigation.

Inevitably, issues of race surfaced in Ribble's classroom. Rayner V. Snead (Law 1942), a student in Ribble's course in 1941, posed the question: "Is anti-lynching bill constit.? It is drawn in a sense to get negro vote & places penalty on local officers who allow such & places a penalty on county in which a lynching occurs." The answer, Snead noted via Ribble, was that "such matters should be left to local officers & to state." Snead went on to observe that Ribble gave "2–1 odds" that the Supreme Court would "sustain [an] Anti-Lynching bill." Ribble covered an array of states' rights topics, including the vote and literacy tests, believing it "O.K. to give certain testss [*sic*] to see whether a person is qualified to vote." On the topic of Jim Crow laws generally, Ribble believed the Supreme Court would uphold them, adding the curious caveat, "these laws must not discriminate."[33]

During the 1950s, the description for Ribble's constitutional law course remained largely unchanged. But the menu of elective courses related to constitutional law began to grow. In the 1950–51 academic year, a seminar for second- and third-year students focused on "theory and principles of self-government, as originally developed in the federal constitution, and as affected by modern pressures for social legislation."[34] In the 1958–59 academic year, the Law School offered a seminar examining constitutional litigation.[35] The year before, in 1957–58, the Law School had begun offering its first seminar on civil rights as such, covering such topics as "freedom of speech and of the press, religious liberty, loyalty programs . . . right of association, equal protection . . . due process and other rights in criminal procedure," as well as the "scope of state and federal power" generally.[36] This addition came seven years after Gregory H. Swanson (Law 1951), an LLM (master of laws) student, integrated UVA and UVA Law in 1950, after first having been denied admission by the University and then having sued the Board of Visitors in federal court.[37]

The quickening pace of the Warren Court's decisions in the 1960s manifestly affected those who wrote constitutional law casebooks and, in turn, those who taught constitutional law classes. As the civil rights movement gathered momentum, the justices found themselves thrust into more highly charged issues of constitutional law. Harvard law professor and former solicitor general of the United States Archibald Cox remarked, the "civil rights movement required that the Court preside over parts of a social and political revolution seeking accomplishment within the frame of constitutionalism." The resulting tensions, he said, "strained the process of constitutional adjudication," profoundly influencing the course of constitutional interpretation.[38] The Warren Court transformed the political question doctrine; reshaped the Fourth, Fifth, and Sixth Amendments to provide the accused more robust protections; expanded speech rights; devised the rule that measures impinging on a fundamental right required strict scrutiny; and more.

The deluge of opinions from the Warren Court prompted changes in constitutional law textbooks and in the classroom. William B. Lockhart, Yale Kamisar, and Jesse H. Choper, the authors of a leading casebook, were forced in 1970 to publish a third edition just three years after the second had appeared, rather than publish a four hundred-page supplement.[39] A reviewer of the 1964 edition noted the book's estimate that "over half the cases were less than ten years old, and twenty percent of them less than five years old as of March 1, 1964, the cut-off date for inclusion in the book."[40] By 1968, all of the new or revised constitutional law casebooks had supplements to keep up with the latest Supreme Court decisions.[41]

Successive editions of the joint effort of Noel Dowling and Gerald Gunther, the casebooks used in the 1960s by Professor A. E. Dick Howard (Law 1961), who began teaching constitutional law courses in 1964, illustrated the evolving nature of the constitutional law curriculum. Frank Strong observed that, compared to previous editions (the most recent being 1959), the 1965 version was "an entirely new and different casebook."[42] Gunther and Dowling's 1970 casebook was published at the close of the Warren Court. Nearly half of the book's 1,500 pages focused on "Individual Rights." The book's chapter on equal protection carried the subtitle "The Expanding Contours of Constitutional Equality." In his preface, Gunther referred to that chapter as "one of the edition's major innovations."[43]

Due to the subject's growth in 1965, the UVA Law School's long-range curriculum committee decided to expand the course in constitutional law by an additional credit hour. The committee explained, "Developments in the areas of racial discrimination, civil rights, and reapportionment, for example, cannot be adequately covered under the present allocation."[44]

The 1960s also saw an expansion in course offerings related to constitutional law, including Constitutional Litigation, Civil Rights, and Constitutional Law Problems. Some focused explicitly on matters of race. For example, Professor Edward A. Mearns Jr.'s (Law 1958) Civil Rights course was described as a "study of the legal problems of the American Negro, with particular emphasis on recent civil rights legislation." Professor Howard's Constitutional Law Seminar was explicit in its focus on Warren Court decisions, as was the newly created course Advanced Criminal Procedure.[45]

Beyond the Classroom

Aside from what they learned in the classroom, law students were exposed to journals and newspapers published at the Law School. These included the *Virginia Law Register*, published between 1895 and 1928 (when it was absorbed into the *Virginia Law Review*), and the *Virginia Law Weekly*.[46] Run by student editors and writers who studied with Raleigh Minor and then with F. D. G. Ribble, the *Register* viewed the world of constitutional law through the lens of states' rights. That attitude was especially explicit in the journal's reaction to the Supreme Court's decision in *Berea College v. Kentucky*, a 1908 ruling in which the Fuller Court upheld a state's right to forbid private educational institutions, chartered as corporations, from admitting both Black and white students.[47] The *Register* applauded the decision, saying the court "occasionally lets a star shine, which arouses hope in the breast of the faithful watchers who have not entirely abandoned the doctrine of State Rights. We hail the decision in the case of Berea."[48]

Two years after *Berea*, the Supreme Court upheld a Kentucky law requiring segregation of interstate railway passengers.[49] The *Register* was pleased: "The Supreme Court of the United States has definitely pointed a way to carriers of passengers, by which they may conform to enlightened public sentiment with regard to an intermixture of the two races even on interstate coaches, without fear of rendering themselves liable for damages."[50]

A new perspective was evident, however, when, in 1949, Dean F. D. G. Ribble asked Armistead L. Boothe (Law 1930) to write an article on civil rights for the *Virginia Law Review*.[51] Boothe's article was ahead of its time; he predicted the Supreme Court would declare segregated schools and Virginia's poll tax to be unconstitutional.[52]

As litigation to achieve desegregation in public schools gained momentum, the Law School's newspaper, the *Virginia Law Weekly* (*VLW*), became a forum for local opinion. Its circulation extended beyond that of the student body, reaching alumni and even other law schools.[53] In the wake of *Brown v. Board of Education,* columns and articles in the *VLW* highlighted such topical news items as a report by the Institute of Government at the University of North Carolina on alternative plans to implement *Brown* and Professor Hardy Dillard's address in California on how sociological and psychological studies, like those used in *Brown,* should be used in legal contests.[54] The *VLW* gave prominent attention to local events, including Thurgood Marshall's talk to the local NAACP and a speech by the Louisville, Kentucky, superintendent of public schools about desegregation in Charlottesville.[55]

Whatever might have been the racial attitudes of UVA law students in the early years of the century, a heightened sensitivity to racial discrimination is evident in the *VLW*'s reaction when the Law School's softball team was prevented from playing a game in 1957 at Richmond's Byrd Park because "a negro law student was in the line-up." The *VLW* was appalled: "That the presence of a negro on an athletic team in Byrd Park could be thought a threat to the public peace is a sad comment on popular feeling. That future contests might be barred because a negro once participated is equally shocking." It was, the paper asserted, a case of "unreasoned prejudice. . . . The mere existence of this social canker of racism in Virginia today is both frightening and discouraging."[56]

In the 1960s, the *VLW* continued to reflect robust student interest in constitutional issues, especially those touching matters of race. In 1960, high-profile columnist President-elect John F. Kennedy, whose brothers

Robert F. Kennedy (Law 1951) and Edward "Ted" M. Kennedy (Law 1959) attended UVA Law, wrote that, as president, he would avoid "racism in reverse" by not considering race or religion in making cabinet appointments.[57] When unsuccessful Senate candidate Edward H. McCormick attacked Ted Kennedy for attending an "almost totally segregated" law school, the *VLW* emphasized that the University had quietly pursued accepting students regardless of race since 1951, producing results "of far greater significance to us than we may readily realize."[58]

The *Virginia Law Review* (*VLR*) was a forum for students and professors to expound on matters of race and the Warren Court.[59] For example, an obtuse opinion in *Swain v. Alabama* held that racial disparity in jury pools and the absence for decades of any Black jurors serving at trial in Talladega County, Alabama, did not "make out a prima facie case of invidious discrimination under the Fourteenth Amendment."[60] A student Note in the *VLR* was acerbic: "There seems to be no rational basis for the Court's insistence on blinding itself to the continuing total white control of the processes of justice in most of the South, or to the central role which this particular form of discrimination plays in the larger framework of equal protection."[61]

From Massive Resistance to a New State Constitution

One measure of the Law School's place in the development of constitutional law in the Commonwealth is the conspicuous role played by its graduates in public life, especially in matters of race. Robert Y. Button (Law 1922) is one such figure. A loyal member of the Harry F. Byrd Organization, Button served as Virginia's attorney general from 1961 to 1969. During his tenure, that office lost such notable Supreme Court cases as *NAACP v. Button*, *Griffin v. County School Board of Prince Edward County*, and *Loving v. Virginia*. Button characterized the Voting Rights Act of 1965 as "among the most dangerous pieces of legislation" ever enacted by Congress.[62]

More consequential was the public career of J. Lindsay Almond (Law 1923). The nadir of Almond's time in public life came when, as governor from 1958 to 1962, he carried out Virginia's massive resistance laws by closing schools in Warren County, Charlottesville, and Norfolk.[63] Yet

Virginia governor Mills Edwin Godwin Jr. (Law 1939) speaking at the 1969 Commission on Constitutional Revision in Williamsburg, Virginia. (Arthur J. Morris Law Library Special Collections, University of Virginia)

Almond also recognized that, ultimately, Virginia would have to comply with the federal courts' rulings. Years later, the General Assembly recognized Almond for having moved state policy from defying federal orders to complying.[64]

Especially notable was the mark Mills E. Godwin Jr. (Law 1938), twice governor of Virginia, left on constitutionalism in his native state. Settling into law practice in Suffolk, Godwin entered politics in the era of the Byrd machine.[65] As a state senator, Godwin became a key figure in Virginia's massive resistance to school desegregation. When the General Assembly convened in special session in 1956, Godwin was against any compromise on the issue.[66] He maintained that integration was a "cancer eating at the very life blood" of Virginia's public schools.[67] As time passed, however, Godwin shifted his tone. In 1959, he advised Virginia Democrats to focus on the Commonwealth's "great good" rather than "sulk about dead issues" like preventing desegregation.[68]

In the 1960s, Godwin's political instincts seemed to take him to more moderate political grounds. Running for governor in 1965, Godwin showed further signs of moving away from Byrd machine traditions of tight-fisted spending. He spoke in favor of increasing teachers' salaries, enhancing state support for colleges and universities, improving mental hospitals, and combating pollution.[69] As governor, Godwin put education center stage, earning the title "the education governor."[70]

1971 Constitution

In his welcoming address to the General Assembly in January 1968, Governor Godwin called attention to the effect of the "inexorable passage of time" on Virginia's constitution.[71] Acting on Godwin's recommendation, the Assembly authorized him to create an eleven-member Commission on Constitutional Revision.[72] Godwin forthwith named eleven distinguished Virginians to the commission, designating former Governor Albertis S. Harrison Jr. (Law 1928), as chairman. The commissioners were a distinguished group, including two former governors of Virginia

Members and staff of the Virginia Commission on Constitutional Revision gathered on the steps of Clark Hall, 1968. (Arthur J. Morris Law Library Special Collections, University of Virginia)

(Harrison and Colgate Darden), a future justice of the Supreme Court of the United States (Lewis F. Powell Jr.), a future justice of the World Court at the Hague (Hardy Dillard), and one of Virginia's leading civil rights attorneys (Oliver W. Hill). Five of the eleven commissioners—Harrison, Dillard, Albert V. Bryan Jr. (Law 1950), George M. Cochran (Law 1936), and J. Sloan Kuykendall (Law 1931)—were graduates of the University of Virginia's Law School.

Moving promptly to their task, the commissioners appointed a UVA Law professor, A. E. Dick Howard (also a graduate of the Law School), as their executive director. The Law School was the commission's nerve center. The commission was divided into five subcommittees, each having a practicing lawyer or a law professor as counsel. Two of those counsel—Thomas S. Currier and Peter W. Low (Law 1963)—were members of UVA's law faculty. A recent UVA Law graduate, Hullihen W. Moore (Law 1968), served as the executive director's assistant. During the summer of 1968, a team of researchers produced about 150 memoranda. Twelve of the eighteen research associates were UVA Law students.[73] The commission was also supported by Frances Farmer, UVA Law librarian and first female faculty member, who was appointed as librarian to the commission.[74]

By the fall of 1968, a tentative draft for a revised constitution had taken shape. In addition to approving the text of the revisions, the commissioners sifted and approved detailed commentaries to explain their proposals. On January 1, 1969, the commission delivered a report to the governor, General Assembly, and the people of Virginia. In this report, the commissioners took as their text the admonition of Thomas Jefferson:

> I am certainly not an advocate for frequent & untried changes in laws and constitutions. I think moderate imperfections had better be borne with; because when once known, we accommodate ourselves to them, and find practical means of correcting their ill effects. But I know also that laws and institutions must go hand in hand with the progress of the human mind. As that becomes more developed, more enlightened, as new discoveries are made, new truths disclosed, and manners and opinions change with the change of circumstances, institutions must advance also, and keep pace with the times.[75]

LAURENCE BECK
Class of 1971

NANCY BUC
Class of 1969

WILLIAM CHRISTOPHER
Class of 1970

JOHN DEFAZIO
Class of 1969

CHARD GARNETT III
Class of 1968

RICHARD HOGAN
Class of 1969

GAIL MARSHALL
Class of 1968

NANCY MATTOX
Class of 1969

HULLIHEN MOORE
Class of 1968

TAYLOR REVELEY III
Class of 1968

ROBERT STEIN
Class of 1968

DANIEL WINTERBOTTOM
Class of 1969

UVA Law School students who served as research associates for the Virginia Constitutional Revision Commission, 1968. (Arthur J. Morris Law Library Special Collections, University of Virginia)

The commission emphasized the place of a state constitution in democratic self-government: "The Commission has proceeded on the assumption that the people of Virginia want to shape their own destiny . . . they want a constitution which makes possible a healthy, viable, responsible government."[76]

To that end, the commission made various important recommendations. These included committing the Commonwealth to quality education for its youth and, drawing upon the language of Thomas Jefferson's Bill for the More General Diffusion of Knowledge, including education among the fundamentals recognized by the Bill of Rights.[77] For the first time in Virginia's history, the Bill of Rights would have a clause forbidding discrimination on the basis of race, color, or national origin. Apportionment of seats in Congress and in the General Assembly would be based on population—and districts would be contiguous and compact, an obvious riposte to partisan gerrymandering. Cities and counties with a population over 25,000 would be able to exercise all powers not denied them. In a new environmental conservation article, the revised constitution would make environmental quality public policy in Virginia. In addition to specific recommendations, the commission proposed a general overhaul of the constitution. Applying the principle that a constitution embodies fundamental law, the commission recommended excising a vast amount of essentially statutory language, much of which had been included during the revision of 1901–2. Overall, the result was a crisper, more coherent document half the length of the existing constitution.

When the commissioners reported in January 1969, Godwin declared most of their recommendations to be "consistent, soundly reasoned, and profoundly documented." Looking to Virginia's future, Godwin described the decision before the General Assembly: "It is no longer a Virginia of magnolias and mint juleps that awaits your decisions, but a Virginia at last coming into her own after nearly three-quarters of a century of wandering in the wilderness of Reconstruction and rebuilding, a Virginia now sought after by new industry and new citizens alike."[78] Called into special session in March 1969, the General Assembly approved the bulk of the commission's proposals.[79] The *Washington Post,* initially skeptical, commended the legislature: "The General Assembly has risen above itself. It has produced a document that, with all its shortcomings, would have been inconceivable in Virginia a decade or even five years ago."[80]

When the General Assembly convened at their 1969 session, twenty-six of the House of Delegates' one hundred members were graduates of UVA's Law School, and fourteen of the forty senators had their law degrees from UVA.[81] These individuals were prominent in the sessions' debates. In contrast with the 1901–2 Convention, UVA Law graduates in the 1969 session voiced their respect for the federal courts. For example, a tuition grant provision of the existing constitution had been ruled unconstitutional by the Fourth Circuit because of its use during massive resistance to circumvent the Supreme Court's school desegregation ruling.[82] In considering tuition grants for students with disabilities to attend private schools, the 1969 legislators debated whether reenacting tuition grants of any kind was consistent with the Equal Protection Clause. UVA Law alumni delegates D. French Slaughter Jr. (Law 1953) and Julien J. Mason (Law 1940) particularly emphasized the importance of respecting federal rights and deferring to the federal courts.[83]

After a second approval at the 1970 regular session, the revised constitution was ready to go to the people in referendum. Governor A. Linwood Holton asked A. E. Dick Howard, who had served as the General Assembly's counsel during the revision process, to head up the referendum campaign. Howard assembled a staff for what became known as "Virginians for the Constitution."[84]

The group's statewide steering committee symbolized the broad consensus of support for the proposed constitution. Godwin was honorary chairman, and his Republican successor, Holton, served as chairman. All three men who had sought the Democratic Party's nomination for governor in 1969—William C. Battle (Law 1947), Henry E. Howell Jr. (Law 1943), and Fred G. Pollard (Law 1942)—agreed to serve on the steering committee. These three differed in many ways, but they had one thing in common: all three held their law degrees from the University of Virginia. They received support from campaign committees created at the county and city levels. Four UVA Law students—Tim W. Finchem (Law

Professor A. E. Dick Howard (Law 1961) teaching at the Law School on North Grounds in an undated photograph. (Arthur J. Morris Law Library Special Collections, University of Virginia)

1973), Thomas A. Schultz Jr. (Law 1972), Fred D. Smith Jr. (Law 1972), and Carl W. Tobias (Law 1972)—served as liaisons between the campaign's central office and the local committees.

Editorial pages weighed in. The Washington, DC, *Evening Star* urged its Virginia readers to rally to the cause "lest a priceless opportunity for advancement be lost."[85] When the Commission on Constitutional Revision issued its report, the *Richmond Times-Dispatch* said the proposed constitution would represent a "spiritual cleanup," sweeping away "the last vestiges of the policies of racial segregation and voter restriction that dominated the 1902 Constitution."[86] On election day, the new constitution was overwhelmingly adopted, receiving 72 percent approval.[87]

Epilogue: Professor A. E. Dick Howard's Reflections

When I first stepped into the classroom at the Law School, I had just spent two years clerking for Justice Hugo L. Black at the United States Supreme Court. As fortune would have it, when I began my clerkship in 1962, Felix Frankfurter had left the court, and Arthur J. Goldberg had taken his place. That shift in seats brought with it the heyday of the Warren Court. The liberal majority's pursuit of such values as fairness, racial justice, and the open society changed the face of constitutional law. Inevitably, beginning my academic career at such a momentous time helped shape my sense of what it was that I was meant to do in teaching constitutional law.

By the time the 1960s ended, I had gone from simply talking about constitutions to helping make one—Virginia's 1971 constitution. The ensuing years have brought other adventures—briefing and arguing constitutional cases in state and federal courts, advising successive governors and state legislators, chairing the Smithsonian Institution's symposium marking the US Constitution's bicentennial, and comparing notes with drafters at work on new constitutions in countries around the world, especially in postcommunist Central and Eastern Europe. The seeds for those constitutional moments were planted in the company of some remarkable leaders and thinkers, such as Hugo Black, Lewis Powell, Hardy Dillard, and others.

What lessons have I learned? How do I view the world of constitutional law? Here are a few thoughts and impressions.

Seeing the work of the Warren Court firsthand taught me about the malleability of constitutional law—how cases take shape in the hands of skilled advocates and engaged judges. I better understand why scholars, judges, and others argue about ideas such as originalism and the "living constitution."

Being at Justice Black's elbow convinced me of how personalities matter, especially on the Supreme Court. Black combined a love for history, the ability to write in direct language, the ability to get along with other justices, and a constitutional vision. Small wonder that he became one of the most influential justices of all time. My interest in judicial personality has led me to teach, for many years, a seminar on Supreme Court justices and the art of judging. Each semester, my students and I have sat in on oral arguments at the Supreme Court and had private audiences with one of the justices—visits that students will remember for the rest of their lives (as they have told me).

History enlarges our understanding of constitutional law. Early in my career, I wrote a book, *The Road from Runnymede,* musing on the Magna Carta's influence on American constitutional law.[88] Now, when I teach a basic course in constitutional law, I spend the first week engaging the students on constitutional history in England and America, all before embarking on *Marbury v. Madison* (1803).

Having a hand in the making of Virginia's constitution opened my eyes to how constitutions come to be—before any judges get to interpret them. I had the privilege of being directly involved in every stage of the crafting of the Constitution of Virginia—the study commission's proposals, the legislature's response to those proposals, and the campaign for the constitution's approval. I better understand the craftmanship required to write a good constitution, the politics that influence how legislators debate and vote, and the hopes and fears of ordinary citizens. Context matters.

A study of constitutionalism in America is incomplete without understanding the place of state constitutions, both in American history (when the state constitutions of the Revolutionary era preceded the Philadelphia convention) and in our own time (when the Roberts Court has taken federal courts out of the business of reviewing challenges to partisan gerrymandering).

Working with constitution makers in other countries has taught me about comparative constitutionalism. Again, context matters. The more I learned about Hungary's Golden Bull (1222), the revolutions of 1848, the sense of loss felt because of the Treaty of Trianon (1920), and the corrosive legacy of the communist era, the better I understood the forces shaping debate over a postcommunist constitution in Hungary. Back in Charlottesville, I began teaching a course on comparative constitutional law in 1991. That course evolved into a new course titled Constitutionalism: Nation, Culture, and Constitutions, where we enquire what people, here and abroad, mean when they talk about the "nation."

As this account of Virginia since 1902 suggests, our graduates have been at the heart of constitutional development in the Commonwealth. I connect constitutionalism with civic education, with civic virtue, with self-government by a free people. I loved chairing Virginia's Commission on the Bicentennial of the United States Constitution because it brought the welcome opportunity to take constitutional conversation out of law schools and various courts and to the people in local communities. In my teaching, my scholarship, and my engagement in constitutionalism in this country and elsewhere, I have taken as my lodestar the admonition in Virginia's 1776 Declaration of Rights: "That no free government, nor the blessings of liberty, can be preserved to any people, but by . . . frequent recurrence to fundamental principles."

Notes

We are grateful for research and helpful suggestions from Meggan F. Cashwell and the Special Collections staff at UVA Law. We also drew inspiration from members of informal constitutional law seminars in the spring and fall of 2022—Christian Alcorn, Holly Bard, Jonathan Duval, Sean Gray, Meaghan Haley, Hunter Heck, Reece Henry, Jeffrey Horn, Donna Faye Imadi, Morgan Maloney, Elana Oser, Ashley Reed, Frances Skardon, Andrew Tynes, and Regina Zheng.

1. Paul E. Herron, *Framing the Solid South: The State Constitutional Conventions of Secession, Reconstruction, and Redemption, 1860–1902* (Lawrence: University Press of Kansas, 2017); Michael Perman, *Struggle for Mastery: Disenfranchisement in the*

South, 1888–1908 (Chapel Hill: University of North Carolina Press, 2001); Dorothy Overstreet Pratt, *Sowing the Wind: The Mississippi Constitutional Convention of 1890* (Jackson: University Press of Mississippi, 2018).

2. See Elizabeth R. Varon, "The Civil War and Reconstruction, 1861–1877," in this volume, on the history of the Civil War and Reconstruction and the role that UVA Law professors played in perpetuating Lost Cause ideology through their teaching and mentorship.
3. James H. Lindsay, ed., *Report of the Proceedings and Debates of the Constitutional Convention, State of Virginia: Held in the City of Richmond, June 12, 1901, to June 26, 1902* (Richmond: Hermitage Press, 1906).
4. J. N. Brenaman, *A History of Virginia Conventions* (Richmond: J. L. Hill Printing, 1902), 96–104. This list was compiled with the assistance of Special Collections staff at the Arthur J. Morris Law Library. Each graduate of UVA Law is listed with their graduation year in parentheses throughout the chapter.
5. Lindsay, *Report of the Proceedings*, 2:2966.
6. Lindsay, *Report of the Proceedings*, 1:1535.
7. Lindsay, *Report of the Proceedings*, 1:1674.
8. Pratt, *Sowing the Wind*.
9. *The Constitution of Virginia Framed by the Convention Which Met in Richmond, Virginia on Tuesday, December 3, 1867* (Richmond: Office of the New Nation, 1868).
10. Williams v. Mississippi, 170 U.S. 213 (1898).
11. Virginia Commission on Constitutional Revision, *The Constitution of Virginia: Report of the Commission on Constitutional Revision to His Excellency, Mills E. Godwin, Jr., Governor of Virginia, the General Assembly of Virginia, and the People of Virginia* (Richmond: Michie, 1969), 23 (hereafter cited as CCR).
12. Richard Lowe, *Republicans and Reconstruction in Virginia, 1856–70* (Charlottesville: University Press of Virginia, 1991); Hanes Walton Jr., Sherman C. Puckett, and Donald Richard Deskins, *The African American Electorate: A Statistical History* (Thousand Oaks, CA: CQ Press, 2012), 360 (indicating African Americans represented 46.8 percent of voters in Virginia in 1867); A. E. Dick Howard. "50 Years On, Does Virginia's 1971 Constitution Still Meet the Challenge?," *Virginia Bar Association* 47, no. 2 (Fall 2020): 16–18; A. E. Dick Howard, "'For the Common Benefit': Constitutional History in Virginia as a Casebook for the Modern Constitution-Maker," *Virginia Law Review* 54, no. 5 (June 1968): 816–902.
13. Wythe Holt, *Virginia's Constitutional Convention of 1901–1902* (New York: Garland, 1990), 233–34.
14. Brent Tarter, *The Grandees of Government: The Origins and Persistence of Undemocratic Politics in Virginia* (Charlottesville: University of Virginia Press, 2013); V. O. Key Jr., *Southern Politics in State and Nation* (New York: A. A. Knopf, 1949), 17–33.
15. *Catalogue of the Officers and Students of the University of Virginia, Session of 1844–45* (Philadelphia: C. Sherman, 1845), 17.
16. "Report of the Committee on Legal Education," Annual Report of the American Bar Association 18 (1895): 309–34.
17. University of Virginia, *Department of Law: Catalogue 1903–1904, Announcements, 1904–1905*, Bulletins of the University of Virginia, n.s., vol. 4, no. 3 (Charlottesville: University of Virginia, 1904), 7 (starting in 1915, UVA published this bulletin series as part of the University of Virginia Record; hereafter cited as *LSR* for *Law School Record*).

18. Thomas M. Cooley and Andrew C. McLaughlin, *The General Principles of Constitutional Law in the United States of America,* 3rd ed. (Boston: Little, Brown, 1898), iii.
19. *LSR,* 1911, 8.
20. *LSR,* 1921, 9.
21. Henry Campbell Black, *Handbook of American Constitutional Law,* 2nd ed. (St. Paul, MN: West, 1895), iii.
22. Black, *Handbook of American Constitutional Law,* x.
23. UVA Law's course roster lists at least eight courses taught during the 2022–23 academic year that are in some way derivative of a typical constitutional law course: Administrative Law, Civil Rights Litigation, Criminal Procedure, Constitutional Law II: Religious Liberty, Constitutional Law II: Poverty, Constitutional Law II: Survey of Civil Liberties, Constitutional Law II: Freedom of Speech and Press, and Constitutional Law and Economics.
24. John Ritchie, "F. D. G. Ribble." *Virginia Law Review* 57, no. 1 (February 1971): 1–2.
25. F. D. G. Ribble, *State and National Power over Commerce* (New York: Columbia University Press, 1937).
26. See G. Edward White, "Poised between a Regional and a National Law School, 1920–1960," in this volume, for more on UVA Law's initial resistance and then gradual transition to the case method in the 1930s.
27. Dean's Annual Report, 10 January 1931, Deans' Papers, RG–32-100-78, Arthur J. Morris Law Library Special Collections, University of Virginia (hereafter cited as LLSC).
28. Lawrence B. Evans, *Leading Cases on American Constitutional Law,* 2nd ed. (Chicago: Callaghan, 1925).
29. Noel T. Dowling, *Cases on Constitutional Law,* 2nd ed. (Chicago: Foundation Press, 1941).
30. Dowling, *Cases on Constitutional Law,* vii.
31. Everard H. Smith Jr. Student Notebook, 1948, F. D. G. Ribble, Constitutional Law, Student Notebooks, RG–32–400, LLSC.
32. Dowling, *Cases on Constitutional Law,* vii.
33. Rayner V. Snead Student Notebook, 16 October 1941, 18 January 1942, F. D. G. Ribble, Constitutional Law, Student Notebooks, RG–32–400, LLSC.
34. *LSR,* 1951, 46.
35. *LSR,* 1959, 50.
36. *LSR,* 1957, 47.
37. For the history of desegregation at UVA Law, see the chapter by Risa Goluboff, Randall N. Flaherty, and Biruktawit M. Assefa, "Gregory H. Swanson and the Integration of the University of Virginia School of Law," in this volume.
38. Archibald Cox, *The Warren Court: Constitutional Decision as an Instrument of Reform* (Cambridge, MA: Harvard University Press, 1968), 24.
39. William B. Lockhart, Yale Kamisar, and Jesse H. Choper, *Constitutional Law: Cases—Comments—Questions,* 3rd ed. (St. Paul, MN: West, 1970), ix.
40. Charles W. Quick, review of *Constitutional Law: Cases, Comments & Questions,* by William B. Lockhart, Yale Kamisar, Jesse H. Choper, *Michigan Law Review* 64, no. 3 (January 1966): 569.
41. Harold Norris, "Introduction," of a roundtable on constitutional law, *Journal of Legal Education* 20, no. 4 (1968): 485–87.
42. Frank Strong, review of *Cases and Materials on Constitutional Law,* by Noel T. Dowling and Gerald Gunther, *Journal of Legal Education* 18, no. 4 (1966): 461.

43. Gerald Gunther and Noel T. Dowling, *Cases and Materials on Constitutional Law,* 8th ed. (Mineola, NY: Foundation Press, 1970), xix, xiii.
44. Report of the Long-Range Curriculum Committee, 1 June 1965, Papers of Frederick D. G. Ribble, MSS-77-1, LLSC.
45. *LSR,* 1966, 53, 58.
46. Ronald J. Fisher, "One Hundred Years of Law Reviewed," *Virginia Law Review* 100, no. 1 (March 2014): 4–5, 5n20.
47. Berea College v. Kentucky, 211 U.S. 45 (1908).
48. Editorial, "The Berea College Case," *Virginia Law Register* 14, no. 8 (December 1908): 643.
49. Chiles v. Chesapeake & Ohio Ry. Co., 218 U.S. 71 (1910).
50. Editorial, "Right of Carriers to Separate the Races," *Virginia Law Register* 16, no. 5 (September 1910): 387.
51. J. Douglas Smith, "'When Reason Collides with Prejudice': Armistead Lloyd Boothe and the Politics of Moderation," in *The Moderates' Dilemma: Massive Resistance to School Desegregation in Virginia,* ed. Matthew D. Lassiter and Andrew B. Lewis (Charlottesville: University Press of Virginia, 1998), 24–25.
52. Megan Rosenfeld, "He Was 'Right Too Soon,'" *Washington Post,* 29 July 1978; Armistead L. Boothe, "Civil Rights in Virginia," *Virginia Law Review* 35, no. 7 (November 1949): 928–75.
53. *LSR,* 1949, 27.
54. Brown v. Board of Education of Topeka, 347 U.S. 483 (1954); Editorial, "Publication Views Some Alternative Segregation Plans," *Virginia Law Weekly,* 2 December 1954 (hereafter cited as *VLW*); "Dillard Addresses Calif. Conference," *VLW,* 20 September 1956.
55. "Thurgood Marshal Talks to NAACP," *VLW,* 13 October 1955; "J.B.M. Presents . . . McCarran-Walter Act," *VLW,* 10 December 1953; H. Foster Pettit, "Dr. Omer Carmichael Leads Louisville towards Peaceful School Integration," *VLW,* 11 October 1956; "Article in Virginia Quarterly Review Suggests Relocation as Racial Solution," *VLW,* 4 April 1957.
56. "Negro's Presence Causes Transfer of Softball Game," *VLW,* 9 May 1957.
57. John F. Kennedy, "DICTA: Kennedy Talk Shows Approach to Conflicts," *VLW,* 10 November 1960. For more on the Kennedy family's relationship to UVA Law, see "The Kennedys at Virginia," *UVA Magazine* (Winter 2009), https://perma.cc/CZX6-SNWZ.
58. "No Third Appomattox . . . ," *VLW,* 18 October 1962.
59. *LSR,* 1918, 3.
60. Swain v. Alabama, 380 U.S. 202, 206 (1965). This decision was later overruled by Batson v. Kentucky, 476 U.S. 79 (1986).
61. F. R. D., "*Swain v. Alabama:* A Constitutional Blueprint for the Perpetuation of the All-White Jury," *Virginia Law Review* 52, no. 6 (October 1966): 1159.
62. NAACP v. Button, 371 U.S. 415 (1963); Griffin v. School Board, 377 U.S. 218 (1964); Loving v. Virginia, 388 U.S. 1 (1967). See also Robert Y. Button, *The Constitutionality of the Voting Rights Act of 1965: A Response to the Attorney General of the United States* (Richmond: Virginia Commission on Constitutional Government, 1965), 5.
63. "Nine Schools Close in Three Cities; Thousands without Classrooms," *Southern School News,* October 1958.
64. "Almond Dies at 87; Accepted Mixing," *Richmond Times-Dispatch,* 15 April 1986.

65. M. Carl Andrews, *No Higher Honor: The Story of Mills E. Godwin Jr.* (Richmond, VA: Dietz Press, 1970), 29, 32.
66. "Support for Stanley Stand Requested," *Richmond News Leader,* 9 August 1956.
67. "27 Backers of Stanley Plan Speak Out at Public Hearing," *Richmond Times-Dispatch,* 5 September 1956.
68. "Reconcile Differences, Godwin Tells Party," *Richmond Times-Dispatch,* 18 October 1959.
69. Frank B. Atkinson, *The Dynamic Dominion: Realignment and the Rise of Two-Party Competition in Virginia, 1945–1980,* 2nd ed. (Lanham, MD: Rowman and Littlefield, 2006), 171, 175.
70. James L. Bugg Jr., "Mills Edwin Godwin, Jr.: A Man for All Seasons," in *The Governors of Virginia 1860–1978,* ed. Edward Younger and James Tice Moore (Charlottesville: University Press of Virginia, 1982), 373.
71. Mills E. Godwin Jr., "Address to the General Assembly," 10 January 1968, in Senate Docket no. 1, 1968 Session (Richmond, 1968).
72. H. J. Res. 3 in *Acts and Joint Resolutions of the Assembly of the Commonwealth of Virginia,* 1968 Session (Richmond, 1968), 2:1568.
73. The UVA Law student research associates included Laurence D. Beck (Law 1971), Nancy L. Buc (Law 1969), William G. Christopher (Law 1970), John T. Defazio (Law 1969), Richard W. Garnett III (Law 1968), Richard W. Hogan (Law 1969), Gail S. Marshall (Law 1968), Nancy A. Mattox (Law 1969), W. Taylor Reveley III (Law 1968), Robert M. Stein (Law 1968), and Daniel A. Winterbottom (Law 1969).
74. A. E. Dick Howard, interview by Frances Farmer, 9 March 1983, University of Virginia School of Law Oral History Project, RG-32-405, LLSC.
75. CCR, 8–9; see also Thomas Jefferson to "Henry Tompkinson" (Samuel Kercheval), 12 July 1816, in James P. McClure and J. Jefferson Looney, eds., *The Papers of Thomas Jefferson Digital Edition* (Charlottesville: University of Virginia Press, Rotunda, 2008–25), Retirement Series, 10:226–27, https://rotunda.upress.virginia.edu/founders/TSJN-03-10-02-0128-0002.
76. CCR, 11.
77. CCR, 99, 255–56, 96, 117, 229, 321–22, 9–10. On Jefferson, see McClure and Looney, *Papers of Thomas Jefferson,* Main Series, 2:526–35, https://rotunda.upress.virginia.edu/founders/TSJN-01-02-02-0132-0004-0079.
78. Mills E. Godwin Jr., "Address to the General Assembly Extra Session," 26 February 1969, in *Proceedings and Debates of the Virginia House of Delegates Pertaining to Amendment of the Constitution: Extra Session 1969, Regular Session 1970* (Richmond: Virginia General Assembly House of Delegates, 1972), 5, 11.
79. *Proceedings and Debates,* 815–80.
80. Editorial, *Washington Post,* 26 April 1969.
81. See the University of Virginia Law Alumni Association's *1972 Directory of Alumni of the Law School* (Charlottesville: Michie, 1972). UVA Law Special Collections staff compiled this list, using the roll call for the General Assembly and comparing it to the directory.
82. A. E. Dick Howard, *Commentaries on the Constitution of Virginia* (Charlottesville: University Press of Virginia, 1974), 2:951.
83. *Proceedings and Debates,* 302–4, 314.
84. The discussion in this and the following paragraph draws from A. E. Dick Howard

and William Antholis, "The Virginia Constitution of 1971: An Interview with A. E. Dick Howard," *Virginia Magazine of History and Biography* 129, no. 4 (2021): 346–89.

85. Editorial, *Evening Star* (Washington, DC), 27 October 1970.

86. "Revised State Constitution Offered by Commission Headed by Harrison," *Richmond Times-Dispatch,* 12 January 1969.

87. A. E. Dick Howard, Harry M. Bradley, and Tim Finchem, *Virginia Votes for a New Constitution* (Roanoke: Virginia Western Community College, 1973).

88. A. E. Dick Howard, *The Road from Runnymede: Magna Carta and Constitutionalism in America* (Charlottesville: University of Virginia Press, 1968).

Gregory H. Swanson and the Integration of the University of Virginia School of Law

Risa Goluboff, Randall N. Flaherty, and Biruktawit M. Assefa

ON SEPTEMBER 15, 1950, Gregory H. Swanson enrolled in the LLM (master of laws) program at the University of Virginia School of Law.[1] A graduate of Howard University Law School and a practicing Virginia attorney, his credentials had earned him unanimous approval for acceptance by the Law School's graduate committee. When the University's Board of Visitors (BOV) subsequently denied Swanson's admission based on his race, he sued the University in federal court under the Fourteenth Amendment and won his right to enroll. Swanson attended the Law School during the 1950–51 academic year as the first Black student to integrate the University of Virginia and its Law School and to enroll on an integrated basis at any previously white law school in the former Confederacy.[2] With an LLM degree, he hoped to teach. A native Virginian, Swanson believed that his admission to his state university would be "a triumph in the struggle to break down segregation and discrimination or to bring about equalization in education facilities."[3]

Swanson's attendance at UVA was transformative for the Law School, its student body, and its curriculum. His presence as a Black man in a previously all-white institution challenged the idea of a justly "separate but equal" society that had been taught in the Law School's curriculum since the 1896 *Plessy v. Ferguson* case and had deep connections to the Law School's founding principles.[4] When Thomas Jefferson founded UVA

Gregory H. Swanson (Law 1951) enrolls and registers for classes as a graduate law student at UVA, September 15, 1950. Pictured with student Eugene Nuckols (Law 1951). (Albert and Shirley Small Special Collections Library, University of Virginia)

more than a century earlier, he had not conceived of Swanson, or any other Black American, as a student. Jefferson's ambitious goal, as David T. Konig has described in this volume, was to educate students for leadership and service to the new democracy he had helped establish.[5] Within twenty years of the University's founding, Jefferson expected that UVA alumni would constitute a majority in the Virginia legislature and carry the school's doctrines to other states, thus leavening "the whole mass."[6] But Jefferson's intentions for who would study at his university and lead his nation were narrow. The university he built was exclusively for white men, and it taught legal justifications for slavery.[7] After emancipation, *Plessy's* separate but equal principle further justified and entrenched this practice of racial exclusion.

With occasional exceptions, the white perspectives from which these ideas originated dominated the intellectual life of Clark Hall in the decades leading up to Swanson's admission in 1950.[8] Swanson justified integration and his own right to attend UVA as continuous with Jefferson's own ideas. "It is the true spirit of Jefferson," he stated in a 1951 interview, "that there is a consciousness and concerted effort on the part of students to concern themselves about the welfare and future of this country and the complete enjoyment of equality by all American citizens."[9]

The evolution of the Law School student body that Swanson referenced, and of the law curriculum they encountered and helped shape, was gradual. Proceeding in fits and starts, it was responsive to changes in the world, in legal theory, and in law. Though the student body remained resoundingly white and male for some time after Gregory Swanson's enrollment, Swanson's story is an important inflection point in this history. His admission to and integration of the Law School would have a profound and long-lasting effect on the school and its curriculum. Beyond UVA, it was a product of and a catalyst for broader changes in American race relations and civil rights in the mid-twentieth century.

Gregory Swanson, Esquire

When Gregory Swanson applied to the LLM program at UVA in 1949, he knew that he was joining a civil rights movement and that he might make history. He was twenty-six years old and a recent graduate of Howard University Law School, where he had been immersed in Howard's curricular focus on training civil rights lawyers. Howard Law School's unique approach had been the legacy of Charles Hamilton Houston's leadership. Houston had studied law at Harvard in the emerging tenets of legal realism, a legal theory that spread from its epicenter at Yale Law School and understood law as an instrument of social engineering with material civil and economic consequences.[10] At the helm of Howard Law School between 1929 and 1935, Houston centered the curriculum around the "functional teaching of law" to educate lawyers who could meet the practical demands of the Black struggle for equality.[11] In 1936, Howard introduced a research-intensive civil rights course, the first of its kind in American law schools, under the guidance of Professor James M. Nabrit Jr.[12]

As a college and law student, Swanson spent seven years at Howard in the 1940s. He enrolled as an undergraduate in 1941, graduated with an AB in political science in 1945, and matriculated immediately to Howard Law School. He was a member and officer of Howard's chapter of the Alpha Phi Alpha (APA) fraternity and active in the Kappa Sigma Debating Society.[13] In law school, Swanson took Constitutional Law and Civil Rights with Nabrit, both of which were required. He took Conflict of Laws with professor and civil rights lawyer Herbert Reid.[14] Swanson graduated in 1948 with his LLB (bachelor of laws) and began his legal career.[15]

In his first year out of law school, Swanson worked for Hill, Martin, and Robinson in Richmond, Virginia, the preeminent civil rights litigation firm in the American South. Under principals Oliver W. Hill, Spotswood W. Robinson III, and Martin A. Martin—also law graduates of Howard—the firm served as counsel to the NAACP of Virginia in challenging racial segregation in all forms, especially in education. After celebrating the 1948 Supreme Court rulings outlawing all-white primaries and racially restrictive housing covenants, the firm worked on salary inequality between white and Black Virginia teachers and litigation for equal school facilities for Black children in Virginia's Gloucester and King Counties.[16]

In September 1949, Swanson returned to his hometown of Danville, Virginia, and began clerking for Jerry L. Williams, a prominent civil rights attorney and lawyer for the Danville chapter of the NAACP.[17] Even while in law school, Swanson had expected to continue his legal education with graduate work. While clerking for Williams, Swanson received an offer to join the faculty at a law school, likely the Terrell Law School. The offer was contingent on Swanson earning a graduate law degree.[18] In the fall of 1949, Swanson initiated his application to UVA to join the LLM program. "My primary reason stems from the desire to teach law," Swanson wrote to the Committee on Admission.[19] Though UVA had never enrolled a Black student, it was the only Virginia school with a graduate program in law at the time.

Legal Education at UVA

When Swanson applied, the Law School had recently added its LLM graduate program to enhance its national standing. By the 1940s, as G. Edward White discusses in a prior chapter, UVA Law School was making a conscious effort to both deepen its regional prominence in the American South and secure a spot as a leading national law school.[20] As dean from 1939 to 1963, Frederick D. G. Ribble, himself a 1921 Law School graduate, invested in a new LLM program as part of this strategy. Ribble tasked Professor Garrard Glenn with studying LLM programs at peer, elite institutions such as Columbia, Harvard, and Yale as models.[21] In 1945, the Law School implemented its own program, requiring for admission an LLB degree "with high rank" from an accredited law school.[22] The 1949–50 catalog that Swanson requested and received as he considered his application to UVA described the LLM program as an opportunity for those interested in exploring specialized legal research, expanding their legal education, or preparing to teach law. In consultation with a faculty advisor, LLM students would attend select law school courses and develop independent thesis projects.[23]

The program was a logical fit for Swanson, especially because between 1945 and 1950 the Law School was expanding the depth and renown of its faculty in the areas of tax and corporate law that Swanson hoped to explore. The Law School was keen to bring the legal issues of the day into legal education, particularly the practice of law in government and business. This period also saw the formation of the Student Legal Forum and the *Virginia Law Weekly* (*VLW*) for that purpose, as well as regular topical articles in the *Virginia Law Review*.[24] In Ribble's 1947 annual report to the University president, he outlined three areas for expansion in the formal law curriculum—international law, business and labor law, and legal philosophy—all of which responded to "developments in our civilization abroad and at home."[25] The Law School subsequently added or greatly expanded its course catalog to include Taxation, Foreign Commercial Transactions, Conflict of Laws, Legal Philosophy, Local Government Law, State and Local Taxation, and Aviation Law.[26] Many of these classes reflected the Law School's curricular embrace of topics that would train lawyers for an increasingly industrialized and corporate society with practice-based pedagogy.

By 1950, the curriculum required second-year students to take a number of new courses, including Constitutional Law.[27] The decision marked a return to former curricular practice. The topic of constitutional law had been obligatory for graduation through the nineteenth century. UVA and its law school peers exhibited a heightened interest in constitutional law by the early twentieth century. As A. E. Dick Howard and Catherine A. Ward have noted, Ribble took the class over from Raleigh C. Minor (Law 1890) in 1924.[28] In accordance with the realist emphasis on teaching legal practice, the Law School in 1949 also offered an elective Constitutional

Law seminar in which students tried cases currently before the Supreme Court using actual briefs.[29] The course was taught by Donald R. Richberg, a labor lawyer who had helped write the National Industrial Recovery Act and the Taft-Hartley Act.[30]

The Law School thus embraced the realist's emphasis on practice-based classes, but like many white or predominantly white law schools, it did not follow Howard's lead in adopting the more political strands of realism that would prompt a critique of prevailing constitutional doctrines on issues of race. The formal curriculum maintained a conservative respect for teaching long-standing principles, specifically the separate but equal doctrine. For instance, a 1910 edition of Henry Black's *Handbook on American Constitutional Law,* used by student Francis W. Payne (Law 1916) in Minor's 1915 Constitutional Law class, includes heavy annotations in the civil rights chapter. Underlining and various "NB" notations, reminding the reader to note well, appear in the margins by sections on the constitutionality of segregated schools under the Fourteenth Amendment.[31]

Ribble continued teaching the validity of the separate but equal doctrine in his Constitutional Law classes into the 1940s using Noel T. Dowling's popular *Cases on Constitutional Law.*[32] In 1938, after the Supreme Court announced in *Missouri ex rel. Gaines v. Canada* that the University of Missouri could not cure the lack of equality in state legal education by sending Black students to out-of-state law schools, Dowling added the case to his 1941 and 1946 editions. Student notes show that Ribble taught this case pursuant to the Supreme Court ruling, as an example of the state's failure to uphold equal protection for Gaines, not as evidence of any error in the *Plessy* logic itself. Notes by law student Rayner V. Snead (Law 1942), likely from Ribble's 1941 seminar, recorded the following from Ribble's lecture: "Gaines won on ground that he had to leave state to get legal educ. & he was denied equal protection of laws." Building on his *Gaines* discussion, Ribble argued more broadly that segregation would be upheld because the separate but equal principle was not discriminatory: "I agree that the Sup. Ct. will uphold Jim Crow law. All laws take some liberties, but these laws must not discriminate."[33] Judge Collins J. Seitz (Law 1940), whose 1952 decision in *Gebhart v. Belton* regarding Delaware schools found segregation unequal and called for immediate remedy, took Ribble's Constitutional Law class in the late 1930s.[34] Confirming Snead's notes and the Law School curriculum's broader approach to civil rights, Seitz recalled that when Ribble taught constitutional law, there was never a discussion of Justice John Marshall Harlan's dissent in *Plessy v. Ferguson*, and there was no questioning of the separate but equal principle.[35]

Desegregation in Higher Education

Gaines was the first Supreme Court case to vindicate a claim of race discrimination in higher education, but by the time Swanson decided to apply to UVA in 1949, it was not the only one. Indeed, Swanson's decision resulted not only from his own career goals—the need for a graduate degree to secure the teaching job he wanted—but also from his sense that the moment had come for UVA to desegregate. After submitting his first application materials in November 1949, Swanson wrote to George Marion Johnson, dean of the Howard University Law School, that he expected to hear in reply "the usual answer referring to the laws of Virginia requiring the segregation of the races, and that if such educational opportunities are desired, the same may be obtained by attending some out of state institution through grant-in-aid from the state." Under usual circumstances, Swanson would accept this "compromise," he wrote to Johnson. Though Swanson admitted that he had "no vehement desire to attend the University of Virginia," he thought the timing seemed propitious to challenge the constitutionality of segregation in a state graduate school.[36]

Swanson was correct. More than fifteen years had passed since the University had received, and rejected, its first application on record from a prospective Black student. Alice Jackson's 1935 application to UVA's master's program in French joined several applications to universities in North Carolina, Tennessee, and Maryland as part of an NAACP litigation strategy to insist on the "equal" part of the *Plessy's* "separate but equal" principle. If the Equal Protection Clause of the Fourteenth Amendment countenanced racial segregation only when the state offered substantially equal facilities and services to Black individuals, the NAACP sought to hold southern states to that constitutional promise.[37] The ultimate goal was to improve Black life under Jim Crow by rendering "separate but equal" too expensive and unworkable to maintain.

Jackson's application to UVA was one of the NAACP's earliest efforts to make such arguments in the context of graduate education. Though Virginia had established Black grammar and high schools, as well as the Virginia State College for Negroes, it offered no opportunities for prospective Black graduate students in 1935. A memo to the University's administration that Professor Ribble authored before he became dean concluded that Virginia law prohibited UVA from admitting Black graduate students. Virginia's constitution and statutes outlawed mixed schools, he wrote, and the University of Virginia, as an arm of the state, had no power to admit Black students unilaterally.[38] After the University's BOV rejected Jackson's application, the NAACP threatened to sue. Following models enacted in other southern states, the Virginia General Assembly passed the Dovell Act in 1936. The act supplemented tuition for Black Virginians to attend graduate programs in other states if the graduate program they sought was not otherwise available to them in Virginia.[39] Jackson used Dovell Act funds to earn a master's degree in English and literature at Columbia University.[40]

Also in 1936, the NAACP celebrated its first success in a graduate education case when the Maryland Court of Appeals agreed with Donald G. Murray's argument against his exclusion from the all-white University of Maryland Law School.[41] *Gaines* followed two years later, echoing *Murray*'s prohibition on states using out-of-state facilities to circumvent the bare requirements of the "separate but equal" regime. Both cases left open the possibility that states could discharge their obligations by establishing segregated in-state programs for Black students.[42] Over the next decade, as the NAACP's higher education litigation strategy largely stalled, multiple states nonetheless relied on out-of-state tuition programs rather than desegregate state graduate programs. In Virginia, 4,964 Black students from 1936 to 1950 used these tuition grants for out-of-state graduate education after being excluded from in-state programs.[43] UVA alone paid supplemental out-of-state tuition for hundreds of Black graduate students—including law students—to whom it denied admission.[44]

By the time Swanson applied to UVA more than a decade after *Gaines*, much had changed in the political status of civil rights advocacy, and the time seemed ripe for change in the legal status of discriminatory graduate education. World War II's domestic and international dimensions gave Black civil rights greater salience in mainstream political discourse. Alongside this new political power came new energy and resources for legal change, as lawyers in the NAACP, the Department of Justice's fledgling Civil Rights Section, and elsewhere experimented with legal arguments to challenge Jim Crow. During the 1940s, the Supreme Court vindicated Black civil rights in cases about peonage, union discrimination, police brutality, voting rights, and interstate transportation.[45] In legal education, the Association of American Law Schools (AALS) had made a slow and moderate response to the civil rights movement through the 1930s, but the topic of segregation was growing in importance. Ribble served as AALS secretary-treasurer from 1948 to 1949 and as president-elect in 1949. He noted that annual meetings in these years were becoming a forum for member discussions on desegregation, although the AALS would not formally take up the issue of segregation in legal education until 1950.[46]

Renewed momentum in the NAACP's campaign against discrimination in higher education in 1948 and 1949 set the stage for Swanson's application to UVA. In January 1948, the University of Arkansas became the first formerly white institution of higher education to enroll a Black student since Reconstruction, though it segregated Silas H. Hunt from his law school classmates. That same month, the Supreme Court decided a higher education case for the first time in a decade. In response to the University of Oklahoma's rejection of Ada Sipuel Fisher's application to its law school, the court reaffirmed its decision in *Gaines*. *Sipuel v. Board of Regents* evinced the court's willingness to reenter the constitutional fray on the question of desegregation while still allowing higher education institutions to maintain racially segregated educational facilities within graduate programs.[47] How equal these separate provisions needed to be, and whether any separate institution could actually be equal, were open questions the NAACP pushed to answer.

A year and a half after *Sipuel*, the NAACP convinced the Supreme Court to grant certiorari in two cases it hoped would answer these questions, *Sweatt v. Painter* and *McLaurin v. Oklahoma State Regents*.[48] As the court would later note in *Sweatt*, both cases "present[ed] different aspects of [one] general question: to what extent does the Equal Protection Clause of the Fourteenth Amendment limit the power of a state to distinguish between students of different races in professional and graduate education in a state university?"[49] In *Sipuel*, the court had reaffirmed its constitutional disapproval of the widespread practice of subsidizing out-of-state education for Black students. These new cases might further narrow the options available to UVA in Swanson's case—by heightening the standard for providing a truly equal separate program, requiring admission to white programs on a segregated basis, or even requiring both admission and integration.

The Changing Legal Landscape and Swanson's Application to Virginia Law

With *Sipuel* decided, Hunt admitted to a segregated University of Arkansas School of Law, and *Sweatt* and *McLaurin* at the Supreme Court, Swanson completed his application to UVA in January 1950. As he prepared his materials, Swanson had been monitoring *Sweatt* and *McLaurin*, as well as *Henderson v. United States*, a case challenging the constitutionality of racial segregation on trains.[50] His packet included recommendations from Howard's Dean Johnson and Professor Nabrit.[51] UVA Law School faculty member Leslie H. Buckler, chairman of the committee on graduate studies, was convinced enough that Swanson's application would earn his committee's approval that he invited Swanson to Charlottesville for an in-person meeting even before the committee had deliberated.[52] Swanson's qualifications did earn him unanimous approval for admission to the Law School from Buckler's graduate studies committee.[53] On January 19, 1950, the committee brought the matter of Swanson's application before a full meeting of the law faculty. With one dissenting vote among the twelve faculty members in attendance, the law faculty approved the committee's decision and sent the matter to UVA President Colgate W. Darden, as "directed" for "such cases," for a final decision.[54]

Darden moved slowly in making that decision, highlighting differences in outlook between the nationally situated Law School and the larger University, the state's flagship institution of public higher education. Given the increasingly national profile of the Law School and the growing national orientation of its faculty, Law School administration and faculty had a keen interest in adhering both to federal constitutional principles and to law school admissions criteria that were becoming more standardized through the AALS. The Supreme Court was expected to support integration in *Sweatt* and *McLaurin*, and Swanson met the qualifications for admission with ease. From the University president's office, however, where regional audiences and Virginia's powerful pro-segregation political machine led by Harry Byrd held more sway, waiting for the Supreme Court to decide *Sweatt* and *McLaurin* helped preserve UVA's public standing within state politics as a protector of segregation. Even if desegregation was coming, Darden and the BOV preferred a court order to voluntary desegregation.

The Supreme Court's decisions in *Sweatt* and *McLaurin* on June 5, 1950, looked likely to force the issue. In *Sweatt*, Texas had established a separate law school for Black students, though its resources were not equal to those of the highly regarded University of Texas Law School. Even more than the material inequalities between the two schools, the NAACP emphasized, and the court echoed, were the intangible "qualities which are incapable of objective measurement but which make for greatness in a law school": the reputation of the faculty, the quality of the administration, the strength of the alumni network, and "the interplay of ideas and the exchange of views with which the law is concerned." On these grounds, the *Sweatt* court required Texas to admit Sweatt to the formerly all-white state law school.[55]

McLaurin pushed the reasoning yet further. Even after George W. McLaurin began graduate school in education at the University of Oklahoma, the university went to great lengths to segregate him from white students in the classroom and other school facilities—as it had Ada Sipuel.[56] The question McLaurin's treatment raised was whether segregation within a desegregated program was constitutional. The court said no. This treatment diminished McLaurin's education and inhibited "his ability to study, to engage in discussions and exchange views with other students, and, in general, to learn his profession."[57] Taken together, *Sweatt* and *McLaurin* raised the standard of equality required to satisfy the "separate but equal requirement" so high that it might be impossible to meet. Anticipating *Brown v. Board of Education* four years later, NAACP Special Counsel Thurgood Marshall concluded, "The complete destruction of all enforced segregation is now in sight."[58]

Sweatt and *McLaurin* seemed to prompt action at UVA. Just after the court's decisions in June 1950, Darden brought the matter of Swanson's application to the BOV, and together they solicited the advice of Virginia Attorney General J. Lindsey Almond (Law 1923). Almond informed them that Virginia segregation law likely applied only to K–12 education, not to graduate programs.[59] "Grave doubt arises as to . . . whether there 'is a legal duty imposed upon' your Board to deny admission under facts shared by you."[60] Almond concluded that under recent Supreme Court decisions, "it is manifest that a denial of admission to the applicant under the facts stated by you could not be successfully defended if appropriate action is instituted in the Federal Courts."[61]

Almond's legal analysis notwithstanding, on July 14, 1950, the BOV denied Swanson's application to UVA.[62] On July 29, Professor Emerson G. Spies, who was serving as acting Law School dean that summer, wrote to Swanson to inform him of the decision.[63] UVA's official statement referenced the Virginia Constitution and state laws. Despite Almond's conclusions and the recent Supreme Court decisions, Darden and the BOV maintained their position that Virginia law left them no choice in the matter. As Darden wrote to a number of people in the summer of 1950, "the Board felt . . . that until a competent court had set aside the Virginia provision they were not at liberty to assume that it was unconstitutional and take action in direct contravention to it."[64]

This choice to force court action was not lost on observers.[65] In Norfolk, columnist Vivian Carter Mason of the Black newspaper the *Journal and Guide* emphasized that UVA's decision to deny Swanson's application had been a choice, not a dictate. The BOV "had a key in their hands which could have unlocked the door to UVA," Mason wrote upon hearing of Swanson's initial denial for admission. "They would have been forerunners of the day when all men are free citizens in a free world unhampered by superficial and unjust barriers" if they had cited *Sweatt* to allow Swanson's admission. Instead, they chose to keep the door closed.[66]

Members of the Law School community joined the critique. Law student Margaret Gordon Seiler (Law 1951) called out the BOV tactic of privileging state law over federal and regretted the potential backlash it would have on the national reputation of the Law School. "In the face of a direct conflict between Federal and State law, it is at least debatable whether the duty of the State agent is to uphold State law in the face of the certain knowledge of the supremacy of the Supreme Court's interpretation of constitutional principles," she wrote of the Swanson case in a letter to the *VLW*. Seiler believed a better decision would have been to admit Swanson and force legal verification of this decision through any potential ensuing lawsuit. Seiler lamented that the Law School now appeared complicit in the decision and, consequently, parochial. "As it was," she wrote, "the law school, which enjoys a national reputation, was placed in the unfortunate light of appearing to resist the law, which, if controversial, is certainly clear in this case."[67]

Swanson v. UVA

With UVA's rejection, Swanson turned to the courts. Swanson's legal counsel included Thurgood Marshall, Spotswood Robinson, Oliver Hill, Martin A. Martin, Howard Law School Dean George M. Johnson, and Howard Law Professor James A. Washington Jr., with assistance from the NAACP.[68] Under Robinson's leadership, Swanson filed a complaint and motion for preliminary injunction in the US District Court for the Western District of Virginia, Charlottesville Division, to gain admission to UVA Law School for the fall 1950 semester.[69]

For the remainder of the summer, lawyers for the two sides conferenced under the expectation, shared by the three-judge court, that the case could be concluded before the start of UVA's fall semester.[70] In August 1950, opposing counsel met to "prepare a final judgment which [UVA] would not consent to, but would not oppose."[71] Swanson's original complaint brought action on behalf of "all Negro citizens of the United States residing in the state of Virginia similarly situated, who are duly qualified for admission to the University of Virginia."[72] The UVA defendants countered that Swanson's action applied only to Black students qualified to apply for graduate legal education at UVA, particularly since Virginia offered "separate but equal" alternatives to Black students in other fields of study.[73] Both sides agreed to limit the class action to graduate applicants to the Law School.[74] Spotswood Robinson was confident in gaining Swanson's admission at the conclusion of the trial, and Swanson began to plan for the temporary closing of his Martinsville office. He wrote to Howard professors Nabrit and Herbert Reid asking whether a contract law paper he had written at Howard might be an appropriate topic to explore further for a potential LLM thesis.[75]

On September 5, 1950, after a very brief court hearing, the district court ruled in favor of Swanson's admission to UVA Law School. The court order allowed Swanson to enroll immediately and barred UVA from denying admission to "any other Negro similarly situated."[76] With Swanson's admission achieved in court, Swanson and his legal team proceeded first to the green outside the federal courthouse, the then-home of the city's Robert E. Lee statue, and took a group photograph. Next, they went to the UVA Lawn, where photographers took pictures of the all-Black counsel and UVA's first Black student at the base of a statue of Thomas Jefferson.[77]

A Law Student at UVA

On September 15, 1950, Swanson registered as a graduate student at the University of Virginia School of Law.[78] The local Charlottesville newspaper declared, "The all-white tradition of the University of Virginia was ended here yesterday with the enrollment of Gregory Hayes Swanson."[79] Swanson had already reviewed the course catalog that summer to select his classes. So certain was Buckler of the outcome of the hearing that he had met with Swanson immediately before to map out a likely program of study.[80] In fall 1950, Swanson took three classes with professors Mortimer M. Caplin (Law 1940) (the first Jewish law professor at UVA), Laurens H. Rhinelander, and Buckler and worked on his thesis topic. He was nervous about being called on in class but proud of his first delivery. After meeting with his thesis advisor, Professor T. Munford Boyd (Law 1923), Swanson wrote to his friend, "I have the impression we should get along extremely well."[81] He wrote home to his sister that he had befriended a fellow LLM classmate and that he "had a carrel along with several others in the law school library stacks, for private study."[82] He had lunch every day with two friends in the UVA Commons Cafeteria.[83] Swanson and fellow LLM student Walter H. Beaman (Law 1951) had numerous chats about their shared interest in tax law.[84]

Swanson took the initiative to participate in University life, driven by his acute awareness of his status as the only Black student in residence at UVA that year and by his intention to normalize this presence for the University community.[85] "I am endeavoring to participate [in] the University activities as much as possible so that the students can get used to the idea of a Negro being here," Swanson wrote to his sister in September 1950.[86] Quickly upon beginning his studies at UVA, Swanson joined the UVA YMCA. In October 1950, he was an organizing member of the YMCA's new Committee for Racial Understanding.[87] Swanson attended lectures and football games, where he sat in the desegregated student section with friends from the YMCA and also heard racial epithets hurled at him. He was a season ticket holder to the University's Tuesday Evening Concert Group at Cabell Hall.[88] He attended Unitarian church services near UVA Grounds. Invitations began arriving from around Virginia to speak at churches and NAACP meetings about his case and about Black civil rights.[89]

In other words, the spaces of the University were legally open to Swanson without segregation, and he made a point to inhabit them. His

Gregory H. Swanson with Robert C. Angus (College 1951), a friend from the UVA YMCA, standing on the UVA Lawn. (Moorland-Spingarn Research Center, Howard University)

presence created opportunities to push integration at the University even further. In spring 1951, the Law School's Student Legal Forum, under the organization's president Robert F. Kennedy (Law 1951), invited Black Nobel Prize winner Dr. Ralph J. Bunche to give a talk at UVA. Virginia law required segregation in public assemblies, and Bunche was known to refuse invitations to segregated events. As Kennedy worked to convince Dean Ribble and UVA President Darden to integrate the event, he cited the *McLaurin* ruling and the inference from it that UVA could not segregate Black attendees at a public educational function.[90] In a March 1951 letter to Darden on the matter, Kennedy also cited the importance of Gregory Swanson and the precedent that Swanson had already set by attending Law School events alongside his white peers. Bunche came, and his lecture that spring was the first fully integrated public event at UVA. Reports at the time estimated that Black attendees comprised a third of the audience in Cabell Hall.[91]

Integrated but Isolated

Swanson integrated the Law School in many ways, but he often felt alone. He participated freely in the seven classes he took as an LLM student and thought the Law School was "one of the best in the country," but he was astounded at the lack of realist teachings on law and society and the few opportunities to "discuss the problems of racial cooperation." He spoke to a Richmond newspaper about his surprise "that there is so little emphasis placed on teaching sociology, which should be directed to the end of helping southerners to completely understand the crisis of our time."[92] At the opening of the fall 1950 semester, the *VLW* decided that it would mention Swanson only within its routine write-up of new graduate students.[93] To law student Margaret Gordon Sieler, this policy treated Swanson like any other student and exemplified "the dignified and friendly incorporation of this newcomer into the student body."[94] At once accepting of Swanson as a lawyer, this policy also effaced the student body's need to engage in Swanson's personal experience as a Black Virginian, and it was alienating. Swanson's LLM colleague Beaman recalled, for example, that when he would see Swanson in the large gathering spaces of the Law School, Swanson was most often alone.[95] For understanding and support, Swanson largely looked to his network outside of UVA.

Swanson bristled at the paternalistic ease with which some white students and residents told him what he should expect for his civil rights. Bunche's 1951 talk surfaced some of this tension within the student body. Bunche argued that US segregation policies and incidents of racial prejudice jeopardized US foreign relations, and he decried the gradual approach to desegregation. The talk sparked a counter-article by the *VLW* editorial board praising "the success which we believe has so far attended the gradual approach" and claiming that the existence of progress was more important than the rate of progress. Calling on Black Americans to assume the burdens of segregation, the editorial read: "So long as [minorities in America] assume the burdens as well as the benefits of democratic life—even though others similarly situated, except for race or creed, might receive more of the benefits and less of the burdens—we may be sure that this country's unity in time of peril will continue."[96] In a letter to the *VLW* editor, Swanson critiqued the *VLW*'s praise for gradualism. He wrote, "Of course, it cannot be reasonably expected that the Negro will sleep and simultaneously dream of enjoying the 'inalienable' rights *in future*. If the *contra* is true, then he comes committed to long and protracted litigation."[97] Swanson circulated the *VLW* editorial to the NAACP's *Crisis* and other Black newspapers and heard in return agreement that the original article "boils down to the same old hackneyed southern argument that Negroes should be 'patient' and not rush things."[98]

Swanson's correspondence with white Charlottesville resident Sarah Patton Boyle highlights his encounters with such views. Boyle, a staunch moderate and spouse of a UVA drama professor, had been moved by Swanson's court case and began corresponding with him in September 1950. She felt her letters would welcome him to UVA. She began with unsolicited advice: "Watch that high vocabulary," she offered alongside the warning that "the thing most ridiculed in the educated Negro by educated Whites is his rejection of the simplicity which we fight desperately to acquire."[99] Although Boyle framed herself as an ally to Swanson that fall, her interactions with him reveal the deep barriers to inclusion that Swanson faced beyond the legal opening of University spaces. There were limits to Boyle's willingness to integrate that she felt no need to hide, most especially in housing. After hearing of a movement to get Swanson housing in the UVA dorms, Boyle called instead for gradualism: "If we can't at this point be filled with gratitude that you're here at all, I doubt if this additional minor victory would make us happy either. I'll bet you agree with me that the surest step toward getting what we want is to be grateful—but visibly grateful—for what we get."[100] Swanson pulled back from the correspondence.[101] To a friend, Swanson wrote that while Boyle's heart may have been in the right place, "she possesses strains of paternalism which I utterly deplore."[102] Only later, sparked by her interactions with Swanson, would Boyle transform into a national advocate for civil rights.[103]

The issues he faced in finding housing epitomized Swanson's physical and social distance from the rest of the University. Whereas contemporary Law School directories show most law student residencies bunched around Copeley Hill or the neighborhoods off Rugby Road and Jefferson Park Avenue, Swanson lived on his own at the Carver Inn, a Black hotel in Charlottesville's former Black neighborhood of Vinegar Hill. He lamented the relative lack of social interaction.[104] Swanson made the long walk from the Carver Inn to the Law School each day and noted at the time the novel significance of his trek as a Black student: "It is difficult to stop realizing that I am on the spot as well as a stranger in this town. I walk to the Univ. each day, a mile or more—good exercise, and the whites also stop to stare at me, for they realize that I am going to the Univ. I should like to read their minds. Sometimes, I feel that I do."[105]

Swanson regularly faced subtle acts of racism. He heard repeated claims that desegregation was legally justified but fundamentally regrettable.[106] Swanson wrote to his sister in fall 1950: "It can hardly be said that my presence here has caused a disturbing influence, but my presence is not unnoticed. Yet, there is no perceptible indication of any form of hostility: it is one of those things in the undercurrent; you can't put your finger on it, but you know that [it] is there."[107] Other acts of racism were explicit. After overhearing a UVA student say in casual conversation that

The Carver Inn on Preston Avenue in Charlottesville, 1961. Gregory H. Swanson rented a room here while pursuing his LLM at UVA Law. (Albert and Shirley Small Special Collections Library, University of Virginia)

"we should get that nigger out of the law school," Swanson reflected to a friend about this underlying current of racial prejudice. Discussing the UVA Honor System, Swanson wrote: "I evaluate it in terms of how the students treat others, such as myself, for example. To pledge not to steal, lie, cheat, etc. and yet be permitted under the same pledge to say humiliating things about another student puts the Honor System in question."[108]

Much like the experience of Elizabeth N. Tompkins (Law 1923) and the first women at UVA Law School in the 1920s, important aspects of the larger social community of the Law School, and the spaces for those social interactions, were closed to Swanson.[109] The APA fraternity had been so important to Swanson at Howard, but at UVA he was excluded from fraternities and their functions. On the same day that news appeared in the *VLW* of the Law School spring dance at the privately owned Fry's Spring Beach Club, Swanson wrote to President Darden in hopes of hearing that Darden supported Swanson's legal right to attend dance parties put on by UVA student groups. Darden's response provided no such support.[110]

Onward from UVA

In the summer of 1951, after completing five courses that spring at the Law School, Swanson returned to Martinsville, Virginia, and reopened his law practice.[111] UVA's LLM program required graduate students to be in residence at the Law School for only one year, so Swanson had always planned to leave Charlottesville after the spring 1951 semester.[112] Per the LLM program guidelines, his next task was to draft a prospectus. Then he had two years to complete his thesis.[113] All of this was to happen after Swanson and his LLM peers returned to their jobs and lives beyond Charlottesville.

Back at his law practice, Swanson completed his prospectus and worked with Buckler through fall 1952 to draft a paper.[114] In April 1952, Buckler wrote to Swanson asking if he had made any progress, "or has practice intervened?"[115] Swanson's situation was common. "I am quite in sympathy with people who find, after they have finished their residence, that they are carried into new activities to an extent which precludes their ever completing their graduate work," Buckler wrote to Swanson in 1952.[116] Though Swanson did send an introduction of his thesis to Buckler in May 1951, and a draft of his thesis exists in Swanson's papers at Howard University, he did not hand in a completed thesis prior to the two-year deadline. Like many of his peers, he never received his LLM degree.[117] It turned out that the LLM program was poorly structured for the legal professionals who participated in it. None of the four other LLM students who started with Swanson finished their degrees. Of the twenty-nine LLM students at the Law School during the 1950s, only six received degrees. For Swanson, the closing of Terrell Law School in December 1950 also eliminated his initial reason for pursuing his LLM degree—to join the school's faculty.[118]

The work of lawyering took precedence, and Swanson immediately found meaningful legal work. In May 1951, as his LLM classes concluded, Swanson took up the defense of Albert Jackson, a Black Charlottesville man accused of raping a white woman.[119] Swanson accepted Jackson's case at a time of striking disparities in the severity of sentencing for rape convictions between white and Black men in Virginia.[120] Swanson argued that Jackson's confession had been obtained under duress, and he referenced Jackson's recent discharge from the US Army due to psychological issues. After Jackson's conviction and sentence to death, Swanson, Hill, Martin, and Robinson, with support from the NAACP, took the case to the Supreme Court of Virginia.[121] The appeal was unsuccessful. Jackson was put to death in August 1952.[122] After interviewing Swanson at the trial's start in 1951, the *VLW* wrote: "Mr. Swanson . . . feels an advocate for his race and has a deep sense of responsibility wherever his services are needed, whether in the courtroom or in the community."[123]

Swanson's lack of an LLM degree did not hinder his ability to build a long and successful career in law and civil rights after UVA. In 1957, he moved his private practice to Alexandria, Virginia. In 1961, he joined the Internal Revenue Service under Commissioner Mortimer Caplin, Swanson's former UVA Law School tax professor. It was Swanson's old colleague Robert F. Kennedy who helped him reconnect with Caplin. At the IRS, Swanson served in the office of the chief counsel for the Washington, DC, region until his retirement in 1984.[124] Throughout his life, Swanson continued to advocate for Black civil rights. He was an active member of the Virginia Chapter of the NAACP and served as head of the Martinsville branch.[125] Swanson also served in the Virginia Voters League, a statewide organization dedicated to Black suffrage.[126] He remained involved in his fraternity, APA, which supported Black students and Black civil rights.[127] In 1984, Swanson returned to UVA as the keynote speaker for a Martin Luther King Jr. program sponsored by APA's UVA chapter.[128] Swanson passed away on July 26, 1992, survived in his immediate family by Betty Swanson, his wife, and his two daughters, Karen and Camille Swanson. Today, a portrait of Gregory Swanson adorns the front hallway of the Law School, and the school bestows an annual award in his name to a student who demonstrates "courage, perseverance and a commitment to justice."[129]

Swanson's Legacy

The desegregation cases of 1950 definitively clarified long-standing uncertainties about which options a state could pursue to keep higher education formally segregated. After the Supreme Court's first foray in *Gaines* in 1938, very little had changed in the higher education opportunities southern states offered Black students. But over the course of two years, from 1948 to 1950, the court insisted on desegregation within formerly white graduate institutions. All-Black institutions that a state might hastily establish in response to litigation could no longer be considered equal. Swanson's attendance at UVA was integrated from the moment of his enrollment. Sipuel and McLaurin attended their law schools on an integrated basis. There was no going back.

Far beyond graduate education, *Sweatt, McLaurin,* and *Swanson* proved pivotal to the NAACP's evolving legal strategy. In the immediate aftermath of those victories, the NAACP committed to a head-on challenge to segregation that would culminate in *Brown v. Board of Education* four years later.[130] Swanson's story, as well as those of the many other persistent and brave Black student plaintiffs, is thus an overlooked but critically important part not only of UVA's history but of the history of civil rights more generally.

Swanson desegregated UVA and its law school, but further progress in diversifying student enrollment at UVA and UVA Law School was slow. Swanson's court victory immediately opened the door for Walter N. Ridley (Educ 1953) to enroll in UVA's doctoral program in education, for which there was no counterpart at any of the state's Black colleges. At the same moment, however, Robert A. Smithey, who had applied in summer 1950 to UVA's master's program in English, still found his application referred to the English graduate program at Virginia State College.[131] In 1954, with *Brown* pending before the Supreme Court, John F. Merchant (Law 1958) applied to UVA to join the Law School's LLB (later JD [Juris Doctor]) program. Merchant was a student at Virginia Union University (VUU) at the time. He had applied at the request and encouragement of VUU Vice President Samuel D. Proctor, who felt strongly that the first Black graduate of UVA's law school should be a VUU alum.[132] Proctor's faith in Merchant was not misplaced, and Merchant indeed became the Law School's first Black graduate in 1958. With the Supreme Court's 1956 *Frasier* decision, which held that *Brown* applied to undergraduate education, UVA admitted its first three Black undergraduate students, two of whom would graduate in 1959.[133] In 1960, Fisk University graduate and Virginia native Isaac C. Hunt Jr. (Law 1962) enrolled at the Law School and became its second Black graduate. Asked why he had applied to UVA in a

John F. Merchant (Law 1958), first Black graduate of UVA Law, pictured in 1958. (Arthur J. Morris Law Library Special Collections, University of Virginia)

2015 interview, Hunt stated, "It was my state law school."[134] As Claudrena Harold writes, it would be decades before Black law student enrollment at UVA increased beyond a few pioneers like these students every year.[135] Not until 1967 did the Law School admit its first Black woman student, Elaine Jones (Law 1970). Even fifteen years after *Sweatt* and *McLaurin,* Jones expected to be rejected and given state money to attend a law program outside of Virginia.[136] These early cohorts of Black students, alongside the growing community of women law students, would push for important future changes in the student and faculty composition of the Law School and its curriculum.[137]

In the meantime, curricular growth at UVA Law School was slowly underway. The Law School made incremental but notable changes to expand its teaching on civil rights, particularly with practice-based engagement. In 1952, Ribble became involved in the school desegregation case of *Davis v. Prince Edward County School Board* in support of the plaintiffs.[138] After attending the 1952 Supreme Court arguments for *Davis,* he had his Constitutional Law seminar students argue the case in class in fall 1952. Noting this assignment, the *VLW* reported that the case "had aroused much general interest."[139] In January 1953, Ribble brought the *Davis* counsel to the Law School to argue the case again before a packed crowd in Mural Hall.[140] A few years later, in 1956, the Law School instituted a new civil rights seminar taught by lecturer Charles A. Horsky, who had served as counsel for Fred Korematsu alongside the American Civil Liberties Union in the World War II internment case of *Korematsu v. United States*.[141]

These changes were as much Swanson's legacy at UVA as they were a product of *Brown* and the developments that followed. Not all that transpired at UVA or in Virginia in the decade after Swanson studied there continued straight down the path Swanson had paved, however. Even as other Black students followed in Swanson's footsteps and the curriculum began to incorporate civil rights, school desegregation across Virginia stalled in the face of the state's massive resistance campaign. Though Virginia had been willing to put up only a minimum legal barrier to Swanson's law school admission, the same was not true for K–12 education. As A. E. Dick Howard and Catherine A. Ward outline, many UVA Law School alums would go on to play significant roles in constructing and supporting massive resistance.[142]

Swanson detested this delay of justice. He was acutely aware of his legacy at UVA, his contributions to desegregation, and how much more work needed to be done. In the immediate aftermath of his departure from Charlottesville, he pushed back against an emerging narrative that he had failed by not completing his degree. Darden stated in his 1952 testimony in the *Davis* case that Swanson had "dropped out before the end" of his first year, and the press was quick to repeat this framing.[143] Swanson wrote immediately to Darden that he had not withdrawn and had indeed completed his residency requirement.[144] Darden's false narrative would nonetheless prove difficult to dislodge, receding only with renewed public interest in Swanson's story since 2015.[145]

Swanson had experienced both the promise and the limits of integration at UVA in 1950–51 and knew there was more to achieve: "[I] fully participated in classroom discussions and used all campus facilities—cafeterias, libraries. I just picked my classroom seat at random as everyone else did. I attended concerts, lectures, and football games but never attempted to attend any social affairs." Interviewed for a 1958 *Washing-*

ton Post article at the height of massive resistance, Swanson acknowledged the importance of formal integration under law but added that only face-to-face interaction across racial lines would engender "respect for human personality" and move the bar forward from what Swanson had experienced in 1950–51.[146] Throughout his life, Swanson remained committed to the deliberate, difficult work that advanced the cause his attendance at UVA had vindicated. After reconnecting briefly with Sarah Patton Boyle in 1961 on the topic of desegregation as Boyle drafted her autobiography, Swanson noted, as he had in 1950, that true integration required systemic change. He wrote: "It would require a painful maturation of many economic, political and social forces before integration would become entrenched."[147]

Notes

1. We are ever grateful to the Swanson family for preserving and bringing light to Gregory H. Swanson's story and for donating an important collection of Swanson's legal and personal papers to the UVA Law Library in 2023. We thank Kim Forde-Mazrui for his work to tell Gregory Swanson's history and to deepen the Law School's relationship with the Swanson family. We are also indebted to J. Gordon Hylton (Law 1977), who conducted significant research into Swanson's life and UVA experience in support of the Law School's inaugural Gregory H. Swanson Award in 2018. We rely on and note Hylton's work throughout this chapter.
2. Silas Hunt was the first Black student to attend a previously white university in a former Confederate state when he enrolled at the University of Arkansas School of Law in 1948, but he took segregated classes in the law school basement. Richard A. Buckelew, "Silas Herbert Hunt (1922–1949)," Encyclopedia of Arkansas, Central Arkansas Library System, https://perma.cc/76E4-BK4J. From 1948 to 1950, a number of southern states admitted Black students to select graduate programs at previously white state universities, but with separate classroom, dining, or library spaces. John A. Hardin, *Fifty Years of Segregation: Black Higher Education in Kentucky, 1904–1954* (Lexington: University Press of Kentucky, 1997), 97, 99; Edith Mae Irby Jones interview by Scott Lunsford, 3 April 2006, Arkansas Memories Project, Pryor Center for Arkansas Oral and Visual History, University of Arkansas, https://perma.cc/ZC6T-NWY2. In the immediate aftermath of the *Sweatt* decision in June 1950, John Sanders Chase and Horace Lincoln Heath enrolled on an integrated basis in non-law graduate programs at the University of Texas for the summer session, followed quickly by six additional Black graduate students. Heman Marion Sweatt enrolled at the University of Texas Law School on September 19, 1950, four days after Swanson's enrollment at UVA. Gary M. Lavergne, *Before Brown: Heman Marion Sweatt, Thurgood Marshall, and the Long Road to Justice* (Austin: University of Texas Press, 2010), 260. Ada Sipuel Fisher and George McLaurin both attended the University of

Oklahoma School of Law on an integrated basis in the aftermath of the *McLaurin* decision.

3. Gregory H. Swanson (cited hereafter as GHS) to F. D. Wilkinson, 30 January 1950, Gregory Swanson Papers, Moorland-Spingarn Research Center, Howard University, Washington, DC (cited hereafter as GSP).
4. Plessy v. Ferguson, 163 U.S. 537 (1896).
5. David Thomas Konig, "Jeffersonian Foundations of Legal Education in Virginia, 1779–1845," in this volume.
6. Thomas Jefferson to James Madison, 17 February 1826, James Madison Papers, 1723 to 1859, Library of Congress (cited hereafter as LOC).
7. For Jefferson's views on the founding of, and the student body for, UVA, see Cameron Addis, *Jefferson's Vision for Education, 1760–1845* (New York: Peter Lang, 2003); Andrew J. O'Shaughnessy, *The Illimitable Freedom of the Human Mind: Thomas Jefferson's Idea of a University* (Charlottesville: University of Virginia Press, 2021). See also Justene Hill Edwards, "Teaching the Laws of Slavery, 1826–1865," in this volume.
8. Other students from non white communities preceded Swanson at UVA Law School. Napoleon Breedlove Ainsworth, a member of the Choctaw Nation, attended the Law School from 1881 to 1882 and was the first UVA and Law School student to publicly self-identify as an Indigenous American; see Kelly Fleming, "Alumnus Profile: Napoleon Breedlove Ainsworth, Lawyer and Choctaw Nation Official," *MoreUs* (blog), 29 November 2018, Arthur J. Morris Law Library, University of Virginia, Charlottesville, https://perma.cc/5EXF-AUHB. Ryosuke Hiraoka of Japan and Yan Huiqing of China both attended the Law School for the 1899–1900 session; see University of Virginia, *Department of Law Catalogue 1899–1900* (Roanoke, VA: Stone Printing and Manufacturing, 1900) 22, 24. In 1920, UVA also admitted its first three women law students, as Anne M. Coughlin recounts in "'This Mob of Men': The Road to Coeducation at the University of Virginia School of Law, 1870–1923," in this volume, and Elizabeth Nelson Tompkins from that cohort became the Law School's first female graduate in 1923.
9. GHS statement to Gary Ferguson, GSP.
10. Kenneth W. Mack, *Representing the Race: The Creation of the Civil Rights Lawyer* (Cambridge, MA: Harvard University Press, 2012), 43; Genna Rae McNeil, *Groundwork: Charles Hamilton Houston and the Struggle for Civil Rights* (Philadelphia: University of Pennsylvania Press, 1984), 76–85; Laura Kalman, *Legal Realism at Yale, 1927–1960* (Chapel Hill: University of North Carolina Press, 1986), 3.
11. Mack, *Representing the Race,* 44–45. Mack offers the critical reminder that race-based civil rights law in this time, including at Howard, was primarily focused on rights for straight Black men; Margaret Edds, *We Face the Dawn: Oliver Hill, Spottswood Robinson, and the Legal Team That Dismantled Jim Crow* (Charlottesville: University of Virginia Press, 2018), 67–68. For the work of the cadre of lawyers who constructed the foundations for civil rights law in this period, see Mark V. Tushnet, *Making Civil Rights Law: Thurgood Marshall and the Supreme Court, 1936–1961* (New York: Oxford University Press, 1994).
12. Mack, *Representing the Race,* 227; Edds, *We Face the Dawn,* 66.
13. "Alpha Phi Alpha News," 10 April 1942, and "Alpha Phi Alpha," 30 November 1943, *Howard University Hilltop;* "Biographical Sketch," GSP.
14. GHS to George Johnson, 17 August 1950, GSP.

15. *Catalogue of the Officers and Students of Howard University, 1942–43* (Washington, DC: Howard University, 1944); *Catalogue of the Officers and Students of Howard University, 1948–49* (Washington, DC: Howard University, 1949), 634.
16. Primaries: Rice v. Elmore, 165 F.2d 387 (4th Cir. 1947); Housing covenants: Shelley v. Kraemer, McGhee v. Sipes, 334 U.S. 1 (1948); Edds, *We Face the Dawn*, 173, 180–82.
17. "G. H. Swanson, New Attorney," *Journal and Guide* (Norfolk, VA), 11 March 1950.
18. Swanson wrote in his 1949 application to UVA Law that a "very fine teaching position" was being held for him. GHS to Committee on Admission, 6 December 1949, GSP. According to J. Gordon Hylton, Swanson received this offer from the Terrell Law School, which was a Black law school in Washington, DC. In a 1958 interview, Swanson claimed that he had hoped to teach at the Howard University School of Law at the time of his application to UVA Law. Susanna McBee, "First Negro to Attend U. of Virginia Sees Need for 'Massive Assistance,'" *Washington Post and Times Herald*, 1 September 1958.
19. GHS to Committee on Admission, 6 December 1949, GSP.
20. G. Edward White, "Poised Between a Regional and a National Law School, 1920–1960," in this volume; Dean's Annual Report, 20 January 1946, 20 January 1947, Deans' Papers, RG-32-100-78, Arthur J. Morris Law Library Special Collections, University of Virginia (hereafter cited as LLSC; the Dean's Annual Reports hereafter cited as *DAR*).
21. For Ribble's support for the LLM program see *DAR*, 20 January 1944.
22. University of Virginia, *The Department of Law: Record for 1944–1945, Announcements and Courses 1945–1946*, University of Virginia Record, n.s., 31, no. 3 (Charlottesville: University of Virginia, 1945), 12–13 (hereafter cited as *LSR* for *Law School Record*).
23. *LSR*, 1950, 13; *DAR*, 20 January 1946; Stelle Carter to GHS, 15 October 1949, GSP.
24. Ronald Andrew Bassford, *The Student Legal Forum at the University of Virginia School of Law: The First Fifty Years, 1947–1997* (Charlottesville: Law School Foundation, 2000), 4–5. See also articles from 1946 symposium on "Integrating Law and Other Learned Professions" in *Virginia Law Review* 32, no. 4 (June 1946); "Mr. Jefferson's Law School to Have Student Weekly Paper for First Time since Founding," *Virginia Law Weekly*, 27 May 1948 (hereafter cited as *VLW*).
25. *DAR*, 20 January 1946, 5–6; *DAR*, 20 January 1947, 7, 13.
26. *DAR*, 20 January 1948, 12–15.
27. *LSR*, 1950, 39.
28. A. E. Dick Howard and Catherine A. Ward, "Constitutional Law at the University of Virginia: Between State Constitutional Bookends, 1902–1971," in this volume.
29. *LSR*, 1950, 43.
30. Frank Annunziata, "Donald R. Richberg and American Liberalism: An Illinois Progressive's Critique of the New Deal and Welfare State," *Journal of the Illinois State Historical Society (1908–1984)* 67, no. 5 (November 1974): 530–47.
31. Henry Campbell Black, *Handbook of American Constitutional Law* (St. Paul, MN: West, 1910), 555, 557. A note in the copy held by the UVA Law Library Special Collections states that it was owned by Francis Payne and then bequeathed to Law School Dean William Minor Lile "for use in his law school." The handwriting of the annotations matches Payne's signature at the front of the text.
32. Dowling was Ribble's graduate advisor at Columbia. Noel T. Dowling, *Cases on Constitutional Law* (Chicago: Foundation Press, 1946).

33. Rayner V. Snead Student Notebook, 18 January 1942, 120–21, Professor F. D. G. Ribble's Constitutional Law Class, Student Notebooks, RG-32-400, LLSC; Missouri *ex rel.* Gaines v. Canada, 305 U.S. 337 (1938).
34. Gebhart v. Belton, 91 A.2d 137 (1952).
35. Collins J. Seitz, interview by A. Leon Higginbotham Jr., 21 February 1986, William A. Elwood Civil Rights Lawyers Project, Albert and Shirley Small Special Collections, University of Virginia (cited hereafter as SSCL), https://avalon.lib.virginia.edu/media_objects/pr76f345z.
36. GHS to George Marion Johnson, 30 November 1949, GSP.
37. *Plessy,* 163 U.S. 537 (1896); Frederick D. Loomis Jr., "State Policy and Planning Systems: Responses to the Legal Mandate to Desegregate Higher Education in Virginia and South Carolina," (PhD diss., Pennsylvania State University, 1994), 43.
38. The memo draft held at LLSC does not provide information on who requested this memo or how it was used. F. D. G. Ribble, "A Memorandum on the Eligibility of Negroes for Admission as Students in the Graduate Department of the University of Virginia," 1936, Box 7, Papers of Frederick D. G. Ribble, MSS 77 1, LLSC.
39. "An Act to provide equal educational facilities for certain persons denied admission to Virginia, State colleges, universities, and institutions of higher learning," in *Acts of the General Assembly of the Commonwealth of Virginia,* 1936 Session (Richmond, 1936), 561; U.S. Civil Rights Commission, *Equal Protection of the Laws in Public Higher Education* (Washington, DC: s.n., 1960), 15.
40. "Virginia Moves Cautiously," *Journal and Guide,* 7 March 1936; Peter Wallenstein, "Desegregation in Higher Education," *Encyclopedia Virginia,* Virginia Humanities, https://perma.cc/N5HA-W6B8.
41. Pearson et al. v. Murray, 182 A. 590 and 169 Md. 478 (1936).
42. *Gaines,* 305 U.S. at 350.
43. Marian P. Capps, "The Virginia Out-of-State Graduate Aid Program, 1936–1950," *Journal of Negro Education* 25, no. 1 (Winter 1956): 29.
44. Maurice Apprey and Shelli M. Poe, eds., *The Key to the Door: Experiences of Early African American Students at the University of Virginia* (Charlottesville: University of Virginia Press, 2017).
45. Risa L. Goluboff, *The Lost Promise of Civil Rights* (Cambridge, MA: Harvard University Press, 2007), 43.
46. Association of American Law Schools, *Proceedings of the Annual Meeting of the Association of American Law Schools* (Washington, DC: AALS, 1949), v; Ribble to Ben Gay, 20 November 1951, Box 31, Papers of the President, RG-2/1/2.581, SSCL; Robert A. Leflar, "Legal Education: Desegregation in Law Schools," *American Bar Association Journal* 43, no. 2 (February 1957): 145.
47. Sipuel v. Board of Regents, 332 U.S. 631 (1948).
48. Sweatt v. Painter, 339 U.S. 629 (1950); McLaurin v. Oklahoma State Regents, 339 U.S. 637, 640 (1950).
49. *Sweatt,* 339 U.S. at 631.
50. Henderson v. United States, 339 U.S. 816 (1950).
51. GHS to George Johnson, 9 January 1950, GSP; George Johnson to Leslie Buckler, 10 January 1950, GSP; James Nabrit to Leslie Buckler, 11 January 1950, GSP.
52. Leslie Buckler to GHS, 9 January 1950, GSP.
53. UVA Law School Faculty Meeting Minutes, 19 January 1950, Deans' Papers.
54. UVA Law School Faculty Meeting Minutes, 19 January 1950.

55. *Sweatt,* 339 U.S. at 634–35.
56. Ada Lois Sipuel Fisher, *A Matter of Black and White: The Autobiography of Ada Lois Sipuel Fisher* (Norman: University of Oklahoma Press, 1996), 152; *McLaurin,* 339 U.S. 637, 640.
57. *McLaurin,* 339 U.S. at 641.
58. "A Turning Point in 1950," Separate Is Not Equal: Brown v. Board of Education, Smithsonian National Museum of American History, https://perma.cc/T5Y4-73V8.
59. University of Virginia Board of Visitors Official Minutes, 1947–57, 9 June 1950, Box 3, RG-1/1/1.384, SSCL (cited hereafter as BOV Minutes).
60. J. Lindsey Almond to Colgate Darden, 10 July 1950, BOV Minutes.
61. Almond to Darden, 10 July 1950, BOV Minutes; The contents of Almond's letter also appeared in the press at the time. See "Va. U. Turns Down Negro's Application," *Daily Press* (Newport News, VA), 15 July 1950.
62. BOV Minutes, 14 July 1950.
63. Emerson Spies to GHS, 29 July 1950, GSP.
64. Colgate Darden to Arthur D. Morse, 21 August 1950, Box 28, Papers of the President, RG-2/1/2.562, SSCL.
65. The Associated Press reported that although Swanson had expected the ruling, he felt that the BOV's decision "would prolong the tedious legal efforts by Negroes to gain full education facilities" in Virginia. See "Swanson Uncertain on Course after University Denial," *The Bee* (Danville, VA), 17 July 1950.
66. Vivian Carter Mason, "The Door Was Not Unlocked; 'The Applicant Is a Colored Man,'" *Journal and Guide,* 22 July 1950.
67. Margaret Gordon, letter in "Reader's Forum," *VLW,* 28 September 1950.
68. Memorandum, Spottswood Robinson to Thurgood Marshall, 3 August 1950, Box 247, NAACP Legal Defense and Education Fund Records, LOC.
69. Complaint, Swanson v. Rector & Visitors of Univ. of Va., No. 30 (W.D. Va. 5 September 1950), Box 42, Papers of Judge John Paul, MSS-81-7, LLSC.
70. Judge John Paul to Hill, Martin, and Robinson, 16 August 1950, GSP; J. Lindsey Almond to Judge John Paul, 31 August 1950, Box 42, Papers of Judge John Paul; Spottswood Robinson to Thurgood Marshall et al., 16 August 1950, Box 247.
71. Spottswood Robinson to Robert Carter, 22 August 1950, Box 247.
72. Complaint at 3, *Swanson,* No. 30 (W.D. Va. Sept. 5, 1950).
73. Answer to Defendants to Bill of Complaint at 2–4, *Swanson,* No. 30 (W.D. Va. Sept. 5, 1950).
74. Memorandum, Robinson to Marshall, 3 August 1950; Agreed Statement of Facts, *Swanson,* No. 30 (W.D. Va. Sept. 5, 1950).
75. GHS to George Johnson, 17 August 1950, GSP.
76. Judgment at 3, *Swanson,* No. 30 (W.D. Va. Sept. 5, 1950).
77. "U. of Virginia's First Negro Student on Famed Campus," *Journal and Guide,* 16 September 1950.
78. "Martinsville Negro Lawyer Is Admitted to University," *Richmond Times-Dispatch,* 16 September 1950.
79. "Swanson Enrolls without Incident," *Daily Progress* (Charlottesville, VA), 16 September 1950.
80. Leslie Buckler to GHS, 7 January 1950, and 26 August 1950, GSP; GHS to Stelle Carter, 6 September 1950, GSP.

81. GHS to Sybil, 24 and 28 September 1950, GSP. On Caplin, see Sarah-Jane Lorenzo, "Remembering Mortimer Caplin '40," *VLW*, 9 October 2019.
82. GHS to Marquerite Swanson, 28 September 1950, GSP.
83. GHS to Marquerite Swanson, 28 September 1950.
84. Walter H. Beaman, written recollection of Gregory Swanson, August 2004, given to the UVA Law Library, Alumni Biographical Files, RG-32-406, LLSC.
85. Walter N. Ridley had followed Swanson's lead and applied for graduate study after Swanson won his case. Though Ridley also attended UVA that fall in the School of Education, he commuted and was only in Charlottesville part time; Apprey and Poe, *Key to the Door*, 101–2.
86. GHS to Marquerite Swanson, 28 September 1950.
87. YMCA meeting minutes, 16 October 1950, GSP.
88. The Tuesday Evening Concert Group, Season Ticket 1950–1951; YMCA service programs, various dates, GSP.
89. Eudora D. Lias, "Ellison, Gregory Swanson Heard in Charlottesville," *Journal and Guide*, 4 November 1950.
90. Untitled memorandum, 1951, Box 31, Papers of the President.
91. "Bunche Warns of USA Isolationism in Cabell Address," *VLW*, 5 April 1951.
92. Statement to Gary Ferguson, GSP.
93. "The Report of Dean Ribble to the Law School Alumni," *VLW*, 26 October 1950.
94. Gordon, letter in "Reader's Forum," *VLW*.
95. Walter H. Beaman, written recollection of Gregory Swanson, August 2004.
96. "Bunche Warns of USA Isolationism in Cabell Address," *VLW*; "Of Dive Bombers and Dr. Bunche," *VLW*, 5 April 1951.
97. GHS to Sherwood S. Cadwell (Law 1951), 16 April 1951, GSP.
98. James Ivy to GHS, 17 April 1951, GSP; George Schuyler to GHS, 19 April 1951, GSP.
99. Sarah Boyle to GHS, 4 and 6 September 1950, GSP.
100. Boyle to GHS, 10 September 1950, GSP; underline in original. Excerpt also printed in Sarah Patton Boyle, *The Desegregated Heart: A Virginian's Stand in Time of Transition* (New York: William Morrow, 1962), 65.
101. GHS to Sarah Boyle, 7 September 1950, GSP.
102. GHS to Sybil, 24 September 1950, GSP.
103. Boyle, *Desegregated Heart*.
104. Swanson had arranged this accommodation through correspondence with Charlottesville minister Benjamin Bunn and T. J. Sellers, editor of the *Charlottesville Tribune* and the *Roanoke Times*, two local Black newspapers. GHS to T. J. Sellers, 6 and 9 September 1950, GSP; Benjamin Bunn to GHS, 12 September 1950, GSP; GHS to Marquerite Swanson, 28 September 1950.
105. GHS to Marquerite Swanson, 28 September 1950.
106. See interview with Edward Murr, president of Law School student council, "Fair Treatment of Negro Law Student Urged," *Richmond News Leader*, 9 September 1950.
107. GHS to Marquerite Swanson, 28 September 1950.
108. GHS to Sybil, 24 September 1950.
109. For more on the first women to attend UVA Law School, see Coughlin, "'This Mob of Men.'"
110. GHS to Darden, 12 April 1951, and Darden to GHS, 12 April 1951, Box 31, Papers of the

President; "Law School Dance Initiates Program for Gala Weekend," *VLW,* 12 April 1951.

111. Research notes by J. Gordon Hylton.

112. GHS to Darden, 4 March 1952, GSP; GHS to Sybil, 24 September 1950.

113. *LSR,* 1949, 16.

114. GHS to Buckler, 16 May 1951, GSP; Buckler to GHS, 16 October 1952, GSP.

115. Buckler to GHS, 28 April 1952, GSP.

116. Buckler to GHS, 18 October 1952, GSP.

117. "Swanson, Gregory," 1 October 2015, Manuscript Division, Paper 187, http://dh.howard.edu/finaid_manu/187; GHS to Buckler, 16 May 1951.

118. According to conversation with J. Gordon Hylton.

119. "Gregory Swanson Will Defend in Rape Case," *VLW,* 11 June 1951; see GHS's file on the Albert Jackson case in Gregory H. Swanson Papers, MSS-2024-01, LLSC.

120. Donald Partington found that of the fifty-six men executed in Virginia for rape or attempted rape from 1908 to 1963, all were Black. Donald H. Partington, "The Incidence of the Death Penalty for Rape in Virginia," *Washington and Lee Law Review* 22, no. 1 (Spring 1965): 43–75. Lisa Dorr substantiated these statistics with her own research and argued, for this reason, that "rape cases became part of the struggle for civil rights." Lisa Lindquist Dorr, *White Women, Rape, and the Power of Race in Virginia, 1900–1960* (Chapel Hill: University of North Carolina Press, 2004), 211, 293n16. See also Eric W. Rise, *The Martinsville Seven: Race, Rape, and Capital Punishment* (Charlottesville: University Press of Virginia, 1995).

121. Legal Department Monthly Report, March 1952, Part 01: Supplement, 1951–55, Group I, Administrative File, Executive Office Reports 1951–55, National Association for the Advancement of Colored People Records, 1842–2019, LOC.

122. "Local Restaurant Employee Raped," *Daily Progress,* 7 May 1951; "Swanson Will Ask Verdict of Death for Rape Be Set Aside," *Daily Progress,* 5 July 1951; Jackson v. Commonwealth, 193 Va. 664 (Va. 1952).

123. "Gregory Swanson Will Defend."

124. "Gregory H. Swanson, 68, Lawyer with IRS, Dies," *Washington Post,* 31 July 1992; Internal Revenue Service, *Chief Counsel Office Directory* (Spring 1984), 67, 13.

125. "Swanson Asks Support for NAACP Va. School Program," 24 May 1951, "Swanson Blasts Negro Press; Cites 'Reactionary Stand,'' 19 May 1951, and "Virginia State Conference—NAACP," 28 August 1954, Part 26: Selected Branch Files, 1940–55, Series A: The South, Virginia State Conference, 1951 and 1954, National Association for the Advancement of Colored People Records, 1842–2019; Edds, *We Face the Dawn,* 283.

126. "Virginia NAACP Delegates to Air Social Change Issues," *Journal and Guide,* 9 October 1954.

127. J. Gordon Hylton compiled this information on Swanson's service to Alpha Phi Alpha, particularly during 1951–53 (email on file with authors); "Lawrenceville Alphas to Present Dr. Daniel," *Journal and Guide,* 5 April 1952.

128. "Martin Luther King, Jr. Memorial Program," *Daily Progress,* 27 January 1984.

129. "Gregory H. Swanson, 68, Lawyer with IRS, Dies"; "Gregory H. Swanson Award," UVA Law, https://www.law.virginia.edu/students/gregory-h-swanson-award.

130. Brown v. Board of Education of Topeka, 347 U.S. 483 (1954).

131. Ridley would become the first Black student to graduate from UVA in 1953. "U.Va. Enrolls Negro, Ph.D. Candidate," *Richmond News Leader,* 27 September 1950; "Norfolk Negro Seeking Admission to University," *Norfolk Virginian-Pilot,* 15 September 1950.

132. John F. Merchant, *A Journey Worth Taking: An Unpredictable Adventure* (self-pub., Xlibris, 2012), 79–80, 91.

133. Board of Trustees of University of NC v. Frasier, 350 U.S. 979 (1956); "New Ruling Goes Far beyond University Policy on Negroes," *Daily Progress,* 6 March 1956.

134. Isaac C. Hunt Jr., interview by Will Thomas, 21 July 2015, Securities and Exchange Commission Historical Society, interview transcript, https://perma.cc/ZS5X-JQ2E.

135. See Claudrena Harold, "We Demand: Student Advocates for Curricular Change, 1960–1980," in this volume.

136. Elaine Jones, interview by Julieanna L. Richardson, 6 March 2007, interview A2006.151, transcript, The HistoryMakers Digital Archive, https://www.thehistorymakers.org/biography/elaine-jones-41; U.S. Civil Rights Commission, *Equal Protection of the Laws,* 17.

137. Harold, "We Demand."

138. Davis v. County School Board of Prince Edward County, 149 F. Supp. 431 (E.D. Va. 1957).

139. "Dean Ribble Hears Sup. Court Debates in Explosive Case," *VLW,* 11 December 1952.

140. "Cooperation Necessary," *VLW,* 15 January 1953.

141. Korematsu v. United States, 323 U.S. 214 (1944); "Faculty Increased by Nine New Men," *VLW,* 20 September 1956.

142. See Howard and Ward, "Constitutional Law at the University of Virginia."

143. Transcript of Record, *Davis,* 457; see William B. Foster Jr., "More Negroes Enter White State-Supported Colleges," *Richmond News Leader,* 25 September 1952, and "Many Virginia Schools Now Admitting Negroes," *Philadelphia Tribune,* 7 October 1962.

144. GHS to Darden, 4 March 1952.

145. David A. Maurer, "Commemoration Recalls Effort to Desegregate UVA Law School," *Daily Progress,* 24 October 2015.

146. McBee, "First Negro to Attend U. of Virginia Sees Need for 'Massive Assistance.'"

147. Boyle to GHS, 17 November 1961, and GHS to Boyle, 1961, Gregory H. Swanson Papers, LLSC; Boyle, *Desegregated Heart.*

We Demand

STUDENT ADVOCATES FOR CURRICULAR CHANGE, 1960–1980

Claudrena Harold

ON FEBRUARY 17, 1969, a small but influential group of student leaders at the University of Virginia held a four-hour strategy session at which they discussed the best way to advance the fight for racial justice on Grounds. After careful deliberation and intense debate, the students finalized an eleven-point program, a combination of specific demands and broad sweeping proposals aimed at transforming the University politically, intellectually, and economically.[1] Among the students' demands were the integration of African Americans into all areas of campus life, the elimination of application fees for low-income students, a public statement from the athletic director confirming his commitment to recruit African American athletes and coaches, the formation of a Black studies program by the fall of 1970, and the hiring of an African American as associate dean of admissions. The program also addressed the concerns of UVA's non-academic employees, many of whom were African American. A testament to the influence of organized labor on campus activists, student leaders demanded that Virginia legislators "raise the minimum wage scale for all non-academic University employees in the state and allow the University of Virginia the option of raising its own pay scale." They also called for elected officials to "pass legislation to the effect that University employees have the right to organize employee associations, collective bargaining agreements, strike, and affiliate with national unions."

Now, the students argued, was the time for action. "If we want to change the racist nature of the University," Arthur "Bud" Ogle (College 1971), Student Council (Studco) president, insisted, "we have to take the necessary action ourselves."[2] Heeding Ogle's call, UVA students staged mass demonstrations, confronted state leaders in Richmond, and demanded that University administrators comply fully with the Civil Rights Act of 1964.[3]

This tidal wave of activism sweeping the University was not confined to the undergraduate student body. As Law School Dean Monrad G. Paulsen quickly discovered, the spirit of dissent permeated Clark Hall as well. On February 19, the Law School's Student Advisory Council (SAC) registered its "support of and sympathy with the lawful and nonviolent achievement of racial justice" in academics and employment. Since its formation in 1936, SAC had functioned as a liaison between students, faculty, and administrators. Charged with promoting law students' academic and professional growth, SAC leaders felt compelled to address one of the biggest issues facing higher education: racial integration. Noting that the "feelings of law leaders should be expressed," SAC emphasized the necessity of "a vigorous stand on behalf of justice for minority groups."[4] The fight for justice, SAC also recognized, entailed confronting the entrenched racism and sexism within the Law School itself. Though the Civil Rights Act of 1964 had outlawed discrimination based on race and sex, the composition of the school's faculty and student body remained overwhelmingly white and male.

"It was not a welcoming environment," remembered Elaine R. Jones (Law 1970), the first African American woman to graduate from the Law School.[5] When Jones entered UVA Law in 1967, she was one of eleven women and one of two African Americans in her class. These abysmally low numbers would not go unchallenged. By the time Jones graduated from UVA Law in the spring of 1970, there existed a well-organized coalition of student activists committed to increasing the presence of women and African Americans in the Law School, diversifying the faculty, and building the institutions needed to advance their political vision. Moved by the political fervor of the civil rights, anti-war, women's liberation, and Black Power movements, these students were determined to transform legal education and, by extension, the legal profession.

As described in the pages that follow, law student activism forms an important chapter in the fascinating story of institutional change at the Law School between 1960 and 1980. During these politically charged years, UVA Law students, professors, and administrators clashed over curricular reform, shared governance, minority recruitment, and faculty hiring. These battles were not unique to the University of Virginia. Historian Laura Kalman comments:

> Open the newspapers published at elite law schools during the period, and you will find common themes beneath the dust. United in their condemnation of their education as sterile, dissatisfying, and needlessly competitive, law student agitators sought to end hierarchy and alienation. They agitated for community, citizenship, democracy, and relevance. They fretted about American, as well as academic, politics. They worried constantly about the draft, they grappled with racial injustice, they confronted sexual inequality (though it chiefly concerned women), they saw their professors as symbols of the system and society, and they wondered how they could serve the larger world.[6]

These students bore the imprint of a social milieu that shaped their vision of the transformative possibilities of legal education: the 1960s.

The Civil Rights Movement and Law Student Activists

The 1960s was a time of significant change at UVA Law and within larger society. The civil rights movement transformed the political, economic, and social landscape of post–World War II America. Across the South, African American activists relied on nonviolent direct action, mass demonstrations, litigation, and economic boycotts to dismantle the Jim Crow system. A major turning point for the movement came on February 1, 1960, when four college students from North Carolina Agricultural and Technical State University (NC A&T) conducted a sit-in at the F. W. Woolworth store in downtown Greensboro. Joseph A. McNeil, Franklin E. McCain, Ezell A. Blair, and David L. Richmond entered Woolworth, sat down at the "whites only" lunch counter, and placed an order for coffee. Though the shocked waitress denied their request and ordered them to leave, the students remained seated until the store closed.[7] Over the next two days, dozens of students joined the NC A&T four at Woolworth's segregated lunch counter. By the fourth day, students were also targeting the Kress chain store, which, like Woolworth, had segregated lunch counters. The Greensboro sit-in quickly ignited demonstrations across the South. By the third week of February, the sit-in wave had spread to cities in South Carolina, Florida, Tennessee, Georgia, and Virginia.[8]

Far from passive observers, several UVA Law students who confronted the school's racist practices and policies had political roots in this sit-in movement. One such student was James F. Gay (Law 1968). On Friday, February 12, 1960, Gay and thirty-seven other Black protesters staged a sit-in at the whites-only lunch counter of the F. W. Woolworth store in Norfolk, Virginia. The students attempted to place an order, but the waitress refused to serve them. Gay and his fellow protesters remained seated until the store closed. The next day, they returned to Woolworth, but the store manager had roped off its lunch counter. The students pressed on to another nearby store, S. S. Kresge. In the days ahead, they also targeted W. T. Grants.[9]

"We believed in direct action to confront the system," Gay later recalled.[10] He also believed in the litigation strategies of the NAACP. Gay served as the president of the NAACP's youth chapter and helped increase the chapter's membership by over 300 percent.[11] After graduating from Booker T. Washington High School, he enrolled at Norfolk Division of Virginia State College (Norfolk State). There he majored in chemistry and was a charter member of Alpha Phi Alpha Fraternity. A scholar activist, Gay spoke several times before Norfolk City Council on issues such as civil rights and discrimination.[12]

After graduating from Norfolk State in 1965, Gay enrolled at UVA Law, where he immersed himself in student politics. In 1966, he was elected as the Law School representative on the University's Studco, becoming the first African American to hold a Studco position. He was a member of the Virginia Legal Research group and John Bassett Moore Society of International Law and participated on the International Law Moot Court Team and the Lile Moot Court Competition.[13] As one of Studco's most outspoken members, Gay embraced the opportunity to address UVA's racism and advocated full compliance with the Civil Rights Act of 1964. Thanks largely to his persistence and legal advice, Studco declared all businesses that practiced racial segregation or exclusion off-limits to UVA organizations receiving fiscal support from Studco. Passed by a vote of ten to four on May 2, 1967, the resolution played a critical role in the desegregation of University student life at the undergraduate and graduate level.[14]

Gay's time at the Law School overlapped with the arrival of several students with deep commitments to or deep roots in the Black freedom struggle. This distinguished group included Harold M. Marsh (Law 1966), Elaine Jones, Robert A. Williams (Law 1969), Lester V. Moore Jr. (Law 1969), and James Benton (Law 1970). A native of Norfolk, Benton participated in several civil rights demonstrations as a student at Booker T. Washington High School. He was also involved in the Student Nonviolent Coordinating Committee (SNCC) during his undergraduate studies at Temple University in Philadelphia.[15] Harold M. Marsh, the younger brother of civil rights attorney Henry L. Marsh, was no stranger to political protest and civil rights litigation. Together with Samuel W. Tucker and Oliver W. Hill, Henry Marsh worked tirelessly to tear down the legal edifice of white supremacy in Virginia.[16] Likewise, civil rights was also a family affair for Robert A. Williams, whose father Jerry was an attorney for the NAACP in Danville. In fact, Gregory H. Swanson (Law 1951), the first African American admitted to UVA in 1950, clerked in Williams's law firm.[17] As a youth, Robert Williams led a sit-in at the all-white public library. Years later, he credited his dinner conversations and consultations with his father and community elders about "what was possible and what we could accomplish through the law" with pushing him to challenge Jim Crow segregation.[18] As was the case with Williams, Elaine Jones's political consciousness predated her arrival at UVA. As a child, Jones experienced the sting of white racism and anti-Blackness not just in her hometown of Norfolk. At the age of seven, she had her first brush with northern racism when her family was denied a hotel room during a visit to Chicago. Jones's childhood encounters set her on a career path focused on racial justice. "That's when I decided that my career had to be civil rights. Things had to change."[19]

Though Jones and her peers envisioned the law as a major agent of change, they all had reservations about attending UVA Law School. "Nobody applied to the University of Virginia," Benton later recalled. "It was not a place that was considered welcoming to us." He graduated from Temple University and applied to Northwestern for graduate study in mathematics. After a year in Evanston, Benton decided to apply to UVA Law. Benton received encouragement from a notable alumnus, Robert C. Nusbaum (Law 1948). In the late 1950s, Nusbaum leveraged his political and financial resources to fight against massive resistance to the integration of Norfolk public schools. Later, as founder of the Aid Fund, he offered scholarships to African American students attending college. One of the beneficiaries of Nusbaum's generosity was Benton, who after years of opposition to returning south, warmed to the idea of studying law in his native state. Ultimately, UVA Law School's prestigious reputation, along with its lower tuition relative to other top-tier institutions, sealed the deal.[20]

Whereas race was the principal concern for Benton, Elaine Jones had to consider both her race and gender status when applying to law school. Though the Civil Rights Act had banned discrimination based on race and sex, Jones questioned whether her application would even receive serious consideration. "I said, 'You know, I doubt that Virginia will admit me, although they should. I'm a daughter of Virginia and my grades are good.' But I said, 'They won't. And what they will do,' I thought, 'is pay my tuition to go to school elsewhere.' Because that had been the policy of the State of Virginia. I thought, 'Elaine, you're on your way to law school elsewhere with Virginia picking up the tab.' So, I applied to Virginia. And . . . they admitted me."[21]

As the only African American woman in the Law School at the time, Jones experienced both racism and sexism. It was not always easy to decipher the source of a hostile stare from an undergraduate walking across the lawn, a terse response from a professor during class, or a fellow law student's refusal to share notes during a study session. She later remembered, "I didn't know what was race and what was gender discrimination. . . . Because it was coming at us from every classroom. The discussions, the hypotheticals, everything. So, sitting in the ladies room with my six white sisters, sitting there listening to them talk about their experiences, I was trying to figure out what was gender, what was race. Whatever was left over after their discussion, I realized, was race."[22]

To navigate this complex world, as well as the typical challenges of law school, Jones leaned heavily on her African American peers. "We were a close-knit group . . . there were four men and me. And we all asked the one in the third-year class, 'How have you made it?' But we would come together. And . . . the five of us were the nucleus for others [Black graduate students in other schools]." Jones was especially close to James Benton. "We were in different study groups . . . and then we came together and compared what we both got from each study group, so we helped one another in that way." This support system was crucial in an environment that often felt isolating for students of color. "There were . . . some [white students] who really befriended me," Jones acknowledged, but "most ignored me."[23]

Curricular Change

Despite these challenges, Jones and other African American students entering the Law School in the 1960s appreciated the rigor and diversity of their intellectual experiences and legal training. "The Law School was not rocked like Berkeley or Columbia," Professor A. E. Dick Howard (Law 1961) admitted, "but there was a sense that students should have more choice, fewer requirements, that somehow required courses were onerous."[24] In 1965, the faculty curriculum committee proposed eliminating Agency and Partnership and Negotiable Instruments as required courses, combining Legislation and Administrative Law into a single required course, and requiring third-year students to write a research paper.[25] To improve the experiences of first-year law students, the committee also recommended returning all of Civil Procedure to the first year, transferring Criminal Law to the second year, adding a new course, Legal Institutions, and redesigning Legal Method to include only research and writing. Over the next few years, there were other changes in response to student demands and developments at other top-tier law schools. For example, in 1968, the number of course requirements for rising second- and third-year students were reduced.[26]

There was also a growing sense of the need for courses that addressed social and policy issues. The 1960s witnessed the introduction of such courses as Environmental Law, Law and the Politics of Action, Law and Poverty, and Law in Modern Society.[27] One of the strongest proponents of policy-oriented and interdisciplinary legal study was Professor Mason

Willrich, an expert on energy law who came to UVA Law in 1965. He commented, "Legal education in the future in the nation's great law schools must produce a man that is just as sophisticated in the policy process as he is in the judicial process. . . . Few important decisions do not contain a mixture of political, economic, and social implications, and have national and international dimensions."[28] Willrich was not alone in his call for pedagogical innovation. Moving from Columbia University to UVA Law in the fall of 1968, Dean Paulsen also embraced change: "We are living in a day with pressing problems, and any law school worth its salt will pay attention to them."[29] Paulsen created his Law and the Politics of Action seminar in response to the rise of the New Left and its impact on national politics. Students enrolled in the seminar investigated why "the New Left and other activist groups have rejected the traditional political system in favor of the non-electoral political methods of protest, demonstration, and resistance."[30] In this course, students had the opportunity to reflect on how nonviolent protest, mass demonstrations, and resistance either strengthened or imperiled democratic dialogue and rule.

Along with the increase of socially relevant seminars came the expansion of the school's clinical education program through the creation of the Legal Aid Society. The first steps toward the formation of a legal aid clinic were in fall 1965, when a small group of students expressed interest in using Law School resources to provide legal assistance, advice, and representation to low income and vulnerable populations. Taking the lead in this initiative was Gail S. Marshall (Law 1968), F. Hayden Curry (Law 1967), David S. Fitzpatrick (Law 1967), Thomas G. Livesay (Law 1967), Wallace C. Winter (Law 1967), and Peter F. Windrem (Law 1968). The students began drafting a report calling for a legal aid clinic in Charlottesville. Combined with studying legal aid clinics at other law schools, the students surveyed various community leaders and residents about the need for such a clinic. Counted among the most supportive was Drewary Brown, president of the Charlottesville chapter of the NAACP. "A lot of problems could be avoided if the poor had a place to turn to for advice," Brown informed the students. Other supporters believed the provision of legal services to disadvantaged groups would also alter their views of the law more broadly. According to Reverend Robert B. Albritton of Charlottesville's Westminster Presbyterian Church, a legal aid society could help the poor and marginalized communities "discover the legal system as a protector of rights rather than a visitor of vengeance."[31]

Beyond its value as a public good, a legal aid clinic would also enhance the educational experiences of law students. John C. Lowe (Law 1967), who two years after graduating from UVA Law filed suit to overturn the University's male-only undergraduate admissions policy, was an outspoken advocate for legal aid.[32] "Presently at the law school," he stated, "there is no directive program aimed at teaching counseling and interviewing techniques to the law student." This curricular shortcoming could easily be corrected. As he explained, "A very excellent vehicle for teaching law students interviewing and counseling techniques and giving them experience in these functions is the legal aid clinic."[33]

On March 3, 1966, students submitted their report to the executive committee of the Charlottesville-Albemarle Bar Association.[34] Less than a year later, the association accepted the students' report and established the Charlottesville Legal Aid Society. Seventy students signed up to participate in the program, but the director limited the number to forty. To promote the program and inform the public of its legal services, students visited various churches and civic organizations. Under the leadership of its first two directors, Myron P. Simmons (Law 1968) and Michael J. Fox (Law 1969), the Legal Aid Society made substantial progress. "As the society completes its second year at the Law School, progress and growth are readily apparent," Lawrence S. Fullerton (Law 1974) noted in spring 1969. "Clients have been coming to the Court Square office at a rate triple that of last year, the office hours have been doubled, and an answering service has been added to handle after hours calls. But a more important and meaningful growth has been the expansion of Legal Aid's activities in solving problems of the poor."[35] The society provided legal services in several areas, including domestic relations, landlord-tenant disputes, and employment.

Black Law Students Association

Such work pleased but hardly satisfied many progressive students seeking to leverage the resources of the Law School for social change. If truly committed to providing everyone with access to justice, then the Law School must address its own issues, most notably the low number of women and African Americans in the student body. In 1966, only 8 of the 247 members of the incoming class were women.[36] The next year, the incoming class had two African Americans. Only a handful of African Americans and women were admitted each year until the end of the 1960s.

The Law School's demographic profile began to shift in 1968, the year President Lyndon B. Johnson abolished draft deferments for graduate students. To compensate for the anticipated decline in enrollment, UVA Law began admitting more students, including women. The first-year class in 1968 had 24 female students out of 303, three times as many women as the preceding year's class.[37] Coupled with the gradual increase in women's enrollment was a more concerted effort to recruit African American students. Not long after Paulsen assumed the deanship in 1968, Elaine Jones and James Benton invited him to lunch to discuss ways to increase the number of Black students and faculty at the Law School. In response to the growing call for more diversity, UVA supplemented its admission program with outreach and recruitment at historically Black colleges and universities (HBCUs).[38] The next recruiting season, Professor Charles Whitebread and Jones visited several HBCUs, including Virginia State, Howard, and Norfolk State. The results were immediate. The incoming class of 1969 included thirteen African American students, one of whom was Jones's younger sister Gwendolyn L. Jones (Law 1972).

Feeling as if the moment was ripe for substantive change, these African American students intensified the call for more Black students at Virginia Law. Like their counterparts across the nation, they also demanded more Black professors. On October 2, 1970, the Law Student Council passed a resolution endorsing the "appointment of blacks to faculty of the School of Law of the University of Virginia." In response, the faculty's Appointments Committee assured the Law Student Council that it was "continuing to search actively for black lawyers who may qualify."[39]

On October 9, 1970, the *Virginia Law Weekly* (*VLW*) weighed in on the council's resolution. Though sympathetic to the demand for more Black professors, the *VLW*'s editorial board expressed concern about the resolution tenor. "The student resolution, by its implication of dereliction, does a serious injustice to the existing law school faculty, and in particu-

UVA Law student Gwendolyn L. Jones (Law 1972) accepts the Constance Baker Motley Scholarship Award of the NAACP Legal Defense and Education Fund from Professor Emerson G. Spies (left) and Dean Monrad G. Paulsen (right). (Arthur J. Morris Law Library Special Collections, University of Virginia)

lar, to the faculty committee on appointments and tenure. Students promulgating the resolution have apparently overlooked, or intentionally ignored the fact that the committee has made a sincere and conscious policy decision in favor of actively and persistently seeking qualified black candidates for appointments to the law faculty."[40] After defending the tenure and appointments committee, the *VLW* cautioned against lowering standards to hire more Black professors. The demand for more Black faculty, the paper insisted, "must be tempered with the recognition that the criteria for appointment to the faculty at the University of Virginia Law School, or any law school, must include elements beyond skin color." In an increasingly competitive world, UVA Law students deserved to learn from the very best legal minds, the editors claimed: "It is one thing to establish dual standards to accommodate minority students who are otherwise denied quality legal education, but quite another to establish dual standards in areas where far more is at stake than the opportunity and future of a single individual."[41]

Predictably, the *VLW*'s editorial elicited a strong rebuttal from Black students. Livid at the editorial's "insidious invocations of Black inferiority," Black students dismissed it as "an inaccurate, retrogressive, uninformed, ill-reasoned voicing of liberal ideology actually undergirded by prejudiced attitudes."[42] The patronizing tone and content of the editorial was "an insult to every competent Black lawyer, to every Black alumnus of the Virginia Law School, and to those Black law students presently enrolled here." So focused on defending the faculty's reputation for "conscientious progressivism," the *VLW* not only misrepresented the views of Black students but simplified the complexity of the meritocracy discussion. As the Black students explained: "It has never been suggested, by the resolution or by those who promulgated it, that skin color should be the only criterion for appointment to the faculty. We insist that it not be used as the sole bar to appointment. For over a year, the Black law students, to no avail, have inquired persistently as to what constitutes the criteria for acceptance to the law faculty. In view of the heterogenous nature of the law faculty, with its wide range of educational, professional, and experiential competence, it is difficult to discern the criteria used to appoint faculty members."[43] The issue at hand, the students insisted, was not the absence of qualified African American applicants who met UVA's lofty standards but rather one of institutional will and commitment. "At Virginia," the students concluded, "we need a change of heart, a firmer and less rhetorical commitment to equal opportunity which will be reflected by the hiring of Black law professors here in the halls where justice is taught."[44]

If nothing else, the students' razor-sharp critique of the *VLW* underscored their determination to set the terms of the debate on desegregation, establish their own criteria on whether the Law School was making progress in minority recruitment, and speak and act in their own interests. The students' response also provided a window into the self-determinist ethos that animated the formation of one of the most important student groups to emerge during this period: the UVA chapter of the Black American Law Students Association (BALSA, later BLSA).

Founded in 1968 at New York University Law School, BALSA pursued three interrelated goals: promote, protect, and defend the interests of Black law students, advance the Black liberation struggle, and transform the legal system. Under the astute leadership of its founder Algernon Cooper, BALSA quickly branched out to other universities, including Howard, Columbia, and Yale.[45] The UVA BALSA chapter was officially founded on October 16, 1970. At the founding meeting, BALSA members elected Albert L. Preston (Law 1971) as their convener rather than president. Gloria H. Bouldin (Law 1973) held the position of secretary, and Gwendolyn Jones, Bobby N. Vassar (Law 1972), and Leonard L. McCants (Law 1972) were selected as committee chairs. BALSA shared its major goals via the *VLW:* "stimulate recruitment of black students and professors," "aid Black students at the University by identifying problem areas and working to alleviate them," facilitate meaningful communication and dialogue about critical racial issues among all students and provide legal assistance to the Black community in Charlottesville.[46]

The importance of BALSA, according to founding member Bobby Vassar, cannot be overstated. Combined with providing students with a deeper sense of belonging, BALSA provided a vehicle "to face the challenges we were facing from a unified, organized, recognized context. . . . It was our sphere of operation for how we would channel our efforts to change not only the University, but the world around us." The unique circumstances of the post–Jim Crow era demanded the formation of

1971 members of the Law School's Black American Law Students Association (BALSA). Left to right: Bobby N. Vassar (Law 1972), Jerry L. Williams (Law 1973), John W. Scott Jr. (Law 1973), Stephanie J. Valentine (Law 1973), Arthur C. McFarland (Law 1973), Charles E. Walker (Law 1973), and Leroy W. Bannister (Law 1973). Gwendolyn L. Jones (Law 1972) is not pictured. (*Virginia Law Weekly* and Arthur J. Morris Law Library Special Collections, University of Virginia)

BALSA: "There was no other avenue for us to operate . . . even though we certainly had white students who were very strong allies."[47]

Wasting no time in establishing its presence on Grounds, BALSA closed out the fall semester of 1970 with a three-day minority prelaw conference for undergraduates. Thanks to planning by students James E. Ghee (Law 1972) and Barbara A. Bailey (Law 1971), the conference was an overwhelming success. The list of participants included Walter Leonard, assistant dean of Harvard Law School, Ronald R. Davenport, dean of Duquesne University Law School, and feminist and civil rights activist Florynce R. Kennedy. There was also a strong alumni presence. Elaine Jones, Robert Williams, Henry Marsh, and James Gay participated in the historic gathering as panelists and moderators.[48] "This was no symposium of empty rhetoric," raved David B. Hagan, "but a realistic and hard minded attack on very real problems."[49]

Virginia Law Women

By 1970, African Americans were not the only group seeking to transform the culture and politics of the Law School. With the second wave of the feminist movement in full swing, UVA Law also witnessed an upsurge in women's activism. Though the Law School had opened its doors to women in 1920, it remained a male-dominated space rife with sexism. "The Law School was not uniformly welcoming," remembered Nancy L. Buc (Law 1969). "A lot of the students thought we were, as they put it, taking up a space a man could have had." Her experiences with faculty were mixed. "There were some faculty members who were very unhappy about having women at the Law School, some were approving—and hired us as their student assistants—and some were at least neutral." The environment of the Law School was slowly changing, but sexism remained a constant reality for women students. "I had a good time in law school," Buc admitted. "But you were always sort of aware that if you were a woman in the Law School in 1966 to 1969, that you were at least a curiosity and sometimes a villain."[50]

These feelings were especially acute when on the job market. "I had interviews with a whole bunch of law firms that basically told me they didn't hire women," Buc recalled. "And I would say to them, 'Well, what did you interview me for?'"[51] Buc was not alone in her frustrations. The *VLW* put the school's placement office on notice about the urgent need to address law firms' entrenched sexism. Written by J. Carolyn Burgess (Law 1972), a 1970 article provided numerous examples of sexual discrimination during the interview process. Whereas men were rarely questioned about their career intentions, women were routinely asked, "Why did you come to law school?" and "Do you intend to practice law as a career?" No matter how effectively female interviewees answered these questions, law firm representatives refused to treat them as equal to their male counterparts. One law firm representative asked four women "What sort of childbirth covenant would you be willing to sign?" Another representative asked a female interviewee if she was dating anyone in the Law School. One recruiter from Florida communicated his firm's resolve to never hire another woman after its first and only female lawyer married and then left the firm. Upon hearing these complaints, Dean Paulsen and the Law School's placement director Albert R. Turnbull (Law 1962) reiterated the Law School's commitment to gender equity and equal opportunity for all students. The visiting law firms, Turnbull assured students, had been given a handbook detailing the school's policy against sex-based discrimination.[52]

These reassurances were not enough; neither were progressive students' episodic responses to the entrenched sexism within the Law School. Change required collective action and sustained organization. Mary Jane McFadden (Law 1974) started Law School with a deep awareness of the legal fight for gender equality at UVA, a determination to maintain her activist stance, and a deep desire to build community among other women students. No stranger to protest politics, McFadden had been actively involved in the anti-war movement during her undergraduate years at The Ohio State University (OSU). When OSU shut down after the Kent State murders, McFadden was a part of the negotiating team setting the terms for the university's reopening. The political experience and lessons acquired at OSU proved useful as McFadden remained committed to social justice work. "When I graduated, I thought going to law school was a way of gaining voice, being able to advocate. And it was." A couple of months before the start of classes, McFadden contacted every current and incoming woman law student about the possibility of organizing to protect and advance their interests. The response to McFadden's call was anything but encouraging. Only two women wrote back, and they both issued a cautionary warning about disrupting the status quo.[53]

And yet, McFadden's political convictions grew stronger upon her arrival at UVA. "Walking across Grounds . . . there was still a lot of hostility coming from some of the male students," she recalled.[54] McFadden joined a small cohort of women law students committed to change. In October 1971, she was one of six students who attended the historic "Women In and Under the Law," conference, held at Duke University Law School. The other attendees from the Law School were Ellen A. Bass (Law 1973), Elizabeth H. Trimble (Law 1973), Bobara E. Liles (Law 1974), Diane L. Hermann (Law 1972), and Margaret A. Wilson (Law 1974). At the

VIRGINIA LAW WEEKLY

Vol. XXIV, No. 19 Charlottesville, Virginia, Friday, March 24, 1972 Twenty-five Cents

A Light Moment During Serious Confrontation

Confront 'Chauvinists'

Women Law Students Discuss Possible Female Faculty Post

Women law students attend a meeting with the Law School dean and administrators to discuss a possible female faculty position, 1972, from coverage in the *Virginia Law Weekly*. (*Virginia Law Weekly* and Arthur J. Morris Law Library Special Collections, University of Virginia)

gathering, Ruth Bader Ginsburg, then a professor at Rutgers Law School, delivered the keynote address in which she discussed the legal status of women, the percentage of women in law school, and other issues.[55] Years later, McFadden remembered the historic conference as a symbol of the energy and hope engulfing women across the nation. "It was exciting. It was a time when people were creatively thinking about possibilities."[56]

Upon their return from Duke, these women organized the Virginia Law Women.[57] Foremost on their agenda was expanding the number of female faculty. For quite some time, a common refrain among female law students was the dearth of women on the faculty. During the first fifty years of coeducation at the Law School, only three women had been on the teaching faculty: Frances Farmer, Priscilla Richardson Apperson (Law 1962), and Gail Marshall. In 1963 Farmer, who had begun working at the Law School as senior cataloguer and executive secretary in 1942, was elected to the general faculty as an associate professor, becoming the first female law professor in the school's history.[58] In 1962, Priscilla Apperson became the second woman to teach at the Law School and the first on a full-time basis.[59] Gail Marshall was appointed as a lecturer in 1968 and then promoted to assistant professor the following year.[60] Marshall, a founding member of Legal Aid, also continued to work closely with the organization.

Additionally, there was a noticeable curricular gap in the late 1960s and early 1970s on critical legal issues related to women: sex discrimination in the workplace, reproductive rights, and the Equal Rights Amendment, to name a few. In 1972 the Law School introduced the seminar Women and the Law, a three-credit course supervised by Dean Paulsen and Professor Wadlington but listed in the catalog as led by lecturer Elinor Gammon Vaughter (Law 1969).[61] Topics for the course included "the Women's Rights Amendment, legal problems of child care, control of reproduction, Family Law and women's equality, equal employment opportunity, and the Feminist Movement."[62] Over time, these topics seeped into other Law School courses, including Civil Liberties, Constitutional Law, and Family Law. It bears noting that women law students were vital to the creation and intellectual vibrancy of Women and the Law. They recommended lecturers, topics, and readings. Simply put, they anchored the course.[63]

As part of their effort to address curricular gaps, as well as promote the hiring of more women on the faculty, women law students also sought a greater share in the culture and governance of the University. Few were more assertive than Linda G. Howard (Law 1973), a native of Ettrick, Virginia, who received her BA in mathematics from Reed College. The daughter of college professors who taught at Virginia State University, Howard possessed a sparkling intellectual curiosity and a quiet yet steady confidence in her abilities. In 1972, she decided to run for president of the Law School Council.[64] Not afraid to challenge tradition, Howard questioned the validity of the Law School's honor system, called for the recruitment of more Black women and men, and asked for an upgraded job placement program.

Howard's campaign pivoted around three goals: increasing the Black presence, hiring more Black and women professors, and ridding the Law School of its elitism. On February 22, 1972, Howard defeated Joseph A. Schwartz (Law 1973) by twenty-two votes to become the first woman and African American president of the Law School Council. Covered extensively in the white and Black press, Howard's victory signaled, for some, a shift in the Law School's culture. Her election elicited commentary from the *Richmond Times–Dispatch, Journal and Guide* (Norfolk), *Daily Progress* (Charlottesville), *Jet, Washington Post,* and other media outlets. The ever-focused Howard concentrated her energy on carrying out her campaign promises. "Hopefully . . . the publicity I've received at the beginning will help me to realize my responsibilities during my term of office."[65]

A month after Howard's election, one of her campaign goals—diversifying the faculty—was the topic of intense debate. On March 16, 1972, the Virginia Law Women convened a meeting with Dean Paulsen to discuss the possibility of hiring a female professor for the 1972–73 academic year. At the meeting, the students explained that an additional female professor would improve student recruitment, enhance the already exceptional job placement and counseling work of Professor Gail Marshall, and elevate the school's reputation nationally. But Dean Paulsen refused to commit to hiring a female professor for the coming year. The discussion turned contentious when BALSA's Leonard McCants stated that hiring a Black man was "more important than 'women's lib crap.'" McCants's comments (which were denounced by other BALSA members) did not sit well with Linda Howard, who shot back "amid a chorus of 'right-ons,' 'What you men don't realize is that women are on the way up!'"[66]

Combined with potentially dividing progressive students in the Law School, McCants's remarks marginalized the gender-specific concerns of African American women law students. Many African American women, including Linda Howard, viewed the demands of BALSA and Virginia Law Women as mutually beneficial. It was also important for BALSA not to alienate allies, particularly those who connected to both the Black freedom struggle and the women's liberation movement. Now more than ever, BALSA needed allies as it intensified its demands for Black faculty.

Around this time, BALSA filed suit with the Department of Health, Education, and Welfare (HEW) charging the Law School with discrimination. In a letter to HEW head Elliot L. Richardson, Bobby Vassar accused the Law School of failing to comply with Title VI of the Civil Rights Act: "Black Students over the past three years have voiced criticisms, sought

The John B. Minor Pre-Legal Society presents a discussion on the role of "Women in Law." Panelists, left to right: Ellen A. Bass (Law 1973), Margaret A. Wilson (Law 1974), Linda G. Howard (Law 1973) (moderator), Freda L. Mandl (Law 1975), and Catherine B. Tackney (Law 1976) at Jefferson Hall (Hotel C) in UVA's Central Grounds, 1973. (*Virginia Law Weekly* and Arthur J. Morris Law Library Special Collections, University of Virginia)

Margaret P. Spencer (Law 1972), Bobby N. Vassar (Law 1972), and Leonard L. McCants (Law 1972) present BALSA's demands to diversify the Law School faculty in March 1972. (*Virginia Law Weekly* and Arthur J. Morris Law Library Special Collections, University of Virginia)

answers, offered suggestions, and have had some direct input into the law faculty recruitment effort. . . . Many of those lawyers named were never contacted or formally approached by the Law School."[67] UVA Law professor Jerry L. Mashaw pleaded for patience. "We are trying," he promised. The committee responsible for minority recruitment and hiring, he explained, had to jettison its original plans after "traditional channels" proved unsuccessful. "So we went back to our sources and told them exactly what we wanted, and the response from the law professors was encouraging."[68] Though he appreciated Professor Mashaw's efforts, Leonard McCants questioned the collective will of the faculty. "This isn't a one-man job," McCants rightly argued.[69]

Breaking the Color Line: The Hiring of Larry Gibson

Moved by the students' political pressure and his own convictions, Dean Paulsen contacted one of his former students, Larry S. Gibson, about joining the faculty as a visiting professor. A graduate of Howard University and Columbia Law School, Gibson had an impressive résumé that included a

Black Students, Law Women Focus On Admissions Process

by Robert W. Cover

Two of the newest student organizations at the Law School are the Black American Law Students Association (BALSA) and the Virginia Law Women. These two organizations are composed of and represent the interests of the two most prominent minorities in the Law School student body--blacks and women.

BALSA Committees

BALSA, organized in 1970, works primarily through its four committees, according to second-year student Dennis L. Montgomery, its convenor (or president). The committee on admissions, chaired by

Montgomery

second-year student Ronald R. Wesley, is trying to increase black enrollment at the Law School. According to Montgomery, admissions is BALSA's most pressing problem. "It's impossible to rationalize the fact that there are only 33 black students here," he said. "We want to double, triple, quadruple the number of black students. One of the great disappointments here has been the total apathy of the student body as a whole to this problem." The committee is working with the Student Admissions Committee and is developing a recruitment brochure on black student life at the Law School. BALSA members also intend to go on recruitment trips to other schools in the South in an attempt to interest more blacks in the Law School.

The committee on education, chaired by second-year student Sheila Jackson Lee, is working to bring more black speakers to the Law School and is trying to establish contact with law firms and corporations interested in hiring black attorneys.

Black Alumni

A black alumni list is being compiled by the finance committee under the chairmanship of second-year student Kester I. Crosse. It intends to publish a monthly newsletter for the black alumni and to seek their assistance in fund-raising efforts. According to Montgomery, there are roughly 50 black alumni of the Law School. The committee also intends to compile sources of financial assistance for both individuals and the organization.

In conjunction with the undergraduate Black Student Alliance, the committee on community/public relations, chaired by second-year student Delores R. Boyd, is operating the New Birth Community Center in downtown Charlottesville with the goal of enriching the cultural background of lower income black children in Charlottesville.

In other activities, BALSA is organizing a statewide conference of all black law students in Virginia to be held here later this month and is planning another faculty reception following a reception in September at which, according to Montgomery, "attendance was very encouraging."

Law Women

The Law Women, organized in 1971, are now working primarily

McFadden

in the areas of recruitment, placement and alumni involvement, according to its president, Mary Jane McFadden. In the recruitment area, panels of speakers are going to many of the women's schools near Charlottesville to talk informally about women and law school. They attempt to interest qualified women in applying to Virginia. The Law Women are also preparing a brochure in cooperation with the Placement Office to be sent to women applicants with the catalogs next year.

Bias In Hiring

The primary emphasis in the placement area is in attempting to detect bias in employment and hiring practices. Every woman who is interviewing this fall may fill out questionnaires on her impressions of each interview and a follow-up questionnaire on the firms which did not grant interviews and those which made positive responses to interviews. The information compiled will be available to women looking for jobs next year and will be used as evidence against firms which are found to discriminate against women.

The Law Women also plan to initiate an alumnae newsletter to be sent to all women alumnae and to compile a list of women alumnae willing to talk to women interested in working in their respective cities.

In fall 1973, the Law School student newspaper covered the work of BALSA and the Virginia Law Women to push for increased Law School recruitment of women and Black students. *Virginia Law Weekly*, October 19, 1973. (*Virginia Law Weekly* and Arthur J. Morris Law Library Special Collections, University of Virginia) clerkship for Federal District Judge Frank A. Kaufman, appointment to the Baltimore School Board, years of experience as a criminal attorney in Baltimore, and a highly publicized victory in a murder case involving Black Panther Charles Wyche. Gibson had come to national attention as the defense attorney for Wyche, who had been charged with first-degree murder, kidnapping, and conspiracy. Though Gibson had some reservations about Charlottesville, he accepted Dean Paulsen's offer to join the faculty in 1972.[70]

Gibson's impact on the Law School's curriculum and clinical education was immediate. In his first semester, he taught the research seminar Problems in Urban Practice for second- and third-year students. Over the course of the semester, students prepared briefs and memos on cases from Maryland and Washington, DC. One group worked on a suit challenging a Maryland statute that eliminated an expectant mother's compensation after her fifth month of pregnancy. Others worked on cases involving juvenile law, loan sharks, and property rights. "Students in the course get a feel for the timing problems of actual, practical client considerations. They are also able to see how an attorney used their work in final pleadings, and the quality of work by legal aid attorneys in most of the cases."[71]

Notably, the semester after Gibson's arrival, the Law School appointed Julius Chambers as a guest lecturer. As the nation's eminent civil rights litigator, Chambers was at the forefront in the struggle for racial justice in the areas of education and employment. A native of Mount Gilead, North Carolina, Chambers possessed a deep commitment to improving the lives of African Americans, particularly workers. After graduating from Peabody High School in 1954, he enrolled in North Carolina Central University, where he majored in history. He then attended the University of Michigan, earning an MA in history. Chambers entered law school at the University of North Carolina at Chapel Hill in 1959 and graduated first in his class of one hundred students. Immersing himself in the world of civil rights litigation after receiving an LLM from Columbia University Law School, Chambers interned with the NAACP Legal Defense and Education Fund in 1963. Shortly thereafter, he opened his own practice in Charlotte, which became the first integrated law firm in North Carolina. In 1971, he argued the landmark *Swann v. Charlotte-Mecklenburg Board of Education* case before the Supreme Court, which ruled in favor of federally mandated busing to desegregate public schools.[72]

In the spring of 1973, Chambers brought his legal expertise to UVA Law School. His Current Civil Rights Litigation seminar focused on Title VII of the Civil Rights Act of 1964 and his most recent employment discrimination case, *Albemarle Paper Co. v. Moody.*[73] In May 1966, Chambers filed EEOC (Equal Employment Opportunity Commission) complaints on behalf of Joseph Moody and three other Black Albemarle Paper workers charging both the company and the union with conspiring to discriminate against African American workers. Over the course of the semester, students broadened their understanding of Title VII and employment discrimination law and litigation.

Lecturer Harry R. Sachse's 1974 class Law and the American Indian was another course that explored the role of the law in advancing the civil rights of marginalized communities.[74] An outspoken advocate of Native American rights, Sachse was a founding partner of Sonosky, Chambers, and Sachse, a law firm devoted to representing Native American tribal interests in state and federal courts and before Congress, state legislatures, and governmental agencies.[75] During the 1970s, Sachse argued several key cases before the Supreme Court, most notably *McClanahan v. Arizona State Tax Commission, Department of Game v. Puyallup Tribe,* and *Morton v. Mancari.*[76] From 1971 to 1976, he served as assistant to the solicitor general of the United States. In spring 1973, he brought his vast expertise to the University of Virginia. His seminar, Law and the American Indian, was divided into two parts. The first consisted of five sessions that provided an overview of Native American law, the changing concept of tribal sovereignty, and the relations between tribes and the state. The ten-session second part focused on Native American water rights, conflict within the federal government over tribal resources, and other contemporary issues. The course's contents and tenor reflected Sachse's political concerns, as evident in the description: "Native Americans, after years of silence, have begun to assert their rights both in the courts and elsewhere. Old myths are crumbling as examples of American injustice, cupidity, and misgovernment are made public. But more than new myths are needed if anything constructive is to be done. Existing rights need to be known and enforced and as new directions are taken past pitfalls must be avoided if possible."[77]

A year after hiring Gibson, the Law School added Professor Lillian R. Altree BeVier to the faculty in 1973. A graduate of Stanford Law School, BeVier specialized in constitutional law, torts, real property, and intellectual property. Prior to her arrival at UVA, she was an associate professor of law at the University of Santa Clara School of Law. Not long after her arrival at UVA, BeVier spoke with the *VLW* about her expectations, views on clinical education, and the status of women in the law profession. Though BeVier looked forward to getting to know women law students, she distanced herself from the women's liberation movement. "I tend to view myself not as a woman pursuing a career in law but as me pursuing a career in law," she explained. "At this particular time in my life, my personal resources are fully utilized in being a mother and a teacher, which goes some way to explaining, perhaps, why I am presently disinclined to become involved in the women's movement."[78] A week after the *VLW*'s profile of BeVier, Mary Jane McFadden reminded readers of the role of student activists in pushing for change among the law faculty:

Professor Lillian R. BeVier, the first woman on the Law School's full-time teaching faculty, joined the Law School in 1973 and specialized in constitutional law, torts, real property, and intellectual property. (Arthur J. Morris Law Library Special Collections, University of Virginia)

"With respect to Professor Lillian Altree's [BeVier's] disclaimer of any involvement with the women's movement, I would like to point out that she probably never would have received an offer from the Law School's faculty had it not been for the agitation of the women's group."[79] BeVier later became the second woman to receive tenure at UVA Law and the first to do so as a member of the full-time teaching faculty.[80]

Clinical Legal Education

As the 1970s progressed, change continued to mark the Law School. Perhaps no change was more welcomed by students than the establishment of a clinical legal education program in 1976.[81] Throughout the 1960s and early 1970s, students had demanded more robust clinical education.[82] In 1971, the law students' Educational Policy Committee strongly recommended that the faculty Appointments Committee hire a director of clinical education. The director would develop new clinical programs in needed areas, help oversee existing programs lacking adequate faculty supervision, and advertise clinical opportunities and provide placement for interested students.[83] The students' demands were met with resistance from some faculty who either believed a clinical program could only be effective in a major city or were opposed to the idea of law students working with clients. "It is not a proper function of the Law School to provide legal services to the community," one professor complained. "I don't know how having a client contributes to training."[84]

Students pressed ahead, believing a formal clinical program was especially important given the critical work and success of the Legal Aid Society. Since its formation in 1967, the Legal Aid Society had launched numerous projects in Charlottesville and the surrounding counties, including the Downtown Office Project, the Circuit Rider Project, the Welfare Rights Project, and the Post-Conviction Assistance Project.[85] Law students gained valuable experience in the areas of public interest law and poverty law, provided critical legal service and advice to the poor, the incarcerated, the mentally ill, and rural communities with limited access to legal representation. This important work, law students felt, would be enhanced by the creation of a clinical legal education program with a full-time director.

Elaine R. Jones (Law 1970) (right), standing with fellow Extra Legal Forum members William L. Harris (Law 1969) and Neil G. McBride (Law 1970) in front of a Confederate monument at the Charlottesville courthouse, 1969. (Arthur J. Morris Law Library Special Collections, University of Virginia)

Thanks in part to this student demand, the Law School established a clinical legal education program in 1976. The program, according to Professor Jerry Mashaw, would have three main components: academic-oriented course work that concentrated on "theoretical aspects of advocacy, counseling, negotiations," experiential classes that included "role playing, simulation techniques, and critiques by trained observers," and field work involving "interviews, negotiations, trial preparations, and trials."[86] Not long after announcing the establishment of the program, the Law School selected the program's director, Professor Robert J. Condlin. A graduate of Boston College Law School, Condlin had served as the assistant attorney general of Massachusetts from 1969 to 1971. He then directed and taught clinical programs at Boston College School of Law and at Harvard Law. Condlin was excited about building UVA Law's clinical program in 1976. "Clinical education is the intellectual heart of law study," Condlin told the *VLW*. "Rules and laws have no existence without implementation," and "operational processes are as sophisticated as case analysis."[87]

Through the survey courses, Lawyering Theory and Practice, Lawyer as Negotiator, and Lawyering Process (Criminal Model), Condlin introduced students to the concepts of effective lawyering and reflective analysis. These courses included videotaped moot litigation exercises and intensive classroom discussion. Students could opt to take more focused seminars such as Trial Practice, Civil Litigation, and Securities Litigation. The experiential phase of their clinical education continued through participation in either Civil Practice or Forensic Psychiatry Clinic.[88]

The establishment of the clinical program was a step in a positive direction, but some students wondered if the new director's work would be undermined "because of the indifference or hostility from those more dedicated to the intellectual branch of 'our family."[89] Condlin garnered the respect and admiration of many students, but his time at the Law School would be brief. By 1980, with the departure of Condlin, administrators and students were once again discussing the future of clinical education.[90]

By 1980, the fight for gender and racial equity was far from over. To be sure, the percentage of women attending UVA Law had increased substantially during the 1970s. At the end of the 1970s, women comprised almost 30 percent of the student body. The rate of growth among African Americans and other racial minorities was less impressive. In 1979, racial minorities consisted of only about 5 percent of the student body.[91] Equally frustrating for many African Americans was the composition of the teaching faculty. Samuel Thompson was the only African American on the faculty in that year.[92] BeVier, who was tenured in 1978, was the only woman teaching full-time. Her presence, several law students sarcastically noted, was "the only thing standing between the Law School and a Title VII sex discrimination suit."[93]

Notwithstanding these realities, the period between 1960 and 1980 was a transformative one for the Law School. These years witnessed the development of new political formations within and beyond the Law School, as well as significant curricular revisions and expansions. The social justice work of the Legal Aid Society and its various projects, the organizational and intellectual opportunities available through BALSA and the Virginia Law Women, and the growing number of courses on racial, gender, labor, and human rights issues significantly altered legal education at the University of Virginia. These developments serve as important reminders that the institutional significance (and legacy) of the student activists of the 1960s and 1970s lay not just in enrollment statistics and hiring patterns, but also in their efforts to reimagine legal education, to build institutions and political networks that value gender and racial diversity and equity, and to transform the Law School into a critical site for creating a new and more just world.

Notes

1. Thom Faulders, "Students to Present Proposals for Ending 'Racist Atmosphere,'" *Cavalier Daily* (Charlottesville, VA), 18 February 1969 (hereafter cited as *CD*).
2. "If There's Really a Will," *CD*, 19 February 1969.
3. See Joanne Reckler, "Virginia U. Student Council Backs Protesters' Demands," *Washington Post*, 19 February 1969; Hamilton Crockford, "Godwin's Reply 'Disappoints' U.VA. Students," *Richmond Times-Dispatch*, 13 March 1969; "College Activists Warned," *Richmond Times-Dispatch*, 15 April 1969.
4. "Advisory Council Takes Stand on University Racial Justice," *Virginia Law Weekly*, 27 February 1969 (hereafter cited as *VLW*).
5. Elaine Jones interview by Julienna L. Richardson, 6 March 2007, interview A2006.151, transcript, The HistoryMakers Digital Archive, https://www.thehistorymakers.org/biography/elaine-jones-41.
6. Laura Kalman, *Yale Law School and the Sixties: Revolt and Reverberations* (Chapel Hill: University of North Carolina Press, 2005), 30.
7. Marvin Sykes, "A&T Students Launch 'Sit Down' Demand for Service at Downtown Lunch Counter," *Greensboro (NC) Record*, 2 February 1960.
8. Emanuel Perlmutter, "Sit-Ins Backed by Rallies Here," *New York Times*, 6 March 1960.
9. Leonard E. Calvin, "Forty Years After: Hampton Roads Natives Recall Their Roles in the Movement," *Journal and Guide* (Norfolk, VA), 16 February 2000.
10. Calvin, "Forty Years After."
11. Jeffrey L. Littlejohn and Charles H. Ford, "Southern Discomfort: The Rise and Fall of Civil Rights Attorney James F. Gay, 1942–2008," in *The Seedtime, the Work, and the Harvest: New Perspectives on the Black Freedom Struggle in America*, ed. Jeffrey L. Littlejohn, Reginald K. Ellis, and Peter B. Levy (Gainesville: University Press of Florida, 2018), 59.
12. "James Gay Sr. Obituary," *Virginian-Pilot* (Norfolk), 23 April 2008.
13. "Gay Assumes Role as President of Young Democrats," *VLW*, 6 April 1967.
14. Rod MacDonald, "Lilly Defends Council in Segregation Action," *CD*, 4 May 1967.
15. Eric Williamson, "Benton '70, Retired Judge Who Helped Give Legal Voice to Others, Discusses His Black History Hero," *News*, 2 March 2016, UVA Law, https://www.law.virginia.edu/news/201603/benton-70-retired-judge-who-helped-give-legal-voice-others-discusses-his-black-history.
16. Jeremy M. Lazarus, "Manchester Courthouse Renamed to Honor Henry and Harold Marsh," *Richmond Free Press*, 26 May 2016.

17. Trevor Metcalfe, "University of Virginia Honors Legacy of Danville Native, College's First-Ever African-American Student," *Danville (VA) Register & Bee,* 25 February 2018.
18. Robert A. Williams interview by Emma C. Edmunds, 25 March 2000, transcript, Virginia Center for Digital History, https://perma.cc/2JYZ-UFA9.
19. "Introducing Elaine R. Jones: Nation's Top Civil Rights Lawyer," *Ebony,* June 1993, 67.
20. Mary Wood, "African-American Graduates Recall Life at Law School after Integration," *News,* 1 March 2004, UVA Law, https://www.law.virginia.edu/news/200402/african-american-graduates-recall-life-law-school-after-integration. Nusbaum, an outspoken advocate of racial integration, encouraged the Law School to commit itself to bringing African Americans "into the mainstream of legal education in Virginia" by "recruiting them energetically and subsidizing them to whatever extent necessary." See Robert C. Nusbaum, "Call for Enlightened Racial Policy," *VLW,* 19 September 1968.
21. Stephen J. Wermiel, "Human Rights Hero: Elaine Jones," *Human Rights Magazine* 37, no. 4 (Fall 2010), https://perma.cc/9C3G-8GAX.
22. Wermiel, "Human Rights Hero."
23. Elaine Jones interview by Julian Bond, 1 November 2000, interview transcript, Explorations in Black Leadership, UVA Arts & Sciences, https://perma.cc/369Q-V82N.
24. Mary Wood, "50 Years at UVA: Professors Howard and Low Look Back at Evolution of Law School," *News,* 21 November 2013, UVA Law, https://www.law.virginia.edu/news/201311/50-years-uva-professors-howard-and-low-look-back-evolution-law-school.
25. James F. Andrews, "Curriculum Changes Proposed in Faculty Committee Report," *VLW,* 30 September 1965.
26. University of Virginia, *School of Law: Record 1968–69* 53, no. 14 (Charlottesville: University of Virginia, 1968), 56 (hereafter cited as *LSR*).
27. See *LSR* for 1967–70.
28. "Willrich Discusses Proposed Changes in Teaching Law," *VLW,* 2 March 1967.
29. Samuel M. Bradley, "New Dean Considers Reaction of System to Modern Needs," *VLW,* 19 September 1968.
30. Bradley, "New Dean Considers Reaction of System."
31. Eric Williamson, "How Students Opened a Door for Legal Aid," *News,* UVA Law, 7 November 2017, https://www.law.virginia.edu/news/201711/how-students-opened-door-legal-aid; Gerald L. Baliles, "Law Group Conducts Survey of Area Need for Legal Aid," *VLW,* 16 December 1965.
32. Ruth Serven, "Lawyer Got UVA to Admit Female Undergrads," *Daily Progress* (Charlottesville, VA), 19 October 2017.
33. John C. Lowe, "Law Schools Fail to Prepare Students in Counseling Work," *VLW,* 16 December 1965.
34. Larry M. Wood, "Local Bar Considers Program Proposing Legal Aid Society," *VLW,* 10 March 1966.
35. Lawrence S. Fullerton, "Legal Aid Group Offers Help to Indigent Local Residents," *VLW,* 17 April 1969.
36. *LSR,* 1967, 43.
37. F. Keith Adkinson, "Hershey Announces End of Graduate Deferments: Policy Upsets Law School Admissions; Applies to Present First-Year Class," *VLW,* 22 February 1968; "Record First Year Class Registers: Students Display Regional Diversity, Excellent Records," *VLW,* 26 September 1968; *LSR,* 1970, 53.

38. "Law School Hopes Recruiting Brings Black Applicants," *VLW,* 20 November 1969.
39. "Council Endorses Black Appointees for Law Faculty," *VLW,* 9 October 1970.
40. "Black Professors," *VLW,* 9 October 1970.
41. "Black Professors."
42. "Black Students Respond," *VLW,* 16 October 1970.
43. "Black Students Respond."
44. "Black Students Respond."
45. "Our Story," NBLSA (National Black Law Students Association), https://www.nblsa.org/about.
46. "Blacks Inaugurate BALSA Chapter to Provide Forum," *VLW,* 23 October 1970. See also "1970: Fifty Years of BLSA, Black Law Students Association at the University of Virginia," Arthur J. Morris Law Library Special Collections, University of Virginia (hereafter cited as LLSC), https://perma.cc/H7VZ-KGZ8.
47. Bobby Vassar interview by Claudrena Harold, 14 May 2022, interview transcript, General Law School Oral History Project, RG–32–405, LLSC.
48. David B. Hagan, "Conferees Consider Relevance of Law to Minority Groups," *VLW,* 18 December 1970.
49. "Minority Conference," *VLW,* 18 December 1970.
50. Mary Wood, "Lawyer to Leader: Alumnae Share Stories on Finding Success," *UVA Lawyer* 44, no. 1 (Fall 2019): 39.
51. Wood, "Lawyer to Leader."
52. J. Carolyn Burgess, "Female Students Suffer Sex Bias in Job Market," *VLW,* 18 December 1970.
53. "Mary Jane McFadden," oral history interview with Randall N. Flaherty, Addison R. Patrick, and Mara Guyer, 23 October 2020, *Virginia Law Women 50,* LLSC, https://vlw50.law.virginia.edu/profiles/mary-jane-mcfadden.
54. "Mary Jane McFadden."
55. Kelly Banks, "Women Attend Duke Law Conference," *VLW,* 8 October 1971.
56. "Mary Jane McFadden."
57. "Mary Jane McFadden."
58. "Frances Farmer, 1942–1976," Our History: Former Faculty, Arthur J. Morris Law Library, University of Virginia, https://perma.cc/F2J5-8PJ9.
59. C. M. Radigan and D. A. Mortman, "Six New Members Added to Law School Faculty," *VLW,* 27 September 1962.
60. "Faculty Adds Members; Seven Accept Positions," *VLW,* 9 May 1968.
61. R. Mark Dare, "Paulsen, Wadlington Study Women and the Law," *VLW,* 11 February 1972.
62. *LSR,* 1973, 95.
63. Dare, "Paulsen, Wadlington Study Women and the Law."
64. "Former Student Elected Law School President," *Journal and Guide,* 25 March 1972.
65. "Howard Wins Election after Three Vote Tallies," *VLW,* 25 February 1972; "News Media Besiege Howard after Election," *VLW,* 3 March 1972; "Black Woman Is Elected Law School Student Head," *Jet,* 30 March 1972, 47.
66. Willard P. McCrone, "Women Law Students Discuss Possible Female Faculty Post," *VLW,* 24 March 1972.
67. Thomas J. Wray, "Black Students Request Inquiry by Government," *VLW,* 24 March 1972.
68. Dare, "Black Professor Recruiting Still Unsuccessful," *VLW,* 3 March 1972.

69. Dare, "Black Professor Recruiting Still Unsuccessful."
70. Paul A. Gregory, "Gibson, Saltzburg Assume New Positions on Law School Faculty," *VLW,* 22 September 1972; see also Larry Gibson interview by Racine Tucker Hamilton, 19 October 2004, interview A2004.093, transcript, The HistoryMakers, https://www.thehistorymakers.org/biography/larry-gibson-38.
71. Bill Fang, "Research Seminar Focuses on Urban Legal Reform," *VLW,* 15 December 1972.
72. Richard A. Rosen and Joseph Mosnier, *Julius Chambers: A Life in the Legal Struggle for Civil Rights* (Chapel Hill: University of North Carolina Press, 2016); Swann v. Charlotte-Mecklenburg Bd. of Educ., 402 U.S. 1 (1971).
73. Albemarle Paper Co. v. Moody, 422 U.S. 405 (1975); see also *LSR,* 1973, 91–92.
74. *LSR,* 1974, 89–90.
75. "About," Sonosky, Chambers, Sachse, Endreson & Perry, LLP, 2025, https://perma.cc/9YHU-J5BR.
76. McClanahan v. Arizona State Tax Comm'n, 411 U.S. 164 (1973); Department of Game v. Puyallup Tribe, 414 U.S. 44 (1973); Morton v. Mancari, 417 U.S. 535 (1974).
77. *LSR,* 1974, 89–90.
78. Joseph P. Rapisarda Jr., "Board Appoints Lillian Altree to Position on Law Faculty," *VLW,* 20 April 1973.
79. Mary Jane McFadden, letter to the editor, *VLW,* 27 April 1973.
80. Bill Marmon, "BeVier Named First Woman to Tenured Faculty Position," *VLW,* 14 April 1978.
81. Elizabeth Haile, "Virginia Court Approves Third-Year Practice; Law School Starts Clinical Education Program," *VLW,* 26 September 1975.
82. Ronald D. Castille, "Student Committee Proposes Teaching, Curriculum Changes," *VLW,* 19 February 1970.
83. R. R. Sparks, "After Lengthy Study: Clinical Education Director Search," *VLW,* 30 April 1971.
84. John H. Murray, "Clinical Program Will Provide Training in Behavioral Skills," *VLW,* 27 February 1976.
85. John S. Reed, "Circuit Riders: Legal Aid Expands Responsibility," *VLW,* 27 October 1972; Lawrence S. Fullerton, "Legal Aid Society Announces New Projects to Help Poor," *VLW,* 25 September 1969; "Post Conviction Group Plans Work with Prison Attorneys," *VLW,* 6 October 1972.
86. Murray, "Clinical Program Will Provide Training in Behavioral Skills."
87. "Condlin Directs Next Fall's Clinical Ed Plans," *VLW,* 19 March 1976.
88. *LSR,* 1977, 85–100; *LSR,* 1979, 87, 92, 95.
89. "Clinical Education," *VLW,* 27 February 1976.
90. "Memo Requests Stronger Faculty Commitment to Clinical Education," *VLW,* 29 February 1980.
91. *LSR,* 1980, 62.
92. "Samuel C. Thompson Jr., 1977–1981," Our History: Former Faculty, UVA Law, https://perma.cc/2YJC-TFK4.
93. Marmon, "BeVier Named First Woman."

A New Curriculum for a New Era

THE LAW SCHOOL AT A CROSSROADS, 1970–1997

Meggan F. Cashwell and Addison R. Patrick

IN 1992, Dean Robert "Bob" E. Scott addressed alumni of the University of Virginia School of Law via the *Virginia Law School Report* (renamed *UVA Lawyer* in 1994), a publication that circulated two to three times a year. Scott, appointed dean the year prior, had served on the UVA Law faculty since 1974 and possessed a keen awareness of the school's mission to maintain both national and elite status. In his message, Scott informed alumni that the Law School was "at a crossroads." As Scott saw it, there were two options: "the school moves boldly forward or it falls backward."[1]

For nearly twenty years, Scott had watched UVA Law try to modernize and reform its curriculum and respond to national trends in legal education. Some of these initiatives had proven successful, moving the school, in Scott's opinion, from "being very good to being near the best in everyone's estimation."[2] But Scott thought the Law School could be even better. Scott laid out his plan to create a revitalized institution that would thrive not just in the present day but also in the twenty-first century: "We must try to reshape legal education in a way that will last well into the next generation."[3]

Through the latter half of the twentieth century, students, faculty, and administrators deliberated over the purpose of the Law School and that of the modern lawyer. UVA Law, and all law schools in the United States, had weathered crises. A surplus of lawyers in the 1980s and questions over whether those lawyers were properly trained ignited debates about the structure of legal education. All law schools had to seek answers to complex questions. Was the case method of instruction appropriate beyond the first year? How could law schools balance legal theory and practical training? At a time when legal education was subject to national and local criticisms about the state of the profession, the Law School continued to situate itself as a national institution with an emphasis on the unique qualities that made it "Virginia Law."

These same decades witnessed a push and pull between administrators and students over the diversity of the student body, faculty, and curriculum. Both groups agreed the Law School must strive to be more diverse in its composition and course offerings, but they diverged significantly in their opinions on what diversity meant, how to achieve it, and on what timeline.[4] While women comprised a higher portion of the student body in the 1990s than previous decades, minority enrollment lagged. In 1995, 42 percent of the first-year class were women, 10 percent were African American, and 10 percent represented other ethnic and cultural minority groups.[5] Demands for critical legal studies (CLS) also infiltrated the Law School by way of students who desired a more progressive curriculum. Meanwhile, Law School administrators largely considered CLS a passing fad in legal education.

In the 1980s and 1990s, UVA Law engaged with national conversations about the changing legal landscape. On the ground, it was in the minutiae of decisions and conversations over community and curricular change that a modern law school emerged. At the heart of Scott's vision was a commitment to return to what he saw as Thomas Jefferson's original plan for the Law School—one that gave it a unique mission when compared with its peers. That mission was built on three pillars: a commitment to teaching and mentorship; a law curriculum that tried to balance theory, practice, and interdisciplinary subjects; and an appreciation for the role of place in fostering community. As Jefferson intended, the Law School of tomorrow would not just produce lawyers but public servants.[6] Financial self-sufficiency would be the road to achieve Scott's ambitious vision, allowing the school to use its own resources to hire new faculty, increase financial aid, initiate curricular restructuring, and build a Law Grounds complex in the spirit of Jefferson's Academical Village.[7] By 1997, UVA Law had rebranded itself, emphasizing its Jeffersonian roots in both place and pedagogy.

Interdisciplinary and Clinical Education at UVA Law, 1970–1978

Beginning in the 1970s, the University of Virginia experienced a revival of Jefferson's interdisciplinary education after a long period of growing professionalization. UVA maintained the interdisciplinary nature of its curriculum until the early 1900s, when a greater emphasis on the importance of science in higher education and increasing standards across professions ignited a new era at UVA.[8] While the Lawn remained the nexus of the University, the establishment of new professional schools and the growth of current schools demanded the University expand. Further professionalism of legal education at UVA in this time resulted in the law program moving to its own independent building, first Minor Hall (1911), then Clark Memorial Hall (1932), and finally North Grounds (1974), with each building bigger than the last.[9]

Throughout the 1970s, interdisciplinary education connected professional schools and departments through joint degree programs and new centers. Law combined with urban planning, government, history, philosophy, and sociology, to name a few, in the creation of interdisciplinary masters' programs. Students could apply for a combined JD-MA in economics, history, or business. Over the years, new joint programs came and went depending on faculty availability and student interest. Most law students still pursued just the traditional JD.[10]

In the 1970 catalogue, there were about ninety course offerings, with roughly twenty classes on civil rights, nuclear energy, medicine, and other courses that blended topics on law and adjacent disciplines. At the time, students had to complete a "cultural requirement" by taking at least one of the following courses or seminars: English Legal Thought, Roman Law, Legal Philosophy, Legal Process, Legal History, or Jurisprudence. This requirement had been in place at the Law School since the 1954–55 academic year.[11] As early as 1948, Dean Frederick D. G. Ribble (Law 1921) advocated for Legal Philosophy or Legal History to be a mandatory feature of the curriculum to provide students "the chance to survey . . . the entire field of the operation of law" and allow them to be "a far better constructive critic of [the law's] activities."[12] The 1950 alumni curriculum committee of the Law School had similarly supported this requirement, stating it would help to create a "well-rounded and scholarly lawyer" in addition to the Law School's "bread and butter" courses.[13]

Excluding this addition of the "cultural requirement," the first-year curriculum had changed little in the twentieth century: students had to take Civil Procedure, Contracts, Legislation and Administrative Law, Property, Torts, and Legal Bibliography. In their 2L year students completed Constitutional Law and Criminal Law; 3Ls took Professional Ethics or the Legal Profession. The remaining curriculum was elective, though 1Ls could not enroll in electives at that time.[14]

Beyond the classroom and joint-degree programs, there was a growing set of options to prepare law students for careers in public service. In 1968, the Law School and the National Science Foundation established the Center for the Study of Science, Technology, and Public Policy. Based in the Law School, the center acted as a means for "faculty and students to relate themselves and their work to other schools and departments," as well as to the federal government.[15] The Legal Aid Society (later the Legal Assistance Society, or LAS), established the year prior to support the larger Charlottesville-Albemarle Legal Aid Society, provided hands-on training to law students and helped the community through anti-poverty initiatives.[16] The LAS also spearheaded efforts to establish a third-year practice rule in Virginia, which would allow 3L students in the Commonwealth's four law schools to practice law in the state's courts under specific guidelines.[17] After several failed attempts, all courts in the Commonwealth passed the rule, with the Virginia Supreme Court being the last in June 1975.[18]

Interdisciplinary training and clinical experience were two sides of the same coin, structured to provide practical training and extend the Law School's connection into the wider community. In anticipation of the 1975 passage of the Third Year Student Practice Rule, UVA Law Dean Monrad G. Paulsen established the Joint Faculty-Student-Bar Committee on Clinical Legal Education and the Third-Year Practice Rule in Virginia to provide a plan for clinical education. That year the committee submitted their report, which argued that clinical training would make the third year of law school more valuable and productive. The committee felt hiring a new and skilled faculty member to begin a formal clinical program would build a bridge between standard coursework and practice and make "major positive effects in getting us to rethink our more traditional pedagogic techniques."[19]

As a result of this preliminary report, the faculty agreed to hire a law professor "principally concerned with the creation of a clinical program of high order."[20] That professor was Robert J. Condlin, who joined the faculty from Harvard in fall 1976. In his seminar Clinical Practice, Condlin paired students with local attorneys to "interview parties and witnesses, draft pleadings, negotiate with adversaries, try complete cases and systematically reflect on all these processes."[21] Condlin felt clinical education had the potential to improve attorney-client relations and provide students with a broader worldview by introducing them to societal problems, as well as their professional responsibility to rectify some of those issues.[22]

Emerson G. Spies, dean of the Law School from 1976 to 1980, had mixed feelings about clinical education, calling it "expensive, valuable, and controversial," in his spring 1977 message to alumni.[23] For Spies, the focus had to remain on preparing competent attorneys for the myriad legal issues they might face—which Spies implied was mutually exclusive from clinical experience. Condlin later noted that Virginia Law never warmed to clinical training during his time. Graham B. Strong (Law 1975) took over after Condlin left in 1980 and restructured the program into the Virginia Criminal Practice Clinic. Over the next decade, Virginia Law's clinical offerings remained relatively slim.[24]

Clinical and interdisciplinary education typified the growing electiveness of American law school curricula. But this trend concerned some UVA Law alumni who believed the Law School's curriculum was drifting dangerously from the "fundamentals," such as Taxation and Evidence courses that had long formed the bedrock of the program. Spies assured alumni that curricular changes had been more "modest" than the expanded catalogue conveyed. These slight adjustments had in no way harmed the Law School's reputation, Spies argued.[25]

The Law School's national and elite status was unquestionable, but Spies could not deny that major curricular changes were on the horizon. As G. Edward White observes in this volume, the case method was Virginia Law's core pedagogical model by this time, in line with most all US law schools. Yet Spies and other faculty increasingly felt that students were not being challenged enough via Socratic instruction and that it was not as useful beyond the first year when class sizes were larger. Spies believed that a different curricular approach in the second and third years would enable students to pursue greater specialization and provide faculty more one-on-one time with students. No law school had found a proper alternative to the case method, though some were considering dropping the third year entirely. On this issue, UVA Law was vehemently opposed: "We need more education, not less," Spies insisted. The answer—though undefined at the time—was not simply "tinkering" with the curriculum but reforming it to meet the needs of students, faculty, society, and the bar.[26]

Crises in American Legal Education, 1978–1988

In the final years of his deanship, Spies hoped to find a solution to the Law School's curricular difficulties that would "challenge our students and satisfy our critics."[27] The Long-Range Curriculum Committee, whose participants included faculty, students, and alumni, had been assessing other US law schools. Spies appointed the committee in 1977, chaired by Professor John C. McCoid II, to make concrete suggestions for a path forward.[28] While UVA Law offered more courses and seminars than most of its peer institutions, the committee identified specific areas in which the Law School was not keeping pace: an inordinately high student to faculty ratio; grade inflation; lack of adequate salary and research support for faculty; and insufficient financial aid that disproportionately hindered recruitment of minority students. Larger trends in legal education included smaller classes, specialization, clinical programs, and interdisciplinary training. But the Law School could not excel in these areas without more faculty or funding, the dean and committee thought.[29]

Meanwhile, all US law schools came under further scrutiny in 1978 as national conversations cast doubt over whether law schools were adequately preparing students for practice. The Devitt Committee, appointed by Chief Justice Warren Burger and comprising judges, attorneys, and professors, issued a report with recommendations for improving trial advocacy skills. Those recommendations included more trial advocacy coursework, an additional examination in federal practice subjects, and four trial experiences—which UVA Law administrators considered impossible without a significant increase in resources.[30] The year 1978 also saw the publication of Joel Seligman's *The High Citadel: The Influence of Harvard Law School,* a book Spies referred to as a "serious indictment of legal education." Seligman, a law professor at Northeastern, accused law schools of failing law students and the public by producing generalists and clinging to the case method. UVA Law and other top-tier law schools were mentioned outright in the text.[31]

UVA Law took these criticisms seriously, with the Curriculum Committee continuing its research and recommendations for improvements. Spies cited several accomplishments in his 1980 dean's report, including an expansion of the legal writing program, a new grading system, a policy-oriented tax program, and a corporate litigation course taught by professors Michael P. Dooley and John C. McCoid. Other joint committees were looking into trial advocacy opportunities and clinical education. Still, Spies and other US law school deans did not have immediate solutions for how to increase trial advocacy training or implement innovative curricular models to replace Socratic instruction.[32] Reflecting on his deanship, Spies lamented, "If there has been one disappointment and one objective not fully realized, it has been our failure to satisfy the many critics of legal education and to realize the goals and effect the reforms." In 1980, Spies stepped down and Richard A. Merrill took over as dean with a commitment to maintaining the Law School's national and elite status.[33]

The international recession that hit the United States in the early 1980s meant the small steps the Law School administrators were taking to improve legal education would be curtailed by the need to increase tuition and stretch resources. The class of 1983 comprised 375 students—a number that was staggeringly high compared to earlier decades but represented UVA Law's new but momentary average. The inflationary admission trend in legal education, which started in the 1970s, was felt at the Law School, where the student body hovered around 1,125 and was at risk of increasing due to financial pressures from the University. The reason

"It's frightening, I don't know anyone anymore who isn't a lawyer."

Cartoon featured in the *UVA Lawyer* drawn by Michael Goodman (Law 1980), 1983. (Michael Goodman and *UVA Lawyer*)

for this influx, according to Merrill, was the "lasting impact of the Viet Nam War on student attitudes" and the resulting "rush of students into law schools and away from graduate programs in arts and sciences."[34] Due to the recession, UVA required the Law School to up its tuition by 28 percent ($2,088) for in-state students and 23 percent ($4,588) for out-of-state students in 1982.[35] Moving forward, Merrill forecast a decline in applicants in the coming years, as economic opportunities for practicing attorneys were expected to decline as well.[36] Between 1982 and 1984, law school applications declined nationally by 12 percent.[37]

Merrill credited the drop in applicants, in part, to criticisms that there was an "oversupply" of lawyers in the United States. In 1983, according to a *New York Times* article cited by Merrill, there were roughly 128,000 law students and 606,000 lawyers. This same article, written by Stanford Law graduate David Margolick, laid out the many ways law schools—particularly top law schools—were failing future lawyers and society. Margolick quoted Derek C. Bok, president of Harvard University and former dean of Harvard Law, who argued that too many law students were lured by the promise of prestige and high salaries associated with large law firms, which added "little to the growth of the economy, the pursuit of culture or the enhancement of the human spirit." While clinical training was gaining popularity, Margolick claimed top law schools had been hesitant to adopt it as part of the curriculum given its similarities to apprenticeship and historical connections to poverty law.[38] Virginia Law was mentioned in the article as an example, among other institutions such as Yale, Columbia, and New York University. Merrill noted briefly in his summer 1983 report to alumni that legal education was "entering an era of critical examination," but he did not feel this was of serious concern.[39]

Amid crisis and change, legal scholar Robert M. O'Neil became president of UVA in 1985 and a faculty member at the Law School, where he taught a class on the First Amendment. Law School administrators hoped O'Neil's appointment signaled a closer intellectual connection between the Law School and Main Grounds and that the curricular and admissions challenges facing the school might be addressed by a president with a vested interest in promoting legal education. In his address to the Law School class of 1988, O'Neil acknowledged the inclination of lawyers toward high-powered careers. O'Neil encouraged law students to turn their sights toward underserved areas in the law and to embrace their duty to serve broader society: "I hope and assume you will not need to choose as most of us did between earning a good living . . . and serving the needs of society. You can—and I assume you will—do both."[40]

This call to public service by O'Neil came at a time of long-range planning for the Law School. Taking O'Neil's suggestions to heart, Law School administrators hoped to create more opportunities for placement in the public sector.[41] Long-range planning also meant returning to curricular reform with a committee headed by Professor David A. Martin. In 1987, the Law School implemented changes to the 1L curriculum that resulted in students completing twenty-five credit hours their first year, which left room for two to three elective courses in their second semester. Greater electivity created space in the curriculum for sequential instruction in one of several subject areas. This pedagogical development had already caught on at other top-tier schools. As early as the first year, UVA Law students now had the option to begin a sequenced curriculum in general practice, business law, civil and criminal litigation, civil rights and civil liberties, humanities and the social sciences, international and comparative law, public law, and taxation.[42] Sequential learning represented a significant step forward in providing students a clearer path to specialization.

Alongside curricular reform, Law School administrators desired additional changes to keep the school competitive with national peers: increasing faculty and financial assistance, reducing class sizes, and expanding the physical footprint of the Law School.[43] In spring 1987, UVA Law had the highest student-faculty ratio among peer national law schools at 32:1 (by comparison, Yale's was 14:1 and Michigan's 20/24:1).[44] In 1988, student applications were up by nearly a thousand, an increase that reflected national trends. Merrill acknowledged that this enrollment boom presented new complications, and consequently curricular reform would be necessarily slowed due to the unexpected burdens it presented for faculty and resources.[45] In fall 1988, Thomas H. Jackson replaced Merrill as dean of the Law School. Jackson came from Harvard

University of Virginia law classroom on North Grounds, spring 1989. (Andrea L. Hall and *UVA Lawyer*)

Law—only the second dean in the Law School's history not to come from the Law School faculty—and energetically joined a law school community in the throes of addressing the changing legal landscape.[46] As Jackson took the helm, students would help lead the way toward meaningful and modern curricular change at the Law School over the coming decade.

Students Speak Out on Curricular Reform

The 1987 alterations to the Law School's curriculum, which made room for more electives, were put to the test during its initial year. Students, who had just three years at the Law School, felt a stronger sense of urgency about curricular change relative to many Law School administrators, and students were particularly outspoken on curricular shifts. First-year students were especially affected by the 1987 changes, as the curriculum compressed core courses—such as Civil Procedure, Contracts, Property, and Torts—into fewer credit hours.[47] In the *Virginia Law Weekly* (*VLW*), one 1L student lamented the "feeling of helplessness" this compression produced, as the faculty "pick[ed] out cases in a seemingly haphazard manner in an attempt to cover a year's worth of material in a semester." The speed with which the change was implemented meant that faculty were not uniform in their teaching approach, and students realized that some sections of a course were moving at a quicker or slower pace than others. The students proposed greater uniformity in teaching approaches, more guidance from upper-class peer advisors in course selection, and more available seats in sequential course offerings.[48]

In general, student organizations led the calls for curricular reform, building upon the foundation established by the preceding generation of Black and female student activists. In particular, the Black Law Students Association (BLSA, est. 1970) and Virginia Law Women (est. 1971) spearheaded demonstrations and teach-ins to protest the lack of minority and female faculty members and students at the Law School.[49] Claudrena N. Harold's chapter discusses how student groups organized petitions, invited legal scholars from other law schools, and published opinion pieces in the *VLW* addressed toward the administration. Through the 1980s and into the 1990s, new affinity groups added their voices to the chorus of student protests, including the Gay and Lesbian Law Students Association (now Lambda Law Alliance, est. 1984), Jewish Law Students Association (est. 1985), and the Asian-American Law Students Association (now the Asian Pacific American Law Students Association, est. 1989).[50]

During Merrill's tenure, students advocated for a progressive curriculum that included CLS, feminist legal theory, and more clinical opportunities. The CLS movement interested Virginia Law students starting in at least 1985, although it was generally perceived as radical by the legal establishment.[51] In the spring 1985 report to alumni, Professor Robert Scott acknowledged the "exciting but turbulent times in legal education" in a brief article about the history of legal pedagogy. CLS can trace its roots to legal realism, Scott wrote, particularly the "distinctly nihilistic or anarchic bent" by which scholars sought to "expose the power relationships underlying all legal institutions."[52] Scott speculated that the CLS movement, the "most radical ingredient to be added to this legal stew," would not replace the traditional style of legal education that UVA Law alums had received.[53]

That same spring semester in 1985, faculty voted to rescind the Law School's "cultural requirement," not because they deemed the requirement's core courses of Legal Philosophy or Legal History an unnecessary addition to a robust legal education, but because the requirement was established when there were fewer electives and interdisciplinary options in the curriculum. By contrast, the current curriculum offered over eighty electives with a variety of historical and philosophical approaches to law.[54]

Still, the faculty established a lecture series during the 1986–87 academic year geared toward 1L students "to compensate for the elimination two years ago of a legal philosophies curriculum requirement" and to "assist [1Ls] in understanding the contexts within which the doctrinal content of their courses are set."[55] Topics included "Confessions of a Legal Realist" by Thomas F. Bergin, "Nineteenth Century Underpinnings of Contemporary Legal Thought" by Calvin Woodard, a lecture on law and economics by Scott, one on contemporary rights theory by George A. Rutherglen, one on social science and the law by John T. Monahan, and a lecture on CLS by Gary Peller. Faculty hosted the series again the following year with a few adjustments, including the addition of a lecture on feminist legal theory by Nancy S. Ehrenreich.[56]

Guest lectures also proved a popular method for student groups to inject their legal education with schools of thought unavailable to them at the Law School.[57] To supplement their education in CLS, the Law School chapter of the National Lawyers Guild invited Harvard professor and CLS scholar Duncan Kennedy to speak in October 1986. Kennedy advocated for affirmative faculty hiring practices and greater clinical offerings that redirected law school resources to underprivileged groups.[58] When Peller, whom students recognized as the only CLS scholar on the law faculty, left the Law School in 1988 for another position, students felt a sense of urgency to fill the curricular gap he left behind. Virginia Law Women organized a speakers series during the 1988–89 academic year and invited legal scholars Mary Joe Frug, Mari J. Matsuda, Frances E. Olsen, and Kimberlé W. Crenshaw (joined by Peller) to speak.[59]

Student support for clinical offerings was widespread during this period and less controversial than the CLS movement. Following Condlin's departure, the Virginia Criminal Practice Clinic (CPC) remained popular with students, who voiced their discontent whenever word trickled down that it might be cut from the curriculum due to lack of funding. When the faculty Special Committee on Clinical Education issued a report in April 1982 calling for more trial advocacy courses and suggesting the CPC be reevaluated on a yearly basis, students bristled.[60] In one *VLW* letter to the editor, a student noted that the clinic provided real-world experience handling "every phase of the case including client interviews, factual investigation, legal research, motions practice, negotiation, bail hearings, trials and appeals. [Trial advocacy] seminars handle only trials."[61] The faculty subcommittee report was eventually approved by the entire faculty, and each year students remained staunch in their support of the CPC, as well as the Family Law Clinic (est. 1984).[62] When Jackson took over the deanship in fall 1988, the Law School's clinical offerings included the CPC, the Family Law Clinic, and multiple sections of Trial Advocacy. Other extracurricular groups such as LAS and the Post-Conviction Assistance Project (P-CAP, est. 1971) provided students with the opportunity to develop lawyering skills outside the classroom, albeit not for course credit.[63] In the *VLW,* Michael Allen (Law 1985) decried the Law School's emphasis on courtroom simulation experiences such as Trial Advocacy while withholding course credit for extracurriculars that provided real legal assistance to the community. This deliberate move, Allen argued, "sends the message that [the Law School] prefers to keep its students on the conveyor belt to the corporate law firm."[64]

Amid the bursts of momentum for curricular reform, students consistently called for greater racial diversity at the Law School. When Jackson arrived in fall 1988, only two of the Law School's fifty-four full-time professors were Black. All the others were white.[65] The student body also remained predominantly white, although demographic diversity was gradually improving: 10 percent of the student population identified as Black in fall 1988, compared with 2 percent in fall 1970 (in 1988, 1 percent identified as Asian, 0.3 percent as Hispanic, and 0.1 percent as Native American).[66] Compared with other ABA accredited law schools, UVA Law was ahead of the curve: the ABA reported that during the 1985–86 academic year, just 5 percent of students at accredited law schools were Black.[67] Such small numbers, while indicative of a gradual diversification in minority admissions over time, were greatly felt as students navigated the Law School. The entering class in fall 1986, for example, included forty-seven Black students, but the next year's entering class dropped to twenty-nine, which students feared was the beginning of a downward trend in minority admissions.[68]

Frustrated by years of slow change in minority enrollment and curricular development, law students from BLSA, Virginia Law Women, the Gay and Lesbian Law Student Association, Law Students for Public Service, and UVA Law's chapter of the National Lawyers Guild wanted to ensure that the incoming dean was made aware of the curricular concerns of Virginia Law students. The groups penned a letter to Jackson a few months prior to his arrival and published it in the *VLW.* The Law School had strayed from Thomas Jefferson's original vision for legal education, they argued, in which the University would be "an arena where a free exchange of ideas could take place." Instead, the students wrote that the Law School prioritized "rights theorists and economic scholars" over other schools of thought. The authors also asserted that hiring more diverse faculty—both demographically and intellectually—would return the Law School to this Jeffersonian vision of a marketplace of ideas.[69]

Like the deans before him, Jackson worked to address internal calls for change with the resources made available to him, while attempting to appease the Law School's numerous stakeholders. In his first letter to alumni in 1988, Jackson identified the major issues he felt the Law School faced: faculty recruitment and retention, female and minority student recruitment, balancing pedagogical diversity with faculty collegiality, and determining how best to craft a curriculum that was both interdisciplinary and rooted in the traditional study of law.[70]

Jackson did not make any immediate changes to the curriculum upon his arrival, and student organizations continued their efforts to advocate for increased demographic and curricular diversity. In a letter to the editor signed by sixteen anonymous students, they again emphasized that demographic and curricular homogeneity rendered UVA Law a "stultifying educational experience" and called for *VLW* readers to sign a petition addressed to law administration demanding greater diversity.[71] Over three hundred students signed the petition, calling for the administration to hire CLS scholars as tenure-track professors, "address the severe under-representation of women and minority faculty members," and expand the school's clinical offerings. They submitted the petition to Jackson in March 1990.[72]

On April 5, 1990, some 250 UVA Law students participated in a class boycott hosted by the newly formed student group Coalition for Diversity. Virginia Law was one of thirty-six law schools across the country that joined this nationwide strike for diversity.[73] Jackson circulated his response to the petition in advance of a meeting with the faculty Appointments Committee, the Coalition for Diversity, and the Student Bar Association. He defended the Law School's curricular offerings and the faculty's efforts to search for scholars of high caliber with a variety of legal interests. Jackson agreed with the importance of actively seeking out more female and minority faculty members who met the standards of teaching and scholarship at UVA Law. As for the lack of clinical offerings, Jackson stated that Virginia Law's approach "has been educationally sound as well as responsive to the most immediate student interest."[74]

The exclusion of student input in curriculum reform resurfaced in fall 1990 when an ad hoc faculty committee, chaired by Scott, published a proposal to revise the curriculum further by reducing four-credit courses to three-credit courses in the name of greater electivity. This would increase faculty leave flexibility and "shift teaching resources

In April 1990, 250 law students gathered on the lawn of the Law School to take part in a nationwide class boycott calling for increased demographic and curricular diversity. (*Virginia Law Weekly* and Arthur J. Morris Law Library Special Collections, University of Virginia)

from first-year to elective courses." The proposal also suggested increasing the size of first-year sections.[75] This move would reduce some of the faculty's course load, allowing them to increase elective courses offered in the curriculum without decreasing the student-faculty ratio. Students met with Scott to voice their concerns. Several students feared that compressing the 1L curriculum further in favor of electives would deteriorate the "solid foundation in the all-important 'basics' of the law." They also criticized the lack of student input in crafting the proposal.[76] The faculty agreed to a compromise that would increase faculty opportunities for leave time as well as curricular offerings without altering the 1L curriculum.[77]

The spring semester saw a second student strike and boycott sponsored by the Coalition for Diversity, calling for the same increased demographic and curricular diversity as the year prior, although students acknowledged faculty efforts to chip away at the issues.[78] Then, in August

1991, UVA President John T. Casteen III announced that he had appointed Jackson as interim University vice president and provost. With Jackson set to begin his new post in September, the Law School had to fill his position quickly.[79] Law professor Robert Scott was selected to serve as interim dean and was later named dean, with his term beginning February 1992.[80]

In his final report to alumni as dean in 1992, Jackson included the Law School's contribution to the University's new ten-year plan, in which he outlined where he felt legal education was headed. Jackson recognized the limitations of a high student-faculty ratio, which he hoped would decrease to 20:1 over the next ten years (it was 28:1 at the time). New faculty members increased the diversity of the Law School's curricular offerings, bringing in new perspectives from other disciplines such as history, psychology, and philosophy, while enabling smaller class sizes. Jackson believed that innovative curricular formats, such as course sequencing and team teaching, were remedies to the ongoing issue of what to do about the third year of law school. And key to the Law School's next era under the leadership of Scott, Jackson emphasized the symbiotic relationship between the Law School's twin missions: teaching and research. Virginia Law's ongoing commitment to these two missions, Jackson wrote, would ensure that UVA continued to produce lifelong legal professionals prepared to become leaders and thus fulfilling "the Jeffersonian ideal of the lawyer as public servant."[81] The Law School's ability to sustain that commitment, however, had become increasingly dependent on fluctuations in state funding. If the Law School was to weather the ongoing storm of pedagogical change in legal education, it would need to stabilize its income stream.

The Beginning of a New Era at UVA Law: Dean Robert E. Scott, 1991–2001

As his predecessors did before him, Scott began his tenure by assessing the current state of the Law School within the broader context of legal education and delineating his goals for the years to come. In his first report to alumni in 1992, Scott celebrated the renown of the Law School's faculty, both the "wise guardians of the tradition" and the school's growing cohort of young faculty.[82] One of the forthcoming challenges, Scott warned, would be faculty retention and expansion to improve the student-faculty ratio and realize a curriculum "that blends theory with practice, ideas with professionalism, and where courses build upon each other in sequences."[83] Entwining legal practice with theory through course sequencing, team teaching, and greater opportunities for student-faculty mentorship would give the third year of law school more structure, Scott argued, while keeping up with trends in legal education. To achieve this ambitious curricular restructuring, Scott appealed for assistance from alumni to support the $9.5 million acquisition of the building soon to be vacated by UVA's Darden Business School. Purchasing the Darden building would be the first step in creating a new Law Grounds with more faculty offices, smaller classrooms, and an overall greater sense of community. In essence, Law School administration hoped to embed the future of legal pedagogy in the architecture of the forthcoming building renovation.[84]

The crucial piece to Scott's plan was achieving financial self-sufficiency. If UVA Law was able to better control tuition rates, and the revenue accrued from tuition increases, Scott argued that the Law School would be better equipped to increase its financial aid packages, utilize leftover funds to raise faculty base salaries, hire more faculty, improve library services, and adjust curricular offerings to meet the changing needs of the legal profession.[85] With the support of UVA President Casteen and Provost Jackson, Law School administration initiated a three-year plan to increase tuition as well as the percentage of those tuition increases that returned to the Law School. Tuition went up each year until the end of the 1995–96 academic year, when the financial restructuring agreement was complete. At that point, the Law School aimed to stabilize its tuition prices to the traditional 2:3 ratio for in-state to out-of-state students, as well as return its in-state to out-of-state student ratio to 2:3.[86] With the resulting revenue from this fiscal agreement, Law School administration created new financial aid opportunities and began aggressively working to decrease the student-faculty ratio, which by fall 1993 had been reduced to 23:1.[87]

Scott also wasted no time in raising funds for the new Law Grounds. In his reports to alumni, in which he provided updates on fundraising and curricular development efforts, he continuously drew upon the architectural and Jeffersonian history of the Law School to reiterate the inseparability of place and pedagogy. He envisioned the new campus as "a contemporary academical village on North Grounds": a place where, as in the days when the Law School was on the Lawn and later in Clark Hall, students and professors could spontaneously build community simply by running into one another in passing.[88] Renovations began on the newly acquired Darden building first, with construction work on what would become Clay Hall, Hunton & Williams Hall, Spies Garden, and Scott Commons beginning in May 1995.[89] The final building doubled the square footage of the Law School and included classrooms, twenty-two faculty

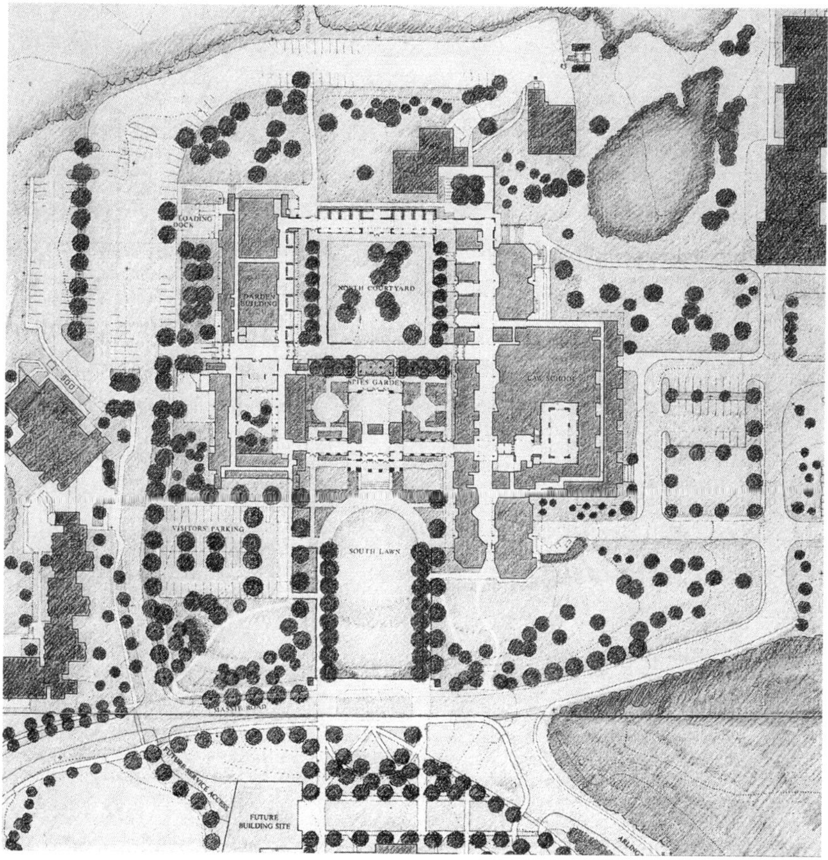

Plan for the Law School's new "Law Grounds" at North Grounds, 1994. (Arthur J. Morris Law Library Special Collections, University of Virginia)

offices, moot court rooms, student lounges, and meeting spaces.[90] With the completion of the Darden building renovation in winter 1997, Scott proclaimed that the Law School was one step closer to reestablishing a "sense of place" for the law community, "a physical identity that embodies the notions of community that uniquely characterize Virginia."[91]

During this time of intense financial and physical reimagining, the Law School also worked to develop a new "curricular blueprint," spearheaded by the faculty Committee on Curricular Enhancement in the New Law Grounds.[92] The committee identified six foci for the curriculum: an emphasis on specialization through course sequences, smaller classes for upper-class students, more courses co-taught by professors and practitioners, curricular internationalization, continued efforts to provide interdisciplinary study, and the integration of new technologies into the classroom.[93] In fall 1994 the Law School inaugurated its "Principles and Practice" team-teaching program, which allowed students to work alongside legal practitioners in fields they might otherwise not be exposed to through the Law School's clinical offerings.[94] To that end, Virginia Law had significantly increased its clinical offerings since the beginning of Scott's deanship. During the 1996–97 academic year the Law School offered the International Human Rights Clinic, the Appellate Litigation Clinic, the Environmental Practice Clinic, the Prosecution Clinical Program, the Psychiatry and Criminal Law Seminar, and the Pro-Bono Public Service Program in addition to its existing Criminal Practice, Family Law, and Forensic Psychiatry clinics.[95] The explosion of opportunities in hands-on legal training was the result of a culmination of factors, including student demand and initiative, but also the recognition on the part of the faculty and administration that law students were increasingly expected to have practical legal experience upon graduation.[96]

With the support of UVA administration, Law School faculty, and alumni, Scott shepherded the Law School through an ambitious period of financial, structural, and curricular transition. Scott also kept communication channels open between administration and students, hosting weekly brown bag lunches to discuss the flurry of changes and address their questions.[97] Students had the opportunity to weigh in on the Law Grounds renovation, and as a result, the finished complex included designated meeting spaces for student groups.[98]

Building a New Generation of Legal Professionals

On November 8, 1997, Law School and University administration addressed a crowd of over eight hundred alumni, faculty, students, and friends at the dedication ceremony for the completed David A. Harrison III Law Grounds. William H. Rehnquist, chief justice of the US Supreme Court at the time, was the keynote speaker. In his opening remarks, Scott asserted that the new facility made a statement about the purpose of Virginia Law, what it had been, and what it would become: "an academic community dedicated to ensuring the ideals of civic virtue, rededicating ourselves to the Jeffersonian ideal of the lawyer as a public citizen."[99] When Rehnquist spoke, he lamented that the practice of law was sometimes more akin to a business than a profession, that hyperspecialization and billable hours had overshadowed a tradition of civility and service.[100]

In a *VLW* article on Rehnquist's speech, Scott acknowledged the perceived ethical and monetary dichotomy in the profession between public and private sector lawyers. But he also acknowledged Virginia Law students' capacity to be a part of the shift away from that reputation: "It is up to law students to challenge that dichotomy when they practice law—to do good wherever they may end up."[101] The Harrison Law Grounds was the setting for that change, and time would tell how the next generation of faculty, administrators, and students would make use of the facility as the Law School rapidly approached a new millennium.

Notes

1. Robert E. Scott, "At a Crossroads," *Virginia Law School Report* 16, no. 2 (Winter 1992): 3–6 (hereafter cited as *VLSR*).
2. Scott, "At a Crossroads," 3.
3. Scott, "At a Crossroads," 6.
4. For more on the struggle for diversity at UVA Law, see Claudrena Harold, "We Demand: Student Advocates for Curricular Change, 1960–1980," in this volume.
5. Robert E. Scott, "Virginia Law's Treasured Resource, The Students," *UVA Lawyer* 19, no. 1 (Winter 1995): 3–5.
6. For more on Jefferson's vision for the Law School, see David Thomas Konig, "Jeffersonian Foundations of Legal Education in Virginia, 1779–1845," in this volume.
7. Scott, "At a Crossroads," 3–6; Robert E. Scott, "A Vision for the Twenty-First Century," *VLSR* 17, no. 1 (Summer 1992): 3–4.
8. University of Virginia, *The University of Virginia Record, School of Law, 1970–1971,*

n.s., vol. 56, no. 11 (Charlottesville: University of Virginia, 1970) (hereafter cited as *LSR* [*Law School Record*]). For more on professionalization at UVA Law, see G. Edward White, "Poised between a Regional and a National Law School, 1920–1960," in this volume.

9. By 1974, UVA Law had 960 students. See *LSR,* 1974, 109. See also Phillip Mills Herrington, *The Law School at the University of Virginia: Architectural Expansion in the Realm of Thomas Jefferson* (Charlottesville: University of Virginia Press, 2017).

10. *LSR,* 1970, 59–62.

11. *LSR,* 1970, 64; *LSR,* 1954, 35.

12. Dean's Annual Report, 20 January 1948, 14, Deans' Papers, RG–32-100-78, Arthur J. Morris Law Library Special Collections, University of Virginia (hereafter cited as LLSC).

13. Paul B. Barringer Jr., "Annual Report of the Committee on Scholarship," *Virginia Law Weekly,* 26 October 1950 (hereafter cited as *VLW*).

14. *LSR,* 1970, 63–65.

15. *LSR,* 1970, 12; "Public Policy Study Center to Open Here," *Daily Progress* (Charlottesville, VA), 6 May 1968.

16. For more on the Legal Aid Society and its establishment at the Law School, see Harold, "We Demand."

17. In an April 17, 1970, meeting the UVA Law faculty unanimously passed a resolution urging the Virginia Supreme Court to adopt the rule, writing: "Resolved, that it be recorded as the opinion of this Faculty that the adoption by the Commonwealth of the American Bar Association Model Rule Relative to Legal Assistance by Law Students would substantially increase the ability of this Law School to prepare its students for the practice of law." See "Law Faculty Urge Rules Permitting Student Practice," *VLW,* 30 April 1970. For the ABA's Model Rule, see Edmund W. Kitch, ed., *Clinical Education and the Law School of the Future* (Chicago: University of Chicago Law School, 1970), 228–65.

18. George K. Walker, "Third-Year Practice Rules in Virginia: Notes for the Practitioner," *University of Richmond Law Review* 11, no. 1 (Fall 1976): 69–85. In brief, the rule allowed eligible law students to appear in court on behalf of any person who had provided their written consent and with the approval of a supervising lawyer. Law students had to complete at least four semesters of coursework, including Criminal Law, Professional Ethics, Evidence, and Procedure, to be eligible. See Memorandum, Joint Faculty-Student-Bar Committee on Clinical Education, 8 January 1975, Papers of Daniel J. Meador, MSS-82-3, LLSC.

19. The committee defined clinical training as "practical legal work, work ordinarily done by lawyers or persons acting in the capacity of lawyers, as opposed to traditional law school study." Memorandum, Joint Faculty-Student-Bar Committee on Clinical Education, 8 January 1975, Meador Papers.

20. Monrad G. Paulsen, "From the Dean: Good News and the Need for Support," *VLW,* 10 March 1975.

21. *LSR,* 1978, 91.

22. "The Man behind Clinical Instruction at Virginia," *VLSR* 1, no. 2 (Fall 1977): 40–41; Gayle Westbrook, "Law School Expands Clinical Programs," *VLW,* 16 February 1979.

23. Emerson G. Spies, "The Dean Reports," *VLSR* 1, no. 1 (Spring 1977): 8.

24. Roger T. Creager, "'New' Clinical Program Will Feature Criminal Practice," *VLW,* 18 April 1980; Robert J. Condlin interview by J. P. "Sandy" Ogilvy, 4 January 2003, transcript, DigitalGeorgetown, Georgetown University Law Library, https://perma.cc/6DKG-9M9K; Spies, "The Dean Reports," 5–10.

25. Spies, "The Dean Reports," *VLSR* 2, no.1 (Winter 1978): 3–4.
26. Spies, "The Dean Reports," *VLSR* 2, no.1 (Winter 1978): 3–4. See also White, "Poised Between a Regional and a National Law School, 1920–1960."
27. Spies, "The Dean Reports," *VLSR* 2, no. 2 (Summer 1978): 3.
28. Emerson G. Spies, "University of Virginia School of Law: Annual Report on Academic Affairs," 1 September 1977–31 August 1978, Records of the Assistant/Associate Dean, RG–32/101–96, LLSC.
29. Spies, "University of Virginia School of Law."
30. Spies, "The Dean Reports: Implications of the Devitt Committee Report," *VLSR* 3, no. 2 (Spring 1979): 3–5.
31. Joel Seligman, *The High Citadel: The Influence of Harvard Law School* (Boston: Houghton Mifflin, 1978); Spies, "The Dean Reports: Challenges Confronting Law Schools," *VLSR* 4, no. 1 (Winter 1980): 3.
32. Spies, "The Dean Reports," *VLSR* 4, no. 1 (Winter 1980), 3.
33. Spies, "The Dean Reports: A Rewarding Five Years," *VLSR* 4, no. 2 (Summer 1980): 4.
34. Richard A. Merrill, "The Dean Reports: State of the Law School," *VLSR* 5, no. 1 (Fall 1980): 3.
35. Merrill, "The Dean Reports," *VLSR* 6, no. 2 (Spring 1982): 3.
36. Merrill, "Another Year Unfolds," *VLSR* 7, no. 1 (Fall 1982): 4.
37. Merrill, "University Appoints President," *VLSR* 9, no. 2 (Spring 1985): 3–4.
38. David Margolick, "The Trouble with America's Law Schools," *New York Times*, 22 May 1983.
39. Merrill, "Dean's Potpourri Highlights Honor System," *VLSR* 7, no. 2 (Summer 1983): 5.
40. Merrill, "New President, Alumni Loyalty," *VLSR* 10, no. 1 (Winter 1985): 3–4.
41. Merrill, "Planning for the Future," *VLSR* 11, no. 2 (Winter 1987): 4.
42. Jacqueline Miller, "Faculty Implements Upperclass Curriculum," *VLW*, 6 November 1987. See also "Suggested Course Sequence and Thesis Options," University of Virginia School of Law, 13 November 1987; "Appendix B: Memorandum to Students Introducing Course Sequences and Thesis Options," undated, David A. Martin Papers, MSS-98-1, LLSC.
43. Merrill, "Planning for the Future," 4–5.
44. Merrill, "New Chairs, Student Body Size, Building Expansion," *VLSR* 11, no. 3 (Spring 1987): 5.
45. Merrill, "Admissions and Curriculum Reform," *VLSR* 12, no. 2 (Spring 1988): 3–4.
46. The first non-UVA dean was Monrad G. Paulsen (1968–75).
47. Jacqueline Miller, "First-Year Curriculum Changed," *VLW*, 14 November 1986.
48. Joe Pankowski Jr., "Work Needed on First-Year Curriculum," *VLW*, 25 March 1988.
49. For more on the founding and early history of BLSA and Virginia Law Women, see Harold, "We Demand."
50. Mary Pat Seery, "GALLSA Members Optimistic," *VLW*, 13 April 1984; Marcia Pope, "Jewish Law Students Form Group," *VLW*, 22 March 1985; Shireen K. Lewis, "Virginia Law Women Speakers' Committee: In Memory of Professors Mary Jo Frug and Denise Carty-Bennia," 1993, Records of the Virginia Law Women, RG–32–209/2010, LLSC. As of 2023, there are multiple affinity organizations at UVA Law catering to the needs of Asian law students, including the Korean American Law Student Association, the South Asian Law Student Association, and Women of Color.

51. For an early history of the CLS movement, see Richard W. Bauman, *Ideology and Community in the First Wave of Critical Legal Studies* (Toronto: University of Toronto Press, 2002).
52. Robert E. Scott, "The Critical Challenge in Legal Education," *VLSR* 9, no. 2 (Spring 1985): 6–7.
53. Scott, *"Critical Challenge,"* 9.
54. *LSR,* 1985, 72.
55. "Philosophy Lectures Scheduled," *VLW,* 26 September 1986.
56. Jacqueline Miller, "Law and Philosophy Lectures Begin," *VLW,* 25 September 1987.
57. This was true during this period and throughout the Law School's history. See, for example, Ronald Andrew Bassford, *The Student Legal Forum at the University of Virginia School of Law: The First Fifty Years, 1947–1997* (Charlottesville: University of Virginia Law School Foundation, 2000).
58. Nancy Green, "Kennedy Discusses CLS Goals," *VLW,* 17 October 1986.
59. Holly Hexter, "Frug Addresses Law School Students," *VLW,* 21 October 1988; Judy Lee, "Prof. Mari Matsuda Urges Focus in Law on Alternative Consciousness of the Oppressed," *VLW,* 7 April 1989; "Frances Olsen to Speak on the Sex of Law," *VLW,* 7 April 1989; "Announcements," *VLW,* 21 April 1989.
60. John Mitchell, "Criminal Clinic's Existence Depends on Future Funds," *VLW,* 19 February 1982; Douglas Sgarro, "Committee Finds Trial Institutes & Seminars Needed," *VLW,* 16 April 1982.
61. David Godofsky, letter to the editor, *VLW,* 23 April 1982.
62. Jay Barker, "Clinics' End Decried," *VLW,* 22 March 1985; Jay Barker, "Merrill: No Decision Made on Clinical Programs Yet," *VLW,* 29 March 1985; Jim Crane, "Optimism Unaffected by Family Feud," *VLW,* 15 November 1985.
63. P-CAP was founded to assist persons incarcerated in the Virginia penal system and enabled third-year students who qualified under Virginia's Third-Year Student Practice Rule to appear in federal district courts and before the Fourth Circuit Court of Appeals. See "Profiles of Three Activities Presented: J. B. Moore, Post Conviction, and Law Women," *VLW,* 17 September 1976; Mary Pat Seery, "P-CAP Gets Law Students into Court," *VLW,* 1 February 1985.
64. Michael Allen, letter to the editor, *VLW,* 17 February 1984.
65. University of Virginia, *Data Digest, 1988–1989* (Charlottesville: University of Virginia, 1988), 72.
66. University of Virginia, *Data Digest, 1988–1989,* 38; University of Virginia, *Statistical Information, November 1970* (Charlottesville: University of Virginia, 1970), 55.
67. Emily Couric, "Blacks in Law," *VLSR* 11, no. 1 (Fall 1986): 6.
68. Catharina Min, "Largest Class Ever Enrolls," *VLW,* 4 September 1987.
69. "A Plea for Diversity," *VLW,* 8 April 1988.
70. Thomas H. Jackson, "Challenges Ahead," *VLSR* 13, no. 1 (Fall 1988): 3–6.
71. "Faculty Diversity," *VLW,* 16 February 1990.
72. Jackson, "New Developments Affect Community," *VLSR* 14, no. 3 (Spring 1990): 3–11.
73. "Around North Grounds," *VLW,* 1 April 1990; Shoshana Davids, "Diversity Strike Draws Hundreds," *VLW,* 13 April 1990; Jackson, "New Developments Affect Community," 6.
74. Jackson, "New Developments Affect Community," 10–11.
75. Scott Vance, "Major Curricular Changes Proposed," *VLW,* 11 November 1990.

76. David F. Dabbs, Shoshana R. Davids, Thomas R. Kauffman, Andrew G. Macchione, John L. Moore, Jonathan E. Perkel, Lisa A. Shook, and Winston B. Sitton, "Law School Should Reject Committee's Curriculum Proposal," *VLW*, 11 November 1990.
77. Jeff Brueggeman, "Faculty Approves Upperclass Curriculum Changes, Required First-Year Courses Left Unchanged at Four Hours," *VLW*, 30 November 1990.
78. Jeff Brueggeman, "Students to Strike for Law School Diversity," *VLW*, 29 March 1991; Dave Dabbs, "Law Students Strike for Diversity," *VLW*, 12 April 1991.
79. "Law School Dean Jackson Appointed Interim Provost," *VLW*, 23 August 1991.
80. "Professor Robert Scott Named Acting Dean of Law School," *VLW*, 30 August 1991; Jeffrey Stern, "Professor Robert Scott Named Dean," *VLW*, 21 February 1992.
81. Jackson, "Designing Our Future," *VLSR* 16, no. 1 (Summer 1991): 3–9.
82. Scott, "At a Crossroads," 4.
83. Scott, "At a Crossroads," 4. The student-faculty ratio was 28:1 in fall 1991. In fall 2022, it was 6.2:1. See Jackson, "Designing Our Future," 7; "Facts and Statistics," UVA Law, https://www.law.virginia.edu/facts-and-stats/overview.
84. Scott, "At a Crossroads," 3–6. For a complete history of the development of the David A. Harrison III Law Grounds, see Herrington, *Law School at the University of Virginia*, 159–201.
85. Scott, "At a Crossroads," 6.
86. Robert E. Scott, "The Challenge to Be the Best," *UVA Lawyer* 20, no. 2 (Spring 1996): 3–5. By spring 1996, state revenue only made up 4.7 percent of the Law School's operating budget.
87. Wes Enders, "Dean Addresses Tuition Increases and 'Privatization,'" *VLW*, 15 October 1993.
88. Scott, "Vision for the 21st Century," 3–4.
89. "Law Grounds Construction Schedule Firmed Up," *UVA Lawyer* 19, no. 2 (Spring 1995): 6.
90. Herrington, *Law School at the University of Virginia*, 198–99.
91. Robert E. Scott, "The Lawyer as Public Citizen," *UVA Lawyer* 21, no. 1 (Winter 1997): 3–5.
92. Robert E. Scott, "Community & Curricular Challenges," *VLSR* 18, no. 1 (Summer 1993): 3–5; Robert E. Scott, "The Internationalization of Virginia Law," *UVA Lawyer* 19, no. 2 (Spring 1995): 3–5.
93. Scott, "Community & Curricular Challenges," 3–5.
94. Robert E. Scott, "Legal Education's Changing Market," *UVA Lawyer* 18, no. 2 (Summer 1994): 4; Coke Morgan Stewart, "Frontiers in Legal Education: Principles and Practice at U.Va.," *VLW*, 24 February 1995.
95. Cathy L. Eberly, "Beyond the TV Camera's Reach: Virginia's Criminal Law Program," *UVA Lawyer* 20, no. 1 (Winter 1996): 13–20.
96. R. A. Sturgell, "Law School Responds to Pro Bono Proposal," *VLW*, 4 February 1994; Laurel Carter and Larry DeGraaf, "Administration Hopes New Program Will Enrich Curriculum," *VLW*, 29 April 1994.
97. Shoshana Davids, "Acting Dean Scott Opens Lines of Communication with Student Leaders," *VLW*, 11 October 1991; Jeff Stern, "Acting Dean Scott Reiterates Bold Plan for Law School," *VLW*, 18 October 1991; Christopher Bowen, "Students, Faculty Gather to Discuss Issues of Diversity at the Law School," *VLW*, 22 November 1991; Enders, "Dean Addresses Tuition Increases and 'Privatization.'"

98. Elise Bryant, "Student Input Needed on Darden Acquisition," *VLW*, 26 March 1993; Scott, "Virginia Law's Treasured Resource."
99. Fred Bowyer, "Law School Community Dedicates Law Grounds," *VLW*, 14 November 1997.
100. Kristina Dell, "Rehnquist Reflects on the Legal Profession," *VLW*, 14 November 1997.
101. Dell, "Rehnquist Reflects."

Epilogue

BECOMING THE TWENTY-FIRST CENTURY LAW SCHOOL, 1997–2024

Risa Goluboff

I ARRIVED AS a newly minted untenured law professor at the University of Virginia School of Law in 2002.[1] What I knew about my new professional home was that it was a public and national law school known for its robust and pluralist intellectual community; that it had particular faculty strengths in legal history and law and economics; that it boasted a collegial culture, in part because of its location in a picturesque and cosmopolitan college town; and that my new colleagues welcomed me with open arms. I did not, however, know much about the school's history, despite being a legal historian myself. I did not know which of the attributes I observed were of long standing and which were of recent vintage. I did not know how long it had been a national law school, what it had taken to become such, or what had remained constant over time.

What I have learned since—as a faculty member for sixteen years, as dean for eight, and through my involvement with the research and publication of this volume—is both how much has changed since UVA's founding more than two hundred years ago and what has endured. For much of its history, UVA was a distinctly regional, and even more distinctly Virginian, institution, bound up in the currents of southern history. When Thomas Jefferson founded UVA in 1819, he imagined a school that would educate the white men of the South to become lawyers and public servants for the new American republic. The exclusive homogeneity of the school, along with Jefferson's architectural plans for residential learning, made for a tight-knit community committed to a regionally constrained vision of law and politics dependent on and intertwined with slavery, white supremacy, and patriarchy.

In important and obvious ways, as the essays in this volume reveal, the Law School has departed from that founding vision over the past two hundred years. It is now indisputably a national institution even as it continues to pride itself on its engagement with and service to the Commonwealth of Virginia. Perhaps most significantly, it has fundamentally transformed who participates in its education along geographic, racial, ethnic, gender, and other demographic and intellectual dimensions.

In other ways, however, even as the Law School has changed, critical foundational characteristics endure. The collegial culture born of homogeneity now flourishes in a community heterogeneous along so many dimensions. The Law School continues to foster a cohesive community that prizes the free exchange of ideas, even in the face of recent national and global polarization and strife. Moreover, far more pedagogical continuity can be found than one might expect. From the beginning, Jefferson forged his own pedagogical path of teaching law as part of the University's broad liberal arts curriculum. Within short order, however, the curriculum had to make room for training in the practical and professional legal skills its new students sought. Regardless of the tension between those two approaches, Jefferson's overarching goal for his new university was to educate students to engage in public service to the new democracy.[2] Over the past two hundred years, these three aspects of legal education—thinking of law as part of the liberal arts, providing practical training, and encouraging public service—have ebbed and flowed, both at UVA and in legal education more generally. Today, an embrace of all three largely characterizes UVA's pedagogical mission and, indeed, the educational mission of national law schools generally in the twenty-first century.

The most recent quarter century of this history, from the dedication of the Law School's current facilities in 1997 to the present, has crystallized both these changes and these continuities. The past twenty-five years have extended and intensified the transformations of the prior twenty-five, cementing UVA's position as one of only a handful of either public or southern law schools among top national law schools. At the same time, recent decades have been tumultuous ones, and national and global developments have stimulated change along new frontiers.

This most recent chapter of the Law School's history is the subject of this epilogue. It is also very much my chapter. The deans who led the school were my deans, the faculty my colleagues, the students my students. I am a primary source—as observer and participant—for the developments I describe here.

I am also the embodiment of many of them. I am the first woman dean, the first Jewish dean, and the first to hold a PhD in a separate field alongside my legal education. I am a northeasterner and a civil rights historian, educated at leading national universities. One hundred years before my arrival, I would not have been welcome here. Even fifty years earlier, I would have been a significant outlier. I am both a product of and an additional reason for the UVA Law School of the twenty-first century.

Given both my historical interests and my place in UVA's history, it was perhaps overdetermined that I would spend no small part of my time as dean learning about the history of this leading institution of higher education in, and of, the South. This volume is an important part of that project. The history told here is honest, sometimes brutally so. I am proud of this institution, proud that we can examine our past with unflinching eyes. Such self-reflection seems necessary to me, both as a historian who wants to better understand the past on its own terms and as a recent dean who believes that reckoning with that past will enable this perpetual institution to become the best possible version of itself.

UVA as a National Law School

When I joined the faculty in 2002, the Law School was already and definitively a national institution. It attracted students and faculty with the highest levels of achievement from around the country. Students entering the Law School in 2000 came from forty-four states and generally launched their careers in major cities, both in and outside of the South. With graduates practicing in thirty-three states and Washington, DC, UVA was one of only two schools nationwide at the time with graduates at each of the country's top one hundred law firms.[3] The Law School drew its faculty from prominent law schools in every region, and its curriculum emphasized training in law generally, rather than Virginia law specifically. Ever since *US News and World Report* began publishing law school rankings in 1987, UVA had been ranked among the top fourteen law schools in the country.[4]

Over the past twenty-five years, UVA has cemented this national status. Though the values embedded in national rankings like *US News* have recently come under fire, including from UVA, such rankings continue to hold considerable influence. We are the only law school in a public university and the only law school in the South to remain in the *US News* top ten every year of the new millennium (most recently tied for number four). Our faculty consistently places among the most influential in academic scholarship, and other rankings regularly place us in the top five in the nation for career prospects, quality of life, professors, classroom experience, and selectivity.[5] Our student-faculty ratio, a data point previous deans viewed as a sign of national status, has improved from 23:1 in 1993 to 5.5:1 thirty years later.[6] Virtually every incoming class in recent years has surpassed the previous one in terms of academic achievement. Students today are more geographically varied than ever before, hailing from 40 states and 144 undergraduate institutions.

The Law School is equally national in where it sends its graduates. UVA Law alumni reside and practice in every state in the union. (Indeed, the wide dispersion of our alumni makes UVA more "national" geographically than many of its peers, whose alumni concentrate in a few large cities.) Overwhelming majorities begin their careers at major national law firms, as well as in judicial clerkships, the federal government, and state and local governments and nonprofit organizations across the country.[7] Federal judicial clerkships have become a new marker of national stature, and UVA regularly ranks in the top five both for federal clerkships generally and for Supreme Court clerkships in particular.[8] Such national achievement continues well into graduates' careers. UVA Law is second in the number of alumni in the nation's top one hundred law firms, third in chief legal officers at the country's top five hundred companies, and sixth for the number of graduates serving as US attorneys, federal judges, state attorneys general, and solicitors general.[9]

All of this success has been facilitated by the financial self-sufficiency that Dean Robert E. Scott envisioned and that his successor, John C. Jeffries Jr., implemented around the turn of the twenty-first century. Under the terms the Law School negotiated with the University of Virginia and the Virginia General Assembly, the Law School, along with UVA's Darden School of Business, has forfeited University and Commonwealth subsidies, gained substantial control over its finances, and contributed a portion of its tuition revenue to the University.[10] Every dean since Jeffries—Paul G. Mahoney, myself, and my successor Leslie C. Kendrick—has maintained and articulated the importance of financial self-sufficiency to the Law School's continued success and stature.[11]

We remain a proud public law school committed to serving the Commonwealth, but our financial footing now more closely resembles our private than our public peers. Like law schools attached to private universities, we rely on market-based tuition, philanthropic gifts, and endowment spending as our main sources of revenue.[12] Tuition thus increased early in the twenty-first century from what had been historically low, publicly subsidized levels to market rates with a discount for in-state students. Building on the pioneering work of David H. Ibbeken (Law 1971) beginning in 1979, the Law School Foundation also dramatically expanded and professionalized its fundraising apparatus. Under Ibbeken and his successor Luis Alvarez, the school has maintained a vigorous annual giving program, with levels of alumni participation that are among the highest at American law schools.[13] Moreover, three major capital campaigns have built an endowment to rival UVA's private peers. Scott completed a $203 million campaign in 2000, which was at the time the most successful capital campaign in the history of American legal education. In 2012, Mahoney completed an eight-year capital campaign that surpassed its $150 million goal, raising $173.9 million despite the headwinds of the Great Recession.[14] And in 2024, we surpassed our $400 million goal fifteen months before the end of a six-year campaign, ultimately raising the second-largest total in the history of any law school. The $831 million endowment is currently the fifth largest of any American law school.[15]

The leadership of the Law School over the past several decades has similarly reflected and crystallized its national status. Like Scott, the school's twenty-first century deans have each been UVA-grown scholars with national reputations. The personal histories of these deans—Jeffries, Mahoney, myself, and Kendrick—bear various markers of educational achievement and national scholarly distinction, from Ivy League alma maters to Rhodes Scholarships. We all clerked for justices on the United States Supreme Court, and, deepening trends of the later twentieth century, we are all nationally engaged and recognized scholars.[16]

Our geographical range is a measure of the continued shift to national stature as well. Jeffries and Kendrick are southerners (from North Carolina and Kentucky, respectively), Mahoney is a midwesterner (from Missouri), and I am a northeasterner (from New York). At the same time, we have continued the almost unbroken pattern of deans emerging from the ranks of our own faculty.[17] All four of us began our teaching careers at the Law School and were longtime members of the faculty, as well as recipients of University teaching awards, before becoming dean. Jeffries and Kendrick are UVA Law graduates themselves (classes of 1973 and 2006, respectively). We are all, then, representative of UVA both in having arrived here already the product of prominent national institutions and in our homegrown commitment to UVA's unique values of pluralism and collegiality.

Transforming the People of UVA Law School

As the essays in this volume have shown, the most significant change over the Law School's history, one that is both a cause and a product of cementing its place in the pantheon of national law schools, was the expansion of who was included in the academic community of students, faculty, and staff. Increased opportunity for both students and faculty has become an essential characteristic of legal education generally in the late twentieth and early twenty-first centuries, and the same has been true at UVA. As earlier chapters in this volume show, that transformation began more than a century ago with the admission of women. But integration and inclusion proceeded slowly and fitfully for decades, with real demographic change occurring only in the past fifty years and accelerating in the past twenty-five.[18]

The class of 2026 reflects these demographic changes, as well as the enhanced student quality that a broader applicant pool has made possible. A majority of the incoming class, 53 percent, identified as women, while 36 percent identified as people of color and 19 percent as LGBTQ+. These percentages are significantly higher than even a decade ago, when the percentage of students of color and women remained largely as they had been since the 1990s—typically in the mid-20s and low- to mid-40s, respectively.[19] It was not until 2020 that women comprised a majority of the entering class, reflecting the predominance of women among college graduates. Current students also bring more pre–law school experience, with 74 percent of the incoming class of 2026 having some postgraduate experience before starting at the Law School, compared with 63 percent ten years earlier.[20] In addition, 30 percent of the class were first-generation graduate or professional students, and 10 percent were first-generation college students. The Law School continues to expand access to legal education as part of the 2030 strategic plan for "A Great and Good University" led by former UVA Law faculty member and then UVA President James E. Ryan (Law 1992). In 2022, for example, we launched the Roadmap Scholars Initiative, for first-generation and low-income college students to learn about legal education, become competitive applicants to the country's top law schools, and ultimately succeed as law students and lawyers.[21] Expanding opportunity to a broader pool of applicants has enhanced the academic excellence of the Law School and resulted in ever higher academic credentials among our student body—which attained a median LSAT of 171 and undergraduate GPA of 3.94 for the class of 2026.

As the Law School has welcomed this wider range of students, student organizations of all kinds have proliferated. By 2023, students had established more than seventy organizations, running the gamut from racial, ethnic, and religious affinity groups to first-generation and LGBTQ+ and veterans groups, to political and ideological organizations such as the Federalist Society and the American Constitution Society, to the North Grounds Softball League and the Libel Show.[22] As prior chapters show, the mere presence of students who had been previously excluded did not lead initially, inevitably, or naturally to their embrace as full members of the UVA Law community. Belonging has taken aspiration, reflection, and intentionality. These student organizations, as well as the student self-governance that has long been a hallmark of UVA, have been a critically important part of both fostering belonging for all students and advocating for the Law School as an institution to do the same.

The Law School's excellence and national stature have also been enhanced by twenty-first-century changes in faculty and leadership demographics at UVA. In 2002, women comprised 23 percent of the faculty and people of color around 9 percent.[23] In 2024, those numbers were 37 percent and 19 percent, respectively. In 2009, faculty member M. Elizabeth Magill (Law 1995) became the first woman to serve as vice dean in the school's history.[24] In 2016, I became the first woman and first Jewish dean, and I was succeeded in 2024 by Kendrick, who shares both of those attributes. As women have graduated from the Law School in larger numbers, they have become more visible and engaged as donors, especially in the most recent capital campaign. Alumnae such as Nancy L. Buc, one of only eight women of the class of 1969, and Martha Lubin Karsh, class of 1981 (together with her husband, Bruce A. Karsh, class of 1980), became the first to endow professorships in their names. There are now about fifty endowments either named for or endowed by alumnae of the Law School.[25]

The people who have come to study, teach, and work at UVA Law School, in other words, could not have been imagined by, and were in fact actively excluded by, Thomas Jefferson and many of the faculty and Law School leaders who succeeded him. As prior chapters have shown, it was not that the Law School's inhabitants were entirely homogeneous—both enslaved people and the wives and daughters of faculty also lived and worked at the University. But those who held formal positions as students and teachers—those who belonged as equals—long were.[26] The most significant transformation of this law school, without which it could not and would not have become a national law school, has been its transformation from a public institution whose definition of "public" was cramped by hierarchical, subordinating, and prejudiced notions of race, sex, class, and region (as well as other characteristics) to one whose "public" is all-encompassing and committed to creating access and opportunity for all.

The Twenty-First-Century Law School and Jefferson's Three Approaches to Legal Education

At the same time that the Law School has departed from Jefferson's vision of a regional institution for the education of white men by expanding who participates on an equal footing, a fair bit of what has made UVA a national law school echoes and continues its founding vision. Indeed, much of what makes any law school a national one in the twenty-first century has come to reflect UVA's own history. During the late nineteenth and early twentieth centuries, UVA lagged (though eventually joined) Harvard and its other peers in adopting Christopher Columbus Langdell's case method of legal education—focused on carefully reading judicial opinions to learn to "think like a lawyer." UVA did not similarly lag behind as law schools displaced the Langdellian approach from its longstanding dominance over the law school curriculum in the late twentieth and twenty-first centuries.[27] Though the Socratic method remains an important component of contemporary law teaching and continues to capture both the professional and popular imagination, the approach has lost much of its actual dominance of the law school curriculum. The rise of legal movements such as law and economics, critical approaches to the law, and others; the changing demographics and advocacy of students; developments in the social science of effective pedagogy; changing approaches to the academic study of law; and the evolving needs of the legal profession have led to a proliferation of alternative approaches to legal education.[28]

Indeed, the national law school of the twenty-first century now incorporates all three of the approaches to legal education that were present from the early days of UVA: the teaching of law as part of a liberal arts education, which now takes the form of interdisciplinarity; practical preparation for legal practice; and a mission to produce leaders for and public servants of a (then and now) fragile democracy.[29] Although each of these approaches began their modern ascendance prior to the twenty-first century both at UVA and in legal education more generally, they have reached maturity during this most recent period. A perceived incompatibility between a liberal arts and a more practical approach to law has given way to a sense that national law schools should offer both. And a commitment to supporting public service with substantial resources has become a significant marker of national status.

Jefferson's First Approach: The Embrace of Law as a Liberal Art in the form of Modern Interdisciplinarity

When Jefferson established UVA, its "law department" was an integral part of the University's liberal arts curriculum. This stood in contrast to the apprenticeship-based approach of freestanding "proprietary" law schools of the same period.[30] Though UVA quickly made room for the kind of practical training its students sought, its continued attachment to its liberal arts approach eventually placed it outside the mainstream of more law-specific approaches. In particular, UVA's extended resistance to the Langdellian revolution contributed to the sense that it was a regional, old-fashioned, and traditional place.[31] Indeed, over the course of the nineteenth century and well into the twentieth, law schools were more closely connected both intellectually and institutionally to the legal profession and the practice of law than to the rest of the universities with which they were often affiliated. Although trends began to change in the late twentieth century, as recently as 2000 the vast majority of law professors across the country were trained exclusively in law. They came to law teaching after judicial clerkships and brief stints in legal practice.[32]

In recent years, however, Jefferson's vision of law as a liberal art has taken on new life in the form of the interdisciplinary study of the law, both at UVA and elsewhere. At UVA, the Law School moved physically further from the rest of the University in 1974, but the scholarship its faculty produces and the legal training it offers has moved closer to it since then. Although teaching had long dominated the law school mission, especially at UVA, research and scholarship became increasingly important to both that mission and UVA's growing national stature under Deans Monrad G. Paulsen, Richard A. Merrill, Thomas H. Jackson, and Scott. That emphasis has continued to deepen in the past twenty-five years, with the hiring of esteemed faculty from across the country.

Moreover, becoming or remaining a national law school during this period has entailed increased hiring of faculty with formal doctoral training in complementary cognate fields alongside their law degrees—economics, psychology, politics, history, philosophy, literature, and more.[33] UVA has been no exception to either the existence of interdisciplinarity in the twentieth century or its expansion in the twenty-first. When I joined the UVA Law faculty in 2002, one of the things I knew was that UVA boasted renowned legal historians and economists. My arrival brought the total number of professors with PhDs to eleven.[34]

Two decades later, that number has almost doubled: twenty of the resident UVA Law faculty hold PhDs, plus another forty-three with other advanced degrees in cognate fields (compared with eighteen in 1997).[35] Though I was the first UVA Law School dean with a doctoral degree in a cognate field, it is already clear that I will not be the last: Leslie Kendrick holds a DPhil from Oxford in English literature.[36] Alongside this increased emphasis on the scholarly mission and the increased hiring of interdisciplinary faculty, the Law School began to create centers of academic excellence to highlight faculty work, facilitate collaboration, and engage students in such work. As of 1997, there were six such centers and programs. By 2024, there were twenty-five.

This increased interdisciplinarity has moved the Law School closer to the University not only intellectually but also institutionally, through joint appointments, co-teaching, cross-listing of courses, and student and faculty engagement in pan-University institutes and centers.[37] The number of dual degrees law students can pursue with other schools (at UVA and beyond) has also increased substantially. For much of the Law School's history, the only available degree was the LLB, which became the JD in 1970, and since 1945 the master of laws (LLM) and doctor of juridical science (SJD). In 1997, the Law School offered seven dual degrees; in 2024, sixteen.

The Law School curriculum itself has unsurprisingly followed faculty and student interest in interdisciplinary study. All law schools to some extent, but especially national schools, now offer more courses in critical theories, the humanities, and the social sciences.[38] Small seminars have displaced a substantial portion of large Socratic lecture courses, and students learn the disciplinary approaches of multiple methodologies alongside the analytical reasoning of blackletter fundamentals. The result is a legal education attuned not only to the logic of the law but also to the big picture within which that logic operates. Though the particular form of this broad interdisciplinary approach has changed, the modern national law school has very much embraced Jefferson's law as a liberal art.

Jefferson's Second Approach: The Modern Embrace of Practical Education in the Wake of the Great Recession

At around the same time law schools expanded the curriculum toward new intellectual and interdisciplinary horizons, they also began to offer far more practical training than ever before. Though those impulses may seem to point in different directions, their simultaneous rise has been more complementary than competitive. In the Langdellian law school, not only interdisciplinary and theoretical context—Jefferson's law as a liberal art—but also the nuts and bolts of legal practice were often left out. Where the former had been considered the province of other parts of the university, the latter were traditionally left to employers to provide. That has changed dramatically in recent years. Though clinical and experiential education had been developing in law schools for some time before the Great Recession of 2008—they began at UVA in the 1970s, and John Jeffries substantially expanded them in the early 2000s—their growth accelerated in its wake.[39] Just months after Paul Mahoney became dean, the recession jolted law practice and legal education.

One consequence of the struggling legal market that accompanied the recession was a reduction in the ability of financially strapped law firms to provide the kind of practical training to new lawyers they had long offered. In response, the American Bar Association (ABA), the accreditor of law schools, and the dominant New York state bar established new practical and "experiential" course requirements for law students. This shifted practice-oriented training from legal employers to law schools.[40] By 2010, 85 percent of law schools regularly offered students the opportunity to engage with clients via clinical programs, and at least half reported offering ten or more types of professional skills opportunities.[41]

Here at UVA, practical training had been a staple of the curriculum since just after its founding. In recent decades, such training ranged from Scott's Principles and Practice courses to Jeffries's founding of the Law and Business Program to Mahoney's founding of the Program in Law and Public Service. The Law School has also expanded access to practitioners through "short courses" in recent decades—now to the tune of 170 per year. Students participate in part- and full-time externships for credit in Charlottesville, through our Semester in DC program, and through student-initiated national and international opportunities. Students gain additional training through pro bono service—they logged more than sixteen thousand hours of such service during the 2022–23 school year.

The primary vehicle for exposing our students to real clients and legal practice is our clinical education program. Begun as a student-initiated legal aid society in 1967, the number of clinics expanded to seven by 1997, sixteen by 2008, and twenty-four today.[42] Often established in response to student interest and advocacy, current clinics range from traditional, legal aid direct client service work to policy clinics to transactional law clinics to problem-solving clinics. They provide support to tenants, entrepreneurs, criminal defendants, and government attorneys, among many others, largely in Charlottesville, but also elsewhere in the Commonwealth, the nation, and even the world.

The more than 200 courses that make up the UVA Law School curriculum in any given year are both more numerous than in prior years—in the 2000–2001 academic year, there were 147—and more varied.[43] Courses are now roughly evenly split into thirds between lecture courses, small seminars, and experiential opportunities.[44] What once seemed a conflict between the academic and the practical now has given way to complementarity. The Socratic method still dominates much of the first-year curriculum and our imagination about legal pedagogy. But it has ceded its monopoly over legal education as it now stands. UVA in the twenty-first century, like its peers, is far less Langdell's law school than it is Jefferson's.

Jefferson's Third Approach: The Modern Embrace of the Law School's Public Service Mission

As much as the increase in clinical education was spurred by regulatory requirements for practical training, it was equally spurred by a renewed commitment, at UVA and elsewhere, to serving the public. The increase in clinical and experimental education leads not only to greater fluency with the practice of law but also greater understanding of the human dimension on which several of the essays in this volume touch. It is a critical part of the growing importance of public service to legal education generally and this law school in particular.

The impetus for supporting public service at UVA Law School has existed from the beginning, with Jefferson's hope that his graduates would go on to support the nation's new democracy. For Jefferson, the hope was that these men of the South would ensure southern regional dominance of national politics for generations to come. Indeed, that vision endured, and the Law School always produced public servants, often in Virginia and the South, as several chapters in this volume have shown. But it had long done so largely through articulating its aspirations and offering up alumni as models, rather than through direct institutional support.[45]

In the late twentieth century, both the public service aspirations of UVA graduates and the form of institutional support for public service would change. As to the former, as prior chapters have shown, UVA law graduates shifted from state and regional leadership largely intent on preserving the slavery and segregation of the Old South to leadership across state, regional, and national governments and organizations that is politically and institutionally far more heterogeneous.[46] UVA Law graduates now are prosecutors and public defenders, legal aid lawyers and elected officials, Republicans and Democrats.

Institutional support for public service at UVA began to change in 1980. Students interested in public service careers created new organizations such as Student Funded Fellowships (which became the Public Interest Law Association) and pressed the Law School to provide funding, counseling, networking, and other services and opportunities. In 1997, Scott created the Mortimer Caplin Public Service Center to provide career counseling and support to students interested in public service careers. In response to the September 11, 2001, attacks and a perceived rise in "national pride and solidarity," Jeffries dedicated the 2001–2 school year to "a celebration of public service."[47] Since that time, often in response to student advocacy, the Law School, like its peers, has continued to provide additional investments in our Public Service Center and its personnel, as well as the Program in Law and Public Service. In recent years, we expanded financial support for both summer and postgraduate fellowships, expanded eligibility for our loan forgiveness program, broadened clinical opportunities, and hired additional personnel to support growing numbers of public service students. These developments have not only put postgraduate public service careers within reach for UVA alumni. They have also enabled the Law School to fulfill its mission—and that of all law schools—of serving the public, both by doing so directly and by enabling the service of students, faculty, and alumni alike. They have helped sustain UVA as a national law school in an era when a commitment to public service—a commitment UVA has maintained since its founding—has become a marker of such status.

At times, UVA Law School's commitment to one or the other of the three approaches described above has placed it outside the mainstream of legal education or highlighted the deeply sectional nature of its approach and imagination. That is no longer the case. All three aspects of Jefferson's original vision have come to define modern legal education. Law as a liberal art has become the now widespread interdisciplinary study and teaching of law. Law as legal practice has been deeply embedded in experiential and especially clinical learning in the law school curriculum. And the aspiration of educating lawyers for service to and leadership of what Jefferson hoped to be a dominant South has become a national understanding that law schools educate students for leadership of our democracy, our society, and our world.

It has become clear that what once might have seemed incompatible impulses together help prepare law students to lead and serve in this challenging moment. They help aspiring lawyers of every belief, background, and identity learn to respect opposing views, listen with empathy, and speak with respect. Together, these approaches make advocates and counselors of our students, teach them to take seriously their own humanity and the humanity of others, help them understand law's place in the world, and inculcate in them the civic obligations they incur by virtue of their legal educations.

New Frontiers

As UVA has crystallized its place among national law schools, new frontiers have opened up over the past few decades requiring further change and auguring more change to come. That should not be surprising. These have been turbulent and unprecedented times: the first decade of this century began with the tragedy of September 11 and the ensuing War on Terror in 2001 and continued in 2008 with the election of the first Black president in Barack Obama as well as the Great Recession. The past eight years, my years as dean, have continued to witness rapid change and frequent upheaval, with the shifting politics that led to the election of Donald J. Trump in 2016; the white supremacist violence in Charlottesville in 2017; the global COVID-19 pandemic and then the civil rights protests following the police killing of George Floyd and other Black Americans in 2020; the election of Joseph R. Biden that same year and the subsequent events at the US Capitol on January 6, 2021; the protests accompanying recent violence and war in the Middle East; and the 2024 reelection of Donald Trump. We felt many of these events especially acutely here in Charlottesville—the white supremacist violence of 2017, for example, occurred in our very own community, and I spent the following year leading the University's response. Less acute but also destabilizing developments both nationally and locally were the tectonic changes in Supreme Court personnel and jurisprudence from 2016 on; the consequences of nationally and globally polarized politics for universities, our students, and our faculties; an epidemic of gun violence, especially in schools; a deepening environmental crisis; increasing and alarming rates of anxiety and depression among young people; and the rapidly shifting technological and economic realities of modern life.

These many and varied developments have placed new pressures on all law schools. In the wake of the Great Recession of 2008, for example, the contracting legal market led to increased criticism of legal education and questions about its value. As during a similar moment of economic crisis in the 1980s, critics called again for the elimination of the third year of law school and for greater regulatory oversight. The ABA did substantially increase its oversight and reporting requirements. Those requirements, as well as the increased difficulty of admitting and placing law students in succeeding years and the heightened emphasis on student mental health and well-being, have led to a substantial expansion of professional administrators. Where even a few decades ago faculty performed most administrative functions, law schools now employ significant numbers of professionals to perform the increased variety of functions of the twenty-first century law school.

These changes are related in many ways to the rapid technological change that has penetrated all aspects of legal (and all) education (and society) in recent decades. Technology has shaped and reshaped legal practice, the employment market for our students, and law school pedagogy and operations. Such change accelerated with the COVID-19 pandemic, when UVA, like many institutions, shifted all of its classes online in the span of eight days. Navigating the shift to online, and then to hybrid, learning required creativity as we attempted to preserve our community and collegiality despite not being able to engage readily with one another in person.

National and global politics have posed additional challenges to UVA Law School's unique culture. Universities have become targets of and participants in what have become chronic and severe culture wars. Polarization and threats to democracy in the United States and abroad have resulted in the increased politicization of legal pedagogy, law schools, and higher education more generally. Student activism across the ideological spectrum, ongoing debates about diversity, and the mental health needs of our students have both accompanied and intensified the consequences of this increasing polarization. Here at UVA, the Law School has reinforced our long-standing embrace of an intellectually and ideologically heterogeneous faculty and student body and recommitted to our values of free speech and the robust exchange of ideas. Faculty and administrators have partnered with student organizations to foster civil dialogue across the ideological divide. The Law School has benefited in these efforts from its unique, and hard-fought, transformation from a collegial culture based in homogeneity to an equally collegial culture that celebrates heterogeneity and intellectual and ideological pluralism within a single and singular community.

Within this context, what it meant and means to be a national law school was and is dynamic and ever shifting. The long-standing question that UVA faced during most of its history was whether it would be a regional or national law school or both. The twenty-first century has added a new question: whether, and to what extent, it would become a global law school. Prior to 2003–4, students could get credit for courses taken at international law schools only by petitioning the administration for approval. Today, the law school offers an international dual-degree program, formal study abroad for a semester or during the J-Term, and student-initiated study abroad projects and externships. Students can take advantage of eleven formal study abroad programs from Italy to Japan to Australia to India and beyond. Students also learn from an increasingly international faculty, who themselves participate in three international faculty exchange programs as well as other forms of faculty-initiated global engagement.

As I write, still new frontiers are opening up that will no doubt occupy Leslie Kendrick, who has already identified as key priorities both the future of the legal profession and the professional training of our students. The rise of large language models, like ChatGPT, and other forms of artificial intelligence and technological and digital transformation will affect how teachers teach and students learn, how lawyers and judges practice law, and how professors engage in research and scholarship. Changing economic realities of law firm markets and management—especially recent national and global consolidation—will continue to accelerate and respond to these technological changes. The Supreme Court's recent cases limiting affirmative action in higher education admissions; the ABA's possible elimination of a standardized test requirement for law school admissions; challenges to and changes in *US News* and other rankings; and the advent of fully online degrees are likely to destabilize long-established patterns of law school admissions, matriculation, pedagogy, and culture. For the moment, most national law schools, including UVA, remain committed to in-person JD instruction, though changes to ABA regulations could soon change that. In addition, the complex relationship of law schools and other institutions of higher education to politics, polarization, and challenges to democracy seems here to stay for the foreseeable future.

It is unsurprising that law schools have changed alongside shifts in our political, moral, and economic cultures. It is equally unsurprising that these changes would and do affect who we teach, who does that teaching, what we teach, and how we teach it. This volume describes how UVA Law School has adapted to these changes, as well as to related changes in the legal profession itself. In doing so, it raises questions about legal education more generally and prompts us to ask how law schools can continue to live up to the lofty and critically important aspirations of our profession in the midst of ongoing challenges.

The Stories We Tell

Just as I was becoming dean, I discovered how little I knew about the Law School's history when I learned about Gregory H. Swanson (Law 1951) and the role he played in desegregating the Law School.[48] That realization, combined with my scholarly interests, set the stage for the serious exploration of our institutional history during my time as dean.[49] This volume is an important part of that project. It was conceived before I became dean, but that it comes to fruition just after I step down brings me enormous satisfaction and pride. Knowing our history shapes both who we are today and who we will be in the future.

Indeed, I have come to the conclusion that part of becoming a national law school has entailed knowing, understanding, acknowledging, and telling our history—both the changes and the continuities, the aspirations we still embrace, and the painful failings we repudiate. When the University commemorated its centennial in 1921, the students at UVA Law School remained quite similar to those at its founding. They were all white, largely southern, and almost entirely male. The centennial commemoration was shot through with the white supremacist values and rhetoric dominant in a South intent on venerating the Lost Cause and buttressing the Jim Crow status quo.

One hundred years later, the people both involved and invoked in the Law School's bicentennial commemorations were utterly transformed. Indeed, the 2019–20 school year marked not only two hundred years since the Law School's founding, but also a century since Elizabeth Nelson Tompkins (Law 1923) inaugurated coeducation; seventy years since Gregory Swanson racially integrated the Law School and the University; and fifty years since Elaine R. Jones (Law 1970) became the first Black woman to graduate from the Law School.

At the same time, continuities across the two centuries of our history are both visible and substantial. For all that our pedagogy has changed over that time, in some ways this law school, indeed legal education as a whole, has never been more Jeffersonian than in its current embrace of all three elements present at the school's founding. On a cultural level, as the people of this law school have become heterogeneous in ways that Jefferson and some of his successors could not have comprehended, the school has managed to preserve its long-standing sense of community.

In other words, we are Jefferson's law school, and we are also Elizabeth Tompkins's law school and Gregory Swanson's and Elaine Jones's. We get to make and remake who we are through the stories we tell. As the Law School has commemorated these milestones over the past several years, we have had, and taken, many opportunities to tell our history—to identify both change and continuity. In the end, the history of UVA Law School is the history not only of a single school but of legal education in flux. It is the history of a place (Charlottesville), a region (the South), and a nation. This history challenges us all to better understand ourselves, our profession, our democracy, our society, and our world. In doing so, it offers us opportunities to continue to shape who we are—for our time and the times to come.

Notes

1. Thanks to Haley Gorman for invaluable research assistance and to Randall N. Flaherty and Rich Schragger for their insightful and helpful comments.
2. See David Thomas Konig, "Jeffersonian Foundations of Legal Education in Virginia, 1779–1845," in this volume.
3. University of Virginia School of Law, Career Services brochure (archived 7 February 1998), University of Virginia School of Law (hereafter cited as UVA Law), https://web.archive.org/web/19980207092611/http://www.law.virginia.edu/apply/newbrochure/career.htm.
4. I refer to the top fourteen because the "T14" is the standard category of the most prominent national law schools.
5. UVA Law ranked ninth in the latest Sisk-Leiter faculty impact ranking and led the nation in Supreme Court citations during the 2016 and 2017 terms. Gregory Sisk, Nicole Catlin, Alexandra Anderson, and Lauren Gundersen, "Scholarly Impact of Law School Faculties in 2021: Updating the Leiter Score Ranking for the Top Third," *University of St. Thomas Law Journal* 17 (2022): 1041, 1043; Mike Fox, "UVA Faculty Lead in U.S. Supreme Court Citations," *News,* 1 November 2018, UVA Law, https://www.law.virginia.edu/news/201811/uva-law-faculty-lead-us-supreme-court-citations. See also Matthew Sag, "Forward Looking Academic Impact Rankings for U.S. Law Schools," *Florida State University Law Review* 51 (2024): 798 (ranking Virginia Law sixth in the country for academic influence); "University of Virginia—School of Law," *Princeton Review* (New York: 2024), https://perma.cc/ZZ7Z-42D8.

6. Wes Enders, "Dean Addresses Tuition Increases and 'Privatization,'" *Virginia Law Weekly,* 15 October 1993 (hereafter cited as *VLW*).
7. In 2024, UVA was ranked first in the *Above the Law* ranking and fifth in the ABA Elite 100 employment and federal clerkships rankings. See "Above the Law Top 50 Law School Rankings," *Above the Law,* https://abovethelaw.com/top-law-schools-2024/; Mary Wood, "UVA Law Grads Are Best Employed in Nation, According to New Data," *News,* 28 May 2024, https://www.law.virginia.edu/news/202405/uva-law-grads-are-best-employed-nation-according-new-data.
8. Arthur J. Morris Law Library, "List of University of Virginia Law Alums Who Clerked for the U.S. Supreme Court from 1889 to 2024" (c. 2010–24), Historical Research Collection, RG–32–503, Arthur J. Morris Law Library Special Collections, University of Virginia (hereafter cited as LLSC). See also UVA Law, "Clerkships by Term," 2024, https://www.law.virginia.edu/clerkships#data. See also Karen Sloan, "These Law Schools Dominated the Federal Clerk Hiring Market in 2023," *Reuters,* 25 April 2024.
9. "Law Schools of Choice for AmLaw 100 Firms: Class of 2023," *Firm Prospects,* 6 March 2024, https://perma.cc/MT6V-3CXA; Thomas Lewis, "Insight: Most General Counsels Gain Experience In-House, Harvard Tops Backgrounds," *Bloomberg Law,* 31 January 2020, https://news.bloomberglaw.com/us-law-week/insight-most-general-counsels-gain-experience-in-house-harvard-tops-backgrounds; Adam Feldman, "Law Schools, Judges, and Government Attorneys," *Empirical SCOTUS,* 10 September 2017, https://perma.cc/UC8A-3E8L.
10. Cullen Couch, "The Road to Financial Self-Sufficiency," *UVA Lawyer* 32, no. 1 (Spring 2008): 5–9.
11. Mary Wood, "Eight Years Stronger," *UVA Lawyer* 40, no. 2 (Spring 2016): 29–36; Mary Wood, "The People's Dean," *UVA Lawyer* 48, no. 2 (Spring 2024): 25–32; Nikolai Morse, "Kendrick to Be UVA Law's 13th Dean," *VLW,* 7 February 2024.
12. Denis Binder, "The Changing Paradigm in Public Legal Education," *Loyola Journal of Public Interest Law* 8, no. 1 (Fall 2006): 1–28. See also UVA Law, "Annual Report, 2022–2023," 18 October 2023, https://perma.cc/V43L-KR6V.
13. Tina Lundy, "New Foundation Head Seeks Greater Alumni Participation," *VLW,* 14 September 1979; Evan Mix, "Alumni Donors Bridge Budget Gap," *VLW,* 24 September 2010; UVA Law, "Annual Report, 2022–2023."
14. Robert E. Scott, "Looking Back, Looking Ahead," *UVA Lawyer* 25, no. 1 (Spring 2001): 4; Wood, "Eight Years Stronger," 32.
15. Wood, "People's Dean," 26; I requested capital campaign and endowment numbers from Law School Chief Development Officer Jason Wu Trujillo for the end of fiscal year 2024.
16. Rich Bland, "Jeffries to Succeed Scott as Dean," *VLW,* 22 February 2001; Wood, "Eight Years Stronger"; Wood, "People's Dean"; Morse, "Kendrick to Be UVA Law's 13th Dean."
17. Deans Monrad G. Paulsen (1968–75) and Thomas H. Jackson (1988–91) have been the only deans not drawn from UVA Law faculty.
18. See Anne M. Coughlin, "'This Mob of Men': The Road to Coeducation at the University of Virginia School of Law, 1870–1923"; Risa Goluboff, Randall N. Flaherty, and Biruktawit M. Assefa, "Gregory H. Swanson and the Integration of the University of Virginia School of Law"; Claudrena Harold, "We Demand: Student Advocates for Curricular Change, 1960–1980"; and Meggan F. Cashwell and Addison R. Patrick, "A

New Curriculum for a New Era: The Law School at a Crossroads, 1970–1997," all in this volume.

19. In the class of 2016, 24 percent of students identified as minority and 42 percent identified as women. See Class of 2016 Profile, https://www.law.virginia.edu/admissions/class-2016-profile; Robert E. Scott, "Virginia Law's Treasured Resource, the Students," *UVA Lawyer* 19, no. 1 (Winter 1995): 3–5. See also Cashwell and Patrick, "New Curriculum for a New Era," on the 1990s.
20. See Class of 2026 Profile, https://www.law.virginia.edu/admissions/class-2026-profile; Class of 2016 Profile.
21. University of Virginia, "A Great and Good University: The 2030 Plan," August 2019, https://perma.cc/5F9M-ZRP2; UVA Law, Roadmap Scholars Initiative, https://www.law.virginia.edu/academics/program/roadmap-scholars-initiative.
22. By comparison, there were forty-five student organizations at the Law School in 2002. UVA Law, Graduate Student Record, 2001–2002, "Facts & Statistics," archived 15 October 2002, https://web.archive.org/web/20020804192255/http://www.law.virginia.edu/home2002/html/about/factsstats.htm.
23. UVA Law, Graduate Student Record, 2001–2002, "Facts & Statistics."
24. "Magill Named New Academic Associate Dean," *VLW*, 28 August 2009.
25. UVA Law, "Annual Report, 2022–2023."
26. See David T. Konig, "Jeffersonian Foundations of Legal Education in Virginia, 1779–1845"; Justene Hill Edwards, "Teaching the Laws of Slavery, 1826–1865"; Randall N. Flaherty, "John B. Minor and the Science of Legal Education, 1845–1895"; Elizabeth R. Varon, "The Civil War and Reconstruction, 1861–1877"; Laura F. Edwards, "Coverture and the Virginia Law Professors: The Nineteenth Century"; Coughlin, "'This Mob of Men,'" all in this volume.
27. G. Edward White, "Poised between a Regional and a National Law School, 1920–1960," in this volume; Joel Seligman, *The High Citadel* (Boston: Houghton Mifflin, 1978), 33–38.
28. For student activism as a force for curricular change, see Harold, "We Demand"; for the influence of legal movements on the UVA Law School curriculum, see Cashwell and Patrick, "New Curriculum." For legal pedagogy changes in response to shifting demographics of students and faculty, see essays from a 2022 *Virginia Law Review* symposium on the future of legal pedagogy, especially Molly Bishop Shadle, Sophie Trawalter, and J. H. Verkerke, "Gender Differences in Law School Classroom Participation: The Key Role of Social Context," *Virginia Law Review Online* 108 (2022): 30–54, https://perma.cc/VR5Z-UPXF; Anne M. Coughlin and Molly Bishop Shadel, "The Gender Participation Gap and the Politics of Pedagogy," *Virginia Law Review Online* 108 (2022): 55–71, https://virginialawreview.org/articles/the-gender-participation-gap-and-the-politics-of-pedagogy/; and Risa Goluboff, "Symposium: Forward," *Virginia Law Review Online* 108 (2022): 24–53, https://virginialawreview.org/articles/foreword-2022/.
29. See UVA Law, Courses, https://www.law.virginia.edu/courses; cf., for example, Harvard Law School, Courses, https://hls.harvard.edu/courses/?page=1; Columbia Law School, Courses, https://www.law.columbia.edu/academics/courses; Yale Law School, Courses, https://courses.law.yale.edu.
30. See Konig, "Jeffersonian Foundations of Legal Education."
31. White, "Poised between a Regional and a National Law School"; Seligman, *High Citadel*, 33–38. Justice Louis Brandeis described Langdell's focus, which became

central to Harvard's curriculum and those of the scores of law schools nationwide that followed in his footsteps, as the following: "[Legal instruction] should [aim] to teach the student to think in a legal manner in accordance with the principles of the particular branch of law. [The instructor] should seek to inculcate and develop in legal reasoning the habit of intellectual self-reliance." Seligman, *High Citadel,* 35, 43–44.

32. Justin McCrary, Joy Milligan, and James Phillips, "The Ph.D. Rises in American Law Schools, 1960–2011: What Does It Mean for Legal Education?," *Journal of Legal Education* 65, no. 3 (Spring 2016): 543, 553.
33. McCrary, Milligan, and Phillips, "Ph.D. Rises," 553 (noting that 28 percent of law professors at the top thirty-four law schools hold PhDs, compared to 5 percent of all law professors in 1989). See also Lynn M. LoPucki, "Dawn of the Discipline-Based Law Faculty," *Journal of Legal Education* 65, no. 3 (Spring 2016): 506, 507. "The overall trend is unmistakable. Ph.D. hiring is increasing rapidly."
34. University of Virginia School of Law Faculty and Administration Directory, 1992–93, Box 4, Directories of the University of Virginia School of Law, RG–32–502, LLSC.
35. Resident Faculty, University of Virginia School of Law, 2024–25, https://www.law.virginia.edu/faculty; University of Virginia School of Law Faculty & Administration Directory, 1997–98, Box 4, LLSC.
36. Former deans Robert E. Scott and Frederick Deane Goodwin Ribble (Law 1921) both held SJDs.
37. See generally Kim Diana Connolly, "Elucidating the Elephant: Interdisciplinary Law School Classes," *Washington University Journal of Law & Policy* 11, no. 1 (January 2003): 19–22.
38. See UVA Law, Courses; cf., for example, Harvard Law School, Courses; Columbia Law School, Courses; Yale Law School, Courses. See also Brian H. Bornstein, "Law and Social Science: How Interdisciplinary Is Interdisciplinary Enough?," in *The Witness Stand and Lawrence S. Wrightsman, Jr.,* ed. Cynthia Willis-Esqueda and Brian H. Bornstein (New York: Springer Science & Business Media, 2016), 117–18.
39. "Public Service the Virginia Way," *UVA Lawyer* 32, no. 1 (Spring 2008): 14–18. One of the earliest experiential learning programs at UVA Law was the student-led creation of a local legal aid chapter in 1967. See Eric Williamson, "How Students Opened a Door for Legal Aid," *News,* 7 November 2017, https://www.law.virginia.edu/news/201711/how-students-opened-door-legal-aid. See also Harold, "We Demand"; Peter A. Joy, "The Uneasy History of Experiential Education in U.S. Law Schools," *Dickinson Law Review* 122, no. 2 (Winter 2018): 551, 574; Daniel Thies, "Rethinking Legal Education in Hard Times: The Recession, Practical Legal Education, and the New Job Market," *Journal of Legal Education* 59, no. 4 (May 2010): 598–99.
40. Joy, "Uneasy History of Experiential Education," 576–80. See, e.g., American Bar Association, *ABA Standards and Rules of Procedure for Approval of Law Schools: 2024–2025* (Chicago: American Bar Association, 2024), 20–24.
41. Catherine L. Carpenter, ed., *A Survey of Law School Curricula: 2002–2010* (Chicago: American Bar Association, 2012), 16.
42. For more on legal aid at UVA Law, see Harold, "We Demand."
43. In the 2000–2001 academic year, UVA Law offered 147 courses across seventeen subject concentrations. "University of Virginia School of Law Course Offering Directory: 2000–2001," 31–34, 60–84.
44. See UVA Law, Courses.

45. Konig, "Jeffersonian Foundations of Legal Education"; Flaherty, "John B. Minor"; Varon, "Civil War and Reconstruction."
46. A. E. Dick Howard and Catherine A. Ward, "Constitutional Law at the University of Virginia: Between State Constitutional Bookends, 1902–1971," in this volume.
47. John C. Jeffries Jr., "Public Service in Challenging Times," *UVA Lawyer* 26, no. 2 (Fall 2002): 3.
48. See Goluboff, Flaherty, and Assefa, "Gregory H. Swanson."
49. Slavery and the UVA School of Law: A History, LLSC, https://slavery.law.virginia .edu/; Virginia Law Women Oral History Project, *Virginia Law Women 50,* LLSC, https://vlw50.law.virginia.edu/; "An Oral History of Lambda Law Alliance," *MoreUs* (blog), Arthur J. Morris Law Library, UVA Law, https://perma.cc/UG8E-YF6X; see generally https://avalon.lib.virginia.edu/collections/bn999721k. The Law School currently offers a research seminar, in collaboration with the UVA history department, on the history of race and slavery on our North Grounds landscape (HIST 5706/LAW 9364).

CONTRIBUTORS

BIRUKTAWIT M. ASSEFA (Law 2024) is an associate at Williams & Connolly in Washington, DC. While pursuing her JD, Assefa served as the 2023–24 editor-in-chief of the *Virginia Law Review* and as education chair for the Black Law Students Association. Assefa holds a BA in political science and an MPH, both from Yale University. Before attending UVA Law, she helped launch and worked as a researcher at the SEICHE Center for Health and Justice, a collaboration between Yale School of Medicine and Yale Law School.

MEGGAN F. CASHWELL is a historian of the nineteenth-century United States and the Alvin V. and Nancy Baird Curator of Historical Collections at the University of Virginia Claude Moore Health Sciences Library. In her current role, Cashwell leads her department's efforts to make accessible an extensive collection of manuscripts, rare books, artifacts, and institutional records that chronicle the history of the health sciences. Cashwell received her MA and PhD in history from Duke University. She was a postdoctoral research associate in legal history for the Arthur J. Morris Law Library Special Collections at the University of Virginia, where she spearheaded this book project.

ANNE M. COUGHLIN is the Lewis F. Powell Jr. Professor of Law at the University of Virginia. Her primary research and teaching interests are in the areas of criminal law, criminal procedure, feminist jurisprudence, and law and humanities. She is coauthor of the casebook *Criminal Law* (2015) and has written a number of articles exploring intersections among criminal law, criminal procedure, and feminist theory. Coughlin led the Molly Pitcher Project, which challenged the ban on women in military combat. She clerked for Judge Jon O. Newman of the US Court of Appeals for the Second Circuit and for US Supreme Court Justice Lewis F. Powell Jr.

LAURA F. EDWARDS is a scholar of legal history and is the Class of 1921 Bicentennial Professor in the History of American Law and Liberty at Princeton University. She is the author of several books in legal history including *The People and Their Peace: Legal Culture and the Transformation of Inequality in the Post-Revolutionary South* (2009), which won the Southern Historical Association's Charles S. Sydnor Award and the American Historical Association's Littleton-Griswold Prize. Her most recent book, *Only the Clothes on Her Back: Textiles, Law, and Commerce in the Nineteenth-Century United States* (2022), addresses the role of textile production and ownership as tools for expanding women's historical legal power.

RANDALL N. FLAHERTY (GSAS 2008, 2014) serves as law school historian and head of the Arthur J. Morris Law Library's Special Collections at the University of Virginia School of Law. She is a historian of the early national United States whose recent work explores the history of American legal education. Flaherty oversees the department's efforts to study and share the history of UVA Law and make accessible the Law Library's collection of legal history materials. She spearheads a number of public and institutional history projects, including The Historical Landscape of North Grounds and Slavery & The University of Virginia School of Law.

RISA GOLUBOFF is the David and Mary Harrison Distinguished Professor of Law and a professor of history at the University of Virginia. She served as the twelfth, and the first female, dean of the University of Virginia School of Law from 2016 to 2024. Her scholarship and teaching concentrate on American constitutional and civil rights law, with a particular emphasis on their historical evolution throughout the twentieth century. Goluboff is the author of *The Lost Promise of Civil Rights* (2007), which won the Order of the Coif Biennial Book Award, and *Vagrant Nation: Police*

Power, Constitutional Change, and the Making of the 1960s (2016), which was recognized with multiple awards, including the American Historical Association's Littleton-Griswold Prize. Before joining UVA Law, Goluboff clerked for Judge Guido Calabresi and US Supreme Court Justice Stephen Breyer.

CLAUDRENA HAROLD is the associate dean for the social sciences and Edward Stettinius Professor of History at the University of Virginia. She is the author of three books, *When Sunday Comes: Gospel Music in the Soul and Hip-Hop Eras* (2020); *New Negro Politics in the Jim Crow South* (2016); and *The Rise and Fall of the Garvey Movement in the Urban South, 1918–1942* (2007). In 2018, she coedited the volume *Charlottesville 2017: The Legacy of Race and Inequity*. Harold heads the digital project *Black Fire at UVA* and has written, produced, and codirected nine short films with Kevin Everson on the history of Black student activism at UVA.

JUSTENE HILL EDWARDS is an associate professor of history at the University of Virginia. She specializes in African American history, specifically the influence of slavery on Black economic life in the United States. Hill Edwards is the author of *Savings and Trust: The Rise and Betrayal of the Freedman's Bank* (2024), which chronicles the rise and fall of the Freedman's Savings and Trust Company, and *Unfree Markets: The Slaves' Economy and the Rise of Capitalism in South Carolina* (2021), which explores the economic lives of enslaved people as active participants in their local economies. She is the recipient of the Mellon New Direction Fellowship and a 2022 Carnegie Fellow.

A. E. DICK HOWARD (Law 1961) is the Warner-Booker Distinguished Professor of International Law Emeritus at the University of Virginia School of Law and specializes in constitutional law, comparative constitutionalism, and the US Supreme Court. Howard has been counsel to the Virginia General Assembly and a consultant to state and federal bodies, including the US Senate Judiciary Committee. From 1982 to 1986 he served as counselor to the governor of Virginia, and he chaired Virginia's Commission on the Bicentennial of the United States Constitution. Howard is the author of numerous books, articles, and monographs, including *The Road from Runnymede: Magna Carta and Constitutionalism in America* (2015) and *Commentaries on the Constitution of Virginia* (1974).

LAURA KALMAN is a distinguished research professor of history at the University of California, Santa Barbara, and a past president of the American Society for Legal History. Her scholarship spans the intersection of law and history, with a particular focus on the US Supreme Court and legal developments in the twentieth century. Among her notable works are *FDR's Gambit: The Court-Packing Fight and the Rise of Legal Liberalism* (2022); *The Long Reach of the Sixties: LBJ, Nixon, and the Making of the Contemporary Supreme Court* (2017); and *The Strange Career of Legal Realism* (1996).

DAVID T. KONIG is an emeritus professor of law and history at Washington University in St. Louis. He specializes in Anglo-American legal history, with a focus on property law, the Second Amendment, and the law of freedom and slavery. He is a leading authority on Thomas Jefferson and the development of law in colonial, Revolutionary, and early national America. He has edited the legal papers of Thomas Jefferson for The Papers of Thomas Jefferson and is completing a book on Jefferson's legal thought and practice. Konig is the author and editor of several books, including his most recent, *Jefferson's Legal Commonplace Book*, which he coedited for the *Papers of Thomas Jefferson Second Series* (2019).

LOREN S. MOULDS (GSAS 2006, 2014) is a historian of twentieth-century American political development and is head of Digital Scholarship & Preservation at the University of Virginia School of Law, where he is responsible for the development and interpretation of the Arthur J. Morris Law Library's digital scholarship projects as well as the promotion, creation, and preservation of its digital archival collections. Moulds received his MA and PhD from the University of Virginia. He serves as codirector of the Farmer Postdoctoral Fellow in Digital Humanities at the UVA Law Library, notably directing the book, authored by Philip Mills Herrington, *The Law School at the University of Virginia: Architectural Expansion in the Realm of Thomas Jefferson* (2017).

ADDISON R. PATRICK (College 2020) is the curatorial specialist at the Arthur J. Morris Law Library Special Collections at the University of Virginia School of Law. Patrick leads the Law Library's oral history program, through which she collaborates with students, alumni, faculty, and staff to document and preserve the history of the Law School. She enables the discovery of this history through physical exhibitions, digital projects, and other outreach initiatives. She received her MS in Information Sciences from the University of Tennessee, Knoxville.

ELIZABETH R. VARON is Langbourne M. Williams Professor of American History and associate director of the John L. Nau III Center for Civil War History at the University of Virginia. Varon has published widely on the Civil War and Reconstruction. Her book *Appomattox: Victory, Defeat, and Freedom at the End of the Civil War* (2013) was the winner of the 2014 Library of Virginia Literary Award for Nonfiction as well as the 2014 Daniel M. and Marilyn W. Laney Prize of the Austin Civil War Roundtable. Her most recent book is *Longstreet: The Confederate General Who Defied the South* (2023).

CATHERINE A. WARD (Law 2023) is a judicial law clerk for the US Court of Appeals for the Third Circuit. Previously, she served as a law clerk for the US District Court for the Western District of Virginia. Ward earned her JD from the University of Virginia School of Law and graduated Order of the Coif. She was a Rotary Global Grant Scholar at the University of Cambridge, from which she received her MPhil in education, globalisation, and international development. Ward's areas of professional interest include education, legal history, and state constitutional law. She earned her BA from Duke University.

G. EDWARD WHITE (Law 1970) is the David and Mary Harrison Distinguished Professor of Law at the University of Virginia School of Law. White is an authority in legal history and American culture and has served as a Guggenheim Fellow and a senior fellow of the National Endowment for the Humanities. White has published twenty books, including the three-part series *Law in American History,* earning honors such as the Silver Gavel Award from the American Bar Association, the James Willard Hurst Prize, and the Littleton-Griswold Prize. White has served as editor of the *Studies in Legal History* series and held advisory roles with Oxford University Press.

INDEX

Italicized page numbers refer to illustrations.